SAMS Teach Yourself

Microsoft®
Visual Basic® .NET 2003

in 24 Hours

James Foxall

COMPLETE STARTER KIT

SAMS   800 East 96th St., Indianapolis, Indiana, 46240 USA

Sams Teach Yourself Microsoft® Visual Basic® .NET 2003 in 24 Hours, Complete Starter Kit

Copyright © 2003 by Sams Publishing

International Standard Book Number: 0672325373

Library of Congress Catalog Card Number: 2003102957

Printed in the United States of America

First Printing: June 2003

06 05 04   6   5   4

Sams Publishing offers excellent discounts on this book when ordered in quantity for bulk purchases or special sales. For more information, please contact

U.S. Corporate and Government Sales

      1-800-382-3419   corpsales@pearsontechgroup.com

For sales outside of the U.S., please contact International Sales

      1-317-428-3341   international@pearsontechgroup.com

Trademarks

All terms mentioned in this book that are known to be trademarks or service marks have been appropriately capitalized. Sams Publishing cannot attest to the accuracy of this information. Use of a term in this book should not be regarded as affecting the validity of any trademark or service mark.

Warning and Disclaimer

ASSOCIATE PUBLISHER
Michael Stephens

EXECUTIVE EDITOR
Candace Hall

DEVELOPMENT EDITOR
Mark Renfrow

MANAGING EDITOR
Charlotte Clapp

PROJECT EDITOR
Rebecca Lansberry

COPY EDITOR
Mike Henry

INDEXER
Mandie Frank

PROOFREADER
Mike Henry

TECHNICAL EDITOR
Bill Hatfield

TEAM COORDINATOR
Cindy Teeters

MEDIA DEVELOPER
Dan Scherf

INTERIOR DESIGNER
Gary Adair

COVER DESIGNER
Alan Clements

PAGE LAYOUT
Eric S. Miller

Contents at a Glance

Introduction 1

Part I The Visual Basic .NET Environment 3

Hour 1 Jumping In with Both Feet: A Visual Basic .NET Programming Tour 5

2 Navigating Visual Basic .NET 29

3 Understanding Objects and Collections 59

4 Understanding Events 81

Part II Building a User Interface 97

Hour 5 Building Forms—The Basics 99

6 Building Forms—Advanced Techniques 121

7 Working with the Traditional Controls 149

8 Using Advanced Controls 179

9 Adding Menus and Toolbars to Forms 197

Part III Making Things Happen—Programming 217

Hour 10 Creating and Calling Code Procedures 219

11 Using Constants, Data Types, Variables, and Arrays 241

12 Performing Arithmetic, String Manipulation, and Date/Time Adjustments 265

13 Making Decisions in Visual Basic Code 287

14 Looping for Efficiency 303

15 Debugging Your Code 317

16 Designing Objects Using Classes 337

17 Interacting with Users 355

18 Working with Graphics 375

Part IV Working with Data 395

Hour 19 Performing File Operations 397

20 Controlling Other Applications Using Automation 415

21 Working with a Database 425

Part V Deploying Solutions and Beyond   **447**

Hour 22	Deploying a Visual Basic .NET Application	449
23	Introduction to Web Development	461
24	Building a Real-World Application	469
Appendix A	The 10,000-Foot View	489
Appendix B	Answers to the Quizzes	497
	Index	507

Contents

Introduction   1

Part I The Visual Basic .NET Environment   3

Hour 1 Jumping In with Both Feet: A Visual Basic .NET Programming Tour   5

Starting Visual Basic .NET 6

Creating a New Project 7

Understanding the Visual Studio .NET Environment 10

Changing the Characteristics of Objects 11

    Naming Objects 12

    Setting the Text Property of the Form 12

    Giving the Form an Icon 13

    Changing the Size of the Form 14

    Adding Controls to a Form 15

Designing an Interface 17

    Adding a Visible Control to a Form 17

    Adding an Invisible Control to a Form 19

Writing the Code Behind an Interface 21

    Letting a User Browse for a File 21

    Terminating a Program Using Code 24

Designating a Startup Object 25

Running a Project 25

Summary 27

Q&A 27

Workshop 28

    Quiz 28

    Exercises 28

Hour 2 Navigating Visual Basic .NET   29

Using the Visual Studio .NET Start Page 30

    Creating New Projects 31

    Opening an Existing Project 32

Navigating and Customizing the Visual Basic Environment 33

    Working with Design Windows 33

Working with Toolbars 38

    Showing and Hiding Toolbars 38

    Docking and Resizing Toolbars 39

Adding Controls to a Form Using the Toolbox 40

Setting Object Properties Using the Properties Window 41
   Selecting an Object and Viewing Its Properties 42
   Viewing and Changing Properties...42
   Working with Color Properties 44
   Viewing Property Descriptions 46
Managing Projects 46
   Managing Project Files with the Solution Explorer 47
   Working with Solutions..49
   Understanding Project Components 49
   Setting Project Properties 51
   Adding and Removing Project Files 52
A Quick-and-Dirty Programming Primer...54
   Storing Values in Variables 54
   Using Procedures to Write Functional Units of Code 54
   MessageBox.Show() 55
Getting Help 56
Summary 57
Q&A 58
Workshop 58
   Quiz 58
   Exercises 58

Hour 3 Understanding Objects and Collections   59

Understanding Objects 60
Understanding Properties 61
   Getting and Setting Properties...61
   Working with an Object and Its Properties 63
Understanding Methods 68
   Triggering Methods 68
   Understanding Method Dynamism 69
Building a Simple Object Example Project 69
   Creating the Interface for the Drawing Project...69
   Writing the Object-Based Code 70
   Testing Your Object Example Project 74
Understanding Collections 75
Using the Object Browser..77
Summary 78
Q&A 79
Workshop 79
   Quiz 80
   Exercises 80

Hour 4 Understanding Events   **81**

Understanding Event-Driven Programming 82

    Triggering Events 82

    Avoiding Recursive Events 84

    Accessing an Object's Events 85

    Working with Event Parameters 87

Building an Event Example Project 89

    Creating the User Interface 89

    Creating Event Handlers 90

    Testing Your Events Project..93

Keeping Event Names Current 94

Summary 94

Q&A 94

Workshop 95

    Quiz 95

    Exercises 95

Part II Building a User Interface   **97**

Hour 5 Building Forms—The Basics   **99**

Changing the Name of a Form 101

Changing the Appearance of a Form 101

    Displaying Text on a Form's Title Bar 101

    Changing a Form's Background Color 102

    Adding an Image to a Form's Background 104

    Giving a Form an Icon 105

    Preventing a Form from Appearing in the Taskbar 107

    Changing the Appearance and Behavior of a Form's Border 108

    Adding Minimize, Maximize, and Control Box Buttons to a Form..............110

    Specifying the Initial Display Position of a Form 111

    Displaying a Form in a Normal, Maximized, or Minimized State 112

    Changing the Mouse Pointer 113

Showing and Hiding Forms 114

    Showing Forms 114

    Understanding Form Modality 116

    Unloading Forms 117

Summary..119

Q&A 119

Workshop 119

    Quiz 119

    Exercises 120

Hour 6 Building Forms—Advanced Techniques   **121**

Working with Controls 122

    Adding Controls to a Form 122

    Manipulating Controls..123

    Creating a Tab Order 136

    Layering Controls (Z-Order) 137

Creating TopMost Windows 139

Creating Transparent Forms 139

Creating Scrollable Forms 140

Creating MDI Forms..142

Setting the Startup Object..146

Summary 147

Q&A 148

Workshop 148

    Quiz 148

    Exercises 148

Hour 7 Working with the Traditional Controls   **149**

Displaying Static Text with the Label Control 150

Allowing Users to Enter Text Using a Text Box 151

    Specifying Text Alignment 152

    Creating a Multiline Text Box...153

    Adding Scrollbars 154

    Limiting the Number of Characters a User Can Enter 155

    Creating Password Fields 156

    Understanding the Text Box's Common Events 156

Creating Buttons 157

    Accept and Cancel Buttons 159

    Adding a Picture to a Button...160

Creating Containers and Groups of Option Buttons 162

    Using Panels and Group Boxes..162

    Presenting Yes/No Options Using Check Boxes...164

    Working with Radio Buttons..165

Displaying a List with the List Box 167

    Manipulating Items at Design Time 168

    Manipulating Items at Runtime..169

    Sorting a List 173

Creating Drop-Down Lists Using the Combo Box 174

Summary..175

Q&A 176

Workshop 177

    Quiz 177

    Exercises 177

Hour 8 Using Advanced Controls **179**

Creating Timers...180

Creating Tabbed Dialog Boxes...182

Storing Pictures in an Image List...185

Building Enhanced Lists Using the List View 186

Creating Columns 187

Adding List Items 187

Manipulating a List View Using Code 190

Creating Hierarchical Lists with the Tree View 191

Adding Nodes to a Tree View 192

Removing Nodes 194

Clearing All Nodes 195

Summary..195

Q&A 195

Workshop 196

Quiz 196

Exercises 196

Hour 9 Adding Menus and Toolbars to Forms **197**

Building Menus..198

Adding Menu Items..198

Moving and Deleting Menu Items 201

Creating Checked Menu Items 201

Programming Menus..202

Implementing Context Menus 204

Assigning Shortcut Keys 206

Using the Toolbar Control 207

Adding Toolbar Buttons Using the Buttons Collection 208

Programming Toolbars 209

Creating Toggle Buttons 209

Creating Separators 211

Creating Drop-Down Menus for Toolbar Buttons 212

Creating a Status Bar 213

Summary..215

Q&A 215

Workshop 216

Quiz 216

Exercises 216

Part III Making Things Happen—Programming   217

Hour 10 Creating and Calling Code Procedures   219

Creating Visual Basic Code Modules 220
Writing Code Procedures 222
    Declaring Procedures That Don't Return Values 223
    Declaring Procedures That Return Values..225
Creating the User Interface of Your Project 226
Calling Code Procedures 227
    Passing Parameters 231
Exiting Procedures 232
Avoiding Infinite Recursion 232
Using Sub Main 233
Working with Tasks 234
Summary..237
Q&A 238
Workshop 238
    Quiz 238
    Exercises 239

Hour 11 Using Constants, Data Types, Variables, and Arrays   241

Understanding Data Types 242
    Determining Data Type 243
    Casting Data from One Data Type to Another 245
Defining and Using Constants 246
Declaring and Referencing Variables 247
    Declaring Variables 247
    Passing Literal Values to a Variable 249
    Using Variables in Expressions 249
    Enforced Variable Declaration and Data Typing..250
    Explicit Variable Declaration..250
    Strict Typing 251
Working with Arrays..251
    Dimensioning Arrays..252
    Referencing Array Variables 252
    Creating Multidimensional Arrays 253
Determining Scope 255
    Understanding Block Scope 255
    Understanding Procedure-Level (Local) Scope 256
    Understanding Module-Level Scope..256
    Using Global Scope..258
    Scope Name Conflicts...259

Declaring Variables of Static Scope 260

Naming Conventions..261

    Using Prefixes to Denote Data Type 261

    Denoting Scope Using Variable Prefixes 262

    Other Prefixes 262

Summary..262

Q&A 263

Workshop 263

    Quiz 263

    Exercises 264

Hour 12 Performing Arithmetic, String Manipulation, and Date/Time

Adjustments   265

Performing Basic Arithmetic Operations with Visual Basic .NET 266

    Performing Addition 266

    Performing Subtraction and Negation..267

    Performing Multiplication 267

    Performing Division 267

    Performing Exponentiation 268

    Performing Modulus Arithmetic 268

    Determining the Order of Operator Precedence 268

Comparing Equalities 270

Understanding Boolean Logic 271

    Using the And Operator..272

    Using the Not Operator 272

    Using the Or Operator 273

    Using the Xor Operator 273

    Manipulating Strings 274

    Concatenating Strings of Text 274

    Using the Basic String Functions 275

Working with Dates and Times 279

    Understanding the Date Data Type 280

    Adding to or Subtracting from a Date or Time..281

    Determining the Interval Between Two Dates or Times...............................282

    Retrieving Parts of a Date 283

    Formatting Dates and Times 283

    Retrieving the Current System Date and Time 284

    Determining Whether a Value Is a Date 285

Summary..285

Q&A 285

Workshop 286

    Quiz 286

    Exercises 286

Hour 13 Making Decisions in Visual Basic Code   **287**

Making Decisions Using If…Then 288

    Executing Code When *Expression* Is False 290

    Using ElseIf for Advanced Decision Making 291

    Nesting If…Then Constructs 292

Evaluating an Expression for Multiple Values Using Select Case 293

    Evaluating More Than One Possible Value in a Case Statement 294

    Building a Select Case Example 295

    Creative Uses of Select Case 297

Branching Within a Procedure Using GoTo 298

Summary 300

Q&A 301

Workshop 301

    Quiz 301

    Exercises 302

Hour 14 Looping for Efficiency   **303**

Looping a Specific Number of Times Using For…Next 304

    Initiating the Loop Using For 304

    Closing the Loop with the Next Statement 304

    Specifying an Increment Value Using Step 305

    Creating a For…Next Example 306

Using Do…Loop to Loop an Indeterminate Number of Times 309

    Creating a Do...Loop 310

    Ending a Do…Loop 310

    Creating a Do…Loop Example 311

Summary 313

Q&A 314

Workshop 314

    Quiz 314

    Exercises 315

Hour 15 Debugging Your Code   **317**

Adding Comments to Your Code 319

Identifying the Two Basic Types of Errors 320

Using Visual Basic .NET's Debugging Tools 323

    Working with Break Points 323

    Using the Command Window 325

    Using the Output Window 329

Writing an Error Handler Using Try…Catch…Finally 330

    Dealing with an Exception 333

    Handling an Anticipated Exception 334

Summary 335

Q&A 335

Workshop 335

    Quiz 336

    Exercises 336

Hour 16 Designing Objects Using Classes   **337**

Understanding Classes 338

    Encapsulating Data and Code Using Classes 338

    Comparing Classes with Standard Modules 339

    Creating an Object Interface 341

Instantiating Objects from Classes 346

    Binding an Object Reference to a Variable 347

    Releasing Object References 351

    Understanding the Lifetime of an Object 352

Summary 353

Q&A 353

Workshop 354

    Quiz 354

    Exercises 354

Hour 17 Interacting with Users   **355**

Displaying Messages Using the MessageBox.Show() Function 356

    Specifying Buttons and an Icon 357

    Determining Which Button Is Clicked 360

    Creating Good Messages..361

Creating Custom Dialog Boxes 361

Using InputBox() to Get Information from a User 365

Interacting with the Keyboard 367

Using the Common Mouse Events 370

Summary 373

Q&A 373

Workshop 373

    Quiz 374

    Exercises 374

Hour 18 Working with Graphics   **375**

Understanding the Graphics Object 376

    Creating a Graphics Object for a Form or Control 376

    Creating a Graphics Object for a New Bitmap 377

Working with Pens 378

Using System Colors 379

Working with Rectangles 382

Drawing Shapes 384
   Drawing Lines 384
   Drawing Rectangles...384
   Drawing Circles and Ellipses 384
   Clearing a Drawing Surface 385
Drawing Text...385
Persisting Graphics on a Form 386
Building a Graphics Project Example 387
Summary 392
Q&A 393
Workshop 393
   Quiz 393
   Exercises 394

Part IV Working with Data   **395**

Hour 19 Performing File Operations   **397**

Using the Open File Dialog and Save File Dialog Controls 398
   Using the Open File Dialog Control 398
   Using the Save File Dialog Control 401
Manipulating Files with the File Object...403
   Determining Whether a File Exists 403
   Copying a File 404
   Moving a File 405
   Deleting a File 406
   Renaming a File...407
   Retrieving a File's Properties 407
Manipulating Directories with the Directory Object 411
Summary 412
Q&A 412
Workshop 413
   Quiz 413
   Exercises 413

Hour 20 Controlling Other Applications Using Automation   **415**

Creating a Reference to an Automation Library 416
Creating an Instance of an Automation Server....................................418
Manipulating the Server 419
   Forcing Excel to Show Itself..419
   Creating an Excel Workbook..419
   Working with Data in an Excel Workbook 419
   Testing Your Client Application 421
Summary 422

Q&A 422
Workshop 423
    Quiz 423
    Exercises 423

Hour 21 Working with a Database **425**

Introducing ADO.NET 426
    Connecting to a Database 427
    Closing a Connection to a Data Source 428
Manipulating Data 429
    Understanding DataTables...429
    Creating a DataAdapter...429
    Referencing Fields in a DataRow 431
    Navigating Records 433
    Editing Records 435
    Creating New Records...435
    Deleting Records 437
    Running the Database Example 438
Using the Data Form Wizard 438
Summary...444
Q&A 444
Workshop 444
    Quiz 445
    Exercises 445

Part V Deploying Solutions and Beyond **447**

Hour 22 Deploying a Visual Basic .NET Application **449**

Creating a Custom Setup Program 450
    Adding the Output of a Project 451
    Adding a File to the Installation Program...................................454
    Adding a Custom Folder to the Install 454
    Creating a Shortcut on the Start Menu 455
    Defining the Build Configuration for the Setup Program............456
    The Common Language Runtime 456
    Building the Setup Program 456
Running a Custom Setup Program 457
Uninstalling an Application You've Distributed..................................459
Summary...459
Q&A 460
Workshop 460
    Quiz 460
    Exercises 460

Hour 23 Introduction to Web Development   461

Understanding ASP.NET 462
Creating Dynamic Web Content with Web Forms 462
    Comparing Windows Forms to Web Forms 463
XML Web Services 465
    Understanding the Technology Behind XML Web Services 465
    Consuming XML Web Services 467
Summary 467
Q&A 467
Workshop 468
    Quiz 468

Hour 24 Building a Real-World Application   469

Building the Interface 470
    Designing the Main Window...470
Building the Menu 471
Building the Toolbar 472
Adding the List View to Display Albums...474
Adding the Browse For Database OpenFileDialog Control................................476
    Designing the Album Dialog Box 476
Writing the Code of the CD Cataloger..479
    Writing Code for the Main Window 479
    Writing Code for the Album Maintenance Dialog Box 484
Testing Your Application 487

Appendix A The 10,000-Foot View   489

The .NET Framework...490
Common Language Runtime 490
Microsoft Intermediate Language..491
Namespaces...492
Common Type System 494
Garbage Collection 494

Appendix B Answers to the Quizzes   497

Hour 1 497
Hour 2 497
Hour 3 498
Hour 4 498
Hour 5 498
Hour 6 499
Hour 7 499
Hour 8 499
Hour 9 500

Hour 10 500
Hour 11 501
Hour 12 501
Hour 13 501
Hour 14 502
Hour 15 502
Hour 16 502
Hour 17 503
Hour 18 503
Hour 19 503
Hour 20 504
Hour 21 504
Hour 22 504
Hour 23 505

Index **507**

About the Author

James Foxall is Vice President of Development and Support for Tigerpaw Software, Inc. (www.tigerpawsoftware.com)—an Omaha, Nebraska, Microsoft Certified Partner specializing in commercial database applications. James manages the Tigerpaw Business Suite, an award-winning CRM product designed to automate contact management, marketing, service and repair, proposal generation, and inventory control and purchasing. James's experience in creating certified Office-compatible software has made him an authority on application interface and behavior standards of applications for the Microsoft Windows and Microsoft Office environments.

James has personally written more than 200,000 lines of commercial production Visual Basic code both in single programmer and multiple programmer environments. He's the author of numerous books, including *Practical Standards for Microsoft Visual Basic* and *MCSD in a Nutshell: The Visual Basic Exams*, and he has written articles for *Access-Office-VBA Advisor* and *Visual Basic Programmer's Journal*. James has a Bachelor's degree in Management of Information Systems (MIS), is a Microsoft Certified Solution Developer, and an international speaker on Microsoft Visual Basic. When not programming or writing about programming, he enjoys spending time with his family, playing guitar, doing battle over the chess board, listening to Pink Floyd, playing computer games, and (believe it or not) programming! You can reach James at www.jamesfoxall.com/forums.

About the Tech Editor

Bill Hatfield is the best-selling author of several books on Microsoft technologies, including *ASP.NET For Dummies*, *Active Server Pages For Dummies,* and *Visual InterDev For Dummies* (Wiley). He's also the editor for two monthly technical journals from Pinnacle Publishing: *Hardcore Visual Studio .NET* and *Hardcore Delphi*. In addition, Bill Hatfield develops courseware and presents corporate training in XML, Web development, and distributed technologies for developers. He also consults on a broad variety of architecture and development projects. He works from his home in Indianapolis, Indiana, where he lives with his wife Melanie, their son Bryce, and daughter Zoe.

Dedication

To my family—Tess, Ethan, and Laura

Acknowledgments

To Candy Hall, Mark Renfrow, Bill Hatfield, and everyone else at Sams who had a hand in this book. Working with all of you was a pleasure!

Tell Us What You Think!

As the reader of this book, *you* are our most important critic and commentator. We value your opinion and want to know what we're doing right, what we could do better, what areas you'd like to see us publish in, and any other words of wisdom you're willing to pass our way.

As an Associate Publisher for Sams Publishing, I welcome your comments. You can e-mail or write me directly to let me know what you did or didn't like about this book—as well as what we can do to make our books stronger.

Please note that I cannot help you with technical problems related to the topic of this book, and that because of the high volume of mail I receive, I might not be able to reply to every message.

When you write, please be sure to include this book's title and author as well as your name and phone or fax number. I will carefully review your comments and share them with the author and editors who worked on the book.

Email: feedback@samspublishing.com

Mail: Michael Stephens
           Sams Publishing
           800 East 96th Street
           Indianapolis, IN 46240 USA

For more information about this book or another Sams title, visit our Web site at www.samspublishing.com. Type the ISBN (excluding hyphens) or the title of a book in the Search field to find the page you're looking for.

Introduction

Visual Basic .NET is Microsoft's latest incarnation of the enormously popular Visual Basic language, and it's fundamentally different from the versions that came before it. Visual Basic .NET is now more powerful and more capable than ever before, and its features and functionality are on par with higher-level languages such as C++. One consequence of this newfound power is added complexity. Gone are the days when you could sit down with Visual Basic and the online Help and teach yourself what you need to know to create a functional program.

Audience and Organization

This book is targeted toward those who have little or no programming experience or who might be picking up Visual Basic .NET as a second language. The book has been structured and written with a purpose: to get you productive as quickly and as smoothly as possible. I've used my experiences from writing large commercial applications with Visual Basic and teaching Visual Basic to create a book that I hope cuts through the fluff and teaches you *what you need to know*. All too often, authors fall into the trap of focusing on the technology rather than on the practical application of the technology. I've worked hard to keep this book focused on teaching you practical skills that you can apply immediately toward a development project. Please feel free to post your suggestions or success stories at www.jamesfoxall.com/forums.

This book is divided into five parts, each of which focuses on a different aspect of developing applications with Visual Basic .NET. These parts generally follow the flow of tasks you'll perform as you begin creating your own programs using Visual Basic .NET. I recommend that you read them in the order in which they appear.

- **Part I** "The Visual Basic .NET Environment" teaches you the Visual Basic .NETenvironment, including how to navigate and access Visual Basic .NET's numerous tools. In addition, you'll learn some key development concepts such as objects, collections, and events.

- **Part II** "Building a User Interface" shows you how to build attractive and functional user interfaces. In this part, you'll learn about forms and controls—the user interface elements such as text boxes and list boxes.

- **Part III** "Making Things Happen—Programming" teaches you the nuts and bolts of Visual Basic .NET programming—and there's a lot to learn. You'll discover how to create modules and procedures, as well has how to store data, perform loops, and make decisions in code. After you've learned the core programming skills, you'll move into object-oriented programming and debugging applications.

- **Part IV** "Working with Data" introduces you to working with a database and shows you how to automate external applications such as Word and Excel. In addition, this part teaches you how to manipulate a user's file system.

- **Part V** "Deploying Solutions and Beyond" shows you how to distribute an application that you've created to an end user's computer. Then the focus is brought back a bit to take a look at Web programming. Hour 24 concludes the book step-by-step instructions to build a complete Visual Basic .NET application. In Appendix A, you'll learn about Microsoft's .NET initiative from a higher, less-technical level.

Conventions Used in This Book

This book uses several conventions to help you prioritize and reference the information it contains:

- **Tips** highlight information that can make your VB programming more effective.

- **Cautions** focus your attention on problems or side effects that can occur in specific situations.

- **Notes** provide useful sidebar information that you can read immediately or circle back to without losing the flow of the topic at hand.

- **New Term** icons signal places where new terminology is first used and defined. Such terminology appears in an *italic* typeface for emphasis.

In addition, this book uses various typefaces to help you distinguish code from regular English. Code is presented in a `monospace` font. Placeholders—words or characters used temporarily to represent the real words or characters you would type in code—are typeset in *`italic monospace`*.

Some code statements presented in this book are too long to appear on a single line. In these cases, a line-continuation character (an underscore) is used to indicate that the following line is a continuation of the current statement.

Onward and Upward!

This is an exciting time to be learning how to program, and it's my sincerest wish that when you finish this book, you feel capable of creating, debugging, and deploying modest Visual Basic .NET programs using many of Visual Basic .NET's tools. Although you won't be an expert, you'll be surprised at how much you've learned. And I hope this book will help you determine your future direction as you proceed down the road to Visual Basic .NET mastery.

I love programming with Visual Basic .NET, and I sometimes find it hard to believe I get paid to do so. I hope you find Visual Basic .NET as enjoyable as I do!

PART I

The Visual Basic .NET Environment

Hour

1   Jumping In with Both Feet: A Visual Basic
    .NET Programming Tour

2   Navigating Visual Basic .NET

3   Understanding Objects and Collections

4   Understanding Events

Hour 1

Jumping In with Both Feet: A Visual Basic .NET Programming Tour

Learning a new programming language can be intimidating. If you've never programmed before, the act of typing seemingly cryptic text to produce sleek and powerful applications probably seems like a black art, and you might wonder how you'll ever learn everything you need to know. The answer is, of course, one step at a time. The first step to learning a language is the same as that of any other activity: building confidence. Programming is part art and part science. Although it might seem like magic, it's more akin to illusion; after you know how things work, a lot of the mysticism goes away, freeing you to focus on the mechanics necessary to produce the desired result.

In this hour, you'll complete a quick tour that takes you step-by-step through creating a complete, albeit small, Visual Basic .NET program. I've yet to see a Hello World program that's the least bit helpful (they usually do nothing more than print `hello world` to the screen—oh, fun). So, instead, you'll create a picture-viewer application that lets you view Windows bitmaps and icons on your computer. You'll learn how to let a user browse for a file and how to display a selected picture file on the screen. Both of these skills will come in handy in the real-world applications that you'll create.

Producing large, commercial solutions is accomplished by way of a series of small steps. After you've finished creating the project in this hour, you'll have a feel for the overall development process and will have taken the first step toward becoming an accomplished programmer.

The highlights of this hour include the following:

- Building a simple (yet functional) Visual Basic .NET application
- Letting a user browse a hard drive
- Displaying a picture from a file on disk
- Getting familiar with some programming lingo
- Learning about the Visual Studio .NET IDE

I hope that by the end of this hour, you'll realize just how much fun it is to program using Visual Basic .NET.

Starting Visual Basic .NET

Before you begin creating programs in Visual Basic .NET, you should be familiar with the following terms:

- *Distributable component*   The final, compiled version of a project. Components can be distributed to other people and other computers and they don't require Visual Basic to run (although they do require the .NET runtime, which I'll discuss in Hour 22, "Deploying a Visual Basic .NET Application"). Distributable components are often called programs. In Hour 22, you'll learn how to distribute the Picture Viewer program that you're about to build to other computers.
- *Project*   A collection of files that can be compiled to create a distributable component (program). There are many types of projects, and complex applications might consist of many projects, such as a Windows Application project, and support dynamic link library (DLL) projects.
- *Solution*   A collection of projects and files that make up an application or component.

In the past, Visual Basic was an autonomous language. This has changed. Now, Visual Basic .NET is part of a larger entity known as the *.NET Framework*. The .NET Framework encompasses all the .NET technology, including Visual Studio .NET (the suite of development tools) and the common language runtime, which is the set of files that make up the core of all .NET applications. You'll learn about these items in more detail as you progress through this book. For now, realize that Visual Basic .NET is one of many languages that exist within the .NET family. Many other languages, such as C#, are also .NET languages, make use of the common language runtime, and are developed within Visual Studio .NET.

NEW TERM   Visual Studio .NET is a complete development environment, and it's called the IDE (short for *integrated development environment*). The IDE is the design framework in which you build applications; every tool you'll need to create your Visual Basic .NET projects is accessed from within the Visual Basic .NET IDE. Again, Visual Studio .NET supports development using many different languages with Visual Basic .NET being the most popular. The environment itself is not Visual Basic .NET, but rather the language you'll be using within Visual Studio .NET *is* Visual Basic .NET. To work with Visual Basic projects, you first start the Visual Studio .NET IDE.

Start Visual Studio .NET now by choosing Microsoft Visual Studio .NET 2003 from within the Microsoft Visual Studio .NET 2003 folder on your Start / All Programs menu.

Creating a New Project

When you first start Visual Studio .NET, you're shown the Start Page tab within the IDE. You can open projects created previously or create new projects from this Start page (see Figure 1.1). For this quick tour, you're going to create a new Windows application, so click the New Project button in the lower-left to display the New Project dialog box shown in Figure 1.2.

If you don't see the Visual Studio.NET Start page, chances are that you've changed the default settings. In Hour 2, "Navigating Visual Basic .NET," I'll show you how to change them back. For now, you can create a new project by choosing New from the File menu and then clicking Project.

FIGURE 1.1

*You can open existing
projects or create new
projects from the
Visual Studio .NET
Start page.*

FIGURE **1.1**

*You can open existing
projects or create new
projects from the
Visual Studio .NET
Start page.*

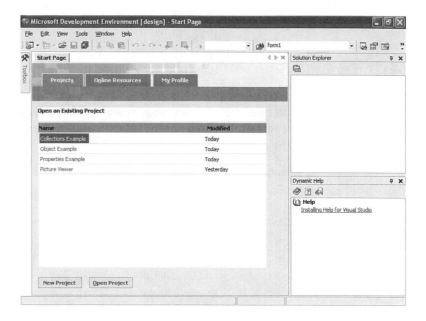

FIGURE **1.2**

*The New Project dia-
log box enables you to
create many types of
.NET projects.*

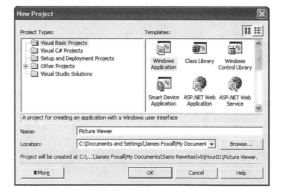

The New Project dialog box is used to specify the type of Visual Basic .NET project to
create. (You can create many types of projects with Visual Basic, as well as with the
other supported languages of the .NET platform.) If the Visual Basic Projects folder isn't
selected, click it to display the Visual Basic project types, and then make sure that the
Windows Application icon is selected (if it's not, click it once to select it). At the bottom
of the New Project dialog box is a Name text box. This is where, oddly enough, you
specify the name of the project you're creating. The Location text box is used to specify
the folder in which to create the project.

When you create the new project, Visual Basic .NET creates a new folder with the same
name as the one you specify in the Name text box under the folder specified in the

Location text box. For example, if you created a project named Music Cataloger and specified the location as c:\temp, the project would be created in a new folder with the path c:\temp\Music Cataloger. If you select the Create Directory for Solution check box, Visual Basic will create a subfolder under Location that contains the solution files (a collection of files referencing multiple projects), and yet another subfolder for your actual project files. This is useful when you build solutions that consist of multiple projects. If the Create Directory for Solution check box isn't visible, click the More button and the dialog box will expand to show this option.

> You should always set the Name and Location values to something meaningful before creating a project, or you'll have more work to do later if you want to move or rename the project. In most cases, the default location is probably fine.

Name your project Picture Viewer by typing **Picture Viewer** into the Name text box. At this time, there's no need to change the location of where the project files will be saved, and there's no need to worry about a separate folder for solution files because your solution will consist of a single project. Go ahead and deselect the Create Directory for Solution check box and click OK to create the new Windows Application project. Visual Basic .NET creates the new project, complete with one form (the gray window with the dots on it) for you to begin building the interface for your application (see Figure 1.3).

> Within Visual Studio .NET, *form* is the term given to the design-time view of windows that can be displayed to a user.

Your Visual Studio .NET environment might look different from that shown in the figures of this hour due to the edition of Visual Studio .NET you're using, whether you've already played with Visual Studio .NET, and other factors such as the resolution of your monitor. All the elements discussed in this hour exist in all editions of Visual Studio .NET, however. (If a window shown in a figure isn't displayed in your IDE, use the View menu to display it.)

FIGURE 1.3

New Windows applications start with a blank form; the fun is just beginning!

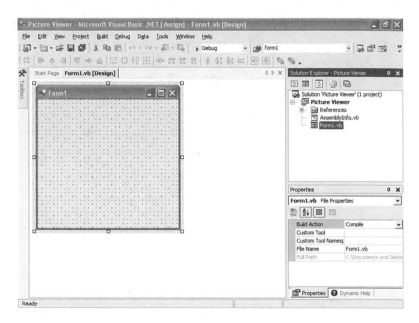

> To create a program that can be run on another computer, you start by creating a project and then compiling the project into a component such as an *executable* (a program a user can run) or a *DLL* (a component that can be used by other programs and components). The compilation process is discussed in detail in Hour 22. The important thing to note at this time is that when you hear someone refer to *creating* or *writing a program*, just as you're creating the Picture Viewer program now, they're referring to the completion of all steps up to and including compiling the project to a distributable file.

Understanding the Visual Studio .NET Environment

The first time you run Visual Studio .NET, you'll notice that the IDE contains a lot of windows, such as the Properties window on the right, which is used to view and set properties of objects. In addition to these windows, the IDE contains a lot of tabs, such as the vertical Toolbox tab on the left edge of the IDE (refer to Figure 1.3). Try this now: Click the Toolbox tab to display the Toolbox window (clicking a tab displays an associated window). You can hover the mouse over a tab for a few seconds to display the window as well. To hide the window, simply move the mouse off the window. To close the window completely, click the Close (X) button in the window's title bar.

You can adjust the size and position of any of these windows, and you can even hide and show them as needed. You'll learn how to customize your design environment in Hour 2.

 Unless specifically instructed to do so, don't double-click *anything* in the Visual Basic design environment. Double-clicking most objects produces an entirely different result than single-clicking does. If you mistakenly double-click an object on a form (discussed shortly), a code window is displayed. At the top of the code window is a set of tabs: one for the form design and one for the code. Click the tab for the form design to hide the code window and return to the form.

The Properties window at the right side of the design environment is perhaps the most important window in the IDE, and it's the one you'll use most often. If your computer display resolution is set to 640×480, you can probably see only a few properties at this time. This makes it difficult to view and set properties as you create projects. I highly recommend that you don't attempt development with Visual Basic .NET at a resolution below 800×600. Personally, I prefer 1024×768 or higher because it offers plenty of work space. To change your display settings, right-click your desktop and select Properties.

Changing the Characteristics of Objects

Almost everything you work with in Visual Basic .NET is an object. Forms, for instance, are objects, as are all the items you can put on a form to build an interface such as list boxes and buttons. There are *many* types of objects, and objects are classified by type. For example, a form is a Form object, whereas items you can place on a form are called Control objects, or controls. (Hour 3, "Understanding Objects and Collections," discusses objects in detail.) Some objects don't have a physical appearance, but exist only in code, and you'll learn about these kinds of objects in later hours.

NEW TERM Every object has a distinct set of attributes known as *properties* (regardless of whether the object has a physical appearance). You have certain properties about you, such as your height and hair color. Visual Basic .NET objects have properties as well, such as Height and BackColor. Properties define the characteristics of an object. When you create a new object, the first thing you need to do is set its properties so that the object appears and behaves in the way you want. To display the properties of an object, click the object in its designer (the main work area in the IDE).

Click anywhere in the default form now and check to see that its properties are displayed in the Properties window. You'll know because the drop-down list box at the top of the properties window will contain the form's name: Form1.

Naming Objects

The property you should always set first for any new object is the Name property. Press F4 to display the Properties window (if it's not already visible), and scroll down to the Design section to see the "(Name)" property. When you first create an object, Visual Basic .NET gives the object a unique, generic name based on the object's type. Although these names are functional, they simply aren't descriptive enough for practical use. For instance, Visual Basic .NET named your form Form1, but it's common to have dozens of forms in a project, and it would be extremely difficult to manage such a project if all forms were distinguishable only by a number (Form2, Form3, and so forth).

> In actuality, what you're working with is a form class, or template, that will be used to create and show forms at runtime. For the purpose of this quick tour, I simply refer to it as a form. See Hour 5, "Building Forms: Part 1," for more information.

To better manage your forms, you should give each one a descriptive name. Visual Basic .NET gives you the chance to name new forms as they're created. Visual Basic .NET created this default form for you, so you didn't get a chance to name it; you must change both the name and the filename of the form. Change the name of the form now by clicking the Name property and changing the text from Form1 to fclsViewer. Notice that this does not change the filename of the form as it's displayed in the Solution Explorer window. Change the filename now by right-clicking Form1.vb in the Solution Explorer window, choosing Rename from the context menu, and changing the text from Form1.vb to fclsViewer.vb. In future examples, I won't have you change the filename each time because you'll have enough steps to accomplish as it is. I do recommend, however, that you always change your filenames to something meaningful in your real projects.

> I use the fcls prefix here to denote that the file is a form class.

Setting the Text Property of the Form

Notice that the text that appears in the form's title bar says Form1. This is because Visual Basic .NET sets the form's title bar to the name of the form when it's first created, but doesn't change it when you change the name of the form. The text in the title bar is determined by the value of the Text property of the form. Click the form once more so that its properties appear in the Properties window. Use the scrollbar in the Properties window to locate the Text property (you'll find it in the Appearance category), and then change the text to **Picture Viewer**. Press the Enter key or click on a different property. You'll see the text in the title bar of the form change.

The Text property was named the Caption property in Visual Basic 6 and earlier versions.

Giving the Form an Icon

Everyone who has used Windows is familiar with icons—the little pictures used to represent programs. Icons most commonly appear in the Start menu next to the name of their respective programs. In Visual Basic .NET, you not only have control over the icon of your program file, you can also give every form in your program a unique icon if you want to.

The instructions that follow assume that you have access to the source files for the examples in this book. They are available at www.samspublishing.com. You can also get these files, as well as discuss this book, at my Web site at www.jamesfoxall.com. You don't have to use the icon I've provided for this example; you can use any icon of your choice. If you don't have an icon available (or you want to be a rebel), you can skip this section without affecting the outcome of the example.

To give the form an icon, follow these steps:

1. In the Properties window, click the Icon property to select it. (It's in the Windows Style category.)

2. When you click the Icon property, a small button with three dots appears to the right of the property. Click this button.

3. Use the Open dialog box that appears to locate the Hour1.ico file or another icon file of your choice. When you've found the icon, double-click it, or click it once to select it and then click Open.

After you've selected the icon, it appears in the Icon property along with the word (Icon). A small version of the icon appears in the upper-left corner of the form as well. Whenever this form is minimized, this is the icon that's displayed on the Windows taskbar. (Note: This doesn't change the icon for the project as a whole. In Hour 22, you'll learn how to assign an icon to your distributable file.)

Changing the Size of the Form

The Properties window currently shows all properties for the form by category (unless you've changed this setting since installing Visual Studio .NET). This is very useful when first learning Visual Basic .NET, but as your skills progress and you begin to commit property names to memory, you might prefer to see the properties listed in alphabetical order (my personal preference). Just above the list of properties in the Properties window is a group of tool buttons. The first button on the left changes the property display to categorical, and should be depressed already (that is, it has a box around it). If not, click it to see the properties listed in categorical order. The button next to this changes the display to alphabetical. Go ahead and click it now to view the properties in alphabetical order. I recommend that you keep the Properties window set to show properties in alphabetical order; doing so makes it easier to find properties that I refer to in the text.

Next, you're going to change the Width and Height properties of the form. The Width and Height values are shown collectively under the Size property; Width appears to the left of the comma, Height to the right. You can change the Width or Height property by changing the corresponding number in the Size property. Both values are represented in pixels (that is, a form that has a Size property of 200,350 is 200 pixels wide by 350 pixels tall). To display and adjust the Width and Height properties separately, click the small plus sign (+) next to the Size property (see Figure 1.4).

FIGURE 1.4

Some properties can be expanded to show more specific properties.

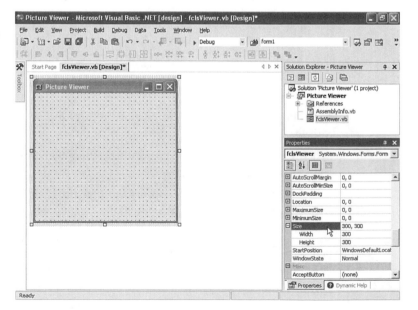

A *pixel* is a unit of measurement for computer displays; it's the smallest visible 'dot' on the screen. The resolution of a display is always given in pixels, such as 800×600 or 1024×768. When you increase or decrease a property by one pixel, you're making the smallest possible visible change to the property.

Change the Width property to **400** and the Height to **325** by typing in the corresponding box next to a property name. To commit a property change, press Tab or Enter, or click a different property or window. Your screen should now look like the one in Figure 1.5.

FIGURE 1.5

Changes made in the Properties window are reflected as soon as they're committed.

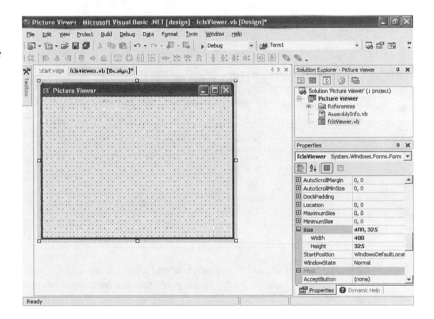

When you first created this project, Visual Basic .NET saved a copy of the source files in their initial state. The changes you've made so far exist only in memory; if you were to turn your computer off at this time (don't do this), you would lose all work up to this point. You should get into the habit of frequently saving your work (committing the changes to disk). Save the project now by choosing Save All from the File menu or by clicking the Save All button on the toolbar—it has a picture of stacked diskettes on it.

Adding Controls to a Form

Now that you've set the initial properties of your form, it's time to create a user interface by adding objects to the form. Objects that can be placed on a form are called *controls*.

Some controls have a visible interface with which a user can interact, whereas others are always invisible to the user. You'll use controls of both types in this example. On the left side of the screen is a vertical tab titled Toolbox. Click the Toolbox tab now to display the Toolbox window (see Figure 1.6). The toolbox contains all the controls available in the project, such as labels and text boxes.

FIGURE 1.6

The toolbox is used to select controls to build a user interface.

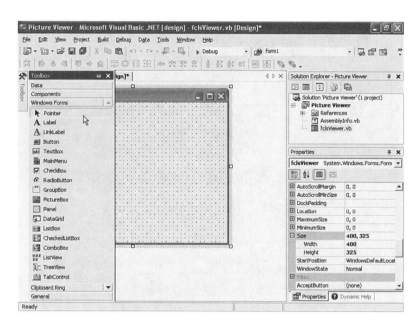

There are three ways to add a control to a form, and Hour 5 explains them in detail. In this hour, you'll use the technique of double-clicking a tool in the toolbox.

The toolbox closes as soon as you've added a control to a form and when the pointer is no longer over the toolbox. To make the toolbox stay visible, click the little picture of a pushpin located in the toolbox's title bar.

Refer to Hour 2 for more information on customizing the design environment.

Your Picture Viewer interface will consist of the following controls:

- Two Button controls (the standard buttons that you're used to clicking in pretty much every Windows program you've ever run)
- A PictureBox control (a control used to display bitmaps to a user)
- An OpenFileDialog control (a hidden control that exposes the Windows Open File dialog box functionality)

Designing an Interface

It's generally best to design the user interface of a form and then add the code behind the interface to make the form functional. You'll build your interface in the following sections.

Adding a Visible Control to a Form

Start by adding a Button control to the form. Do this by double-clicking the Button item in the toolbox. Visual Basic .NET then creates a new button and places it in the upper-left corner of the form (see Figure 1.7).

In Visual Basic 6 and earlier editions, the Button control was called a command button.

FIGURE 1.7

When you double-click a control in the toolbox, the control is added to the upper-left corner of the form.

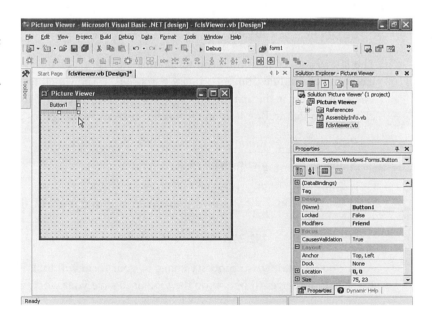

Using the Properties window, set the button's properties as follows. Again, you might want to change the Properties list to alphabetical (if it isn't already) to make it easier to find these properties by name. When you view the properties alphabetically, the Name property is listed first, so don't go looking for it down in the list or you'll be looking awhile.

Property	Value
Name	**btnSelectPicture**
Text	**Select Picture**
Location	**301,10** (Note: 301 is the x coordinate, 10 is the y coordinate.)
Size	**85,23**

You're now going to create a button that the user can click to close the Picture Viewer program. Rather than adding a new button to the form, you're going to create a copy of the button you've already defined. To do this, right-click the button on the form and choose Copy from its shortcut menu. Next, right-click anywhere on the form and choose Paste from the form's shortcut menu. The new button appears centered on the form, and it's selected by default. Change the properties of the new button as follows:

Property	Value
Name	**btnQuit**
Text	**Quit**
Location	**301,40**

The last visible control you need to add to the form is a PictureBox control. A PictureBox has many capabilities, but its primary purpose is to show pictures, which is precisely what you'll use it for in this example. Add a new PictureBox control to the form by double-clicking the PictureBox item in the toolbox and set its properties as follows:

Property	Value
Name	**picShowPicture**
BorderStyle	**FixedSingle**
Location	**8,8**
Size	**282,275**

After you've made these property changes, your form will look like the one in Figure 1.8. Click the Save All button on the toolbar to save your work.

FIGURE 1.8

An application's interface doesn't have to be complex to be useful.

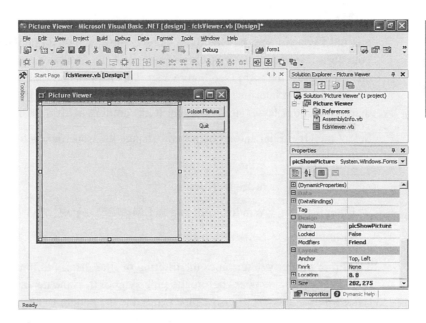

Adding an Invisible Control to a Form

All the controls that you've used so far sit on a form and have a physical appearance when the application is run. Not all controls have a physical appearance, however. Such controls, referred to as *nonvisual controls* (or *invisible-at-runtime* controls), aren't designed for direct user interactivity. Instead, they're designed to give you, the programmer, functionality beyond the standard features of Visual Basic .NET.

To enable the user to select a picture to display, you need to give her the ability to locate a file on her hard drive. You might have noticed that whenever you choose to open a file from within any Windows application, the dialog box displayed is almost always the same. It doesn't make sense to force every developer to write the code necessary to perform standard file operations, so Microsoft has exposed the functionality via a control that you can use in your projects. This control is called the OpenFileDialog control, and it will save you dozens and dozens of hours that would otherwise be necessary to duplicate this common functionality.

Other controls in addition to the OpenFileDialog control give you file functionality. For example, the SaveFileDialog control provides features for allowing the user to specify a filename and path for saving a file.

Display the toolbox and scroll down using the down arrow in the lower part of the tool-box until you can see the OpenFileDialog control, and then double-click it to add it to your form. Note that the control isn't placed on the form, but rather it appears in a special area below the form (see Figure 1.9). This happens because the OpenFileDialog control has no form interface to display to a user. It does have an interface (a dialog box) that you can display as necessary, but it has nothing to display directly on a form.

Select the OpenFileDialog control and change its properties as follows:

Property	Value
Name	**ofdSelectPicture**
Filter	Windows Bitmaps|*.BMP|JPEG Files|*.JPG
Title	**Select Picture**

The Filter property determines the filtering of files displayed in the Open File dialog box. The text that appears before the pipe symbol (|) is the descriptive text of the file type, whereas the text after the pipe symbol is the pattern to use to filter files; you can specify more than one filter type, separated by a pipe. Text entered into the Title property appears in the title bar of the Open File dialog box.

FIGURE 1.9

Controls that have no interface appear below the form designer.

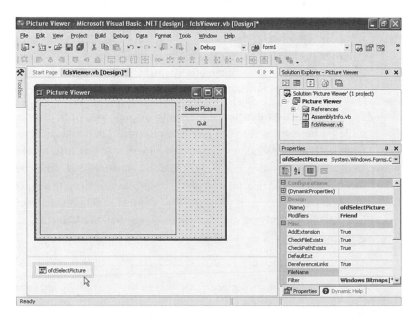

Writing the Code Behind an Interface

1

The graphical interface for your Picture Viewer program is now finished. If you pinned the toolbox open, click the pushpin in the title bar of the toolbox now to close it. You have to write code for the program to be capable of performing actions and responding to user interaction. Visual Basic .NET is an *event-driven* language, which means that code is executed in response to events. These events might come from users, such as a user clicking a button, or from Windows itself (see Hour 4, "Understanding Events," for a complete explanation of events). Currently, your application looks nice, but it won't do a darn thing (sort of like me on Saturday mornings—before kids). The user can click the Select Picture button, for example, until he can file for disability with carpel tunnel syndrome but nothing will happen because you haven't told the program what to do when the user clicks the button. You can see this for yourself now by pressing F5 to run the project. Feel free to click the buttons, but they don't do anything. When you're done, close the window you created to return to Design mode.

You're going to write code to accomplish two tasks. First, you're going to write code that lets the user browse his hard drives to locate and select a picture file and then display the file in the picture box (this sounds a lot harder than it is). Second, you're going to add code to the Quit button that shuts down the program when the user clicks the button.

Letting a User Browse for a File

The first bit of code you're going to write will enable the user to browse his hard drives and select a picture file, and then show the selected picture in the PictureBox control. This code will execute when the user clicks the Select Picture button; therefore, it's added to the Click event of that button (you'll learn all about events in later hours).

When you double-click a control on a form in Design view, the default event for that control is displayed in a code window. The default event for a Button control is its Click event, which makes sense because clicking is the most common action a user performs with a button. Double-click the Select Picture button now to access its Click event in the code window (see Figure 1.10).

NEW TERM When you access an event, Visual Basic .NET builds an *event handler*, which is essentially a template procedure in which you add the code that executes when the event occurs. The cursor is already placed within the code procedure, so all you have to do is add code. By the time you're done with this book, you'll be madly clicking away as you write your own code to make your applications do exactly what you want them to do—well, most of the time. For now, just enter the code as I present it here.

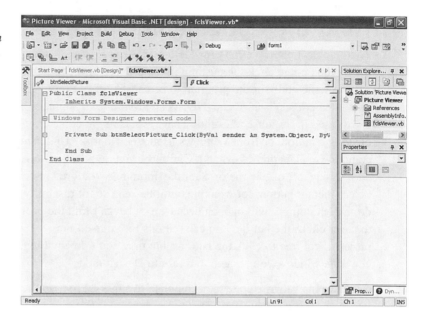

It's very important that you get in the habit of commenting your code, so the first line you're going to enter is a comment. Beginning a statement with an apostrophe designates the statement as a comment; the compiler won't do anything with the statement, so you can enter whatever text you want after the apostrophe. Type the following statement exactly as it appears and press the Enter key at the end of the line:

```
' Show the open file dialog box.
```

The next statement you'll enter triggers a method of the OpenFileDialog control that you added to the form. You'll learn all about methods in Hour 3. For now, think of a method as a mechanism to make a control do something. The ShowDialog method tells the control to show its Open dialog box and let the user select a file. The ShowDialog method returns a value that indicates its success or failure, which we'll then compare to a predefined result (DialogResult.OK). Don't worry too much about what's happening here; you'll be learning the details of this in later hours and the sole purpose of this hour is to get your feet wet. In a nutshell, the ShowDialog method is invoked to let a user browse for a file. If the user selects a file, more code is executed. Of course, there's a lot more to using the OpenFileDialog control than I present in this basic example, but this simple statement gets the job done. Enter the following statement:

```
If ofdselectpicture.ShowDialog = DialogResult.OK Then
```

After you insert the statement that begins with If and you press Enter, Visual Basic .NET automatically creates the End If statement for you. If you type in End If, you'll wind up with two End If statements and your code won't run. If this happens to you, delete one of the statements. You'll learn all about If statements in Hour 13, "Making Decisions in Visual Basic Code."

Time for another comment. Type this statement and remember to press Enter at the end of the code line:

```
' Load the picture into the picture box.
```

Don't worry about indenting the code by pressing the Tab key or using spaces. Visual Basic .NET automatically indents code for you.

This next statement, which appears within the If construct (between the If and End If statements), is the line of code that actually displays the picture in the picture box. (If you're itching to know more about graphics, take a look at Hour 18, "Working with Graphics.")

Enter the following statement:

```
picshowpicture.Image = Image.FromFile(ofdselectpicture.filename)
```

In addition to displaying the selected picture, your program is also going to display the path and filename of the picture in the title bar. When you first created the form, you changed the Text property of the form using the Properties window. To create dynamic applications, properties need to be constantly adjusted at runtime, and this is done using code. Insert the following two statements (press Enter at the end of each line):

```
' Show the name of the file in the form's caption.
Me.Text = "Picture Viewer(" & ofdselectpicture.FileName & ")"
```

After you've entered all the code, your editor should look like that shown in Figure 1.11.

FIGURE 1.11

Make sure your code exactly matches the code shown here.

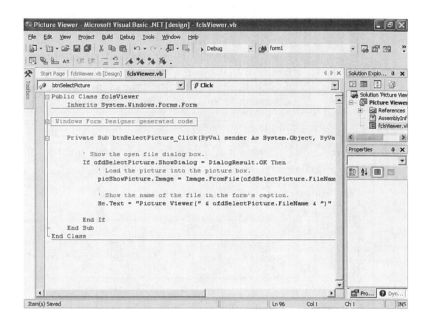

Terminating a Program Using Code

The last bit of code you'll write will terminate the application when the user clicks the Quit button. To do this, you'll need to access the Click event handler of the btnQuit button. At the top of the code window are two tabs. The current tab has the text fclsViewer.vb. This is the tab containing the code window for the form with the filename fclsViewer.vb. Next to this is a tab that contains the text fclsViewer.vb [Design]. Click this tab now to switch from Code view to the form designer. If you receive an error when you click the tab, the code you entered contains an error and you need to edit it to make it the same as shown previously. After the form designer displays, double-click the Quit button to access its Click event.

Enter the following code in the Quit button's Click event handler:

```
Me.Close()
```

The Me.Close statement closes the current form. When the last loaded form in a program is closed, the application shuts itself down—completely. As you build more robust applications, you'll probably want to execute all kinds of clean-up routines before terminating an application, but for this example, closing the form is all you need to do.

Designating a Startup Object

There's one last thing you need to do before you can run your project. Each Visual Basic .NET project has to have an *entry point*—a code procedure that is the first bit of code that executes when the project starts. By default, this startup code is specified as being in the form titled Form1. Earlier, I had you change the name of the default form to fclsViewer. Unfortunately, Visual Basic .NET doesn't change its internal reference and still looks for Form1. This was a known issue in the first release of .NET, and has yet to be corrected. Fortunately, changing this yourself is straightforward. To do so, right-click the project name Picture Viewer in the Solution Explorer and choose Properties from its shortcut menu (be sure to click the Project item, not the Solution item). This displays the Project Property Pages dialog box shown in Figure 1.12. Open the drop-down list for Startup Object, select fclsViewer, and then click OK to save your changes and close the dialog box.

FIGURE 1.12

You designate the Startup object using the Project Property Pages dialog box.

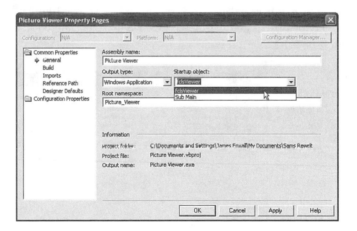

Running a Project

Your application is now complete. Click the Save All button on the toolbar (it looks like a stack of disks), and then run your program by pressing F5. You can also run the program by clicking the button on the toolbar that looks like a right-facing triangle and resembles the Play button on a VCR (this button is called Start, and it can also be found on the Debug menu). Learning the keyboard shortcuts will make your development process move along faster, so I recommend you use them whenever possible.

When you run the program, the Visual Basic .NET interface changes, and the form you've designed appears floating over the design environment (see Figure 1.13).

FIGURE **1.13**
*When in Run mode,
your program executes
the same as it would
for an end user.*

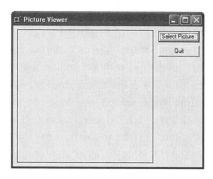

You're now running your program as though it were a standalone application running on another user's machine; what you see is exactly what users would see if they ran the program (without the Visual Studio .NET design environment in the background, of course). Click the Select Picture button to display the Select Picture dialog box (see Figure 1.14). Use the dialog box to locate a picture file. When you've found a file, double-click it, or click once to select it and then click Open. The selected picture is then displayed in the picture box, as shown in Figure 1.15.

FIGURE **1.14**
*The OpenFileDialog
control handles all the
details of browsing for
files. Cool, huh?*

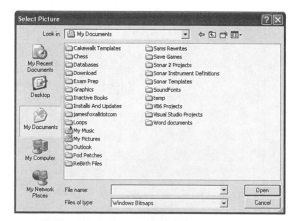

FIGURE **1.15**
*Visual Basic makes it
easy to display pic-
tures with very little
work.*

> If you want to select and display a picture from your digital camera, chances are the format is JPEG, so you'll need to select this from the filter drop-down. Also, if your image is very large, you'll see only the upper-left corner of the image (what fits in the picture box) .

Summary

When you're done playing with the program, click the Quit button to return to Design view.

That's it! You've just created a bona fide Visual Basic .NET program. You've used the toolbox to build an interface with which users can interact with your program, and you've written code in strategic event handlers to empower your program to do things. These are the basics of application development in Visual Basic .NET. Even the most complicated programs are built using this fundamental approach; you build the interface and add code to make the application do things. Of course, writing code to do things *exactly* the way you want things done is where the process can get complicated, but you're on your way.

If you take a close look at the organization of the hours in this book, you'll see that I start out by teaching you the Visual Basic .NET (Visual Studio .NET) environment. I then move on to building an interface, and later I teach you all about writing code. This organization is deliberate. You might be a little anxious to jump in and start writing serious code, but writing code is only part of the equation—don't forget the word *Visual* in Visual Basic .NET. As you progress through the hours, you'll be building a solid foundation of development skills.

Soon, you'll pay no attention to the man behind the curtain—you'll be that man (or woman)!

Q&A

Q Can I show bitmaps of file types other than BMP and JPG?

A Yes. The PictureBox supports the display of images with the extensions BMP, JPG, ICO, EMF, WMF, and GIF. The PictureBox can even save images to a file. Although it can display many types of pictures, it can save files only to BMP format.

Q Is it possible to show pictures in other controls?

A The PictureBox is *the* control to use when you are just displaying images.
However, many other controls allow you to display pictures as part of the control.
For instance, you can display an image on a button control by setting the button's
Image property to a valid picture.

Workshop

The Workshop is designed to help you anticipate possible questions, review what you've
learned, and get you thinking about how to put your knowledge into practice. The
answers to the quiz are in Appendix B, "Answers to the Quizzes."

Quiz

1. What type of Visual Basic project creates a standard Windows program?

2. What window is used to change the attributes (location, size, and so on) of a form
   or control in the IDE?

3. How do you access the default event (code) of a control?

4. What property of a picture box do you set to display an image?

5. What is the default event for a button control?

Exercises

1. Change your Picture Viewer program so that the user can also locate and select
   GIF files. (Hint: Change the Filter property of the OpenFileDialog control.)

2. Alter the form in your Picture Viewer project so that the buttons are side by side in
   the lower-right corner of the form, rather than vertically aligned in the upper-right
   corner.

HOUR 2

Navigating Visual Basic .NET

The key to expanding your knowledge of Visual Basic .NET is to become as comfortable as possible—as quickly as possible—with the Visual Basic .NET design environment. Just as a carpenter doesn't think much about hammering a nail into a piece of wood, performing actions such as saving projects, creating new forms, and setting object properties should become second nature to you. The more comfortable you are with the tools of Visual Basic .NET, the more you can focus your energies on what you're creating with the tools.

In this hour, you'll learn how to customize your design environment by moving, docking, floating, hiding, and showing design windows, as well as how to customize menus and toolbars. You'll even create a new toolbar from scratch. After you've gotten acquainted with the environment, I'll teach you about projects and the files that they're made of (taking you beyond what was briefly discussed in Hour 1, "Jumping In with Both Feet: A Visual Basic .NET Programming Tour"), and I'll introduce you to the design windows with which you'll work most frequently. Finally, I'll show you how to get help when you're stuck.

The highlights of this hour include the following:

- Navigating Visual Basic .NET
- Using the Visual Studio .NET Start Page to open and create projects
- Showing, hiding, docking, and floating design windows
- Customizing menus and toolbars
- Adding controls to a form using the toolbox
- Viewing and changing object attributes using the Properties window
- Working with the many files that make up a project
- How to get help

Using the Visual Studio .NET Start Page

By default, the Visual Studio .NET Start Page shown in Figure 2.1 is the first thing you see when you start Visual Basic (if Visual Basic isn't running, start it now). The Visual Studio .NET Start Page is a gateway for performing tasks with Visual Basic .NET. From this page, you can open previously edited projects, create new projects, and edit your user profile.

FIGURE 2.1

The Visual Studio .NET Start Page is the default entry point for all .NET languages.

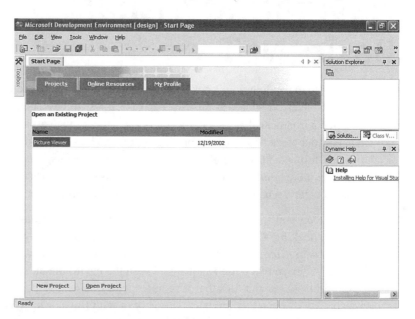

From this page, you can have Visual Basic .NET load the last solution you edited, show the Open Project dialog box, show the New Project dialog box, or show an empty design environment. To view or edit the startup options, choose Options from the Tools menu to display the Options dialog box shown in Figure 2.2. The General section of the Environment folder is selected when the Options dialog box first appears. This section happens to contain the At Startup option. If the Visual Studio .NET Start Page doesn't appear when you start Visual Studio .NET, verify the settings on the Options dialog box; you might need to change At Startup to Show Start Page.

FIGURE 2.2

Use the At Startup setting to control the first thing you see when Visual Studio starts.

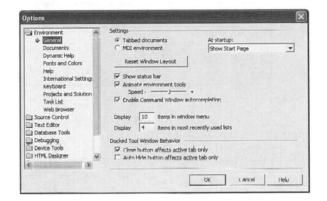

Creating New Projects

To create new projects, click the New Project button in the lower left of the Visual Studio .NET Start Page. This shows the New Project dialog box shown in Figure 2.3. The Project Types list varies from machine to machine, depending on which products of the Visual Studio .NET family are installed. Of course, we're interested only in the Visual Basic Project types in this book.

> You can create many types of projects with Visual Basic .NET, but this book focuses mostly on creating Windows Applications, perhaps the most common of the project types. You will learn about some of the other project types as well, but when you're told to create a new project, make sure that the Windows Application icon is selected unless you're told otherwise.

When you create a new project, be sure to enter a name for it in the Name text box before clicking OK or double-clicking a project type icon. This ensures that the project is created with the proper path and filenames, eliminating work you would otherwise have to do to change these values later. After you specify a name, you can create the new project either by double-clicking the project type template icon or by clicking an icon once to select it and then clicking OK. After you've performed either of these actions, the New Project dialog box closes and a new project of the selected type is created.

FIGURE 2.3

*Use the New Project
dialog box to create
Visual Basic .NET
projects from scratch.*

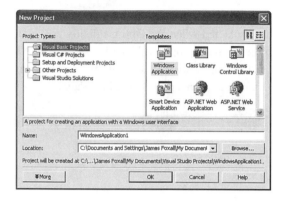

By default, Visual Studio saves all your projects in subfolders of your My Documents
folder. The hierarchy used by Visual Basic .NET is

```
\My Documents\Visual Studio Projects\<Project Name>
```

Notice how the name you give your project is used as its folder name. This makes it easy
to find the folders and files for any given project and is one reason that you should
always give your projects descriptive names. You can use a path other than the default by
specifying it on the New Project dialog box, but you probably won't often need to do this
if you develop alone. If you're on a team of developers, however, you might choose to
locate your projects on a shared drive so that others can access the source files.

> You can create a new project at any time (not just when starting Visual
> Studio .NET) by opening the New submenu on the File menu and choosing
> Project. You can't have multiple projects open at once, however, so if you
> choose to open a project, Visual Basic .NET asks whether you want to save
> changes for the current project and then closes it.

After you enter a project name and choose a location, you click OK to create the project.
Visual Studio .NET then creates the necessary folders and source files, as well as displaying the project in the IDE for you to begin working with it.

Opening an Existing Project

Over time, you'll open more projects than you create. There are essentially two ways to
open projects from the Visual Studio .NET Start Page.

If it's a project you've recently opened, the project name will appear in a list within a
rectangle in the middle of the Start Page (as Picture Viewer does in Figure 2.1). Because

the name displayed for the project is the one given when it was created, this is yet another reason to give your projects descriptive names. Clicking a project name opens the project. I'd venture to guess that you'll use this technique 95% of the time.

To open a project for the first time (such as when opening sample projects), click the Open Project button on the Visual Studio Start Page. This displays a standard dialog box that you can use to locate and select a project file.

As with creating new projects, you can open an existing project at any time, not just when starting Visual Basic, by selecting File, Open. Remember, you can have only one project open at a time, so opening a project causes the current project to be closed. Again, If you've made changes to the current project, you'll get a chance to save them before it's closed.

Navigating and Customizing the Visual Basic .NET Environment

Visual Basic .NET lets you customize many of its interface elements, such as windows and toolbars, enabling you to be more efficient in the work that you do. Create a new Windows Application now by opening the File menu, clicking New, and then choosing Project. This project will be used to illustrate manipulating the design environment. Name this project **Environment Tutorial**. (This exercise won't create anything reusable, but it will help you learn how to navigate the design environment.) Your screen should look like the one shown in Figure 2.4.

Your screen might not look exactly like that shown in Figure 2.4, but it'll be close. By the time you've finished this hour, you'll be able to change the appearance of the design environment to match this figure—or to any configuration you prefer.

Working with Design Windows

Design windows, such as the Properties window and Solution Explorer shown in Figure 2.4, provide functionality for building complex applications. Just as your desk isn't organized exactly like that of your co-workers, your design environment doesn't have to be the same as anyone else's either.

FIGURE 2.4

This is pretty much how the integrated development environment (IDE) appears when you first install Visual Studio.

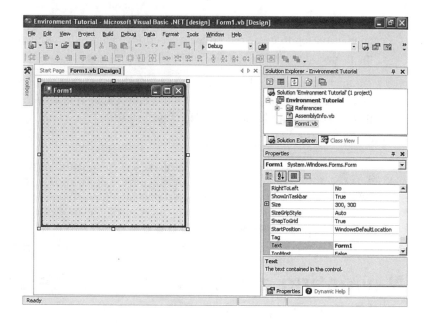

A design window can be placed into one of four primary states:

- Closed—The window is not visible.
- Floating—The window appears floating over the IDE.
- Docked—The window appears docked to an edge of the IDE.
- Automatically hidden—The window is docked, but it hides itself when not in use.

Showing and Hiding Design Windows

When a design window is closed, it doesn't appear anywhere. There is a difference between being closed and being automatically hidden, as you'll learn shortly. To display a closed or hidden window, choose the corresponding menu item from the View menu. For example, if the Properties window isn't displayed in your design environment, you can display it by choosing Properties Window on the View menu (or press its keyboard shortcut—F4). Whenever you need a design window and can't find it, use the View menu to display it. To close a design window, click its Close button (the button on the right side of the title bar with the X on it), just as you would to close an ordinary window.

Floating Design Windows

Floating design windows are visible windows that float over the workspace, as shown in Figure 2.5. Floating windows are like typical application windows in that you can drag them around and place them anywhere you please, even on other monitors when you're using a multiple-display setup. In addition to moving a floating window, you can also change its size by dragging a border.

FIGURE 2.5

Floating windows appear over the top of the design environment.

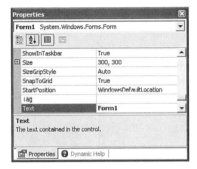

Docking Design Windows

Visible windows appear docked by default. A *docked* window is a window that appears attached to the side, top, or bottom of the work area or to some other window. The Properties window in Figure 2.4, for example, is docked to the right side of the design environment. To make a floating window become a docked window, drag the title bar of the window toward the edge of the design environment to which you want to dock the window. As you drag the window, you'll drag a rectangle that represents the outline of the window. When you approach an edge of the design environment, the rectangle will change shape and "stick" in a docked position. If you release the mouse while the rectangle appears this way, the window will be docked. Although this is hard to explain, it's very easy to do.

> You can size a docked window by dragging its edge opposite the side that's docked. If two windows are docked to the same edge, dragging the border between them enlarges one while shrinking the other.

To try this, you'll need to float a window that's already docked. To float a window, you "tear" the window away from the docked edge by dragging the title bar of the docked window away from the edge to which it's docked. Note that this technique won't work if a window is set to Auto Hide (which is explained next). Try docking and floating windows now by following these steps:

1. Ensure that the Properties window is currently displayed (if it's not, show it by pressing F4). Make sure that the Properties window isn't set to Auto Hide by right-clicking its title bar and deselecting Auto Hide from the shortcut menu (if it's selected), as shown in Figure 2.6.

2. Drag the title bar of the Properties window away from the docked edge. When the rectangle representing the border of the window changes shape, release the mouse button. The Properties window should now float.

3. Dock the window once more by dragging the title bar toward the right edge of the design environment. Again, release the mouse button when the rectangle changes shape. If you dropped the window directly on top of an existing window, you'll create a tabbed window. This is discussed shortly.

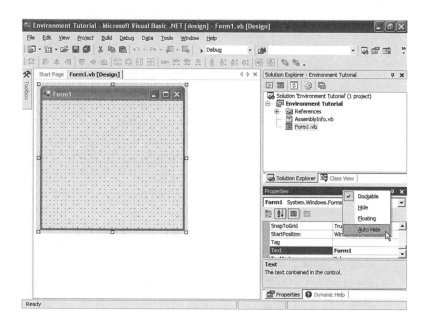

 If you don't want a floating window to dock, regardless of where you drag it to, right-click the title bar of the window and choose Floating from the context menu. To allow the window to be docked again, right-click the title bar and choose Dockable.

Auto Hiding Design Windows

A relatively new feature of Visual Basic .NET's design environment is the capability to auto hide windows. Although you might find this a bit disconcerting at first, after you get the hang of things, this is a very productive way to work because your workspace is freed up, yet design windows are available by simply moving the mouse. Windows that are set to Auto Hide are always docked; you can't set a floating window to Auto Hide. When a window auto hides, it appears as a vertical tab on the edge to which it's docked—much like minimized applications are placed in the Windows taskbar.

Look at the left edge of the design environment in Figure 2.6. Notice the vertical tab titled Toolbox. This tab represents an auto-hidden window. To display an auto-hidden window, move the pointer over the tab representing the window. When you move the pointer over a tab, Visual Basic displays the design window so that you can use its features. When you move the pointer away from the window, the window automatically hides itself—hence the name. To make any window hide itself automatically, right-click its title bar and select Auto Hide from its shortcut menu. You can also click the little picture of a pushpin appearing in the title bar next to the Close button to toggle the window's Auto Hide state.

Performing Advanced Window Placement

The techniques discussed so far in this section have been basic methods for customizing your design environment. Things can become a bit more complicated if you want them to. Such complication presents itself primarily as the capability to create tabbed floating windows like the one shown in Figure 2.5. Notice that at the bottom of the floating window is a set of tabs. Clicking a tab shows its corresponding design window, replacing the window currently displayed. These tabs are created much the same way in which you dock and undock windows: by dragging and dropping.

For instance, to make the Solution Explorer window a floating window of its own, you would drag the Solution Explorer window tab away from the floating window. As you do so, a rectangle appears, showing you the outline of the new window. Where you release the rectangle determines whether you dock the design window being dragged or whether you make the window float. To change a design window into a new tab of an already floating window, drag its title bar and drop it in the title bar of a window that's already floating.

In addition to creating tabbed floating windows, you can dock two floating windows together. To do this, drag the title bar of one window over another window (other than over the title bar) until the shape changes, and then release the mouse. Figure 2.7 shows two floating windows that are docked to one another and a third window that's floating by itself.

Using all the techniques discussed so far, you can tailor the appearance of your design environment in all sorts of ways. There is no one best configuration. You'll find that different configurations work better for different projects and in different stages of development. For instance, when I'm designing the interface of a form, I want the toolbox to stay visible but out of my way, so I tend to make it float, or I turn off its Auto Hide property and leave it docked to the left edge of the design environment. However, after the majority of the interface elements have been added to a form, I want to focus on code. Then I dock the toolbox and make it Auto Hide itself; it's there when I need it, but it's out of the way when I don't. Don't be afraid to experiment with your design windows, and don't hesitate to modify them to suit your changing needs.

FIGURE 2.7

*Floating, docked,
floating and docked—
there are a lot of
possibilities!*

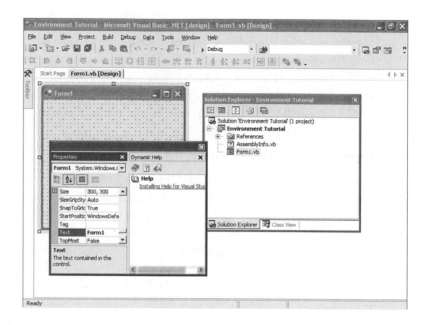

Working with Toolbars

Toolbars are the mainstay for performing functions quickly in almost every Windows program (you'll probably want to add them to your own programs at some point, and in Hour 9, "Adding Menus and Toolbars to Forms," you'll learn how). Every toolbar has a corresponding menu item, and buttons on toolbars are essentially shortcuts to their corresponding menu items. To maximize your efficiency when developing with Visual Basic, you should become familiar with the available toolbars. As your Visual Basic skills progress, you can customize existing toolbars and even create your own toolbars to more closely fit the way you work.

Showing and Hiding Toolbars

Visual Basic .NET includes a number of built-in toolbars you can use when creating projects. Two toolbars are visible in most of the figures shown so far in this hour. The one on the top is the Standard toolbar, which you'll probably want displayed all the time. The second toolbar is the Layout toolbar, which provides useful tools for building forms.

Visual Basic 6 had approximately 5 toolbars; Visual Basic .NET, on the other hand, has more than 20! The toolbars you'll use most often as a new Visual Basic developer are the Standard, Text Editor, and Debug toolbars. Therefore, this hour discusses each of these. In addition to these predefined toolbars, you can create your own custom toolbars to contain any functions you think necessary. You'll learn how to do this later in this hour.

To show or hide a toolbar, choose View, Toolbars to display a list of available toolbars. Toolbars currently displayed appear selected (see Figure 2.8). Click a toolbar name to toggle its visible state.

Right-click any visible toolbar to quickly access the list of available toolbars.

FIGURE 2.8

Hide or show toolbars to make your work more efficient.

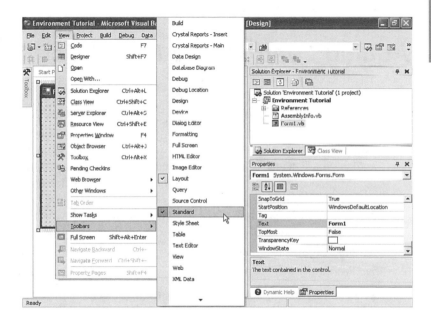

Docking and Resizing Toolbars

Just as you can dock and undock Visual Basic's design windows, you can dock and undock the toolbars. Unlike the design windows, however, Visual Basic .NET's toolbars don't have a title bar that you can click and drag when they're in a docked state. Instead, each docked toolbar has a *drag handle* (a stack of short horizontal lines along its left edge). To float (undock) a toolbar, click and drag the grab handle away from the docked edge. Once a toolbar is floating, it has a title bar. To dock a floating toolbar, click and drag its title bar to the edge of the design environment to which you want it docked. This is the same technique you use to dock design windows.

A shortcut for docking a floating toolbar is to double-click its title bar.

Although you can't change the size of a docked toolbar, you can resize a floating toolbar (a floating toolbar behaves like any other normal window). To resize a floating toolbar, move the pointer over the edge you want to stretch and then click and drag to the border to change the size of the toolbar.

Adding Controls to a Form Using the Toolbox

The IDE offers some fantastic tools for building a graphical user interface (GUI) for your applications. Most GUIs consist of one or more forms (Windows) with various elements on the forms, such as text boxes and list boxes. The toolbox is used to place controls onto a form. The default toolbox you see when you first open or create a Visual Basic project is shown in Figure 2.9. The buttons labeled Data, Components, Windows Forms, and so on are actually tabs, although they don't look like standard tabs. Clicking any of these tabs causes a related set of controls to appear. The default tab is the Windows Forms tab, and it contains many great controls you can place on Windows forms (the forms used to build Windows applications, in contrast to Web applications discussed in Hour 23, "Introduction to Web Development"). All the controls that appear by default on the tabs are included with Visual Basic, and these controls are discussed in detail in Hour 7, "Working with Traditional Controls," and Hour 8, "Using Advanced Controls."

You can add a control to a form in one of three ways:

- In the toolbox, click the tool representing the control that you want to place on a form, and then click and drag on the form where you want the control placed (you're essentially drawing the border of the control). The location at which you start dragging is used for the upper-left corner of the control, and the point at which you release the mouse button and stop dragging becomes the lower-right corner.

- Double-click the desired control type in the toolbox. When you double-click a control in the toolbox, a new control of the selected type is placed in the upper-left corner of the form. The control's height and width are set to the default height and width of the selected control type.

- Drag a control from the toolbox and drop it on a form.

FIGURE 2.9

The standard toolbox contains many useful controls you can use to build robust user interfaces.

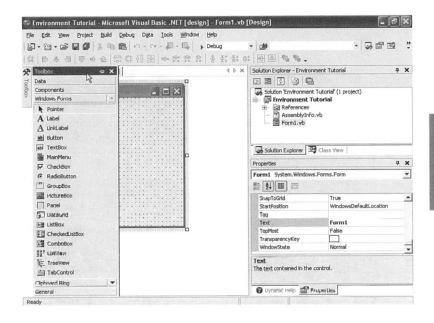

If you prefer to draw controls on your forms by clicking and dragging, I strongly suggest that you dock the toolbox to the right or bottom edge of the design environment or float it. The toolbar tends to interfere with drawing controls when it's docked to the left edge because it obscures part of the form.

The very first item on the Windows Forms tab, titled Pointer, isn't actually a control. When the pointer item is selected, the design environment is placed in a select mode rather than in a mode to create a new control. With the pointer item selected, you can select a control by clicking it to display all its properties in the Properties window—this is the default behavior.

Setting Object Properties Using the Properties Window

When developing the interface of a project, you'll spend a lot of time viewing and setting object properties using the Properties window (see Figure 2.10). The Properties window contains four items:

- An object drop-down list
- A list of properties

- A set of tool buttons used to change the appearance of the properties grid
- A section showing a description of the selected property

FIGURE 2.10

*Use the Properties
window to view and
change properties of
forms and controls.*

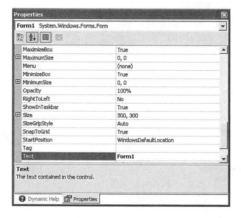

Selecting an Object and Viewing Its Properties

The drop-down list at the top of the Properties window contains the name of the form
with which you're currently working and all the controls (objects) on the form. To view
the properties of a control, select it from the drop-down list or click the control on the
form. You must have the pointer item selected in the toolbox to click an object to select it.

Viewing and Changing Properties

The first two buttons in the Properties window (Categorized and Alphabetic) enable you
to select the format in which you view properties. When you select the Alphabetic
button, the selected object's properties appear in the Properties window in alphabetical
order. When you click the Categorized button, all the selected object's properties are
listed by category. For example, the Appearance category contains properties such as
BackColor and BorderStyle. When working with properties, select the view you're most
comfortable with and feel free to switch back and forth between the views.

The Properties pane of the Properties window is used to view and set the properties of a
selected object. You can set a property in one of the following ways:

- Type in a value
- Select a value from a drop-down list
- Click a Build button for property-specific options

Many properties can be changed by more than one of these methods. For example, color properties supply a dropdown list of colors, but you can enter a numeric color value as well.

To better understand how changing properties works, follow these steps:

1. Start by creating a new Windows Application project. Name this project **Changing Properties**.

2. Add a new text box to a form by double-clicking the TextBox tool in the toolbox. You're now going to change a few properties of the new text box.

3. Select the Name property in the Properties window by clicking it. (If your properties are alphabetic, it will be at the top of the list, not with the Ns.) Type in a name for the text box—call it **txtComments**.

4. Click the BorderStyle property and try to type in the word **Big**. You can't; the BorderStyle property supports selecting values from a list only. You can, however, type a value that exists in the list. When you selected the BorderStyle property, a drop-down arrow appeared in the value column. Click this arrow now to display a list of the values that the BorderStyle property accepts. Select FixedSingle and notice how the appearance of the text box changes. To make the text box appear three-dimensional again, open the drop-down list and select Fixed3D.

5. Select the BackColor property, type in some text, and press the Tab key to commit your entry. Visual Basic .NET displays an Invalid Property Value error. This happens because although you can type in text, you're restricted to entering specific values. In the case of BackColor, the value must be a named color or a number that falls within a specific range. Click the drop-down arrow of the BackColor property and select a color from the drop-down list. (Selecting colors using the color palette is discussed later in this hour, and detailed information on using colors is provided in Hour 18, "Working with Graphics").

6. Select the Font property. Notice that a Build button appears (a small button with three dots on it). When you click the Build button, a dialog box specific to the property you've selected appears. In this instance, a dialog box that enables you to manipulate the font of the text box appears (see Figure 2.11). Different properties display different dialog boxes when you click their Build buttons.

7. Notice that the Size property has a plus sign next to it. This indicates that the property has one or more subproperties. Click the plus sign to expand the property, and you'll see that Size is composed of Width and Height.

By simply clicking a property in the Properties window, you can easily tell the type of input the property requires.

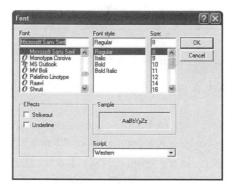

Working with Color Properties

Properties that deal with colors are unique in the way in which they accept values, yet all color-related properties behave the same way. In Visual Basic .NET, colors are expressed as a set of three numbers, each number having a value from 0 to 255. A given set of numbers represents the red, green, and blue (RGB) components of a color, respectively. The value 0,255,0, for example, represents pure green, whereas the value 0,0,0 represents black and 255,255,255 represents white. (See Hour 18 for more information on the specifics of working with color.)

A color rectangle is displayed for each color property in the Properties window; this color is the selected color for the property. Text is displayed next to the colored rectangle. This text is either the name of a color or a set of RGB values that defines the color. Clicking in a color property causes a drop-down arrow to appear, but the drop-down you get by clicking the arrow isn't a typical drop-down list. Figure 2.12 shows what the drop-down list for a color property looks like.

The color drop-down list is composed of three tabs: Custom, Web, and System. Most color properties use a system color by default. Hour 5, "Building Forms—The Basics," goes into great detail on system colors, so I want to mention here only that system colors vary from computer to computer; they're determined by the user when she right-clicks the desktop and chooses Properties from the desktop's shortcut menu. Use a system color when you want a color to be one of the user's selected system colors. When a color property is set to a system color, the name of the system color appears in the property sheet.

The Custom tab shown in Figure 2.13 is used to specify a specific color, regardless of the user's system color settings; changes to system colors have no effect on the property. The most common colors appear on the palette of the Custom tab, but you can specify any color you desire.

FIGURE 2.13

The Custom tab of the color drop-down list lets you specify any color imaginable.

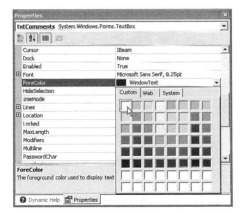

The colors visible in the various palettes are limited by the number of colors that can be produced by your video card. If your video card doesn't support enough colors, some will appear *dithered*, which means they will appear as dots of colors rather than as a true, solid color. Keep this in mind as you develop your applications: What looks good on your computer mind turns to mush if a user's display isn't as capable.

The bottom two rows in the Custom color palette are used to mix your own colors. To assign a color to an empty color slot, right-click a slot in one of the two rows to access the Define Color dialog box (see Figure 2.14). Use the controls on the Define Color dialog box to create the color you want, and then click Add Color to add the color to the color palette in the slot you selected. In addition, the custom color is automatically assigned to the current property.

FIGURE 2.14
The Define Color dialog box enables you to create your own colors.

The Web tab is used in Web applications to pick from a list of browser-safe colors.

Viewing Property Descriptions

It's not always immediately apparent just exactly what a property is or does—especially for new users of Visual Basic .NET. The Description section at the bottom of the Properties window shows a simple description of the selected property (refer to Figure 2.10). To view a description, click a property or value area of a property. For a more complete description of a property, click it once to select it and then press F1 to display Help about the property.

You can hide or show the Description section of the Properties window at any time by right-clicking anywhere within the Properties window (other than in the value column or on the title bar) to display the Properties window shortcut menu and choosing Description. Each time you do this, you toggle the Description section between visible and hidden. To change the size of the Description box, click and drag the border between it and the Properties pane.

Managing Projects

Before you can effectively create an interface and write code, you need to understand what makes up a Visual Basic .NET project and how to add and remove various components from within your own projects. In this section, you'll learn about the Solution Explorer window and how it's used to manage project files. You'll also learn specifics about projects and project files, as well as how to change a project's properties.

Managing Project Files with the Solution Explorer

As you develop projects, they'll become more and more complex, often containing many objects such as forms and modules. Each object is defined by one or more files on your hard drive. In addition, you can build complex solutions composed of more than one project. The Solution Explorer window shown in Figure 2.15 is *the* tool for managing all the files in a simple or complex solution. Using the Solution Explorer, you can add, rename, and remove project files, as well as select objects to view their properties. If the Solution Explorer window isn't visible on your screen, show it now by choosing Solution Explorer from the View menu.

FIGURE 2.15

Use the Solution Explorer window to manage all the files that make up a project.

To better understand the Solution Explorer window, follow these steps:

1. Locate the Picture Viewer program you created in the Quick Tour by choosing File, Open, and then clicking Project.

2. Open the Picture Viewer project. The file you need to select is located in the Picture Viewer folder that Visual Basic created when the project was constructed. The file has the extension .sln (for solution). If you're asked whether you want to save the current project, choose No.

3. Select the Picture Viewer project item in the Solution Explorer (be sure not to click the Project node, not the Solution node). When you do, a button becomes visible toward the top of the window. This button has a picture of pieces of paper and has the ToolTip Show All Files (see Figure 2.16). Click this button and the Solution Explorer displays all files in the project.

Your Solution Explorer should now look like the one in Figure 2.16. Be sure to widen the Solution Explorer window so that you can read all the text it contains.

FIGURE 2.16

*Notice that the form
you defined appears
as two files in the
Solution Explorer.*

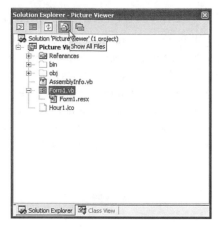

 Some forms and other objects might be composed of more than one file. By default, Visual Basic .NET hides project files that you don't directly manipulate. Click the plus sign (+) next to the form item and you'll see a sub-item titled Form1.resx. You'll learn about these additional files in Hour 5. For now, click the Show All Files button again to hide these related files.

You can view any object listed within the Solution Explorer using the object's default viewer by double-clicking the object. Each object has a default viewer, but might actually have more than one viewer. For instance, a form has a Form Design view as well as a Code view. By default, double-clicking a form in the Solution Explorer displays the form in Form Design view, where you can manipulate the form's interface.

You've already learned one way to access the code behind a form: double-click an object to access its default event handler. You'll frequently need to get to the code of a form without adding a new event handler. One way to do this is to use the Solution Explorer. When a form is selected in the Solution Explorer, buttons are visible at the top of the Solution Explorer window that enable you to display the code editor or the form designer, respectively.

You'll use the Solution Explorer window so often that you'll probably want to dock it to an edge and set it to Auto Hide, or perhaps keep it visible all the time. The Solution Explorer window is one of the easiest to get the hang of in Visual Basic .NET; navigating the Solution Explorer window will be second nature to you before you know it.

Working with Solutions

In truth, the Solution Explorer window is the evolution of the Project Explorer window from Visual Basic 6 and earlier versions, and the two windows are similar in many ways. Understanding solutions is easier to do when you understand projects.

A project is what you create with Visual Basic .NET. Often, the words *project* and *program* are used interchangeably, and this isn't much of a problem if you understand the important distinctions. A *project* is the set of source files that make up a program or component, whereas a *program* is the binary file that you build by compiling source files into something such as a Windows executable file (.exe). Projects always consist of a main project file and can be made up of any number of other files, such as form files, module files, or class module files. The main project file stores information about the project—all the files that make up the project, for example—as well as properties that define aspects of a project, such as the parameters to use when the project is compiled into a program.

What, then, is a solution? As your abilities grow and your applications increase in complexity, you'll find that you have to build multiple projects that work harmoniously to accomplish your goals. For instance, you might build a custom user control such as a custom data grid that you use within other projects you design, or you might isolate the business rules of a complex application into separate components to run on isolated servers. All the projects used to accomplish those goals are collectively called a *solution*. Therefore, a *solution* (at its most basic level) is really nothing more than a grouping of projects. In previous versions of Visual Basic, you created project groups; in Visual Basic .NET, you create solutions. Although the naming is different, the premise is the same.

 You should group projects into a single solution only when the projects relate to one another. If you're working on a number of projects, but each of them is autonomous, work with each project in a separate solution.

Understanding Project Components

As I stated earlier, a project always consists of a main project file, and it might consist of one or more secondary files, such as files that make up forms or code modules. As you create and save objects within your project, one or more corresponding files are created and saved on your hard drive. Each file that's created for a Visual Basic .NET source object has the extension .vb, denoting that it defines a Visual Basic .NET object. Make sure that you save your objects with understandable names, or things will get confusing as the size of your project grows.

With previous editions of Visual Basic (version 6 and earlier), you could easily tell the type of object defined by project file by looking at the extension of the file. For example, form files had the extension .frm. Unfortunately, this is no longer the case and you need to be diligent about giving your files unique names.

All files that make up a project are text files. Some objects need to store binary information, such as a picture for a form's BackgroundImage property. Binary data is stored in an XML file (which is still a text file). Suppose that you had a form with an icon on it. You'd have a text file defining the form (its size, the controls on it, and the code behind it), and an associated resource file with the same name as the form file but with the extension .resx. This secondary file would be in XML format and would contain all the binary data needed to create the form.

If you want to see what the source file of a form file looks like, use Notepad to open one on your computer. Don't save any changes to the file, however, or it might never work again (</insert evil laugh here/>).

The following is a list of some of the components you might use in your projects:

- Modules   Modules enable you to store code procedures without needing a specific form to attach them to.

- Class modules   Class modules are a special type of module that enable you to create object-oriented applications. Throughout the course of this book, you're learning how to program using an object-oriented language, but you're mostly learning how to use objects supplied by Visual Basic .NET. In Hour 16, "Designing Objects Using Classes," you'll learn how to use class modules to create your own objects.

- Forms   Forms are the visual windows that make up the interface of your application. Forms are defined using a special type of class module.

- User controls   User controls (formerly ActiveX controls, which themselves are formerly OLE controls) are controls that can be used on the forms of other projects. For example, you could create a user control with a calendar interface for a contact manager. Creating user controls requires the skill of an experienced programmer; therefore, I won't be covering them in this book.

Setting Project Properties

Visual Basic .NET projects have properties, just as other objects such as controls do. Projects have lots of properties, many of them relating to advanced functionality that I won't cover in this book. You need to be aware, however, of how to access project properties and how to change some of the more commonly used properties.

To access the properties for a project, right-click the project name (Picture Viewer) in the Solution Explorer window and choose Properties from the shortcut menu. Do this now.

> If you select the project in the Solution Explorer, the last menu item on the Project menu will be Properties. If the last thing you selected was a form or other object, this menu item will read *<project name>* properties. These items display the same dialog box.

The Tree View control on the left side of the dialog box is used to display a property page (see Figure 2.17). When you first open the dialog box, the General page is visible. On this page, the setting you'll need to worry about most is the Startup Object property. The Startup Object setting determines the entry point to your application. This can be the name of a form or it can be the text Sub Main. If the name of a form is specified (as it is by default), that form will be loaded and displayed when the project first starts. If Sub Main is specified, you must create a standard module with a procedure called Sub Main, and the code in Sub Main will be the first code executed when the project starts (refer to Hour 10, "Creating and Calling Code Procedures," for more information).

FIGURE 2.17

Project properties let you tailor aspects of the project as a whole.

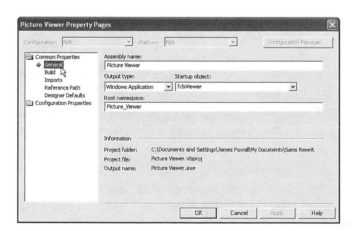

The Output Type option determines the type of compiled component defined by this source project. When you create a new project, you select the type of project to create (such as Windows Application), so this field is always filled in. There might be times when you have to change this setting after the project has been created, and this is the place to do so.

Notice that the project folder, project filename, and output name are displayed on this page as well. If you work with a lot of projects, you might find this information valuable; this is certainly the easiest place to find it.

 The output name determines the filename created when you build an executable. Distributing applications is discussed in Hour 22, "Deploying a Visual Basic .NET Application."

As you work through the hours in this book, I'll refer to the Project Properties dialog box as necessary, explaining pages and items in context with other material.

Adding and Removing Project Files

When you first start Visual Basic .NET and create a new Windows Application project, Visual Basic .NET creates the project with a single form. You're not limited to having one form in a project, however; you can create new forms or add existing forms to your project at will (feeling powerful yet?). You can also create and add code modules and classes, as well as other types of objects.

You can add a new or existing object to your project in one of three ways:

- Choose the appropriate menu item from the Project menu.
- Click the small drop-down arrow that's part of the Add New Item button on the Standard toolbar, and then choose the object type from the drop-down list that displays (see Figure 2.18).
- Right-click the project name in the Solution Explorer window, and then choose Add from the shortcut menu to access a submenu from which you can select object types.

When you select Add *ObjectType* from any of these menus, a dialog box appears, showing you the objects that can be added to the project. Your chosen item is selected by default (see Figure 2.19). Simply name the object and click Open to create a new object of the selected type. To create an object of a different type, click the type to select it, name it, and then click Open.

FIGURE 2.18

This tool button drop-down is one of three ways to add objects to a project.

FIGURE 2.19

Regardless of the menu option you select, you can add any type of object you want using this dialog box.

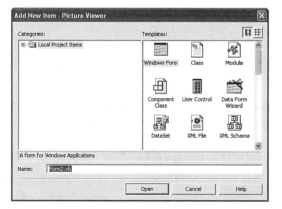

Adding new forms and modules to your project is easy, and you can add as many as you like. You'll come more and more to rely on the Solution Explorer to manage all the objects in the project as the project becomes more complex.

Although it won't happen as often as adding project files, you might sometimes need to remove an object from a project. Removing objects from your project is even easier than adding them. To remove an object, right-click the object in the Solution Explorer window and select Exclude from Project. This removes the object from the file, but doesn't delete the source file from the disk. Selecting Delete, on the other hand, removes the file from the project and deletes it from the disk. Don't select Delete unless you want to totally destroy the file and you're sure that you'll never need it again in the future.

A Quick-and-Dirty Programming Primer

Programming is a complicated task. Everything is so interrelated that it's difficult, if not impossible, to isolate every programming concept and then present the material in a linear fashion. Instead, while learning one subject, you often have to touch on elements of another subject before you've had a chance to learn about the secondary topic. I've made every effort to avoid such forward references, but there are some concepts with which you'll need to be at least slightly familiar with before proceeding. You'll learn the guts of each of these topics in their respective lessons, but you'll need to have at least heard of them before digging any deeper in this book.

Storing Values in Variables

A *variable* is an element in code that holds a value. You might, for example, create a variable that holds the name of a user or the perhaps the user's age. Each variable (storage entity) must be created before it can be used. The process of creating a variable is known as declaring a variable. In addition, each variable is declared to hold data of a specific type, such as text (called a *string*) for a person's name or a number for a person's age. An example of a variable declaration is

```
Dim strFirstName As String
```

This statement creates a variable called strFirstName. This variable is of type String, which means it can hold any text that you choose to put into it. The contents of a variable can be changed as often as desired.

The key primer point to remember: Variables are storage locations that must be declared before use and that hold a specific type of information.

Using Procedures to Write Functional Units of Code

When you write Visual Basic .NET code, you place the code in a procedure. A procedure is a group of code statements that perform a specific function. You can call a procedure from code in another procedure. For example, you might create a procedure that totals the items on an order and another procedure that calculates the tax on the entire sale. There are two types of procedures: procedures that don't return values and procedures that do return values. Some procedures allow data to be passed to them. For example, the tax calculation procedure mentioned previously might allow a calling statement to pass a monetary total into the procedure, and then use that total to calculate tax. When a procedure accepts data from the calling code, the data is called a parameter. Procedures don't have to accept parameters.

A procedure that doesn't return a value is declared using the keyword Sub, and looks like this:

```
Public Sub MyProcedure()
   ' The procedure's code goes here.
End Sub
```

A procedure that returns a value is declared using the keyword Function. In addition, it has a data type specified at the end of the procedure, which denotes the type of data returned by the procedure:

```
Public Function MyProcedure() As String
   ' The procedure's code goes here.
End Function
```

Notice the words *As String*. The keyword As is used to specify a data type. In this example, the function returns a string, which is text.

If a procedure accepts a parameter, it is enclosed in the parentheses. Again, notice how the word As is used to denote the type of data being accepted:

```
Public Function CalculateTax(dblItemTotal As Double) As String
   ' The procedure's code goes here.
End Function
```

MessageBox.Show()

You're almost certainly familiar with the Windows message box—it's the little dialog box that's used to display text to a user (see Figure 2.20). Visual Basic .NET provides a way to display such messages using a single line of code: the MessageBox.Show statement. The following is a MessageBox.Show statement in its most basic form:

```
MessageBox.Show("Text to display goes here")
```

You'll use message boxes throughout this book, and you'll learn about them in detail in Hour 17, "Interacting with Users."

FIGURE 2.20
Visual Basic .NET makes it easy to display simple message boxes like this.

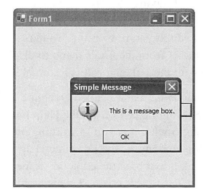

Getting Help

Although Visual Basic was designed to be as intuitive as possible, you'll find that you occasionally need assistance in performing a task. Honestly, Visual Basic .NET is nowhere near as intuitive as its predecessors—with all the additional power and flexibility came complexity. It doesn't matter how much you know, Visual Basic .NET is so complex and contains so many features that you'll have to use Help at times. This is particularly true when writing Visual Basic .NET code; you won't always remember the command you need or the syntax of a command. Fortunately, Visual Basic includes a comprehensive Help feature.

To access Help from within the design environment, press F1. Generally speaking, when you press F1, Visual Basic .NET shows you a Help topic directly related to what you're doing. This is known as *context-sensitive help*, and when it works, it works well. For example, you can display help for any Visual Basic .NET syntax or keyword (functions, objects, methods, properties, and so on) when writing Visual Basic code by typing the word into the code editor, positioning the cursor anywhere within the word (including before the first letter or after the last), and pressing F1. You can also get to Help from the Help menu on the menu bar.

> If your project is in Run mode, Visual Basic .NET's Help won't be displayed when you press F1. Instead, the Help for your application will appear—if you've created Help.

You can have Help display topics directly within the design environment instead of in a separate window. This is a new feature of .NET. Personally, I think this method is considerably inferior to the old style of having Help float above the design environment. When Help is displayed within the design environment, you can't necessarily see the code, form, or other object with which you're working. To make Help float above the design environment, choose Options from the Tools menu to display the Options dialog box, click Help in the Tree view on the left, and select External Help.

Visual Basic .NET includes a new Help feature called Dynamic Help. To display the Dynamic Help window, choose Dynamic Help from the Help menu. The Dynamic Help window shows Help links related to what it is you're working on (see Figure 2.21). For instance, if you select a form, the contents of the Dynamic Help window show you Help links related to forms. If you click a text box, the contents of the Dynamic Help window adjust to show you Help links related to text boxes. This is an interesting feature, and you might find it valuable.

FIGURE 2.21
Dynamic Help gives you a list of Help links related to the task you are performing.

Summary

In this hour, you learned how to use the Visual Studio home page—your gateway to Visual Basic .NET. You learned how to create new projects and how to open existing projects. The Visual Basic environment is your workspace, toolbox, and so much more. You learned how to navigate the environment, including how to work with design windows (hide, show, dock, and float).

You'll use toolbars constantly, and now you know how to modify them to suit your specific needs. You learned how to create new toolbars and how to modify existing toolbars. This is an important skill that shouldn't be overlooked.

Visual Basic .NET has many different design windows, and in this hour, you began learning about some of them in detail. You learned how to get and set properties using the Properties window, how to manage projects using the Solution Explorer, and how to add controls to a form using the toolbox. You'll use these skills often, so it's important to get familiar with them right away. Finally, you learned how to access Visual Basic .NET's Help feature, which I guarantee you'll find very important as you learn to use Visual Basic .NET.

Visual Basic .NET is a vast and powerful development tool—far more powerful than any version that's come before it. Don't expect to become an expert overnight; that's simply impossible. However, by learning the tools and techniques presented in this hour, you've begun your journey. Remember, you'll use most of what you learned in this hour each and every time you use Visual Basic. Get proficient with these basics and you'll be building cool programs in no time!

Q&A

Q How can I easily get more information about a property when the Description section of the Properties window just doesn't cut it?

A Click the property in question to select it, and then press F1—context-sensitive help applies to properties in the Properties window, as well.

Q I find that I need to see a lot of design windows at one time, but I can't find that "magic" layout. Any suggestions?

A Run at a higher resolution. Personally, I won't develop in less than 1024×768. As a matter of fact, all my development machines have two displays, both running at this resolution (or higher). You'll find that any investment you make in having more screen real estate will pay you big dividends.

Workshop

The Workshop is designed to help you anticipate possible questions, review what you've learned, and get you thinking about how to put your knowledge into practice. The answers to the quiz are in Appendix B, "Answers to the Quizzes."

Quiz

1. How can you make the Visual Studio Start Page appear at startup if this feature has been disabled?

2. Unless instructed otherwise, you're to create what type of project when building examples in this book?

3. To make a docked design window appear when you hover over its tab and disappear when you move the mouse away from it, you change what setting of the window?

4. How do you access the Toolbars menu?

5. What design window do you use to add controls to a form?

6. What design window is used to change the attributes of an object?

7. To modify the properties of a project, you must select the project in what design window?

8. Which Help feature adjusts the links it displays to match what it is you are doing?

Exercises

1. Create a custom toolbar that contains Save All, Start, and Stop Debugging—three buttons you'll use often throughout this book.

2. Use the Custom Color dialog box to create a color of your choice, and then assign the color to the BackColor property of a form.

Hour **3**

Understanding Objects and Collections

In Hour 1, "Jumping In with Both Feet: A Visual Basic .NET Programming Tour," you were introduced to programming in Visual Basic .NET by building a Picture Viewer project. You spent the previous hour digging into the integrated development environment (IDE) and learning skills critical to your success with Visual Basic .NET. In this hour, you're going to start learning about some important programming concepts, namely *objects*.

The term *object* as it relates to programming might have been new to you prior to this book. The more you work with Visual Basic .NET, the more you'll hear about objects. Visual Basic .NET, unlike its predecessors, is a true object-oriented language. This hour isn't going to discuss object-oriented programming in any detail—object-oriented programming is a very complex subject and well beyond the scope of this book. Instead, you'll learn about objects in a more general sense.

Everything you use in Visual Basic .NET is an object, so understanding this material is critical to your success with Visual Basic .NET. For example, forms are objects, as are the controls you place on a form; pretty much every element of a Visual Basic .NET project is an object and belongs to a collection of objects. All objects have attributes (called *properties*), most have methods, and many have events. Whether creating simple applications or building large-scale enterprise solutions, you must understand what an object is and how it works. In this hour, you'll learn what makes an object an object, and you'll also learn about collections.

The highlights of this hour include the following:

- Understanding objects
- Getting and setting properties
- Triggering methods
- Understanding method dynamism
- Writing object-based code
- Understanding collections
- Using the Object Browser

> If you've listened to the programming press at all, you've probably heard the term *object oriented*, and perhaps words such as *polymorphism*, *encapsulation*, and *inheritance*. In truth, these new object-oriented features of Visual Basic are very exciting, but they're far beyond Hour 3 (or Hour 24, for that matter). You'll learn a little about object-oriented programming in this book, but if you're really interested in taking your programming skills to the next level, you should buy a book dedicated to the subject after you've completed this one.

Understanding Objects

NEW TERM   Object-oriented programming has been a technical buzzword for quite some time, but as far as Visual Basic programmers are concerned, it became a reality only with Visual Basic .NET (no previous version of Visual Basic was a true OO language). Almost everywhere you look—the Web, publications, books—you read about objects. What exactly is an object? Strictly speaking, an *object* is a programming structure that encapsulates data and functionality as a single unit and for which the only public access is through the programming structure's interfaces (properties, methods, and events). In reality, the answer to this question can be somewhat ambiguous because there are so many types of objects—and the number grows almost daily. However, all objects share specific characteristics, such as properties and methods.

The most commonly used objects in Visual Basic .NET are the form object and the control object. Earlier hours introduced you to working with forms and controls and even showed you how to set form and control properties. In your Picture Viewer project from Hour 1, for instance, you added a picture box and two buttons to a form. Both the PictureBox and the Button controls are *control objects*, but each is a specific type of control object. Another, less-technical example uses pets. Dogs and cats are definitely different entities (objects), but they both fit into the category of Pet objects. Similarly, text boxes and buttons are each a unique type of object, but they're both considered a control object. This small distinction is important.

Understanding Properties

All objects have attributes used to specify and return the state of the object. These attributes are properties, and you've already used some of them in previous hours using the Properties window. Indeed, every object exposes a specific set of properties, but not every object exposes the same set of properties. To illustrate this point, I'll continue with the hypothetical Pet object. Suppose that you have an object, and the object is a dog. This Dog object has a certain properties that are common to all dogs. These properties include attributes such as the dog's name, the color of its hair, and even the number of legs it has. All dogs have these same properties; however, different dogs have different values for these properties. Figure 3.1 illustrates such a Dog object and its properties.

FIGURE 3.1
Properties are the attributes that describe an object.

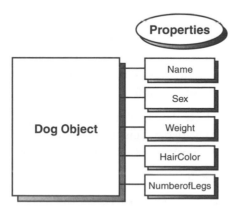

Getting and Setting Properties

You've already seen how to read and change properties using the Properties window. The Properties window is available only at design time, however, and is used only for manipulating the properties of forms and controls. Most getting and changing of properties you'll perform will be done with Visual Basic .NET code, not by using the Properties window. When referencing properties in code, you specify the name of the object first, followed by a period (.), and then the property name, as in the following syntax:

```
{ObjectName}.{Property}
```

If you had a Dog object named Bruno, for example, you would reference Bruno's hair color this way:

```
Bruno.HairColor
```

This line of code would return whatever value was contained in the HairColor property of the Dog object Bruno. To set a property to some value, you use an equal sign (=). For example, to change the Dog object Bruno's Weight property, you'd use a line of code such as the following:

```
Bruno.Weight = 90
```

When you reference a property on the left side of an equal sign, you're setting the value. When you reference a property on the right side of the equal sign, you're getting (reading) the value. In the early days of BASIC, you actually used the word Let when setting values. This made the code easier to read for novices, but it was unnecessarily tedious. Nevertheless, using Let makes the statement clearer, so I'll show the same code statement as before with the word Let:

```
Let Bruno.Weight = 90
```

It's easier to see here that referencing the property on the left side of the equal sign indicates that you're setting the property to some value. The keyword Let is no longer a valid way to make variable assignments. If you enter a code statement that uses Let, you won't receive an error, but the code editor (also known as *the gremlins*) will automatically remove the word Let from the statement for you.

The following line of code places the value of the Weight property of the Dog object called Bruno into a temporary variable. This statement retrieves the value of the Weight property because the Weight property is referenced on the right side of the equal sign.

```
sngWeightVariable = Bruno.Weight
```

Variables are discussed in detail in Hour 11, "Using Constants, Data Types, Variables, and Arrays." For now, think of a variable as a storage location. When the processor executes this statement, it retrieves the value in the Weight property of the Dog object Bruno and places it in the variable (storage location) titled sngWeightVariable. Assuming that Bruno's Weight is 90, as set in the previous example, the computer would process the code statement like this:

```
sngWeightVariable = 90
```

Just as in real life, some properties can be read but not changed. Suppose that you have a Sex property to designate the gender of a Dog object. It's impossible for you to change a dog from a male to a female or vice versa (at least I think it is). Because the Sex property can be retrieved but not changed, it's known as a *read-only* property. You'll often encounter properties that can be set in design view but become read-only when the program is running.

One example of a read-only property is the Height property of the combo box control. Although you can view the value of the Height property in the Properties window, you can't change the value—no matter how hard you try. If you attempt to change the Height property using Visual Basic .NET code, Visual Basic .NET simply changes the value back to the default—eerie.

> The best way to determine which properties of an object are read-only is to consult the online help for the object in question.

Working with an Object and Its Properties

Now that you know what properties are and how they can be viewed and changed, you're going to experiment with properties in a simple project. In Hour 1, you learned how to set the Height and Width properties of a form using the Properties window. Now, you're going to change the same properties using Visual Basic .NET code.

The project you're going to create consists of a form with some buttons on it. One button will enlarge the form when clicked, whereas the other will shrink the form. This is a very simple project, but it illustrates rather well how to change object properties in Visual Basic code.

1. Start by creating a new Windows Application project (from the File menu, choose New, Project).
2. Name the project **Properties Example**.
3. Use the Properties window to change the name of the form to **fclsDrinkMe**. (Click the form to once select it and you'll be able to change its Name in the Properties window.)
4. Next, change the Text property of the form to **Grow and Shrink**.

When the project first runs, the default form will have a Height and Width as specified in the Properties window. You're going to add buttons to the form that a user can click to enlarge or shrink the form at runtime.

Add a new button to the form by double-clicking the Button tool in the toolbox. Set the new button's properties as follows:

Property	Set To
Name	**btnEnlarge**
Text	**Eat Me**
Location	**111,70**

Now for the Shrink button. Again, double-click the Button tool in the toolbox to create a new button on the form. Set this new button's properties as follows:

Property	Set To
Name	**btnShrink**
Text	**Drink Me**
Location	**111,120**

Your form should now look like the one in shown in Figure 3.2.

FIGURE 3.2

Each button is an object, as is the form the buttons sit on.

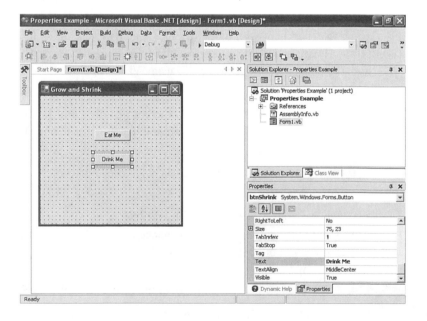

To complete the project, you need to add the small amount of Visual Basic .NET code necessary to modify the form's Height and Width properties when the user clicks a button. Access the code for the Enlarge button now by double-clicking the Eat Me button. Type the following statement exactly as you see it here. Do not press the Enter key or add a space after you've entered this text.

```
Me.Width
```

When you typed the period, or *dot*, as it's called, a small drop-down list like the one shown in Figure 3.3 appeared. Visual Basic .NET is smart enough to realize that Me represents the current form (more on this in a moment), and to aid you in writing code for the object, it gives you a drop-down list containing all the properties and methods of the form. This feature is called *IntelliSense*, and it is relatively new to Visual Basic. When an IntelliSense drop-down box appears, you can use the up and down arrow keys to navigate the list, and press Tab to select the highlighted list item. This prevents you from misspelling a member name thereby reducing compile errors. Now that Visual Basic .NET is fully object-oriented, you'll come to rely on IntelliSense drop-down lists in a big way; I think I'd rather dig ditches than program without them.

FIGURE 3.3

IntelliSense drop-down lists (also called auto-completion drop-down lists) *make coding dramatically easier.*

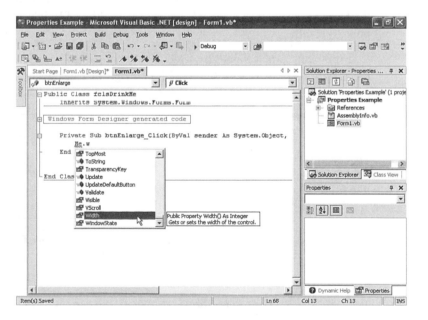

Use the Backspace key to completely erase the code you just entered and enter the following code in its place (press Enter at the end of each line):

```
Me.Width = Me.Width + 20
Me.Height = Me.Height + 20
```

You're probably wondering what *you* have to do with the width and height of the form. Actually the word Me doesn't refer to a person, it refers to the object to which the code belongs (in this case, the form). Me is a *reserved* word; it's a word that you can't use to name objects or variables because Visual Basic has a specific meaning for it. When writing code within a form module, as you're doing here, you should always use the reserved word Me rather than using the name of the form. Me is much shorter than using the full name of the current form, and it makes the code more portable (you can copy and paste the code into another form module and not have to change the form name to make the code work). Also, should you change the name of the form at any time in the future, you won't have to change references to the old name.

Me works only in object-based modules such as form modules; you can't use Me in a standard module, which you'll learn about in Hour 10, "Creating and Calling Code Procedures."

The code you've entered does nothing more than set the Width and Height properties of the form to whatever the current value of the Width and Height properties happens to be, plus 20 pixels.

Redisplay the form designer by selecting the tab named Form1.vb [Design]. Then double-click the Shrink (Drink Me) button to access its Click event and add the following code:

```
Me.Width = Me.Width - 20
Me.Height = Me.Height - 20
```

This code is very similar to the code in the Enlarge_Click event, except that it reduces the Width and Height properties of the form by 20 pixels. Your screen should now look like Figure 3.4.

As you create projects, it's a very good idea to save frequently. Save your project now by clicking the Save All button on the toolbar.

The last step you need to perform is to specify the current form as the Startup object. Do this by right-clicking the Properties Example item in the Solution Explorer, choosing Properties, and then selecting fclsDrinkMe from the Startup object drop-down list. Click OK to close the Property Pages form.

FIGURE 3.4

The code you've entered should look exactly like this.

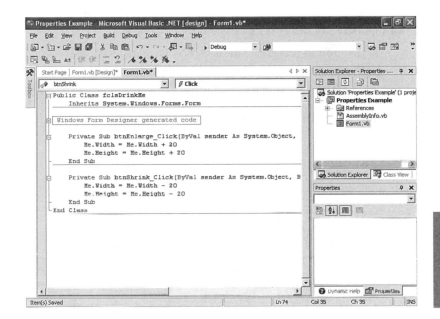

Once again, display the form designer by clicking the tab Form1.vb [Design]. Your Properties Example project is now ready to be run! Press F5 to put the project in Run mode (see Figure 3.5).

FIGURE 3.5

What you see is what you get—the form you created should look just as you designed it.

Click the Eat Me button a few times and notice how the form gets bigger. Next, click the Drink Me button to make the form smaller. When you've clicked enough to satisfy your curiosity (or until you get bored), end the running program and return to Design mode by clicking the Stop Debugging button on the toolbar.

Understanding Methods

In addition to properties, most objects have methods. *Methods* are actions the object can perform, in contrast to attributes that describe the object. To understand this distinction, think about the Pet object example. A Dog object has a certain set of actions that it can perform. These actions, called *methods* in Visual Basic, include barking, tail wagging, and chewing carpet (don't ask). Figure 3.6 illustrates the Dog object and its methods.

FIGURE 3.6
Invoking a method causes the object to perform an action.

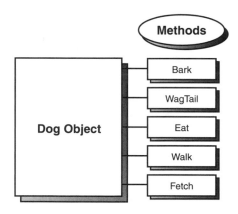

Triggering Methods

Think of methods as functions—which is exactly what they are. When you invoke a method, code is executed. You can pass data to a method, and methods can return values. However, a method is neither required to accept parameters (data passed by the calling code) nor to return a value; many methods simply perform an action in code. Invoking (triggering) a method is similar to referencing the value of a property: You first reference the object's name, and then a dot, and then the method name as shown next:

```
{ObjectName}.{Method}
```

For example, to make the hypothetical Dog object Bruno bark using Visual Basic .NET code, you would use this line of code:

```
Bruno.Bark
```

Methods are generally used to perform an action using an object, such as saving or deleting a record in a database. Properties, on the other hand, are used to get and set attribute values of the object. One way to tell in code whether a statement is a property reference or method call is that the method call will have a set of parentheses after it, as in

```
frmAlbum.ShowDialog().
```

Invoking methods is simple; the real skill lies in knowing what methods an object supports and when to use a particular method.

Understanding Method Dynamism

Properties and methods go hand in hand, and at times a particular method might become unavailable because of one or more property values. For example, if you were to set the NumberofLegs on the Dog object Bruno equal to zero, the Walk and Fetch methods would obviously be inapplicable. If you were to set the NumberofLegs property back to four, you could then trigger the Walk or Fetch methods again.

Building a Simple Object Example Project

3

The only way to really grasp what objects are and how they work is to use them. I've said this before, but I can't say it enough: Everything in Visual Basic .NET is an object. This has its good points and its bad points. One of the bad points is that in some instances, it now takes more code to accomplish a task than it did before—sometimes more characters, sometimes more statements. The functionality of Visual Basic .NET, on the other hand, is head and shoulders above Visual Basic 6. This has the effect of giving Visual Basic .NET a steeper learning curve than any previous version of Visual Basic.

Every project you've built so far uses objects, but you're now going to create a sample project that specifically illustrates using objects. If you're new to programming with objects, you'll probably find this a bit confusing. However, I'll walk you through step-by-step, explaining each section in detail.

The project you're going to create consists of single form with one button on it. When the button is clicked, a line will be drawn on the form beginning at the upper-left corner of the form and extending to the lower-right corner.

In Hour 18, "Working with Graphics," you'll learn all about the drawing functionality within Visual Basic.

Creating the Interface for the Drawing Project

Follow these steps to create the interface for your project:

1. Start Visual Basic .NET.

2. Create a new Windows Application project titled **Object Example**.

3. Rename the default form **fclsObjectExample** (by using the Properties window), and change the form's Text property to **Object Example**.

4. Make this form the Startup object by right-clicking Object Example in the Solution Explorer window, choosing Properties, and then selecting fclsObjectExample from the Startup object drop-down list. Click OK to close the dialog box.

5. Add a new button to the form and set its properties as shown in the following table:

Property	Value
Name	**btnDraw**
Text	**Draw**
Location	**112,120**

Writing the Object-Based Code

You're now going to add code to the Click event of the button. I'm going to explain each statement, and at the end of the steps, I'll show the complete code listing.

1. Double-click the button to access its Click event.

2. Enter the first line of code as follows (remember to press Enter at the end of each statement):

```
Dim objGraphics As Graphics
```

Here you've just created a variable that will hold an instance of an object. Objects don't materialize out of thin air; they have to be created. When a form is loaded into memory, it loads all its controls (that is, creates the control objects), but not all objects are created automatically like this. The process of creating an instance of an object is called *instantiation*. When you load a form, you instantiate the form object, which in turn instantiates its control objects. You could load a second instance of the form, which in turn would instantiate a new instance of the form and new instances of all controls. You would then have two forms in memory, and two of each used control.

To instantiate an object in code, you create a variable that holds a reference to an instantiated object. You then manipulate the variable as an object. The Dim statement you wrote in step 2 creates a new variable called objGraphics, which holds a reference to an object of type Graphics. You learn more about variables in Hour 11.

3. Enter the second line of code exactly as shown here:

```
objgraphics = Me.CreateGraphics
```

CreateGraphics is a method of the form (remember, the keyword Me is shorthand for referencing the current form). Under the hood, the CreateGraphics method is pretty complicated, and I discuss it in detail in Hour 18. For now, understand that the method CreateGraphics instantiates a new object that represents the client area of the current form. The client area is the gray area within the borders and title bar of a form. Anything drawn onto the objGraphics object will appear on the form. What you've done is set the variable objGraphics to point to an object that was returned by the CreateGraphics method. Notice how values returned by a property or method don't have to be traditional values such as numbers or text; they could also be objects.

4. Enter the third line of code as shown next:

```
objgraphics.Clear(system.Drawing.SystemColors.Control)
```

This statement clears the background of the form using whatever color the user has selected as the Windows Control color, which Windows uses to paint forms.

How does this happen? In step 3, you used the CreateGraphics method of the form to instantiate a new graphics object in the variable objGraphics. With the code statement you just entered, you're calling the clear method of the objGraphics object. The Clear method is a method of all Graphics objects used to clear the graphic surface. The Clear method accepts a single parameter: the color you want used to clear the surface.

The value you're passing to the parameter looks fairly convoluted. Remember that "dots" are a way of separating objects from their properties and methods (properties, methods, and events are often called object *members*). Knowing this, you can discern that System is an object (technically it's a namespace, as discussed in Appendix A, "The 10,000 Foot View," but for our purposes it behaves just like an object) because it appears before any of the dots. However, there are multiple dots. What this means is that Drawing is an *object property* of the System object; that is, it's a property that returns an object. So, the dot following Drawing is used to access a member of the Drawing object, which in turn is a property of the System object. We're not done yet, however, because there's yet another dot. Again, this indicates that SystemColors, which follows a dot, is an object of the Drawing method, which in turn is...well, you get the idea. As you can see, object references can and do go pretty deep, and you'll use many dots throughout your code. The key points to remember are

- Text that appears to the left of a dot is always an object (or namespace).

- Text that appears to the right of a dot is a property reference or method call. If the text is followed by a set of parentheses, it's a method call. If not, it's a property.

- Methods can return objects, just as properties can. The only surefire ways to know whether the text between two dots is a property or method is to look at the icon of the member in the IntelliSense drop-down or to consult the documentation of the object.

3

The final text in this statement is the word *Control*. Because Control isn't followed by a dot, you know that it's not an object; therefore, it must be a property or method. Because you expect this string of object references to return a color value to be used to clear the graphic object, you know that Control in this instance must be a property or a method that returns a value (because you need the return value to set the Clear() method). A quick check of the documentation would tell you that Control is indeed a property. The value of Control always equates to the color designated on the user's computer for the face of forms and buttons. By default, this is a light gray (often fondly referred to as *battleship gray*), but users can change this value on their computers. By using this property to specify a color rather than supplying the actual value for gray, you're assured that no matter the color scheme used on a computer, the code will clear the form to the proper system color. System colors are explained in Hour 18.

5. Enter the following statement. (Note: Do not press Enter until you're done entering *all* the code shown here. The code appears on two lines only because of the size restriction of this page.)

```
objgraphics.DrawLine(system.Drawing.Pens.Blue, 0, 0,
                     Me.DisplayRectangle.Width, Me.DisplayRectangle.Height)
```

This statement draws a blue line on the form. Within this statement is a single method call and three property references. Can you tell what's what? Immediately following objGraphics (and a dot) is DrawLine. Because no equal sign is present, you can deduce that this is a method call. As with the Clear method, the parentheses after DrawLine are used to enclose a value passed to the method. The DrawLine accepts the following parameters in the order in which they appear here:

- A pen
- X value of first coordinate
- Y value of first coordinate
- X value of second coordinate
- Y value of second coordinate

The DrawLine method draws a straight line between coordinate one and coordinate two, using the pen specified in the Pen parameter. I'm not going to go into detail on pens here (refer to Hour 18), but suffice it to say that a pen has characteristics such as width and color. Looking at the dots once more, notice that you're passing the Blue property of the Pens object. Blue is an object property that returns a predefined Pen object that has a width of 1 pixel and the color blue.

You're passing 0 as the next two parameters. The coordinates used for drawing are defined such that 0,0 is always the upper-left corner of a surface. As you move to the right of the surface, X increases, and as you move down the surface, Y increases; you can use negative values to indicate coordinates that appear to the left or above the surface. The coordinate 0,0 causes the line to be drawn from the upper-left corner of the form's client area.

The object property DisplayRectangle is referenced twice in this statement. DisplayRectangle is an object of the form that holds information about the client area of the form. Here, you're simply getting the Width and Height properties of the client area and passing them to the DrawLine method. The result is that the end of the line will be at the lower-right hand corner of the form's client area.

6. Lastly, you have to clean up after yourself by entering the following code statement:

```
objgraphics.Dispose()
```

Objects often make use of other objects and resources. The underlying mechanics of an object can be truly boggling and are almost impossible to discuss in an entry-level programming book. The net effect, however, is that you must explicitly destroy most objects when you're done with them. If you don't destroy an object, it might persist in memory and it might hold references to other objects or resources that exist in memory. This means you can create a *memory leak* within your application that slowly (or rather quickly) munches system memory and resources. This is one of the cardinal no-no's of Windows programming, yet the nature of using resources and the fact you're responsible for telling your objects to clean up after themselves makes this easy to do. If your application causes memory leaks, your users won't call for a plumber, but they might reach for a monkey wrench....

Objects that must explicitly be told to clean up after themselves usually provide a Dispose method. When you're done with such an object, call Dispose on the object to make sure it frees any resources it might be holding.

For your convenience, here are all the lines of code:

```
Dim objGraphics As Graphics
objgraphics = Me.CreateGraphics
objgraphics.Clear(system.Drawing.SystemColors.Control)
objgraphics.DrawLine(system.Drawing.Pens.Blue, 0, 0, _
                     Me.DisplayRectangle.Width, Me.DisplayRectangle.Height)
objgraphics.Dispose()
```

The statement calling DrawLine is shown here as two lines of code. At the end of the first line is an underscore (_). This character is a special character called a *line continuation character*, and it tells the Visual Basic compiler that the statement immediately following the character is a continuation of the current statement. You can, and should, use this character to break up long statements in your code.

Testing Your Object Example Project

Now the easy part. Run the project by pressing F5 or by clicking the Start button on the toolbar. Your form looks pretty much like it did at design time. Clicking the button causes a line to be drawn from the upper-left corner of the form's client area to the lower-right corner (see Figure 3.7).

If you receive any errors when you attempt to run the project, go back and make sure that the code you entered exactly matches the code I've provided.

FIGURE 3.7
Simple lines and complex drawings are accomplished using objects.

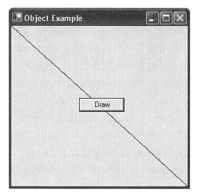

Resize the form, larger or smaller, and click the button again. Notice that the form is cleared and a new line is drawn. If you were to omit the statement that invokes the Clear method (and you're welcome to stop your project and do so), the new line would be drawn, but any and all lines already drawn would remain.

If you use Alt+Tab to switch to another application after drawing one or more lines, the lines will be gone when you come back to your form. In fact, this will occur anytime you overlay the graphics with another form. In Hour 18, you'll learn why this is so and how to work around this behavior.

Stop the project now by clicking Stop Debugging on the Visual Basic .NET toolbar and then click Save All to save your project. What I hope you've gained from building this example is not necessarily that you can now draw a line (which is cool), but rather an understanding of how objects are used in programming. As with learning almost anything, repetition aids in understanding. That said, you'll be working with objects a lot throughout this book.

Understanding Collections

NEW TERM A collection is just what its name implies: a collection of objects. Collections make it easy to work with large numbers of similar objects by enabling you to create code that performs iterative processing on items within the collection. *Iterative processing* is an operation that uses a loop to perform actions on multiple objects, rather than writing the operative code for each object. In addition to containing an indexed set of objects, collections also have properties and might have methods. Figure 3.8 illustrates the structure of a collection.

FIGURE 3.8
Collections contain sets of like objects, and they have their own properties and methods.

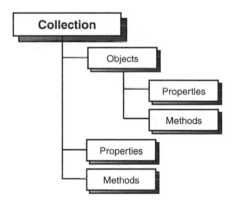

Continuing with the Dog/Pet object metaphor, think about what an Animals collection might look like. The Animals collection might contain one or more Pet objects, or it might be empty (contain no objects). All collections have a Count property that returns the total count of objects contained within the collection. Collections might also have methods, such as a Delete method used to remove objects from the collection and an Add method used to add a new object to the collection.

To better understand collections, you're going to create a small Visual Basic .NET project that cycles through the Controls collection of a form and tells you the value of the Name property of every control on the form. To create your sample project, follow these steps:

1. Start Visual Basic now (if it's not already loaded) and create a new Windows Application project titled **Collections Example**.

2. Change the name of the form to **fclsCollectionsExample** using the Solution Explorer and set the form's Text property to **Collections Example**.

3. Make this form the Startup object by right-clicking Collections Example in the Solution Explorer window, choosing Properties, and then selecting fclsCollectionsExample from the Startup object drop-down list. Click OK to close the dialog box.

4. Add a new button to the form by double-clicking the Button tool in the toolbox. Set the button's properties as follows:

Property	Value
Name	**btnShowNames**
Text	**Show Control Names**
Location	**88,112**
Size	**120,23**

5. Next, add some text box and label controls to the form. As you add the controls to the form, be sure to give each control a unique name. Feel free to use any name you like, but you can't use spaces in a control name. You might want to drag the controls to different locations on the form so that they don't overlap.

6. When you're finished adding controls to your form, double-click the Show Control Names button to add code to its Click event. Enter the following code:

```
Dim intIndex As Integer
For intIndex = 0 To Me.Controls.Count - 1
   MessageBox.Show("Control #" & intIndex & " has of the name " & _
        Me.Controls(intIndex).Name)
Next intIndex
```

> Every form has a Controls collection, which might or might not contain any controls. Even if no controls are on the form, the form still has a Controls collection.

The first statement should look familiar to you by now. As with the Object Example you created earlier, this statement creates a variable to hold a value. Rather than create a variable that can hold an object, as you did in the earlier example, this statement creates a variable that can hold only a number.

The next statement (the one that begins with For) accomplishes a few tasks. First, it initializes the variable intIndex to 0, and then it starts a loop (loops are discussed in Hour 14, "Looping for Efficiency"), incrementing intIndex by one until intIndex equals the number of controls on the form, less one. The reason you subtract one from the Count property is that collections are zero-based—the first item is always item zero. Thus, the first item is in location zero, the second item is in location one, and so forth. If you tried to reference an item of a collection in the location of the value of the Count property, an error would occur because you would be referencing an index that's one higher than the actual locations within the collection.

The MessageBox.Show() method (mentioned in Hour 2, "Navigating Visual Basic .NET," and discussed in detail in Hour 17, "Interacting with Users") is a class of the .NET Framework that's used to display simple dialog boxes with text. The text that you're providing, which the Show method will display, is a concatenation of multiple strings of text. (*Concatenation* is the process of adding strings together; it's discussed in Hour 12, "Performing Arithmetic, String Manipulation, and Date/Time Adjustments.")

Run the project by pressing F5 or by clicking Start on the toolbar. Ignore the additional controls that you placed on the form and click the Show Control Names button. Your program will then display a message box similar to the one shown in Figure 3.9 for each control on your form (because of the loop). When the program is finished displaying the names of the controls, choose Stop Debugging from the Debug toolbar to stop the program, and then save the project.

3

FIGURE 3.9
The Controls collection enables you to get to each and every control on a form.

Because everything in Visual Basic .NET is an object, you can expect to use numerous collections as you create your programs. Collections are powerful, and the quicker you become comfortable using them, the more productive you'll become.

Using the Object Browser

Visual Basic .NET includes a useful tool that enables you to easily view members (properties, methods, and events) of all the objects in a project: the Object Browser (see Figure 3.10). This is extremely useful when dealing with objects that aren't well documented because it enables you to see all the members an object supports. To view the Object Browser, choose Object Browser from the View menu.

The Browse drop-down list in the upper-left corner of the Object Browser is used to determine the *browsing scope*. You can choose Active Project to view only the objects referenced in the active project, or you can choose Selected Components (the default) to view a set of selected objects. The Object Browser shows a preselected set of objects for

Selected Components, but you can customize the object set by clicking the Customize button next to the Browse drop-down list. I don't recommend changing the custom object setting until you have some experience using Visual Basic objects as well as experience using the Object Browser.

FIGURE 3.10

The Object Browser enables you to view all properties and methods of an object.

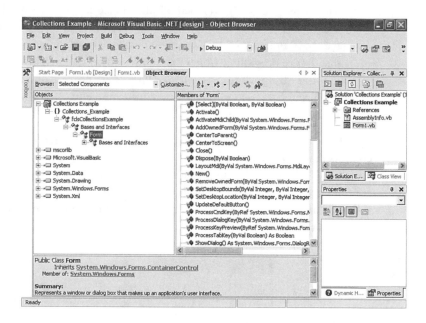

NEW TERM The top-level nodes in the Objects tree are libraries. *Libraries* are usually DLL or EXE files on your computer that contain one or more objects. To view the objects within a library, simply expand the library node. As you select objects within a library, the list to the right of the Objects tree will show information regarding the members of the selected object (refer to Figure 3.10). For even more detailed information, click a member in the list on the right, and the Object Browser will show information about the member in the gray area below the two lists.

Summary

In this hour, you learned all about objects. You learned how objects have properties, which are attributes that describe the object. Some properties can be set at runtime using the Properties window, and most can also be set at runtime in Visual Basic .NET code. You learned that referencing a property on the left side of the equal sign has the effect of changing a property, whereas referencing a property on the right side of the equal sign retrieves a property's value.

In addition to properties, you learned that objects have executable functions, called *methods*. Like properties, methods are referenced by using a dot at the end of an object reference. An object might contain many methods and properties, and some properties can even be objects themselves. You learned how to "follow the dots" to interpret a lengthy object reference.

Objects are often used as a group, called a *collection*. You learned that a collection often contains properties and methods, and that collections let you easily iterate through a set of like objects. Finally, you learned that the Object Browser can be used to explore all the members of an object in a project.

The knowledge you've gained in this hour is fundamental to understanding programming with Visual Basic because objects and collections are the basis on which applications are built. After you have a strong grasp of objects and collections—and you will have by the time you've completed all the hours in this book—you'll be well on your way to fully understanding the complexities of creating robust applications using Visual Basic .NET.

Q&A

Q Is there an easy way to get help about an object's member?

A Absolutely. Visual Basic .NET's context-sensitive Help extends to code as well as to visual objects. To get help on a member, write a code statement that includes the member (it doesn't have to be a complete statement), position the cursor within the member text, and press F1. For instance, to get help on the Count property of the controls collection, you could type Me.Controls.Count, position the cursor within the word Count, and press F1.

Q Are there any other types of object members besides properties and methods?

A Yes. An event is actually a member of an object, although it's not always thought of that way. Not all objects support events, however, but most objects do support properties and methods.

Workshop

The Workshop is designed to help you anticipate possible questions, review what you've learned, and get you thinking about how to put your knowledge into practice. The answers to the quiz are in Appendix B, "Answers to the Quizzes."

Quiz

1. True or False: Visual Basic .NET is a true object-oriented language.

2. An attribute that defines the state of an object is called a _____.

3. To change the value of a property, the property must be referenced on which side of an equal sign?

4. What is the term for when a new object is created from a template?

5. An external function of an object (one that is available to code using an object) is called a

6. True or False: A property of an object can be another object.

7. A group of like objects is called a

8. What tool is used to explore the members of an object?

Exercises

1. Create a new project and add text boxes and a button to the form. Write code that, when clicked, places the text in the first text box into the second text box. Hint: Use the Text property of the text box controls.

2. Modify the collections example in this hour to print the height of all controls, rather than the name.

HOUR 4

Understanding Events

It's fairly easy to produce an attractive interface for an application using Visual Basic .NET's integrated design tools. You can create beautiful forms that have buttons to click, text boxes in which to type information, picture boxes that display pictures, and many other creative and attractive elements with which users can interact. However, that's just the start of producing a Visual Basic program. In addition to designing an interface, you have to empower your program to perform actions in response both to how a user interacts with the program and how Windows interacts with the program. This is accomplished by using *events*. In the previous hour, you learned about objects and their members—notably, properties and methods. In this hour, you'll learn about object events and event-driven programming, and you'll learn how to use events to make your applications responsive.

The highlights of this hour include

- Understanding event-driven programming
- Triggering events
- Avoiding recursive events
- Accessing an object's events

- Working with event parameters
- Creating event handlers
- Keeping event names current

Understanding Event-Driven Programming

With traditional programming languages (often referred to as *procedural* languages), the program itself fully dictates what code is executed as well as when it's executed. When you start such a program, the first line of code in the program executes, and the code continues to execute in a completely predetermined path. The execution of code might branch and loop on occasion, but the execution path is completely determined by the program. This often meant that a program was quite restricted in how it could respond to the user. For example, the program might expect text to be entered into controls on the screen in a predetermined order. This is quite unlike a Windows application in which a user can interact with different parts of the interface—often in any order the user chooses.

NEW TERM Visual Basic .NET incorporates an event-driven programming model. Event-driven applications aren't bound by the constraints of procedural programs. Instead of the top-down approach of procedural languages, event-driven programs have logical sections of code placed within events. There's no predetermined order in which events occur; the user often has complete control over what code is executed in an event-driven program by interactively triggering specific events, such as by clicking a button. An event, along with the code it contains, is called an *event procedure*.

Triggering Events

In the previous hour, you learned that a method is simply a function of an object. Events, in a sense, are really a special kind of method used by an object to signal state changes that might be useful to clients (code using the object). In fact, the Visual Basic .NET documentation refers to events as *methods* quite frequently (something that will no doubt cause a lot of confusion). Events are methods that can be called in special ways—usually by the user interacting with something on a form or by Windows itself—rather than being called from a statement in your code.

There are many types of events and many ways to trigger those events. You've already seen how a user can trigger the event of a button by clicking it. User interaction isn't the only thing that can trigger an event; an event can be triggered in one of the following four ways:

- Users can trigger events by interacting with your program.
- Objects can trigger their own events, as needed.

- The operating system (whichever version of Windows the user is running) can trigger events.

- You can trigger events by calling them using Visual Basic code.

Events Triggered Through User Interaction

The most common way an event is triggered is by a user interacting with a program. Every form, and almost every control you can place on a form, has a set of events specific to its object type. For example, the Button control has a number of events, including the Click event that you've already used in previous hours. The Click event is triggered, and then the code within the Click event executes when the user clicks the button.

The Textbox control enables users to enter information using the keyboard, and it also has a set of events. The Textbox control has some of the same types of events as the Button control, such as a Click event, but the Textbox control also has events not supported by the Button control, such as the TextChanged event. The TextChanged event occurs each time the contents of the text box changes, such as when the user types information into the text box. Because you can't enter text into a Button control, it makes sense that the Button control doesn't have a TextChanged event. Every object that supports events supports a unique set of events.

Each type of event has its own behavior, and it's important to understand the events you work with. The TextChanged event, for example, exhibits a behavior that might not be intuitive to a new developer because the event fires each time the contents of the text box change. If you were to type the following sentence into an empty text box:

```
Visual Basic.Net is very cool!
```

the TextChanged event would be triggered 30 times—once for each character typed— because each time you enter a new character, the contents of the text box are changed. Although it's easy to think that the Change event fires only when you commit your entry, such as by leaving the text box or pressing Enter, this isn't how it works. Again, it's important to learn the nuances and the exact behavior of the events you're using. If you use events without fully understanding how they work, your program might exhibit unusual, and often undesirable, results.

Triggering events (which are just a type of procedure) using Visual Basic code is discussed in detail in Hour 10, "Creating and Calling Code Procedures."

Events Triggered by an Object

Sometimes an object triggers its own events. The most common example of this is the Timer control's Timer event. The Timer control doesn't appear on a form when the program is running; it appears only when you're designing a form. The Timer control's sole purpose is to trigger its Timer event at an interval that's specified in its Interval property.

By setting the Timer control's Interval property, you control the interval (in milliseconds) at which the Timer event executes. After firing its Timer event, a Timer control resets itself and fires its Timer event again when the interval has passed. This occurs until the interval is changed, the Timer control is disabled, or the Timer control's form is unloaded. A common use of timers is to create a clock on a form. You can display the time in a label and update the time at regular intervals by placing the code to display the current time in the Timer event. You'll create a project with a Timer control in Hour 8, "Using Advanced Controls."

Events Triggered by the Operating System

The third way an event can be triggered is by Windows itself. Often, you might not even realize these events exist. For example, when a form is fully or partially obstructed by another window, the program needs to know when the offending window is resized or moved so that it can repaint the area of the window that's hidden. Windows and Visual Basic .NET work together in this respect. When the obstructing window is moved or resized, Windows tells Visual Basic .NET to repaint the form, which Visual Basic .NET does. This also causes Visual Basic .NET to raise the form's Paint event. You can place code into the Paint event to create a custom display for the form, such as drawing shapes on the form using a Graphics object. By doing so, every time the form repaints itself, your custom drawing code executes.

Avoiding Recursive Events

NEW TERM You must make sure never to cause an event to endlessly trigger itself. An event that continuously triggers itself is called a *recursive* event. To illustrate a situation that causes a recursive event, think of the Textbox control's TextChanged event discussed earlier. The TextChanged event fires every time the text within the text box changes. Placing code into the TextChanged event that alters the text within the text box causes the Change event to be fired again, which could result in an endless loop. Recursive events terminate when Windows returns a StackOverflow exception (see Figure 4.1), indicating that Windows no longer has the resources to follow the recursion.

FIGURE 4.1

When you receive a StackOverflow exception, you should look for a recursive event as the culprit.

Recursive behavior can occur with more than one event in the loop. For example, if Event A triggers Event B, which in turn triggers Event A, you can have infinite looping of the two events. Recursive behavior can take place among a sequence of many events, not just one or two.

> Uses for recursive procedures actually exist, such as when writing complex math functions. For instance, recursive events are often used to compute factorials. However, when you purposely create a recursive event, you must ensure that the recursion isn't infinite.

Accessing an Object's Events

Accessing an object's events is simple, and if you've been following the examples in this book, you've already accessed a number of objects' default events. To access an object's events, you double-click the object in Form Design view.

You're now going to create a project to get the feel for working with events. Start Visual Basic .NET, create a new Windows Application project titled **View Events,** and then follow these steps:

1. Change the name of the default form to **fclsViewEvents** and change the Text property to **View Events Example**.

2. Make this form the Startup object by right-clicking View Events in the Solution Explorer window, choosing Properties, and then selecting fclsViewEvents from the Startup object drop-down list. Click OK to close the dialog box.

3. Use the toolbox to add a picture box to the form.

4. Change the name of the picture box to **picText**, and then double-click the picture box to access its event procedures.

Your screen should look like the one in Figure 4.2. Notice the two drop-down lists at the top of the code window: One contains the word picText and the other reads Click. The drop-down list on the left contains a list of all the objects of the current form (including the form and its controls), whereas the list on the right contains all the events for the object selected in the first drop-down list.

Event procedures are created using the events drop-down list in the code editor.

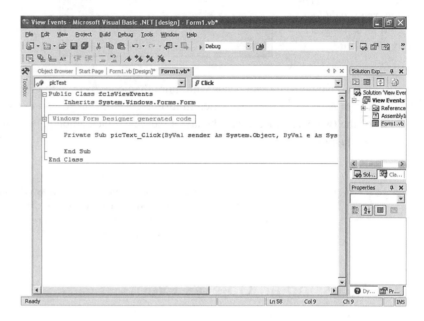

NEW TERM Currently, you're viewing the Click event for the picText object. The cursor is placed within the Click event procedure, ready for you to enter code. The code statement above the cursor is the event declaration. An *event declaration* is a statement that defines the structure of an event. Notice that this event declaration contains the name of the object, an underscore character (_), and then the event name. Following the event name is a set of parentheses. The items within the parentheses are called *parameters,* which are the topic of the next section. This is the standard declaration structure for an event procedure.

Click the events drop-down list (the list on the right), and take a look at all the events that the picture box supports. Select MouseDown from the list and notice how your Code window changes to look like the one shown in Figure 4.3.

When you select an event from the list, Visual Basic .NET creates a new event procedure for that event. The full event declaration is shown here:

```
Protected Sub picText_MouseDown(ByVal sender As System.Object, _
                           ByVal e As System.WinForms.MouseEventArgs)
```

FIGURE 4.3

Visual Basic .NET creates an empty event procedure the first time you select an object's event.

Notice that the new event declaration is similar to the first one in the window in that it's titled with the object's name followed by an underscore. However, the remainder of the event procedure declaration is different. It's the name of the event—in this case, MouseDown.

> The words *Protected* and *Sub* are Visual Basic .NET reserved words that indicate the scope and type of the procedure. Scope and type are discussed in Hour 10.

Working with Event Parameters

NEW TERM As mentioned previously, the items within the parentheses of an event declaration are called *parameters*. An event parameter is a variable that's created and assigned a value by Visual Basic .NET. These parameter variables are used to get, and sometimes set, relevant information within the event. This data may be text, a number, an object—almost anything. Multiple parameters within an event procedure are always separated by commas. As you can see, the MouseDown event has two parameters. When the event procedure is triggered, Visual Basic automatically creates the parameter variables and assigns them values for use in this single execution of the event procedure; the next time the event procedure occurs, the values in the parameters are reset. You use the values in the parameters to make decisions or perform operations in your code.

The MouseDown event of a form has the following parameters:

```
ByVal sender As System.Object
```

and

```
ByVal e As System.WinForms.MouseEventArgs
```

For now, ignore the ByVal keywords. These are discussed in Hour 11, "Using Constants, Data Types, Variables, and Arrays."

NEW TERM The text following ByVal is the name of the parameter, and the string after the word As indicates the type of data the parameter contains. The first parameter, sender, holds a generic object. Object parameters can be any type of object supported by Visual Basic .NET. It's not critical that you understand data types right now, just be aware that different parameter variables contain different types of information. Some contain text, others contain numbers, and still others (many others) contain objects. In the case of the sender parameter, it will always hold a reference to the control causing the event.

The e parameter of the MouseDown event, on the other hand, is where the real action is. The e parameter also holds an object, and in this case the object is System.WinForms.MouseEventArgs. This object has properties that relate to the MouseDown event. To see them, type in the following code, but don't press anything after entering the dot (period):

```
e.
```

When you press the period, you'll get a drop-down list showing you the members (properties and methods) of the e object (see Figure 4.4). Using the e object, you can determine a number of things about the occurrence of the MouseDown event. I've listed some of the more interesting items in Table 4.1.

TABLE 4.1   Commonly Used Members of System.WinForms.MouseEventArgs

Property	Description
Clicks	Returns the number of times the user clicked the mouse button
Button	Returns the button that was clicked (left, middle, right)
X	Returns the horizontal coordinate at which the pointer was located when the user clicked
Y	Returns the vertical coordinate at which the pointer was located when the user clicked

FIGURE 4.4

IntelliSense drop-down lists alleviate the need for memorizing the make up of hundreds of objects.

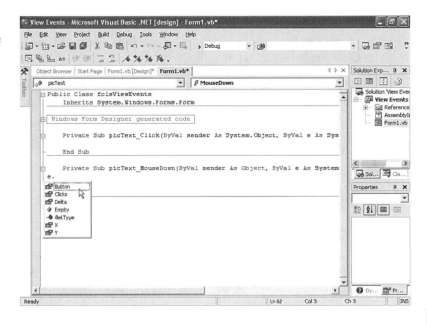

Each time the event occurs, the parameters are initialized by Visual Basic .NET so that they always reflect the current occurrence of the event.

Each event has parameters specific to it. For instance, the TextChanged event returns parameters that are different from the MouseDown event. As you work with events—and you'll work with a *lot* of events—you'll quickly become familiar with the parameters of each event type. You'll learn how to create parameters for your own functions and procedures in Hour 10.

Building an Event Example Project

You're now going to create a very simple project in which you'll use the event procedures of a text box. Specifically, you're going to write code to display a message when a user presses a mouse button on the text box, and code to clear the text box when the user releases the button. You'll be using the e parameter to determine which button the user has pressed.

Creating the User Interface

Create a new Windows application titled **Events Example**. Change the name of the default form to **fclsEventsExample** and set the form's Text property to **Events example**.

Next, make this form the Startup object by right-clicking Events Example in the Solution Explorer window, choosing Properties, and then selecting fclsEventsExample from the Startup object drop-down list.

Add a text box to the form by double-clicking the TextBox tool in the toolbox. Set its properties as follows:

Property	Value
Name	**txtEvents**
Location	**48,120**
Size	**193,20**
Text	**Click Me!**

The only other control you need on your form is a Label. Label controls are used to display static text; users can't type text into a label. Add a new label to your form now by double-clicking the Label tool in the toolbox and then set the Label control's properties as follows:

Property	Value
Name	**lblMessage**
Location	**48,152**
Size	**192,16**
Text	*(make blank)*

Your form should now look like the one in Figure 4.5. It's a good idea to save frequently, so save your project now by clicking the Save All button on the toolbar.

Creating Event Handlers

The interface for the Events Example project is complete—on to the fun part. You're now going to create the event procedures that empower the program to do something. The event that we're interested in first is the MouseDown event. Double-click the text box on the form to access its event procedures. When you double-click a control, the event procedure that's created is always for the default event for the type of control. For text boxes, this is the TextChanged event. You're not interested in the TextChanged event at this time, however. Open the event list (the drop-down list in the upper-right), and then locate and select MouseDown. Visual Basic creates a new MouseDown procedure for the text box (see Figure 4.6).

FIGURE 4.5

A Label control that has an empty Text property can be hard to see unless it's selected.

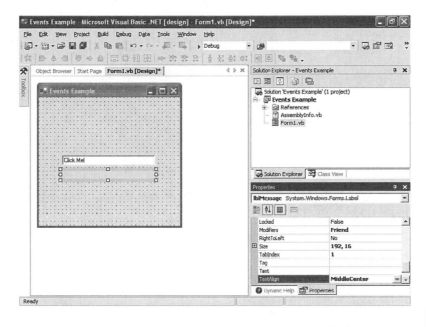

FIGURE 4.6

Each time you select a new event, Visual Basic creates an empty event procedure —if one hasn't been created previously for the control.

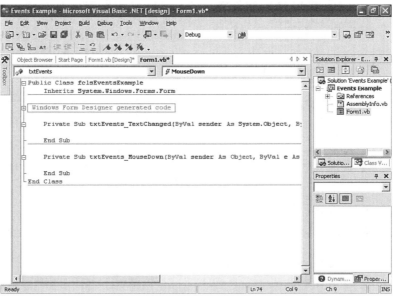

Notice that Visual Basic .NET left the default event procedure it created for you. It's best not to leave dead code (code that isn't used), so delete the TextChanged event procedure now. To fully delete the event procedure, you must delete *all* the following code:

```
Protected Sub txtEvents_TextChanged(ByVal sender As Object, _
                                    ByVal e As System.EventArgs)
End Sub
```

After you've deleted the dead procedure, place the cursor on the line between the Private Sub and End Sub statements of the txtEvents_MouseDown procedure.

Enter the following code into the MouseDown event procedure:

```
Select Case e.Button
   Case MouseButtons.Left
      lblmessage.Text = "You are pressing the left button!"
   Case MouseButtons.right
      lblmessage.Text = "You are pressing the right button!"
   Case MouseButtons.Middle
      lblmessage.Text = "You are pressing the middle button!"
End Select
```

The Select Case construct, which is discussed in detail in Hour 13, "Making Decisions in Visual Basic Code," compares the value of an expression to a list of possible values. In this instance, the expression is the value of e.Button (the Button property of the object e). When this code executes, the expression is compared to each Case statement in the order in which the statements appear. If and when a match is found, the code immediately following the Case statement that was matched gets executed. In a nutshell, the code you wrote looks at the value of e.Button and compares it to three values—one at a time. When the Select Case construct concludes which button has been pressed, it displays a message about it in the Label control.

In a more robust application, you would probably execute more useful and more complicated code. For example, you might want to display a custom pop-up menu when the user clicks with the right button, and perhaps execute a specific function when the user clicks with the middle button. All of this and more this is possible.

The nice thing about objects is that you don't have to commit every detail about them to memory. For example, you don't need to memorize the return values for each type of button (who wants to remember MouseButtons.Left anyway?). Just remember that the e parameter contains information about the event. When you type **e** and press the period, the IntelliSense drop-down list appears and shows you the members of e, one of which is Button. If you select Button and press a space followed by an equal sign, you'll see another drop-down list showing you the possible values of Buttons (you saw this when you entered the code for this procedure). This behavior manifests itself in many ways. For example, each time that you typed the word Case and pressed the spacebar when entering this code, you received a drop-down list showing you possible values. Visual Basic can do this because it knows that the Case statement must evaluate to a value of e.Buttons.

Don't feel overwhelmed by all the object references you'll encounter throughout this book. Simply accept that you can't memorize them all, nor do you need to; you'll learn the ones that are important, and you'll use Help when you're stuck. Also, after you know the parent object in a situation (such as the *e* object in this example), it's easy for you to determine the objects and members that belong to it by using the IntelliSense drop-down lists.

You're now going to add code to the MouseUp event to clear the label's Text property when the user releases the button. First, you'll need to create the MouseUp event procedure. To do this, choose MouseUp from the events drop-down list.

All you're going to do in the MouseUp event is clear the Label control. Enter the following code:

```
lblMessage.Text = ""
```

Testing Your Events Project

Run your project now by pressing F5. If you entered all the code correctly and you don't receive any errors, your form will be displayed as shown in Figure 4.7).

FIGURE 4.7

A simple but functional example.

Click the text box with the left mouse button and watch the label. It will display a sentence telling you that the left button was clicked. When you release the button, the text is cleared. Try this with the middle and right buttons as well. When you click the text box with the right button, Windows displays the standard shortcut menu for text boxes. When this menu appears, you have to select something from it or click somewhere off the menu to trigger the MouseUp event. In Hour 9, "Adding Menus and Toolbars to Forms," you'll

4

learn how to add your own shortcut menus to forms and controls. When you're satisfied that your project is behaving as it should, choose Stop Debugging from the Debug menu or toolbar to stop the project (or click the Close button on your form). Be sure to save your work by clicking Save All on the toolbar.

Keeping Event Names Current

If you've used any version of Visual Basic prior to .NET, you've undoubtedly experienced orphaned events. As you now know, the name of an event procedure is defined by the control's name followed by an underscore and then the event name (such as txtAddress_TextChanged). When you change the name of a control, Visual Basic doesn't change the control's event declarations to reflect the new name, but it does keep the event attached to the control. The way this works is that at the end of each event declaration is the keyword Handles, followed by an object name. The Handles keyword effectively hooks up an event handler to the event of a control. When you change the name of a control, Visual Basic .NET changes the Handles reference, but it doesn't change the event name. Although your code will work, you should manually change the name of the corresponding procedures so that they match the new name of the control; this will help a lot when debugging complicated code.

Summary

In this hour, you learned about event-driven programming, including what events are, how to trigger events, and how to avoid recursive events. In addition, you learned how to access an object's events and how to work with parameters. Much of the code you'll write will execute in response to an event of some kind. By understanding how events work, including being aware of the available events and their parameters, you'll be able to create complex Visual Basic .NET programs that react to a multitude of user and system input.

Q&A

Q Is it possible to create custom events for an object?

A Yes, you can create custom events for your own objects (which you'll learn about in Hour 16, "Designing Objects Using Classes"), and you can also create them for existing objects. Creating custom events, however, is beyond the scope of this book.

Q Is it possible for objects that don't have an interface to support events?

A Yes. However, to use the events of such an object, the object variable must be dimensioned a special way or the events aren't available. This gets a little tricky and is beyond the scope of this book. If you have an object in code that supports events, look in Help for the keyword WithEvents for information on how to use such events.

Workshop

The Workshop is designed to help you anticipate possible questions, review what you've learned, and get you thinking about how to put your knowledge into practice. The answers to the quiz are in Appendix B, "Answers to the Quizzes."

Quiz

1. Name three things that can cause events to occur.
2. True or False: All objects support the same set of events.
3. What is the default event type for a button?
4. Writing code in an event that causes that same event to be triggered, setting off a chain reaction with the event triggered again and again is called what?
5. What is the easiest way to access a control's default event handler?
6. All control events pass a reference to the control causing the event. What is the name of the parameter that holds this reference?
7. What should you do when you change the name of a control?

Exercises

1. Create a project with a single picture box and a text box. In the MouseDown event of the picture box, show the coordinate of the mouse in the text box. (Hint: Use the E parameter in the MouseDown event to get the coordinates.)

2. Create a project with a form and a text box. Add code to the TextChange event to cause a recursion when the user types in text. Hint: Concatenate a character to the end of the user's text using a statement such as

```
txtMyTextBox.Text = txtMyTextBox.Text & "a";
```

The ampersand tells Visual Basic .NET to add the letter a to the end of the existing text box contents.

PART II
Building a User Interface

Hour

5 Building Forms—The Basics

6 Building Forms—Advanced Techniques

7 Working with the Traditional Controls

8 Using Advanced Controls

9 Adding Menus and Toolbars to Forms

HOUR 5

Building Forms—The Basics

With few exceptions, forms are the cornerstones of every Windows application's interface. Forms are essentially windows and the two terms are often used interchangeably. More accurately, *window* refers to what's seen by the user and what the user interacts with, whereas *form* refers to what you see when you design. Forms enable users to view and enter information in a program (such as the form you built in your Picture Viewer program in Hour 1, " Jumping In with Both Feet: A Visual Basic .NET Programming Tour"). Such information may be text, pictures, graphs—almost anything that can be viewed on the screen. Understanding how to design forms correctly will enable you to begin creating solid interface foundations for your programs.

Visual Basic .NET uses a new forms engine called Windows Forms, which is different from the engine used in previous versions of Visual Basic.

Think of a form as a canvas on which you build your program's interface. On this canvas, you can print text, draw shapes, and place controls with which users can interact. The wonderful thing about Visual Basic forms is that they behave like a dynamic canvas; not only can you adjust the appearance of a form by manipulating what's on it, you can also manipulate specific properties of the form itself.

In previous hours, you manipulated the following form appearance properties:

- Text
- Height
- Left
- Top
- Width

The capability to tailor your forms goes far beyond these basic property manipulations, however.

There's so much to cover about Windows forms that I've broken the material into two hours. In this hour, you'll learn the very basics of forms—adding them to a project, manipulating their properties, and showing and hiding them using Visual Basic .NET code. Although you've done some of these things in previous hours, here you'll learn the nuts and bolts of the tasks you've performed. In the next hour, you'll learn more advanced form techniques.

The highlights of this hour include

- Changing the name of a form
- Changing the appearance of a form
- Displaying text on a form's title bar
- Adding an image to a form's background
- Giving a form an icon
- Preventing a form from appearing in the taskbar
- Specifying the initial display position of a form
- Displaying a form in a normal, maximized, or minimized state
- Changing the mouse pointer
- Showing and hiding forms

Changing the Name of a Form

The first thing you should do when you create a new object is give it a descriptive name, so that's the first thing I'll talk about in this hour. Start Visual Basic .NET now (if it's not already running), and create a new Windows Application titled **Forms Example**. Using the Properties window, change the name of the form to **fclsFormsExample**. When you need to create a new instance of this form, you'll use this name rather than the default generic name of Form1. You might have noticed that the tabs in the designer refer to the name of the form file—not the name you give it in code. Change the filename of the form now by right-clicking Form1.vb in the Solutions Explorer, choosing Rename, and then changing the name of the form to **fclsFormsExample.vb** (I prefer not to use spaces in my filenames—old habits, I suppose).

> You should actually change the filename for all the forms in your projects. I haven't done this throughout the book, however, because it adds yet another step to each example and I don't want to complicate things too much.

Changing the Appearance of a Form

The Properties window can actually show two different sets of properties for a form. Right now, it's probably showing the file properties of the form (the properties that describe the physical file(s) on the hard drive). If so, click the form in the designer once again to view its development properties. Take a moment to browse the rest of the form's properties in the Properties window. In this hour, I'll show you how to use the more common properties of the form to tailor its appearance.

> Remember, to get help on any property at any time, select the property in the Properties window and press F1.

Displaying Text on a Form's Title Bar

You should always set the text in a form's title bar to something meaningful. (Note: Not all forms have title bars, as you'll see later in this hour.) The text displayed in the title bar is the value placed in the form's Text property. Generally, the text should be one of the following:

- The name of the program   This is most appropriate when the form is the program's main or only form.

- The purpose of the form   This is perhaps the most common type of text displayed in a title bar. For example, if a form is used to select a printer, consider setting the Text property to **Select Printer**. When you take this approach, use active voice (for instance, don't use **Printer Select**).

- The name of the form   If you choose to place the name of the form into the form's title bar, use the English name, not the actual form name. For instance, if you've used a naming convention and named a form fclsLogin, use the text **Login** or **Login User**.

Change the Text property of your form to **Building Forms Example**. Your form should now look like the one in Figure 5.1.

FIGURE 5.1

Use common sense when setting title bar text.

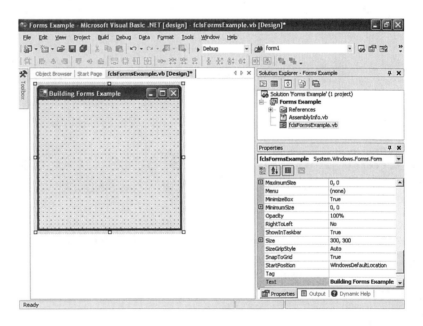

 As with most other form properties, you can change the Text property at any time using Visual Basic code.

Changing a Form's Background Color

Although most forms appear with a gray background (this is part of the standard 3D color scheme in Windows), you can change a form's background to any color you like. To change a form's background color, you change its BackColor property. The

BackColor property is a unique property in that you can specify a named color or an RGB value in the format red, green, blue.

By default, the BackColor property is set to the color named Control. This color is a system color, and might not be gray. When Windows is first installed, it's configured to a default color scheme. In the default scheme for all Windows versions other than XP, the color for forms and other objects is the familiar battleship gray. For XP installations, this color is a light tan (although it still looks gray on most monitors). However, as a Windows user, you're free to change any system color you desire. For instance, some people with color blindness prefer to change their system colors to colors that have more contrast than the defaults so that objects are more clearly distinguishable. When you assign a system color to a form or control, the appearance of the object adjusts itself to the current user's system color scheme. This doesn't just occur when a form is first displayed; changes to the system color scheme are immediately propagated to all objects that use the affected colors.

Change the background color of your form to blue now by deleting the word Control in the BackColor property in the Properties window, and in its place enter **0,0,255** and press Enter or Tab to commit your entry. Your form should now be blue because you entered an RGB value in which you specified no red, no green, and maximum blue (color values range from 0 to 255). In reality, you'll probably rarely enter RGB values. Instead, you'll select colors from color palettes. To view color palettes from which you can select a color for the BackColor property, click the drop-down arrow in the BackColor property in the Properties window (see Figure 5.2).

FIGURE 5.2
All color properties have palettes from which you can choose a color.

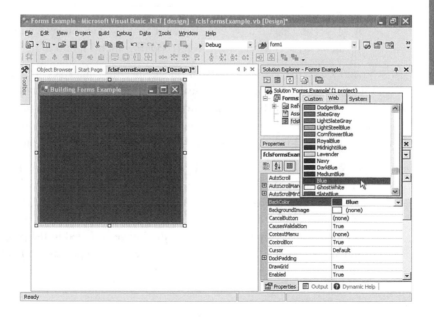

5

System colors are discussed in detail in Hour 18, "Working with Graphics."

When the drop-down list appears, the color blue is selected on the Web tab. This happens because when you entered the RGB value 0,0,255, Visual Basic .NET looked for a named color composed of the same values and it found blue. The color palettes were explained in Hour 2, "Navigating Visual Basic .NET," so I'm not going to go into detail about them here. For now, select the System tab to see a list of the available system colors and choose Control from the list to change the BackColor property of your form back to the default Windows color.

Adding an Image to a Form's Background

In addition to changing the color of a form's background, you can place a picture on it. To add a picture to a form, set the form's BackgroundImage property. When you add an image to a form, the image is painted on the form's background. All the controls that you place on the form appear on top of the picture.

Add an image to your form now by following these steps:

1. Select the form.
2. Click the BackgroundImage property in the Properties window.
3. Click the Build button that appears next to the property (the small button with three dots).
4. Use the Open dialog box that appears to locate and select an image file from your hard drive (I used Blue Lace 16.BMP, which I found in my \Windows folder).

Visual Basic .NET always tiles an image specified in a BackgroundImage property (see Figure 5.3). This means that if the selected picture isn't big enough to fill the form, Visual Basic .NET displays additional copies of the picture, creating a tiled effect. If you want to display a single copy of an image on a form, anywhere on the form, you should use a picture box, as discussed in Hour 8, "Using Advanced Controls."

Notice that to the left of the BackgroundImage property is a small box containing a plus sign. This indicates that there are related properties, or *subproperties*, of the BackgroundImage property. Click the plus sign now to expand the list of subproperties (see Figure 5.3). In the case of the BackgroundImage property, Visual Basic .NET shows you a number of properties related to the image assigned to the property, such as its dimensions and image format. Note that these subproperties are read-only, but not all subproperties that you encounter will be.

FIGURE 5.3

*Background images
are tiled to fill the
form.*

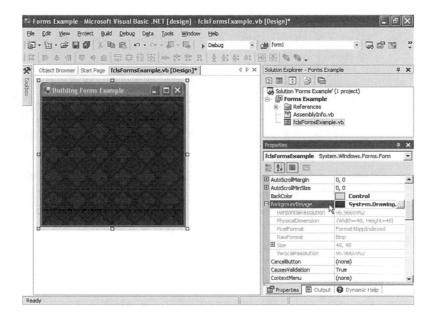

Adding a background image to a form can add pizzazz to a program, but it
can also confuse users by making the form unnecessarily busy. Try to avoid
adding images just because you can. Use discretion and add an image to a
form only when the image adds value to the interface.

5

Removing an image from a form is just as easy as adding the image in the first place. To
remove the picture that you just added to your form, right-click the BackgroundImage
property name and choose Reset from the shortcut menu that appears.

You must right-click the Name column of the property, not the Value column. If you right-click the value of the property, you get a different shortcut
menu that doesn't have a Reset option.

Giving a Form an Icon

The icon assigned to a form appears in the left side of the form's title bar, in the taskbar
when the form is minimized, and in the iconic list of tasks when you press Alt+Tab to
switch to another application. The icon often represents the application; therefore, you
should assign an icon to any form that a user can minimize. If you don't assign an icon

to a form, Visual Basic .NET supplies a default icon to represent the form when it's min-imized. This default icon is generic, unattractive, and doesn't really represent anything—you should avoid it.

In the past, it was recommended that every form have a unique icon that represented the form's purpose. This proved very difficult to accomplish in large applications containing dozens or even hundreds of forms. Instead, it's usually just best to set the icon property of all of your forms to the icon that best represents your application.

You assign an icon to a form in much the same way you assign an image to the BackgroundImage property. Add an icon to your form now by clicking the form's Icon property in the Properties window, clicking the Build button that appears, and selecting an icon file from your hard drive. After you've selected the icon, it appears in the form's title bar to the left.

Run your project by pressing F5. You'll receive a message that there was a build error. Click Yes to continue and you'll get the message shown in Figure 5.4.

FIGURE 5.4

This error is a result of having no valid Startup object.

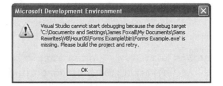

In past hours, I explained that when you change the name of the form, Visual Basic .NET isn't smart enough (yet) to realize that you've done so. If the form was designated as the Startup object, the project will reference the old name, so there's no entry point to the application. Click OK to close the error message dialog box and take a look at the task list; you'll see the error *Sub Main was not found in Forms_Example.Form1*. I've already shown you how to set the Startup object by right-clicking the project name in the Solution Explorer and choosing Properties. If you get this error because you forgot to change the Startup object, the easiest way to fix this is to double-click the task in the Task List (do this now). When you do, Visual Basic displays the handy dialog box shown in Figure 5.5. Choose the Startup object and click OK and you'll be ready to run.

Press F5 again to run the project, and then click the form's Minimize button to minimize it to the taskbar. Look at the form in the taskbar; you'll see both the form's caption and the form's icon displayed (see Figure 5.6).

FIGURE 5.5

Setting a Startup object is easiest from the Task List.

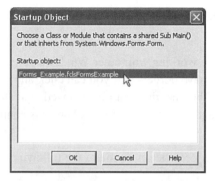

FIGURE 5.6

Assigning meaningful icons to your forms makes your application easier to use.

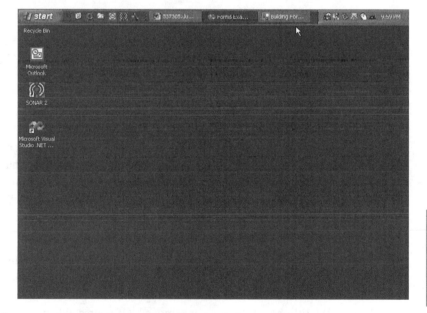

5

Stop the project now by choosing Stop Debugging from the Debug menu.

Preventing a Form from Appearing in the Taskbar

Being able to display an icon for a minimized form is nice, but sometimes it's necessary to prevent a form from even appearing in the taskbar. If your application has a number of palette windows that float over a main form, for example, it's unlikely that you'd want any but your main form to appear in the taskbar. To prevent a form from appearing in the taskbar, set the form's ShowInTaskbar property to False. If the user minimizes a form with its ShowInTaskbar property set to False, he can still get to the application by pressing Alt+Tab even though the program can't be accessed via the taskbar; Visual Basic .NET won't allow the application to become completely inaccessible to the user.

Changing the Appearance and Behavior of a Form's Border

You might have noticed while working with other Windows programs that the borders of forms can vary. Some forms have borders that you can click and drag to change the size of the form, some have fixed borders that can't be changed, and still others have no borders at all. The appearance and behavior of a form's border is controlled by its FormBorderStyle property.

The FormBorderStyle property can be set to one of the following values:

- None
- FixedSingle
- Fixed3D
- FixedDialog
- Sizable
- FixedToolWindow
- SizableToolWindow

Run your project now by pressing F5, and move the mouse pointer over one of the borders of your form. This form has a sizable border, which means that you can resize the border. Notice how the pointer changes from a large arrow to a line with arrows pointing on either side, indicating the direction you can stretch the border. When you move the pointer over a corner, you get a diagonal cursor that indicates you can stretch both of the sides that meet at the corner.

Stop the project now by choosing Stop Debugging from the Debug menu (or click the Close button on the form) and change the form's FormBorderStyle property to None. Your form should look like the one in Figure 5.7. When you choose not to give a form a border, the title bar of the form is removed. Of course, when the title bar is gone, there's no visible title bar text, no control box, and no Minimize or Maximize buttons. Run your project by pressing F5, and notice how the form appears as it did in Form Design view—with no border or title bar. Without a border, the form cannot be resized by the user, and without a title bar, the form cannot be repositioned. It's rarely appropriate to specify None for a form's BorderStyle, but in the event you need to do so, it's entirely possible.

FIGURE 5.7

You can create forms without borders.

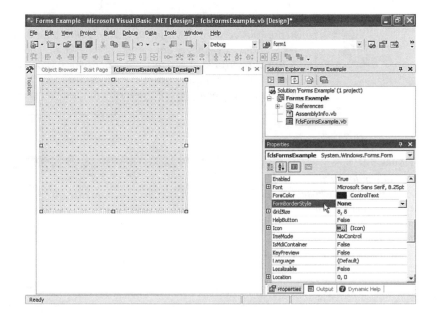

In previous versions of Visual Basic, setting a form's BorderStyle to FixedSingle automatically caused the Maximize and Minimize buttons to be removed from the title bar. This behavior has been changed, and you'll now have to set the Minimize and Maximize properties to False yourself (as discussed in a later section) if you want them hidden.

5

Stop the project (you'll have to do this by clicking the Stop Debugging button on the toolbar because there's no way to close your form) and change the FormBorderStyle to FixedDialog. Press F5 to run the project again, and move the mouse pointer over a border of the form; the mouse pointer won't change, and you won't be able to stretch the borders of the form. Stop the project again and set the form's FormBorderStyle property to FixedToolWindow. This setting causes the title bar of the form to appear smaller than normal and the text to display in a smaller font (see Figure 5.8). In addition, the only thing displayed on the title bar besides the text is a Close button. Visual Basic .NET's various design windows, such as the Properties window and the toolbox, are good examples of tool windows.

In previous versions of Visual Basic, forms with their BorderStyle set to a tool window style never appeared in the taskbar, regardless of the form's ShowInTaskbar property. This behavior has been changed: The ShowInTaskbar property now determines whether the form appears in the taskbar, regardless of the form's BorderStyle property.

FIGURE 5.8
A tool window is a special window whose title bar takes up the minimum space possible.

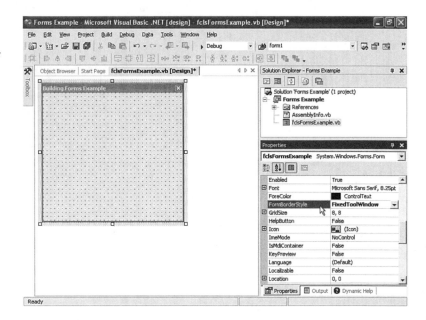

The FormBorderStyle is a good example of how changing a single property can greatly affect the look and behavior of an object. Set the FormBorderStyle of the form back to Sizeable—the default setting for new forms.

Adding Minimize, Maximize, and Control Box Buttons to a Form

Minimize and Maximize buttons make it easy for a user to quickly hide a form or make it fill the entire display. Adding a Minimize or Maximize button to your forms is as easy as setting a property (or two). To add a Minimize button to a form's title bar, set the form's MinimizeBox property to True. To add a Maximize button to a form, set its MaximizeBox property to True. Conversely, set the appropriate property to False to hide a button.

> The form's ControlBox property must be set to True to display a Maximize
> and/or Minimize button on a form. When the ControlBox property of a form
> is set to True, a button with an X appears in the title bar at the right side,
> which the user can click to close the form. In addition, the form's icon is dis-
> played in the left side of the title bar, and clicking it opens the form's system
> menu.

Notice that the title bar of your form shows all three buttons to the far right. From left to
right, these are Minimize, Maximize, and Close. Run the project now and click the icon
in the far left of the title bar to open the control box's menu, as shown in Figure 5.9.
Close the form now by either selecting Close from the menu or clicking the Close button
on the far right of the title bar.

FIGURE 5.9

*Clicking the icon of a
form with a control
box displays a system
menu.*

Changing the MaximizeBox or MinimizeBox property of a form enables or disables the
corresponding item on the system menu in addition to the button on the toolbar. Save
your project now by clicking the Save All button on the toolbar.

Specifying the Initial Display Position of a Form

The location on the display (monitor) where a form first appears isn't random but is controlled by the form's StartPosition property. The StartPosition property can be set to one
of the values in Table 5.1.

5

TABLE 5.1   Values for the StartPosition Property

Value	Description
Manual	The Location property of the form determines where the form first appears.
CenterScreen	The form appears centered in the display.
WindowsDefaultLocation	The form appears in the Windows default location, which is toward the upper left of the display.
WindowsDefaultBounds	The form appears in the Windows default location with its bounds (size) set to the Windows default bounds.
CenterParent	The form is centered within the bounds of its parent form.

It's generally best to set the StartPosition property of all your forms to CenterParent unless you have a specific reason to do otherwise. For the very first form that appears in your project, you might consider using the WindowsDefaultLocation (but I generally prefer CenterScreen).

Displaying a Form in a Normal, Maximized, or Minimized State

Using the Size and Location properties of a form in conjunction with the StartPosition property enables you to display forms at any location and at any size. You can also force a form to appear minimized or maximized. Whether a form is maximized, minimized, or shown normally is known as the form's *state*, and it's determined by the WindowState property.

Look at your form's WindowState property now. New forms have their WindowState property set to Normal by default. When you run the project, as you have several times, the form displays in the same size as it appears in the form designer, at the location specified by the form's Location property. Now change the WindowState property to Minimized. Nothing happens in the Form Design view, but run your project by pressing F5 and you'll see that the form is immediately minimized to the taskbar.

Stop the project and change the WindowState property to Maximized. Again, nothing happens in the form design view. Press F5 to run the project and notice how the form immediately maximizes to fill the entire screen.

When a form is maximized, it fills the entire screen regardless of the current screen resolution being used in Windows.

Stop the project and change the WindowState property back to Normal. You'll rarely set a form's WindowState property to Minimize at design time, but you'll probably encounter situations in which you need to change (or determine) the WindowState at run-time. As with most properties, you can accomplish this using code. For example, the following statement would minimize a form called frmMain:

```
frmMain.WindowState = FormWindowState.Minimized
```

You don't have to remember the names of the values when entering code; you'll get an IntelliSense drop-down list when you type the equal sign.

Changing the Mouse Pointer

You've no doubt used a program that altered the cursor when the pointer was moved over an object. This behavior is prevalent in Web browsers, where the cursor is changed to the shape of a pointing hand when moved over a hyperlink. Using the Cursor property, you can specify the image of the pointer displayed when the pointer is over a form or control.

Click the Cursor property of the form in the Properties window now and a drop-down arrow appears. Click the arrow to view a list of cursors (see Figure 5.10). Selecting a cursor from the list causes the pointer to change to that cursor when positioned over the form. Change the Cursor property of the form to AppStarting and press F5 to run the project. Move the pointer over the form and notice that the cursor changes to the AppStarting cursor while over the form and reverts to the default cursor when moved off the form. Stop the project now and click Save All on the toolbar to save your work.

5

 If it's absolutely necessary to change the default cursor for a form or control, choose a cursor that's consistent in purpose with well-known commercial applications.

FIGURE 5.10

Use the Cursor property to designate the image of the pointer when it's moved over the object.

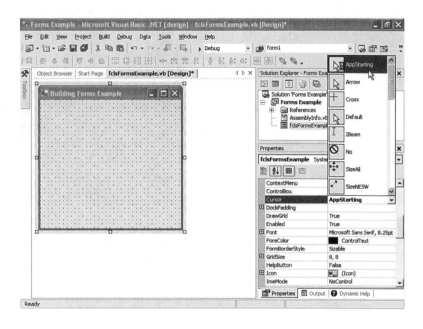

Showing and Hiding Forms

Part III, "Making Things Happen—Programming," is devoted to programming in Visual Basic .NET, and I've avoided going into much programming detail in this hour so that you can focus on the concepts at hand. However, knowing how to create forms does nothing for you if you don't have a way to show and hide them. Visual Basic .NET can display a single form automatically only when a program starts. To display other forms, you have to write code.

Showing Forms

In Visual Basic .NET, everything is an object, and objects are based on classes (see Hour 16, "Designing Objects Using Classes," for information about creating classes). Because the definition of a form is a class, you have to create a new Form object using the class as a template. In Hour 3, "Understanding Objects and Collections," I discussed objects and object variables, and these principles apply to creating forms.

As discussed in Hour 3, the process of creating an object from a class (template) is called *instantiation*. The syntax you'll use most often to instantiate a form is the following:

```
Dim {objectvariable} As New {formclassname()}
```

The three parts of this declaration are

- **The Dim statement** A reserved word that tells the compiler that you're creating a variable. (Refer to Hour 11, "Using Constants, Data Types, Variables, and Arrays," for a complete explanation of using variables.)

- **The name of the variable** This will be the name for the form that you will use in code.

- **The keyword New** Indicates that you want to instantiate a new object for the variable.

Lastly, you specify the name of the class to use to derive the object—your form class. If you have a form class named fclsLoginDialog, for example, you could create a new Form object using the following code:

```
Dim frmLoginDialog As New fclsLoginDialog()
```

Thereafter, for as long as the object variable remains in scope (scope is discussed in Hour 11), you can manipulate the Form object using the variable. For instance, to display the form, you call the Show method of the form or set the Visible property of the form to True using code such as this:

```
frmLoginDialog.Show
```

or

```
frmLoginDialog.Visible = True
```

The easiest way to get the hang of this is to actually do it. To begin, choose Add Windows Form from the Project menu to display the Add New Item dialog box. Change the name of the form to **fclsMyNewForm.vb** (as shown in Figure 5.11), and click Open to create the new form.

5

FIGURE 5.11

When you change the default name of a form, don't forget to leave the .vb extension.

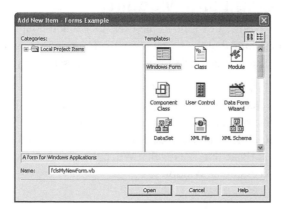

Your project now has two forms, as you can see by viewing the Solution Explorer window. The new form is displayed in the form designer, but right now you need to work with the main form so follow these steps:

1. At the top of the main design area is a set of tabs. Currently, the tab fclsMyNewForm.vb [Design] is selected. Click the tab titled fclsFormsExample.vb [Design] to show the designer for the first form.

2. Add a new button to your form by double-clicking the Button item on the toolbox (be careful not to add the button to the new form by mistake). Set the button's properties as follows:

Property	Value
Name	**btnShowForm**
Location	**112,112**
Text	**Show Form**

3. Double-click the button to access its Click event, and enter the following code:

```
Dim frmTest As New fclsMyNewForm()
frmtest.Show()
```

The first statement creates a new object variable and instantiates an instance of the fclsMyNewForm form. The second statement uses the object variable (now holding a reference to a Form object) to display the form. Press F5 to run the project and click the button. (If the button doesn't appear on the form, you might have accidentally added it to the wrong form). When you click the button, a new instance of the second form is created and displayed. Move this form and click the button again. Each time you click the button, a new form is created. Stop the project now and click Save All on the toolbar.

Understanding Form Modality

You can present two types of forms to the user: modal and nonmodal forms. The modality of a form is determined by how you *show* the form rather than by how you *create* the form (both modal and nonmodal forms are created the same way).

NEW TERM   A *nonmodal window* is one that doesn't cause other windows to be disabled. The forms you created in this example are nonmodal, which is why you were able to continue clicking the button on the first form even though the second form was displayed. Another example of a nonmodal window is the Find and Replace window in Word (and in Visual Basic .NET, as well). When the Find and Replace window is visible, the user can still access other Windows.

When a form is displayed as a modal form, on the other hand, all other forms in the same application become disabled until the modal form is closed; the other forms won't accept any keyboard or mouse input. The user is forced to deal with only the modal form. When the modal form is closed, the user is free to work with other visible forms within the program. Modal forms are most often used to create dialog boxes in which the user works with a specific set of data and controls before moving on. For instance, the Print dialog box of Microsoft Word is a modal dialog box. When the Print dialog box is displayed, the user can't work with the document on the main Word window until the Print dialog box is closed. Most secondary windows in any given program are modal windows.

You can display one modal form from another modal form, but you cannot display a nonmodal form from a modal form.

To show a form as a modal form, you call the form's ShowDialog method rather than its Show method. Change the code in your button's Click event to read:

```
Dim frmTest As New fclsMyNewForm()

frmtest.ShowDialog()
```

When your code looks like this, press F5 to run the project. Click the button to create an instance of the second form. Then move the second form away from the first window and try to click the button again. You can't because you've created a modal form. Close the modal form now by clicking the Close button in the title bar. Now, the first form is enabled again and you can click the button once more. When you're done testing this, stop the running project.

You can test to see whether a form has been shown modally by testing the form's Modal property.

Unloading Forms

After a form has served its purpose, you'll want it to go away. However, *go away* can mean one of two things. First, you can make a form disappear without closing it or freeing its resources (this is called *hiding*). To do so, set its Visible property to False. This hides the visual part of the form, but the form still resides in memory and can still be manipulated by code. In addition, all the variables and controls of the form retain their values when a form is hidden, so if the form is displayed again, the form looks the same as it did when its Visible property was set to False.

Second, you can completely close a form and release the resources it consumes. You should close a form when it's no longer needed so that Windows can reclaim all resources used by the form. To do so, you invoke the Close method of the form like this:

```
Me.Close()
```

In Hour 3, you learned how Me is used to reference the current Form object. Because Me represents the current Form object, you can manipulate properties and call methods of the current form using Me. (Me.Visible = False, and so forth).

The Close method tells Visual Basic .NET not to simply hide the form, but to destroy it completely. If variables in other forms are holding a reference to the form you close, their references will be set to Nothing and will no longer point to a valid Form object (refer to Hour 11 for information about the value Nothing).

Follow these steps to create the close button for your form:

1. Select the fclsMyNewForm.vb [Design] tab to display the form designer for the second form, add a new button to the form, and set the button's properties as follows:

Property	Value
Name	**btnCloseMe**
Location	**112,112**
Text	**Close Me**

2. Double-click the button to access its Click event and then enter the following statement:

    ```
    Me.Close()
    ```

3. Next, run the project by pressing F5. Click the Show Form button to display the second form, and then click the second form's button. The form will disappear. Again, the form isn't just hidden; the form instance is unloaded from memory and no longer exists.

You can create a new form instance by single-clicking the Show Form button on the first form. When you're finished, stop the running project and save your work.

Summary

In this hour, you learned the basics of creating forms. You learned how to add them to your project, how to set basic appearance properties, and how to show and hide them using Visual Basic .NET code. In the next hour, you'll learn more advanced functionality for working with forms. After you've mastered the material in this hour as well as in the next hour, you'll be ready to dig into Visual Basic's controls—that's where the fun of building an interface really begins!

Q&A

Q How many form properties should I define at design time as opposed to runtime?

A You should set all properties that you can at design time. First, it'll be easier to work with the form because you can see exactly what the user will see. Also, debugging is easier because there's less code.

Q Should I let the user minimize and maximize all forms?

A Probably not. First, there's no point in letting a form be maximized if you haven't anchored and aligned controls so that they adjust their appearance when the form is resized. In fact, if a form's contents don't change when a form is resized (including maximized), the form should not have a sizable border or a Maximize button.

Workshop

The Workshop is designed to help you anticipate possible questions, review what you've learned, and get you thinking about how to put your knowledge into practice. The answers to the quiz are in Appendix B, "Answers to the Quizzes."

5

Quiz

1. True or False: The text displayed in the form's title bar is determined by the value in the TitleBarText property.

2. The named color Control is what kind of color?

3. In what three places are a form's icon displayed?

4. A window with a smaller than normal title bar is called a what?

5. For a Minimize or Maximize button to be visible on a form, what other element must be visible?

6. What, in general, is the best value to use for the StartPosition property of a form?

7. To maximize, minimize, or restore a form in code, you set what property?

8. True or False: To display a form, you must create a variable in code.

9. What property do you set to make a hidden form appear?

Exercises

1. Create a semitransparent form with a picture in its background. Does the image become transparent? Add some controls to the form. Does the image appear behind or in front of the controls? (Hint: To create a transparent form, set the form's opacity to something other than 100%—try 50%.)

2. Create a Windows Application with three forms. Give the startup form two buttons. Make the other two forms tool windows, and make one button display the first tool window and the other button display the second tool window.

HOUR 6

Building Forms—
Advanced Techniques

A form is just a canvas, and although you can tailor a form by setting its properties, you'll need to add controls to it to make it functional. In the previous hour, you learned how to add forms to a project, how to set basic form properties, and how to show and hide forms. In this hour, you'll learn all about adding controls to a form, including arranging and aligning controls to create an attractive and functional interface. You'll also learn how to create advanced multiple document interfaces (MDIs) as used in applications such as Photoshop. After you complete the material in this hour, you'll be ready to learn the details about the various controls available in Visual Basic.

The highlights of this hour include

- Adding controls to a form
- Positioning, aligning, sizing, spacing, and anchoring controls
- Creating intelligent tab orders
- Adjusting the z-order of controls
- Creating transparent forms

- Creating forms that always float over other forms
- Creating Multiple Document Interfaces

Working with Controls

Controls are the objects that you place on a form for users to interact with. If you've followed the examples in the previous hours, you've already added controls to a form. However, you'll be adding a lot of controls to forms, and it's important for you to understand all aspects of the process. Following the drill-down in this hour, the next two hours will teach you the ins and outs of the very cool controls provided by Visual Basic.

Adding Controls to a Form

All the controls that you can add to a form can be found in the toolbox. The toolbox appears as a docked window on the left side of the design environment by default. This location is useful when you're only occasionally adding controls to forms. However, when doing serious form-design work, I find it best to dock the toolbox to the right edge of the design environment, where it doesn't overlap so much (if any) of the form I'm working with.

> Remember that before you can undock a toolbar to move it to a new location, you must make sure that it isn't set to Auto Hide.

The buttons on the toolbox are actually considered tabs because clicking one of them displays a specific page of controls. For most of your design, you'll use the controls on the Windows Forms tab. As your skills progress, however, you might find yourself using more complex and highly specialized controls found on the other tabs.

You can add a control to a form in three ways, and you're now going to use all three methods. Create a new Windows Application called **Adding Controls**. Change the name of the default form to **fclsAddingControls** and set its Text property to **Adding Controls**. Next, change the Startup object to point to this form using the Project Property Pages dialog box and follow these steps:

1. The easiest way to add a control to a form is to double-click the control in the toolbox. Try this now: Display the toolbox and double-click the TextBox tool. Visual Basic creates a new text box in the upper-left corner of the form. When you double-click a control in the toolbox (excluding controls that are invisible-at-runtime), Visual Basic creates the new control on top of the last control you just added, with the default size for the type of control you're adding. If there are no other controls

on the form, the new control is placed in the upper-left corner as you've seen here. You're free, of course, to move and size the text box as you please.

2. If you want a little more authority over where the new control is placed, you can drag a control to the form. Try this now: Display the toolbox and then click the Button control and drag it to the form. When the cursor is roughly where you want the button created, release the mouse button.

3. The last and most precise method of placing a control on a form is to draw the control on a form. Display the toolbox now and click the ListBox tool once to select it. Next, move the pointer to where you want the upper-left corner of the list box to appear and then click and hold the mouse button. Drag the pointer to where you want the bottom-right corner of the list box to be and release the button. The list box is created with its dimensions set to the rectangle you drew on the form. This is by far the most precise method of adding controls to a form.

> If you prefer to draw controls on your forms by clicking and dragging, I strongly suggest that you float the toolbox or dock it to the right or bottom edge of the design environment. The toolbox tends to interfere with drawing controls when it's docked to the left edge because it obscures a good bit of the underlying form.

It's important to note that the very first item on the Windows Forms tab, titled Pointer, isn't actually a control. When the pointer item is selected, the design environment is placed in Select mode rather than in a mode to create a new control. With the pointer chosen, you can select a control simply by clicking it, displaying all its properties in the Properties window. This is the default behavior of the development environment.

Manipulating Controls

Getting controls on a form is the easy part. Arranging them so that they create an intuitive and attractive interface is the challenge. Interface possibilities are nearly endless, so I can't tell you how to design any given interface. However, I can show you the techniques to move, size, and arrange controls so that they appear the way *you* want them to. By mastering these techniques, you'll be much more efficient at building interfaces, freeing your time for writing the code that makes things happen.

Using the Grid (Size and Snap)

When you first install Visual Basic, all forms appear with a grid of dots on them. When you draw or move controls on a form with a grid, the coordinates of the control automatically snap to the nearest grid coordinate. This offers some precision when adjusting the

6

size and location of controls. In practical use, I often find the grid to be only slightly helpful because the size or location I want often doesn't fit neatly with the grid locations. You can, however, control the granularity and even the visibility of the grid, and I suggest you do both.

You're now going to assign a higher level of granularity to the grid (the space between the grid points will be smaller). I find that this helps with design because edges aren't so easily snapped to unwanted places.

To adjust the granularity of the grid, you change the form's GridSize property (or the Width and Height subproperties of the GridSize property). Setting the Width or Height of the grid to a smaller number creates a more precise grid, which allows for finer control over sizing and placement, whereas using larger values creates a much coarser grid and offers less control. With a larger grid, you'll find that edges snap to grid points much easier and at larger increments, making it impossible to fine-tune the size or position of a control. Now change the GridSize property of your form to **4,4**. Notice that many more grid dots appear (see Figure 6.1).

FIGURE 6.1

Grids can be distracting.

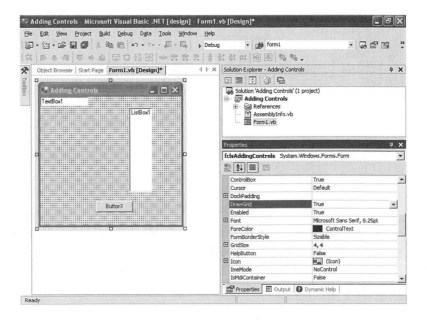

Try dragging the controls on your form or dragging their edges to size them. Notice that you have more control over the placement with the finer grid. Try changing the GridSize to a set of higher numbers, such as **25,25** and see what happens. When you're finished experimenting, change the GridSize values back to **4,4**.

An unfortunate side effect of a smaller grid is that the grid can become quite distracting. Again, you'll decide what you like best, but I generally turn the grids off on my forms. You do this by setting the DrawGrid property of the form to **False**. Try hiding the grid of your form now.

> This property determines *only* whether the grid is drawn, not whether it's active; whether a grid is active is determined by the form's SnapToGrid property.

Selecting a Group of Controls

As your skills increase, you'll find your forms becoming increasingly complex. Some forms might contain dozens, or even hundreds, of controls. Visual Basic has a set of features that makes it easy to align groups of controls.

Create a new Windows Application titled **Align Controls**. Change the name of the default form to **fclsAlignControls** and set its Text property to **Control Alignment Example**. Once again, use the Project Property Pages dialog box to designate this form as your Startup object.

You're now going to add three text boxes to the form by following these steps:

1. Double-click the TextBox tool in the toolbox to add a text box to the form. Set its properties as follows:

Property	Value
Name	**txt1**
Location	**20,20**
Multiline	**True**
Size	**100, 30**
Text	**text box 1**

> If you don't set the Multiline property of a text box to **True**, Visual Basic ignores the Height setting (the second value of the Size property) and instead, keeps the height at the standard height for a single-line text box.

2. Use the same technique (double-click the TextBox item in the toolbox) to add two more text boxes to the form. Set their properties as follows:

6

Text Box 2:

Property	Value
Name	**txt2**
Location	**90,80**
Multiline	**True**
Size	**50,50**
Text	**text box 2**

Text Box 3:

Property	Value
Name	**txt3**
Location	**140,200**
Multiline	**True**
Size	**100,60**
Text	**text box 3**

Your form should now look like the one in Figure 6.2. Save the project by clicking the Save All button on the toolbar.

FIGURE 6.2

It's easy to align and size controls as a group.

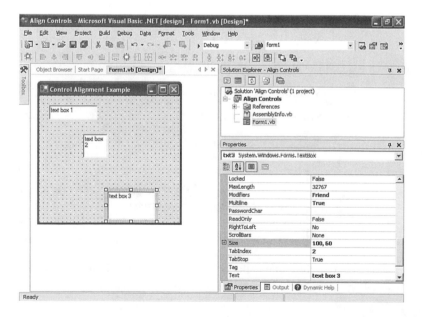

By default, clicking a control on a form selects it while simultaneously deselecting any controls that were previously selected. To perform actions on more than one control, you need to select a group of controls. You can do this in one of two ways, the first of which is to *lasso* the controls. To lasso a group of controls, you first click and drag the mouse pointer anywhere on the form. As you drag the mouse, a rectangle is drawn on the form. When you release the mouse button, all controls intersected by the rectangle become selected. Note that you don't have to completely surround a control with the lasso (also called a *marquee*), you only have to intersect part of the control to select it. Try this now: Click somewhere in the upper-left corner of the form and drag the pointer toward the bottom right of the form without releasing the button (see Figure 6.3). When the rectangle has surrounded or intersected all the controls, release the button and the controls will be selected (see Figure 6.4) .

FIGURE 6.3

Click and drag to create a selection rectangle.

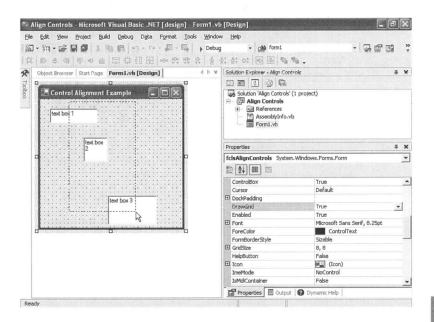

When a control is selected, it has a hatched border and a number of sizing handles (the squares in the hatched border at the corners and midpoints of the control). Pay careful attention to the sizing handles. The control with the black-centered sizing handle is the active control in the selected group. When you use Visual Basic's tools to work on a group of selected controls (such as the alignment and formatting tools), the values of the active control are used. For example, if you were to align the left side of the selected controls shown in Figure 6.4, each of the controls would have its Left property value set to that of the active control. When you use the lasso technique to select a group of controls, you really don't have much influence over which control Visual Basic makes the active control. In this example, you want to align all controls to the control in the middle,

6

so you'll have to use a different technique to select the controls. Deselect all the controls now by clicking anywhere on the form (other than on a control) .

FIGURE 6.4

All selected controls appear with a hatched border and sizing handles.

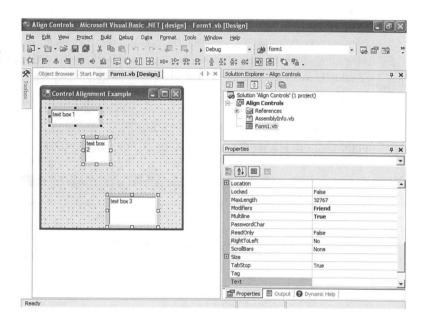

 Not all sizing handles are movable at all times. Before you set the Multiline property of a text box to **True**, for example, Visual Basic .NET won't allow you to change the height of the text box, so only the sizing handles at the left and right edges are movable and therefore colored white.

The second technique for selecting multiple controls is to use the Shift or Ctrl key (either can be used to the same effect); this method is much like selecting multiple files in Explorer. Click the bottom control (txt3) now to select it. (When only one control is selected, it's considered the active control.) Now hold down the Shift key and click the center control (txt2); txt2 and txt3 are now selected. The text box txt2 is now the active control (When more than one control is selected, the active control has its sizing handles set to black so that you can identify it.). When you add a control to a group of selected controls, the newly selected control is always made the active control. Finally, with the Shift key still pressed, click txt1 to add it to the group of selected controls. All the controls should now be selected and txt1 should be the active control.

Clicking a selected control while holding down the Shift key deselects the control.

You can combine the two selection techniques when needed. For instance, you could first lasso all controls to select them. If the active control isn't the one you want it to be, you could hold the Shift key down and click the control you want made active, thereby deselecting it. Clicking the control a second time while still holding down the Shift key would again select the control. Because the control would then be the last control added to the selected group, it would be made active. You're going to do this now. With all three controls selected, hold Ctrl while clicking the second (middle) text box. It will be deselected. Keep holding Ctrl and click the text box once more. Now it will be selected with the rest of the controls, and it will be the active control because it was the last control added to the group.

If you must click the same control twice, such as to deselect and then reselect it, do so s-l-o-w-l-y. If you click too fast, Visual Basic interprets your actions as a double-click and it creates a new event handler for the control.

Aligning Controls

Now that you've selected all three controls, open Visual Basic's Format menu (see Figure 6.5). The Format menu has a number of submenus containing functions to align, size, and format groups of controls. Open the Align submenu now to see the available options (see Figure 6.6).

The top three items on the Align menu are used to align the selected controls horizontally, and the middle three items align the selected controls vertically. The last item, To Grid, snaps the corners of all the selected controls to the nearest grid points. Choose Align Lefts now, and Visual Basic aligns the left edges of the selected controls. Notice how the left edge of the active control is used as the baseline for the alignment (see Figure 6.7) .

6

FIGURE 6.5

Use the Format menu to quickly whip an interface into shape.

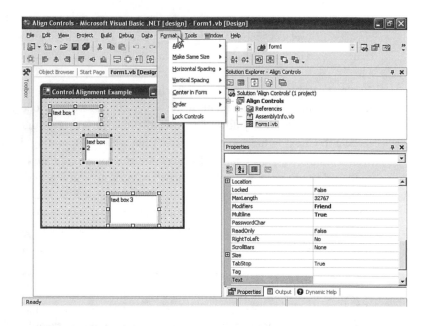

FIGURE 6.6

The Align menu makes it easy to align an edge of a group of controls.

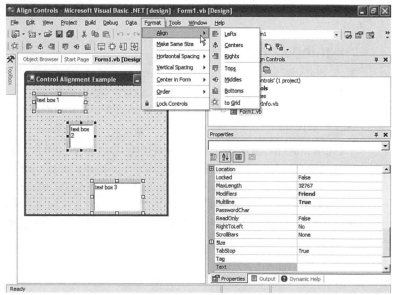

Making Controls the Same Size

In addition to aligning controls, you can also make all selected controls the same size—height, width, or both. To do this, use the Make Same Size submenu on the Format menu (see Figure 6.8). Make all your controls the same size now by choosing Both from the

Make Same Size menu. As with the Align function, the values of the active control are used as the baseline values.

FIGURE **6.7**

The property values of the active control are always used as the baseline values.

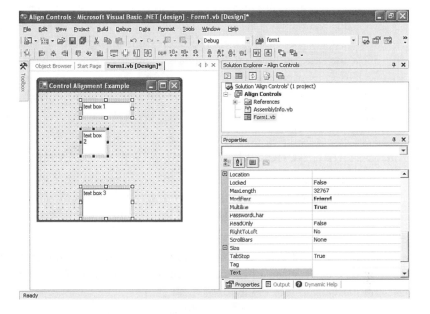

FIGURE **6.8**

Use this menu to quickly make a group of controls the same size.

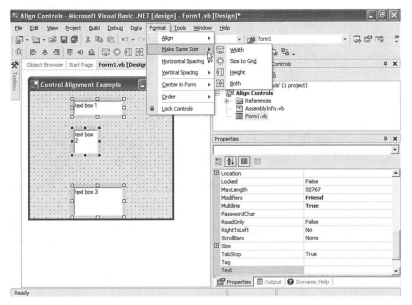

6

Evenly Spacing a Group of Controls

As many a salesman has said, "…and that's not all!" You can also make the spacing between controls uniform using the Format menu. Try this now: Open the Vertical Spacing submenu of the Format menu and then choose Make Equal. All the controls are now evenly spaced. Next, choose Decrease from the Vertical Spacing menu and notice how the spacing between the controls decreases slightly. You can also increase the vertical spacing or completely remove vertical space from between controls using this menu. To perform the same functions on the horizontal spacing between controls, use the Horizontal Spacing submenu of the Format menu. Save your project now by clicking the Save All button on the toolbar.

Setting Property Values for a Group of Controls

The following is a technique that many experienced Visual Basic developers seem to overlook: You can change a property value in the Properties window when multiple controls are selected. This causes the corresponding property to change for all selected controls.

Make sure that all three controls are still selected and then display the Properties window. When a group of controls is selected, the Properties window appears with some modifications (see Figure 6.9):

- No Name property is shown. This occurs because you're not allowed to have two controls with the same name, so Visual Basic won't even let you try.
- Only properties shared by all controls are displayed. If you'd selected a label control and a text box, only the properties shared by both control types would appear.
- For properties where the values of the selected controls differ (such as the Location property in this example), the value is left empty in the Properties window.

Entering a value in a property changes the corresponding property for *all* selected controls. To see how this works, change the BackColor property to a shade of yellow, and you'll see that all controls have their BackColor set to yellow.

Anchoring and Autosizing Controls

Some of my favorite additions to the new forms engine in Visual Basic .NET are the capability to anchor controls to one or more edges of a form and that controls can now size themselves appropriately when the user sizes the form. In the past, you had to use a (usually cumbersome) third-party component or resort to writing code in the form Resize event to get this behavior, but it's an intrinsic capability of Visual Basic .NET's form engine.

FIGURE 6.9

You can view the property values of many controls at once, with some caveats.

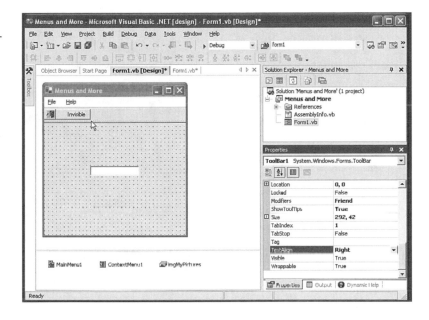

The default behavior is that controls are docked to the top and left edges of their containers. What if you want a control to always appear in the lower-left corner of a form? This is precisely what the Anchor property is designed to handle.

The easiest way to understand how anchoring works is to do it, so follow theses steps:

1. Create a new Windows Application called **Anchoring Example**.
2. Change the name of the default form to **fclsAnchoringExample** and set the form's Text property to **Anchoring Example**.
3. Make the current form the Startup object using the Project Property Pages.
4. Add a new button to the form and name it **btnAnchor**.
5. Run the project by pressing F5.
6. Click and drag the border of the form to change its size.

Notice that no matter what size you change the form to, the button stays in the upper-left corner of the form (see Figure 6.10) .

Stop the running project now by choosing Stop Debugging from the Debug menu. Click the button on the form to select it, click the Anchor property in the Properties window, and then click the drop-down arrow that appears. You'll see a drop-down box that's unique to the Anchor property (see Figure 6.11).

6

FIGURE **6.10**
By default, controls are anchored to the top-left corner of the form.

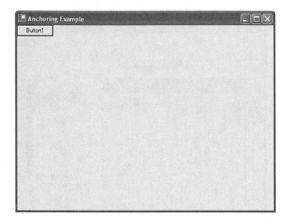

FIGURE **6.11**
You use this unique drop-down box to set the Anchor property of a control.

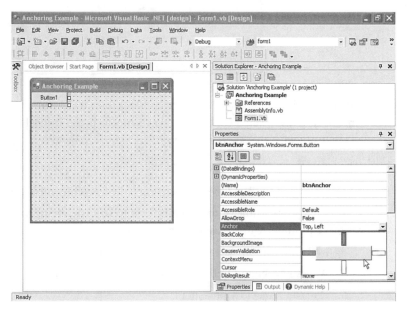

The gray square in the center of the drop-down box represents the control whose property you're setting. The thin rectangles on the top, bottom, left, and right represent the possible edges to which you can dock the control; if a rectangle is filled in, the edge of the control facing that rectangle is docked to that edge of the form.

1. Click the rectangle above the control so that it's no longer filled in, and then click the rectangle to the right of the control so that it is filled in (see Figure 6.12).

2. Click any other property to close the drop-down box. The Anchor property should now read Left, Right.

3. Press F5 to run the project, and then drag an edge of the form to make it larger.

FIGURE 6.12

This setting will anchor the control to the left and right edges.

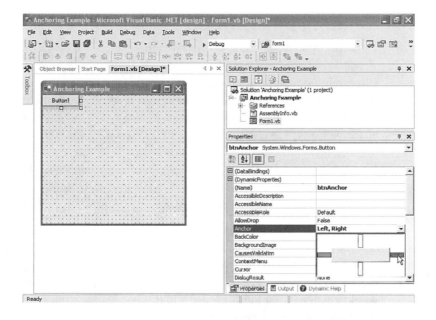

Pretty odd, huh? What Visual Basic has done is anchored the left edge of the button to the left edge of the form and anchored the right edge of the button to the right edge of the form (see Figure 6.13). Really, anchoring means keeping an edge of the control a constant, relative distance from an edge of the form, and it's an unbelievably powerful tool for building interfaces. Now you can make forms that users can resize, but you have to write little or no code to make the interface adjust accordingly. One caveat: Depending on its Anchor setting, a control might disappear if the form is shrunk quite small.

FIGURE 6.13

Anchoring is a powerful feature for creating adaptable forms.

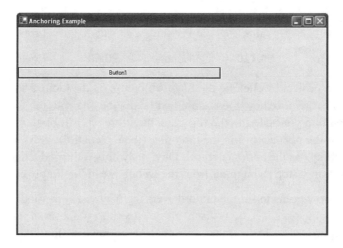

6

Creating a Tab Order

Tab order is something that is often (emphasis on *often*) overlooked by even seasoned Visual Basic programmers. You're probably familiar with tab order as a user, although you might not realize it. When you press Tab while on a form, the focus moves from the current control to the next control in the tab order. This enables easy keyboard navigation on forms. The tab order for controls on a form is determined by the TabIndex properties of the controls. The control with the TabIndex value of 0 is the first control that receives the focus when the form is shown. When you press Tab, the control with the TabIndex of 1 receives the focus. When you add a control to a form, Visual Basic assigns the next available TabIndex value. Each control has a unique TabIndex value, and TabIndex values are always used in ascending order.

If the tab order isn't set correctly for a form, pressing Tab causes the focus to jump from control to control in no apparent order. This really isn't a way to impress users. In the past, the only way to change the tab order for controls on a form was to manually change the TabIndex values. For instance, to make a control the first control in the tab order, you would change its TabIndex property to 0; Visual Basic would then bump the values of all other controls accordingly. This was often a painful process—believe me.

The forms engine in Visual Basic .NET has a far superior way to set the tab order for controls on a form. Create a new Windows Application named **Tab Order**, change the name of the default form to **fclsTabOrder**, and set the Text property of the form to **Tab Order Example**. Next, make this form the Startup object using the Project Property Pages dialog box.

Add three text box controls to the form now and set their properties as follows:

Text Box 1		Text Box 2		Text Box 3	
Property	Value	Property	Value	Property	Value
Location	**90,120**	Location	**90,50**	Location	**90,190**

Save the project by clicking the Save All button on the toolbar and then press F5 to run the project. Notice how the middle text box is the one with the focus. This is because it's the first one you added to the form and therefore has a TabIndex value of 0. Press Tab to move to the next control in the tab order (the top control); press Tab once more and the focus jumps to the bottom control. Obviously, this isn't productive. Stop the project now by choosing Stop Debugging from the Debug menu (or simply close the form).

You're now going to set the tab order via the new visual method. Choose Tab Order from the View menu; notice how Visual Basic superimposes a set of numbers over the controls (see Figure 6.14). The number on a control indicates its TabIndex property value. Now it's very easy to see that the tab order is incorrect. Click the top control. Notice how the number over the control changes to 0. Click the middle control and you'll see its number change to 1. As you click controls, Visual Basic assigns the next highest number to the clicked control. Choose Tab Order from the View menu again to take the form out of Tab Order mode. Run the project again and you'll see that the top control is the first to get the focus, and pressing Tab now moves the focus logically.

FIGURE 6.14

The numbers over each control indicate the control's TabIndex.

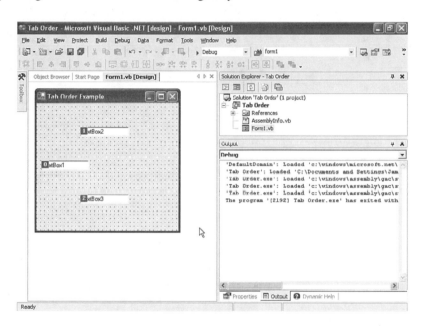

To programmatically move the focus via the tab order, use the SelectNextControl method of a control or a form.

To remove a control from the tab sequence, set its TabStop property to **False**. When a control's TabStop property is set to False, users can still select the control with the mouse but they can't enter the control using the Tab key. You should still set the TabIndex property to a logical value so that if the control receives the focus (such as by being clicked), pressing Tab will move the focus to the next logical control.

Layering Controls (Z-Order)

Tab order and visual alignment are key elements for effectively placing controls on forms. However, these two elements address control placement in only two dimensions—the *x,y* axis. At times, you might need to have controls overlap, although it's rare that

6

you'll need to do so. Whenever two controls overlap, whichever control is added to the form most recently appears on top of the other (see Figure 6.15). You can control the ordering of controls using the Order submenu of the Format menu (see Figure 6.16).

FIGURE 6.15
Controls can overlap.

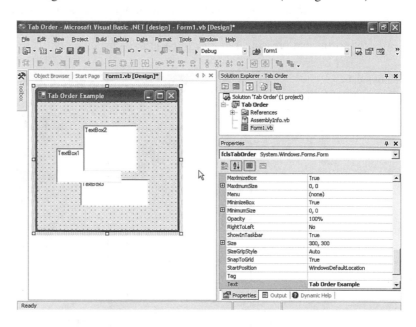

FIGURE 6.16
The Order menu is used to adjust the layering order of overlapping controls.

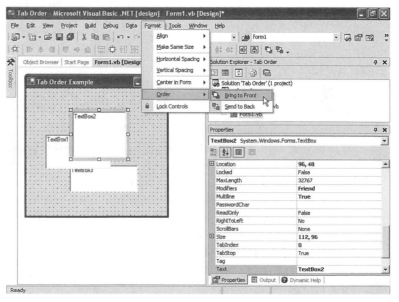

To send a control backward in the layering order, click it once to select it and then choose Send to Back from the Order menu (you can also right-click the control to access the layering commands as well). To bring the control forward in the layering order, select the control and choose Bring to Front from the Order menu.

> You can accomplish the same thing in Visual Basic code by invoking the BringToFront or SendToBack methods of a control.

Creating TopMost Windows

As you're probably aware, when you click a window it usually comes to the foreground and all other windows are shown behind it. At times, you might want a window to stay on top of other windows, regardless of whether it's the current window (that is, it has the focus). An example of this is the Find window in Visual Basic and other applications such as Word. Regardless of which window has the focus, the Find form always appears floating over all other windows. Such a window is created by setting the form's TopMost property to **True**. Not exactly rocket science. However, that's the point: A simple property change or method call is often all it takes to accomplish what might otherwise seem to be a difficult task.

Creating Transparent Forms

A new property of forms that I think is very cool—yet I still can't come up with a reason to use it in a production application—is the Opacity property. This property controls the opaqueness of the form as well as all controls on the form. The default Opacity value of 100% means that the form and its controls are completely opaque (solid), whereas a value of 0% creates a completely transparent form (no real point in that). A value of 50% creates a form that's between solid and invisible (see Figure 6.17). I suppose that you could write a loop that takes the Opaque property from 100% to 0% to fade out the form. Other than that, I don't know where to take advantage of this technique. *But ain't it cool?*

6

FIGURE 6.17

Ghost forms!

Creating Scrollable Forms

A *scrollable form* is one that can display scrollbars when its contents are larger than the physical size of the form. Earlier versions of the Visual Basic form engine lacked the capability to create scrollable forms. It seems odd that this has never been possible before, and I'm personally quite happy to see this feature added. Not only is this a cool yet necessary feature, it's also trivial to implement in your own applications.

The scrolling behavior of a form is determined by the following three properties:

Property	Description
AutoScroll	This property determines whether scrollbars will ever appear on a form.
AutoScrollMinSize	The minimum size of the scroll region (area). If the size of the form is adjusted so that the client area of the form (the area of the form not counting borders and title bar) is smaller than the AutoScrollMinSize, scrollbars will appear.
AutoScrollMargin	This property determines the margin given around controls during scrolling. This essentially determines how far past the edge of the outermost controls you can scroll.

Again, it's easiest to understand this concept by doing it. Create a new Windows Application named **AutoScroll Example**, rename the default form to **fclsAutoScroll**, and set the text of the form to **AutoScroll Example**. Again designate the current form as the Startup object using the Project Property Pages dialog box (tired of doing this yet?).

Add a new Button control to the form by double-clicking the Button tool on the toolbox. Set the button's properties as follows:

Property	Value
Name	**btnTest**
Text	**Test**
Location	**110,120**

Save the project and press F5 to run it. Drag the borders of the control to make it larger and smaller. Notice that no matter how small you make the form, no scrollbars appear. This makes it possible to have controls on the form that are only partially visible or that can't be seen at all (see Figure 6.18).

FIGURE 6.18
Without scrollbars, it's possible to have controls that can't be seen.

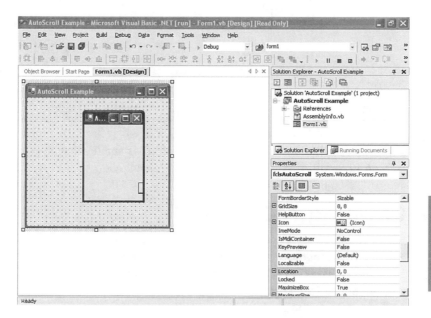

Stop the project now by choosing Stop Debugging from the Debug menu or by closing the form. Change the AutoScroll property of the form to **True**. At this point you still won't get scrollbars because you need to adjust at least one of the other scroll properties. Change the AutoScrollMargin property to **50,50** and run the project once more. Make the form smaller by dragging a border or a corner, and you'll see scrollbars appear (see Figure 6.19). The AutoScrollMargin property creates a virtual margin (in pixels) around all the outermost controls on the form. If the form is sized to within the margin area of one of these controls, scrollbars automatically appear (*voila!*) .

FIGURE 6.19

Scrollbars enable the user to view all parts of the form without changing the form's size.

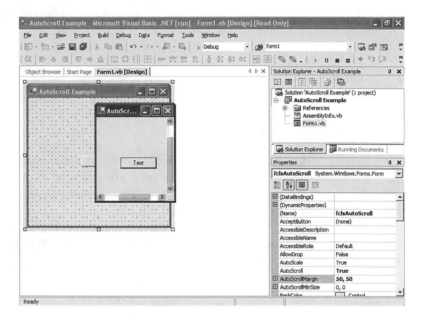

The final property that affects scrolling is the AutoScrollMinSize. Use the AutoScrollMinSize property to create a fixed-size scrolling region. If the form is ever sized such that the visible area of the form is smaller than the scrolling region defined by AutoScrollMinSize, scrollbars appear (again, *voila!*) .

Creating MDI Forms

All the projects you've created so far have been single document interface (SDI) projects. In SDI programs, every form in the application is a peer of all other forms; no intrinsic hierarchy exists between forms. Visual Basic also lets you create multiple document interface (MDI) programs. An MDI program contains one parent window (also called a *container*) and one or more child windows. A classic example of an MDI program is Adobe Photoshop. When you run Photoshop, a single parent window appears. Within this parent window, you can open any number of documents, which appear in child windows. In an MDI program, all child windows share the same toolbar and menu bar, which appears on the parent window. One restriction of child windows is that they can exist only within the confines of the parent window. Figure 6.20 shows an example of Photoshop running with a number of child document windows open.

FIGURE 6.20

Le Collage! MDI applications consist of a single parent window and one or more child windows.

MDI applications can have any number of normal windows (dialog boxes, for example) in addition to child windows.

You're now going to create a simple MDI project. Create a new Windows Application named **MDI Example**. Change the name of the default form to **fclsMDIParent**, change its Text property to **MDI Parent,** and change its IsMdiContainer property to **True**. (If you don't set the IsMdiContainer property to True, this example won't work.) The first thing you'll notice is that Visual Basic changed the client area to a dark gray and gave it a sunken appearance. This is the standard appearance for MDI parent windows, and all visible child windows appear in this area.

Now is a good time to designate this form as the Startup object using the Project Property Pages dialog box. What's that? You're tired of doing this step already? I feel your pain. When I get *really* grumpy about it, I look in the mirror and say, "Suck it up, bucko," and then I also tell myself I really need to start exercising and dieting. Anyway, you can neglect this step and deal with the error that occurs when you try and run the project. In some ways this is easier...

Create a new form by choosing Add Windows Form from the Project menu. Name the form **fclsChild1.vb** and change its Text property to **Child 1**. Add a third form to the project in the same way. Name it **fclsChild2.vb** and set its Text property to **Child 2**.

6

> In previous versions of Visual Basic, you had to set a property of a form to make it an MDI child form. In addition, the property could be set only at design time, so a form was either a child window or a normal window—you couldn't decide at runtime how to show the form, but you can now.

Make sure that the fclsMDIParent parent form is visible in the form designer. If it's not, you can display it by double-clicking it in the Solution Explorer (Form1.vb). Next, double-click the form to access its default event—the Load event. Enter the following code:

```
Dim objChild As New fclsChild1
objChild.MdiParent = Me
objChild.Show()
```

By now, you should know what this code does. The first statement creates a new object variable of type fclsChild1 and initializes it to hold a new instance of a form. The last statement simply shows the form. What we're interested in here is the middle statement. It sets the MdiParent property of the form to the current form (Me always references the current object), which is an MDI parent form because its IsMdiContainer property is set to True. When the new form is displayed, it's shown as an MDI child.

Save your work and then press F5 to run the project. Notice how the child form appears on the client area of the parent form. If you size the parent form so that one or more child windows can't fully be displayed, scrollbars appear (see Figure 6.21). If you were to remove the statement that set the MdiParent property, the form would simply appear floating over the parent form and wouldn't be bound by the confines of the parent (it wouldn't be a child window) .

FIGURE 6.21

Child forms appear only within the confines of the parent form.

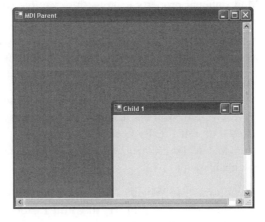

Stop the project by choosing Stop Debugging from the Debug menu and follow these steps:

1. Display the Solution Explorer, and double-click the fclsChild1 form to display it in the designer. Add a button to the form and set the button's properties as follows:

Property	Value
Name	**btnShowChild2**
Location	**105,100**
Size	**85,23**
Text	**Show Child 2**

2. Double-click the button to access its Click event, and then add the following code:

```
Dim objChild As New fclsChild2
objChild.MdiParent = Me.MDIParent
objChild.Show()
```

This code shows the second child form. Note that two differences exist between this code and the code you entered earlier. First, the objChild variable creates a new instance of the fclsChild2 form rather than the fclsChild1 form. The second difference is how the parent is set. Because the child form isn't a parent form, you can't set the second child's MdiParent property to Me because Me doesn't refer to the current form. However, you know that Me.MDIParent references the parent form because this is precisely the property you set to make the form a child in the first place. Therefore, you can simply pass the parent of the first child to the second child, and they'll both be children of the same form.

Any form can be a child form (except, of course, an MDI parent form). To make a form a child form, you set its MDIParent property to a form that's defined as an MDI container.

3. Press F5 to run the project now. You'll see the button on the child form, so go ahead and click it (if you don't see the button, you might have mistakenly added it to the second child form). When you click the button, the second child form appears. Notice how this is also bound by the constraints of the parent form (see Figure 6.22) .

6

The MDI parent form has an ActiveMdiChild property, which you can use to get a reference to the currently active child window.

FIGURE 6.22

Child forms are peers with one another.

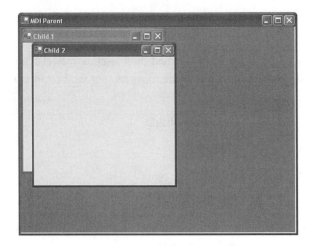

 To make the parent form larger when the project is first run, you set the Height and Width properties of the form either at design time or at runtime in the Load event of the form.

One thing to keep in mind about forms is that you can create as many instances of a form as you want. For instance, you could change the code in the button to create a new instance of fclsChild1. The form that would be created would be the same as the form that created it, complete with a button to create yet another instance. You probably won't apply this technique much now because you're just getting started with Visual Basic. You might find it quite useful in the future, however. For example, if you wanted to create a text editor, you might define the text entry portion as one form but create multiple instances of the form as new text files are opened.

Setting the Startup Object

The Startup object in a Windows Application project is, by default, the first form added to the project. This also happens to be the form that Visual Basic creates automatically when you create a new Windows Application project. Although the Startup object of a project was discussed briefly in a previous hour, and I keep beating it into you with every example, the topic needs a home—so here it is.

Every project must have a Startup object as the entry point to the program. You change the Startup object by right-clicking the project name in the Solution Explorer and choosing Properties. The Startup object property appears on the first property page that displays (see Figure 6.23). Again, when you change the name of a form, Visual Basic .NET doesn't update the Startup object reference—you have to do it yourself.

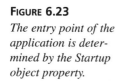

FIGURE 6.23
The entry point of the application is determined by the Startup object property.

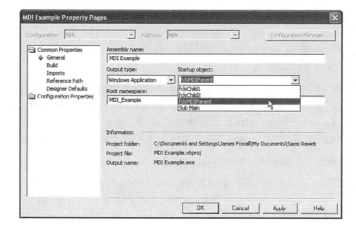

Now, if the Startup object property is set to show a child window, you might not get the behavior you expect when the project starts. The designated form would appear, but it wouldn't be a child because no code would execute to set the MdiParent property of the form to a valid MDI parent form.

If MDI forms still confuse you, don't worry. Most of the applications you'll write as a new Visual Basic programmer will be SDI programs. As you become more familiar with creating Visual Basic projects in general, start experimenting with MDI projects. Remember, you don't have to make a program an MDI program simply because you can; make an MDI program if the requirements of the project dictate that you do so.

Summary

Understanding forms is critical because forms are the dynamic canvases on which you build your user interface. If you don't know how to work with forms, your entire application will suffer. Many things about working with forms go beyond simply setting properties, especially as you begin to think about the end user. As your experience grows, you'll get into the groove of form design and things will become second nature to you.

In this hour, you learned how to do some interesting things, such as creating transparent forms, as well as some high-end techniques, such as building an MDI application. You also learned how to create scrolling forms (an interface element that shouldn't be overlooked), and you spent a lot of time on working with controls on forms, which is important because the primary function of a form is as a place to host controls. In the next two hours, you'll learn the details of many of Visual Basic's powerful controls that will become important weapons in your vast development arsenal.

6

Q&A

Q Do I need to worry about the anchoring and scrolling capabilities of every form I create?

A Absolutely not. The majority of forms in most applications are dialog boxes. A dialog box is a modal form used to gather data from the user. A dialog box is usually of a fixed size, which means that its border style is set to a style that can't be sized. With a fixed-size form, you don't need to worry about anchoring or scrolling.

Q How do I know whether a project is a candidate for an MDI interface?

A If the program will open many instances of the same type of form, it's a candidate for an MDI interface. For instance, if you're creating an image-editing program and the intent is to enable the user to open many images at once, MDI makes sense. Also, if you'll have many forms that will share a common toolbar and menu, you might want to consider MDI.

Workshop

The Workshop is designed to help you anticipate possible questions, review what you've learned, and get you thinking about how to put your knowledge into practice. The answers to the quiz are in Appendix B, "Answers to the Quizzes."

Quiz

1. True or False: The first control selected in a series is always made the active control.
2. How many methods are there to add a control to a form from the toolbox?
3. If you double-click a tool in the toolbox, where on the form is it placed?
4. Which property fixes an edge of a control to an edge of a form?
5. Which property do you change to hide the grid on a form?
6. Which menu contains the functions for spacing and aligning controls?
7. Which property do you set to make a form an MDI parent?

Exercises

1. Use your knowledge of the Anchor property and modify the Picture Viewer project you built in Hour 1, "Jumping In with Both Feet: A Visual Basic .NET Programming Tour," so that the form can be sized. The buttons should always stay the size that they are and in the relative location in which they're placed, but the picture box should change size to show as much of the picture as possible, given the size of the form.

2. Modify the MDI Example project in this hour so that the first child form shows another instance of itself, rather than showing an instance of the second child form.

HOUR 7

Working with the Traditional Controls

The previous two hours described how to work with forms in considerable detail. Forms are the foundation of a user interface, but are pretty much useless by themselves. To create a functional interface, you need to use *controls*. Controls are the various widgets and doodads on a form that a user interacts with. Dozens of different types of controls exist, from the simple Label control used to display static text to the rather complicated Tree View control used to present trees of data like that found in Explorer. In this hour, I'll introduce you to the most common (and simple) controls, which I call *traditional* controls. In the next hour, you'll learn about the more advanced controls that you can use to create professional-level interfaces.

The highlights of this hour include

- Displaying static text with the Label control
- Allowing users to enter text using a text box
- Creating password fields
- Working with buttons

- Using panels, group boxes, check boxes, and option buttons
- Displaying lists with list boxes and combo boxes

Displaying Static Text with the Label Control

Label controls are used to display static text to the user. By *static*, I mean that the user can't change the text directly (but you can change the text with code). Label controls are one of the most common controls used, and fortunately, they're also one of the easiest to use. Labels are most often used to provide descriptive text for other controls, such as text boxes. Labels are also great for providing status-type information to a user, as well as for providing general instructions on a form.

Begin by creating a new Windows Application named **Text Controls**. Change the name of the default form to **fclsTextControls**, and change its Text property to **Text Controls Example**. Next, change the Startup object of the project to fclsTextControls.

Add a new Label control to the form by double-clicking the Label item in the toolbox. The primary property of the Label control is the Text property, which determines the text displayed to the user. When a Label control is first added to a form, the Text property is set to the name of control—this isn't very useful. Set the properties of the new Label control as follows:

Property	Value
Name	**lblMyLabel**
Location	**5,6**
Size	**100,25**
Text	**Labels are for static text!**

Notice how the label's text appears on two lines (see Figure 7.1). This occurs because the text is forced to fit within the size of a new Label control. In most cases, it's best to place label text on a single line. To do that, you could increase the width either by using the Properties window or by dragging the edge of the control, but there's an easier way. Double-click the Label control's AutoSize property now and notice how the label resizes itself automatically to fit the text on a single line. Double-clicking a property that accepts a set number of values cycles the property to the next value. The AutoSize property of new Label controls is False by default, so double-clicking this property changed it to True.

FIGURE 7.1

Labels display text that can't be changed by the user.

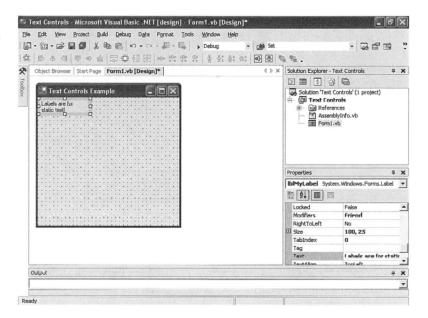

Allowing Users to Enter Text Using a Text Box

A Label control is usually the best control for displaying text that a user can't change. However, when you need to enable users to enter or edit text, the text box is the tool for the job. If you've ever typed information on a form, you've almost certainly used a text box. Add a new text box to your form now by double-clicking the TextBox item in the toolbox. Set the text box's properties as follows:

Property	Value
Name	**txtMyTextBox**
Location	**128,4**
Size	**136,20**

When you create a new text box, its Text property is set to its default name (see Figure 7.2). Unfortunately, the Text property isn't automatically changed when you change the name of the text box (which you should always do), so I recommend that you clear out the Text property of new text boxes. Delete the text in the Text property now and notice that the text box appears empty on the form.

7

FIGURE 7.2

A new text box has its
Text property set to its
default name.

Although you'll probably want to clear the Text property of most of your text boxes at design time, understanding certain aspects of the text box is easier when a text box contains text. Set the text box's Text property to **This is sample text**. Remember to press Enter or Tab to commit your property change.

Specifying Text Alignment

Both the Text Box and the Label controls have a TextAlign property (as do many other controls). The TextAlign property determines the alignment of the text within the control—very much like the justification setting in a word processor. You can select from Left, Center, and Right.

Label controls allow you to set the vertical alignment as well, using their TextAlign property. This works best when AutoSize is set to False.

The TextAlign property replaces the Alignment property of older versions of Visual Basic.

Change the TextAlign property of the text box to Right, and see how the text becomes right-aligned within the text box. Next, change TextAlign to Center to see what center alignment looks like. As you can see, this property is pretty straightforward. Change the TextAlign property back to Left before continuing.

Creating a Multiline Text Box

In the previous hour, I talked about the sizing handles of a selected control. I mentioned how handles that can be sized are filled with white, and handles that are locked appear with a gray center. Notice how only the left and right edges of the text box have white sizing handles. This means that you can adjust only the left and right edges of the control (you can alter only the width, not the height). This is because the text box is defined as a single-line text box, meaning that it will display only one line of text. What would be the point of a really tall text box that showed only a single line of text?

To allow a text box to display multiple lines of text, set its Multiline property to True. Set the Multiline property of your text box to True now, and notice how all the sizing handles become white.

Change the Text property of the text box to **This is sample text. A multiline text box will wrap its contents as necessary.** Press Enter or Tab to commit the property change. Notice how the text box displays only part of what you entered because the control simply isn't big enough to show all the text (see Figure 7.3). Change the Size property to **136,60**, and you'll then see the entire contents of the text box (see Figure 7.4) .

FIGURE 7.3

A text box might contain more text than it can display.

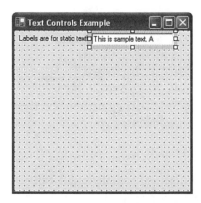

There will be times when you won't want a user to be able to interact with a control. For instance, you might implement a security model in an application, and if the user doesn't have the necessary privileges, you might not want the user to be able to alter data. The Enabled property, which almost every control has, determines whether the user can interact with the control. Change the Enabled property of the text box to False, and press F5 to run the project. Although no noticeable change occurs in the control in Design view, there's a big change to the control at runtime: The text appears in gray rather than black, and the text box won't accept the focus or allow you to change the text (see Figure 7.5).

7

FIGURE 7.4

*A multiline text box
can be sized as large
as necessary.*

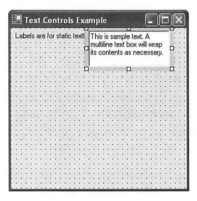

FIGURE 7.4

*A multiline text box
can be sized as large
as necessary.*

FIGURE 7.5

*You can't interact with
a text box whose
Enabled property is
set to False.*

Stop the project now by choosing Stop Debugging from the Debug menu, and then
change the control's Enabled property back to True.

Adding Scrollbars

Even though you can size a multiline text box, there still will be times when the contents
of the control are more than can be displayed. If you believe that this is a possibility for a
text box you're adding to a form, give the text box scrollbars by changing the ScrollBars
property from None to Vertical, Horizontal, or Both.

For a text box to display scrollbars, its Multiline property must be set to
True. Also, if you set the ScrollBars property to Both, the horizontal scrollbar
won't appear unless you also set the WordWrap property to False.

Change the ScrollBars property of your text box to Vertical and notice how scrollbars
appear in the text box (see Figure 7.6).

FIGURE 7.6

If a text box might contain lots of text, give it a scrollbar.

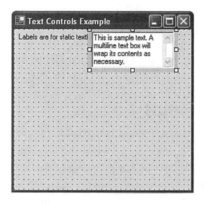

 If you set a text box's AcceptReturn property to True, the user can press Enter to create a new line in the text box. When the AcceptTabs property is set to True, the user can press Tab within the control to create columns (rather than moving the focus to the next control) .

Limiting the Number of Characters a User Can Enter

You can limit the number of characters a user can type into a text box by using the MaxLength property. All new text boxes are given the default value of 32767 for MaxLength, but you can change this as needed (up or down). Add a new text box to the form and set its properties as follows:

Property	Value
Name	**txtRestrict**
Location	**128,80**
MaxLength	**10**
Size	**136,20**
Text	*(make empty)*

Run the project by pressing F5 and enter the following text into the new text box: **So you run and you run.** Be sure to try and enter more than 10 characters of text—you can't (if you can, you're probably entering the text into the text box with scrollbars, rather than into the new text box). All that you're allowed to enter is **So you run** (10 characters). The text box allows only 10 characters, whether that's via entry using the keyboard or a Paste operation. The MaxLength property is most often used when the text box's content

7

is to be written to a database, in which field sizes are usually restricted. (Using a database is discussed in Hour 21, "Working with a Database.")

Stop the project by choosing Stop Debugging from the Debug menu and then click Save All on the toolbar.

Creating Password Fields

You've probably used a password field: a text box that displays an asterisk for each character entered. Any text box can be made a password field by assigning a character to its PasswordChar field. Select the PasswordChar property of the second text box now (txtRestrict) and enter an asterisk (*) for the property value. Run the project once more and enter text into the text box. Now an asterisk is displayed for each character you enter (see Figure 7.7). Although the user doesn't see the actual text contained in the text box, referencing the Text property in code always returns the true text.

FIGURE 7.7

A password field displays its password character for all entered text.

A text box displays password characters only if its Multiline property is set to False. As you can see, the value of the Multiline property affects a number of other properties.

Stop the project by choosing Stop Debugging from the Debug menu. Delete the asterisk from the PasswordChar field, and then save the project by clicking Save All on the toolbar.

Understanding the Text Box's Common Events

You'll rarely make use of the label's events, but you'll probably use text box events quite a bit. The text box supports many different events; Table 7.1 lists the events you're most likely to use regularly.

TABLE 7.1 Commonly Used Events of the Text Box Control

Event	Description
TextChanged	Occurs every time the user presses a key. Use this event to deal with specific key presses (such as capturing specific keys) or when you need to perform an action whenever the contents changes.
Click	Occurs when the user clicks the text box. Use this event to capture clicks when you don't care about the coordinates of the mouse pointer.
MouseDown	Occurs when the user first presses down a mouse button over the text box. This event is often used in conjunction with the MouseUp event.
MouseUp	Occurs when the user releases a mouse button over the text box. Use MouseDown and MouseUp when you need more functionality than provided by the Click event.
MouseMove	Occurs when the user moves the mouse over the text box. Use this event to perform actions based on the movement of the cursor.

Creating Buttons

Every dialog box that Windows displays has at least one button on it. Buttons enable a user to invoke a function with a click of the mouse.

Create a new project named **Button Example**, change the name of the default form to **fclsButtonExample**, and set the form's Text property to **Button Example**. Next, use the Project Property Pages dialog box to designate this form as the Startup object.

Add a new button to the form by double-clicking the Button item in the toolbox. Set the button's properties as follows:

Property	Value
Name	**btnClose**
Location	**104,90**
Text	**Close**

Add a new text box to the form and set its properties as follows:

Property	Value
Name	**txtTest**
Location	**92,40**
TabIndex	**0**
Text	*(make blank)*

7

You're probably starting to see a pattern here. Whenever you add a new control to a form, the first thing you should do is give the control a descriptive name. If the control has a Text property, you should change it to something meaningful as well. Your form should now look like Figure 7.8.

FIGURE 7.8
Users click buttons to make things happen.

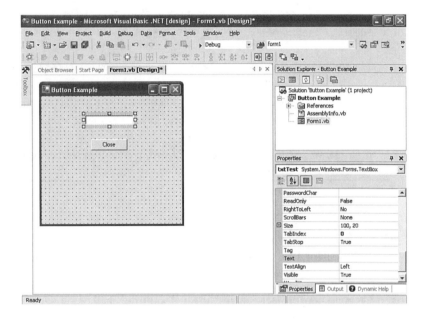

There's no point in having a button that doesn't do anything, so double-click the button now to access its Click event, and then add the following statement:

```
Me.Close()
```

Recall from Hour 5, "Building Forms—The Basics," that this statement closes the current form. Because you'll have only one form in the project, this has the effect of terminating the application. Press F5 to run the project. The cursor appears in the text box, which means the text box has the focus (it has the lowest TabIndex property). Press Enter and note that nothing happens (this will make sense shortly). Next, click the button and the form will close.

You can programmatically trigger a button's Click event, just as though a user clicked it, by calling the button's PerformClick method.

Accept and Cancel Buttons

When creating dialog boxes, it's common to assign one button as the default button (called the Accept button). If a form has an Accept button, that button's Click event is fired when the user presses Enter, regardless of which control has the focus. This is great for dialog boxes in which the user enters some text and presses Enter to commit the data and close the form.

To designate a button as an Accept button, show the AcceptButton property of the form in the Properties window. Notice that it's currently set to (none)—no button has been designated as the Accept button. Click in the property and a drop-down arrow appears. Click the arrow and choose the button (btnClose in this case) from the list.

FIGURE 7.9

You can designate only one button as a form's Accept button.

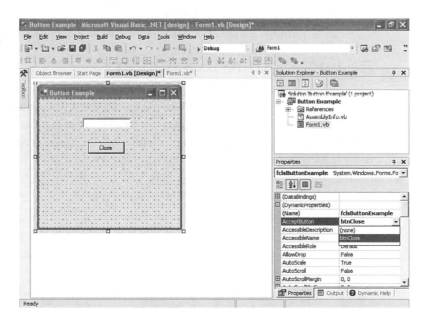

Press F5 to run the project. Again, the text box has the focus. Press Enter, and you'll find that the form closes. Again, pressing Enter on a form that has a designated Accept button causes that button's Click event to fire the same as if the user clicked it with the mouse, regardless of which control has the focus.

The Accept button is a useful concept, and you should take advantage of this functionality when possible. Keep in mind that when you do create an Accept button for a form, you should also create a Cancel button. A Cancel button is a button that fires its Click event when the user presses the Esc key, regardless of which control has the focus. Generally, you place code in a Cancel button to shut down the form without committing

7

any changes made by the user. To designate a button as a Cancel button, choose it as the CancelButton property of the form.

Use the following hints when deciding what buttons to assign as the Accept and Cancel buttons of a form:

- If a form has an OK or Close button, chances are good it should be assigned as the AcceptButton.
- If a form has both an OK and a Cancel button, assign the OK button as the AcceptButton and the Cancel button as the CancelButton (yeah, this is pretty obvious, but it's often overlooked).
- If a form has a single Close or OK button, assign it to both the AcceptButton and CancelButton properties of the form.
- If the form has a Cancel button, assign it to the CancelButton property of the form.

Adding a Picture to a Button

Although it's not standard practice—and you shouldn't overuse the technique because doing so causes clutter and can reduce the usefulness of your interface—it's possible to add a picture to a button. The two primary methods of doing this are to add the picture to the button at design time by loading a picture into the Image property of the control using the Properties window, or binding the button to an image list. I'll discuss loading a picture using the Properties window here, and cover the Image List control in the next hour. (Note: You can load an image at runtime using the technique discussed for the Picture Viewer program in Hour 1, "Jumping In with Both Feet: A Visual Basic .NET Programming Tour.")

To perform this operation, you'll need a small bitmap. I've provided one at www.samspublishing.com and at my Web site www.jamesfoxall.com (the file is called Close.bmp). There's also a set of discussion forums at my site, so feel free to drop by with your questions and comments.

Select the button and display its properties in the Properties window. Click the Image property to select it, and then click the button with the three dots that appears. The Open File dialog box appears, enabling you to find and select a bitmap. Use this dialog box to locate and select the Close.bmp bitmap or another small bitmap of your choosing. Click Open to load the image into the button's Image property, and the picture will appear on your button (see Figure 7.10).

FIGURE 7.10

The Image property is used to display a picture on a button.

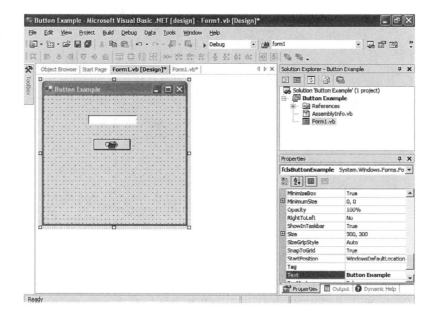

Many controls have an Image property, and for the most part, they all work the same way as the Image property of the Button control.

Notice that there's a problem with how the picture appears on the button: The image overlays the text. This problem is easily corrected.

Although a picture is displayed in the center of a button by default, you can specify the placement using the ImageAlign property. Click the ImageAlign property to display a drop-down arrow, and then click the arrow. The drop-down list contains a special interface for specifying the alignment of the picture (see Figure 7.11). Each rectangle in the drop-down list corresponds to an alignment (center-left, center-center, center-right, and so on). Click the center-left rectangle now and the image will be moved to the left of the text.

7

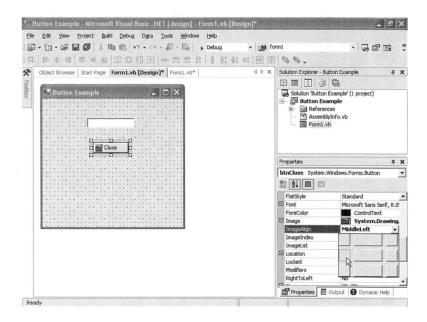

FIGURE 7.11

Click a rectangle to align the picture.

Creating Containers and Groups of Option Buttons

In this section, you'll learn how to create containers for groups of controls using panels and group boxes. You'll also learn how to use the Check Box and Option Button controls in conjunction with these container controls to present multiple choices to a user.

Begin by creating a new Windows Application titled **Options**. Change the name of the default form to **fclsOptions** and set the form's Text property to **Options**. Next, change the Startup object of the project to fclsOptions.

Using Panels and Group Boxes

NEW TERM   Controls can be placed on a form because the form is a *container* object—an object that can host controls. A form isn't the only type of container, however. Some controls act as containers as well, and a container can host one or more other containers. The Panel and Group Box controls are both container controls that serve a similar purpose, yet each is more suited to a particular application.

The Panel control, for the most part, is a slimmed-down version of the Group Box control, so I won't discuss it in depth. If you need a very basic container control without the additional features offered by the Group Box control (such as a border and caption), use the Panel control. The primary exception to this is the panel offers scrolling capabilities just like those found on forms, which group boxes do not support.

In past versions of Visual Basic, the Picture Box control was a container control. This isn't the case in Visual Basic .NET—use a panel instead.

The Group Box is a container control with properties that let you create a border (frame) and caption. Add a new group box to your form now by double-clicking the GroupBox item in the toolbox. When you create a new group box, it has a border by default, and its caption is set to the name of the control.

The Group Box control is like the Frame control of earlier versions of Visual Basic, except that you can't hide the border.

Set the properties of the group box as follows:

Property	Value
Name	**grpMyGroupBox**
Location	**48,16**
Size	**200,168**
Text	**This is a group box**

Your group box should now look like the one in Figure 7.12.

The Group Box is a fairly straightforward control. Other than defining a border and displaying a caption, the purpose of a group box is to provide a container for other controls. The next two sections, "Presenting Yes/No Options Using Check Boxes" and "Working with Radio Buttons," help demonstrate the benefits of using a group box as a container.

7

FIGURE 7.12

A group box acts like a form within a form.

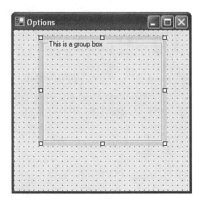

Presenting Yes/No Options Using Check Boxes

A check box is used to display True/False and Yes/No values on a form. You're now going to add a check box to your form—but not in the way you've been adding other controls. As you know by now, double-clicking the CheckBox item in the toolbox will place a new Check Box control on the form. This time, however, you're going to place the check box on the Group Box control.

You can perform any of the following actions to place a control on a group box:

- Add the control to the form, cut the control from the form, select the group box, and paste the control on the group box.
- Draw the control directly on the group box.
- Drop the control on the group box.

You're going to use the third method: dropping a new control directly on the group box. Follow these steps:

1. Click the CheckBox item in the toolbox and drag it to the group box.
2. Release the mouse when you're over the group box.

You should now have a check box on your group box like the one shown in Figure 7.13.

Move the check box around by clicking and dragging it. You'll notice that you can't move the check box outside the group box's boundaries (refer to Figure 7.13). This is because the check box is a child of the group box, not of the form. Set the properties of the check box as follows:

FIGURE 7.13

Container controls hold other controls.

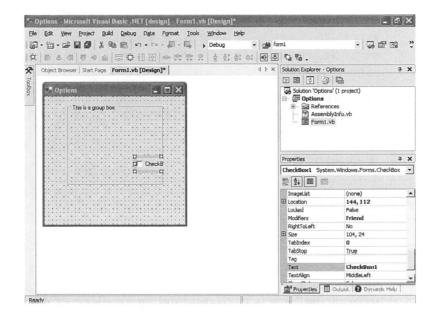

Property	Value
Name	**chkMyCheckBox**
Location	**16,24**
Size	**120,24**
Text	**This is a check box**

When the user clicks the check box, it changes its visible appearance from checked to unchecked. To see this behavior, press F5 to run the project and click the check box a few times.

When you're done experimenting, stop the running project. To determine the state of the check box in code, use its Checked property. You can also set this property at design time using the Properties window.

Working with Radio Buttons

Check boxes are excellent controls for displaying true/false and yes/no values. Check boxes work independently of one another, however; if you have five check boxes on a form, each one of them could be checked or unchecked. Radio buttons, on the other hand, are mutually exclusive to the container on which they're placed. This means that only one radio button per container can be selected at a time. Selecting one radio button

7

automatically deselects any other radio buttons on the same container. Radio buttons are used to offer a selection of items to a user when the user is allowed to select only one item. To better see how mutual exclusivity works, you're going to create a small group of radio buttons.

Open the toolbox and locate the RadioButton item. Next, drag it to the group box to create a new radio button on the Group Box control. Set the properties of the radio button as follows:

Property	Value
Name	**optOption1**
Location	**16,56**
Size	**104,24**
Text	**This is option 1**

You're going to copy this radio button and paste a copy of the control on the group box. Begin by right-clicking the radio button and choosing Copy from its context menu. Next, click the group box to select it, right-click the group box, and choose Paste from its context menu to create a new radio button. Set the properties of the radio button as follows:

Property	Value
Name	**optOption2**
Checked	**True**
Location	**16,80**
Text	**This is option 2**

Now that you have your two radio buttons (see Figure 7.14), run the project by pressing F5.

FIGURE 7.14
Radio buttons restrict a user to selecting a single item.

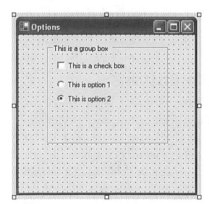

Click the first radio button to select it, and notice how the second radio button becomes deselected automatically (its Checked property is set to False). Two radio buttons are sufficient to demonstrate the mutual exclusivity, but be aware that you could add as many radio buttons to the group box as you want to and the behavior would be the same. The important thing to remember is that mutual exclusivity is shared only by radio buttons *placed on the same container*. To create radio buttons that behave independently of one another, you would need to create a second set on another container. You could easily create a new group box (or panel for that matter) and place the second set of radio buttons on the new container. The two sets of radio buttons would behave independently of one another, but mutual exclusivity would still exist among the buttons within each set.

Stop the running project and save your work.

Displaying a List with the List Box

A list box is used to present a list of items to a user. You can add items to and remove items from the list at any time with very little Visual Basic .NET code. In addition, you can set up a list box so that a user can select only a single item or multiple items. When a list box contains more items than it can show because of the size of the control, scrollbars are automatically displayed.

The cousin of the list box is the combo box, which looks like a text box with a down-arrow button at its right side. Clicking a combo box's button causes the control to display a drop-down list box. Working with the list of a combo box is pretty much identical to working with a list box, so I'll discuss the details of list manipulation in this section, and then discuss the features specific to the combo box in the next section.

Create a new project titled **Lists**. Change the name of the default form to **fclsLists** and set its Text property to **Lists Example**. Next, change the Startup object of the project to fclsLists. Add a new List Box control to the form by double-clicking the ListBox item in the toolbox and then set the properties of the list box as follows:

Property	Value
Name	**lstPinkFloydAlbums**
Location	**72,32**
Size	**160,121**

7

Every item contained in a list box is a member of the list box's Items collection. Working with items, including adding and removing items, is performed using the Items collection. You'll most often manipulate the Items collection using code (which I'll show you a little later in this hour), but you can also work with the collection at design time by using the Properties window.

Manipulating Items at Design Time

The Items collection is available as a property of the list box. Locate the Items property in the Properties window and click it to select it. The familiar button with three dots appears, indicating that you can do advanced things with this property. Click the button now to show the String Collection Editor. To add items to the collection, simply enter the items into the text box—one item to a line.

Enter the following items:

- *Atom Heart Mother*
- *Saucer Full of Secrets*
- *Wish You Were Here*
- *Animals*
- *Echoes*
- *Piper at the Gates of Dawn*

When you're finished, your screen should look like that shown in Figure 7.15. Click OK to commit your entries and close the window. Notice that the list box contains the items that you entered.

FIGURE 7.15

Use this dialog box to manipulate an Items collection at design time.

Manipulating Items at Runtime

In Hour 3, "Understanding Objects and Collections," you learned all about objects, properties, methods, and collections. All this knowledge comes into play when manipulating lists at runtime. The Items property of a list box (and a combo box) is an object property that returns a collection (collections in many ways are like objects—they have properties and methods). To manipulate list items, you manipulate the Items collection.

A list can contain duplicate values, as you'll see in this example. Because of this, Visual Basic .NET needs a mechanism other than an item's text to treat each item in a list as a unique item. This is done by assigning each item in an Items collection a unique index. The first item in the list has an index of 0, the second an index of 1, and so on. The index is the ordinal position of an item relative to the first item in the Items collection, not the top item visible in the list.

Adding Items to a List

New items are added to the Items collection using the Add method of the collection. You're now going to create a button that adds an album to the list. Close the String Collection Editor now, add a new button to the form, and set its properties as follows:

Property	Value
Name	**btnAddItem**
Location	**104,160**
Size	**96,23**
Text	**Add an Item**

Double-click the button to access its Click event and add the following code:

```
lstPinkFloydAlbums.Items.Add("Dark Side of the Moon")
```

Notice that the Add method accepts a string argument—the text to add to the list.

 Unlike items added at design time, items added through code aren't preserved when the program ends.

Press F5 to run the project now and click the button. When you do, the new album is added to the bottom of the list. Clicking the button a second time adds another item to the list with the same album name. The list box doesn't care whether the item already exists in the list; each call to the Add method of the Items collection adds a new item to the list.

7

The Add method of the Items collection can be called as a function, in which case it returns the index (ordinal position of the newly added item in the underlying collection), as in the following:

```
Dim intIndex As Integer
intIndex = lstPinkFloydAlbums.Items.Add("Dark Side of the Moon")
```

Stop the running project and save your work before continuing.

> To add an item to an Items collection at a specific location in the list, use the Insert method. The Insert method accepts an index in addition to text. To add an item at the top of the list, for example, you could use a statement such as `lstPinkFloydAlbums.Items.Insert(0,"Dark Side of the Moon")`. Remember, the first item in the list has an index of 0.

Removing Items from a List

Removing an individual item from a list is as easy as adding an item and requires only a single method call: a call to the Remove method of the Items collection. The Remove method accepts a string, which is the text of the item to remove. You're now going to create a button that will remove an item from the list. Create a new button and set its properties as follows:

Property	Value
Name	**btnRemoveItem**
Location	**104,192**
Size	**96,23**
Text	**Remove an Item**

Double-click the new button to access its Click event and enter the following statement:

```
lstPinkFloydAlbums.Items.Remove("Dark Side of the Moon")
```

The Remove method tells Visual Basic .NET to search the Items collection, starting at the first item (index = 0), and to remove an item when an item is found that matches the specified text. As I stated earlier, you can have multiple items with the same text. In this case, the Remove method will remove only the first occurrence; after the text is found and removed, Visual Basic .NET stops looking. Press F5 to run the project now. Click the Add an Item button a few times to add *Dark Side of the Moon* to the list (see Figure 7.16). Next, click the Remove an Item button and notice how Visual Basic .NET finds and removes one instance of the item.

FIGURE 7.16
The list box can contain duplicate entries, but each entry is a unique item in the Items collection.

To remove an item at a specific index, use the RemoveAt method. For Instance, to remove the first item in the list, you could use a statement such as `lstPinkFloydAlbums.Items.RemoveAt(0)`.

Stop the running project and save your work.

Clearing a List

To completely clear the contents of a list box, use the Clear method. You're now going to add a button to the form that will clear the list when clicked. Add a new button to the form now and set the button's properties as follows:

Property	Value
Name	**btnClearList**
Location	**104,224**
Size	**96,23**
Text	**Clear List**

Double-click the new button to access its Click event and enter the following statement:

```
lstPinkFloydAlbums.Items.Clear()
```

Press F5 to run the project, and then click the Clear List button. The Clear method doesn't care whether an item was added at design time or runtime; Clear() always removes all items from the list. Stop the project and again save your work.

7

> Remember that the Add, Insert, Remove, RemoveAt, and Clear methods are
> all methods of the Items collection, not of the list box itself. If you forget
> that these are members of the Items collection, you might be confused
> when you don't find them when you enter a period after typing a list box's
> name in code.

Retrieving Information About the Selected Item in a List

By default, a list box allows only a single item to be selected by the user at a time.
Whether a list allows multiple selections is determined by the SelectionMode property of
the list box. You'll need to understand how to work with the selected item of the most
common type of list box—a list box that allows only a single selection.

Two properties provide information about the selected item: SelectedItem and
SelectedIndex. It's important to note that these are properties of the list box itself, not of
the Items collection of a list box. The SelectedItem method returns the text of the currently
selected item. If no item is selected, the method returns an empty string. It's desirable at
times, to know the index of the selected item. This is obtained using the SelectedIndex
property of the list box. As you know, the first item in a list has the index of 0. If no item is
selected, SelectedIndex returns –1, which is never a valid index for an item.

You're now going to add a button to the form that, when clicked, displays the selected
item's text and index in the Output window. First, change the Height property of the
form to **320** to accommodate one more button. As you build your interfaces, you'll often
have to make small tweaks such as this because it's nearly impossible to anticipate everything ahead of time. Add a new button to the form and set its properties as follows:

Property	Value
Name	**btnShowItem**
Location	**104,256**
Size	**96,23**
Text	**Show Selected**

Double-click the new button to access its Click event and enter the following statements:

```
Debug.WriteLine(lstPinkFloydAlbums.SelectedItem)
Debug.WriteLine(lstPinkFloydAlbums.SelectedIndex)
```

Press F5 to run the project and click the Show Selected button. Take a look at the Output
window (you might have to show it using Other Windows submenu of the View menu).

You'll see a blank line—the empty string returned by SelectedItem—and you'll also see a –1, which was returned by SelectedIndex. Again, the –1 denotes that no item is selected. Click an item in the list to select it, and then click Show Selected again. This time, you'll see the text of the selected item and its index in the Output window (see Figure 7.17). Stop the running project and save your work.

FIGURE 7.17

The SelectedItem and SelectedIndex proper-
ties make it easy to
determine which item
is selected in a list.

You can set up a list box to allow multiple items to be selected at once. To do this, you change the SelectionMode property of the list box to MultiSimple (clicking an item toggles its selected state) or MultiExtended (you have to hold Ctrl or Shift to select multiple items). To determine which items are selected in a multi-selection list box, you use the list box's SelectedItems collection.

Sorting a List

List boxes and combo boxes have a Sorted property. By default, this property is set to False. Changing this property value to True causes Visual Basic .NET to sort the contents of the list alphabetically. When the contents of a list are sorted, the index of each item in the Items collection is changed; therefore, you can't use an index value obtained prior to setting Sorted to True.

Sorted is a property, not a method. Realize that you don't have to call Sorted to sort the contents of a list; Visual Basic .NET enforces a sort order as long as the Sorted property is set to True. This means that all items added using the Add method or the Insert method are automatically inserted into the proper sorted location, in contrast to being inserted at the end of the list or in a specific location.

7

Creating Drop-Down Lists Using the Combo Box

List boxes are great, but they have two shortcomings. First, they take up quite a bit of space. Second, users can't enter their own values; they have to select from the items in the list. If you need to conserve space, or if you want to enable a user to enter a value that might not exist in the list, use the Combo Box control.

Combo boxes have an Items collection that behaves *exactly* like that of the List Box control (refer to the previous section for information on manipulating lists). Here I'll show you the basics of how a combo box works.

Add a new combo box to the form by double-clicking the ComboBox item in the toolbox. Set the combo box's properties as follows:

Property	Value
Name	**cboAlbums**
Location	**72,8**
Size	**160,21**
Text	*(make blank)*

The first thing you should note is that the combo box has a Text property, whereas the list box doesn't. This works the same as the Text property of a text box. When the user selects an item from the drop-down list, the value of the selected item is placed in the Text property of the text box. The default behavior of a combo box is to allow the user to enter any text in the text box portion of the control—even if the text doesn't exist in the list. I'll show you how to change this behavior shortly.

Select the Items property of the combo box in the Properties window and click the button that appears. Add the following items to the String Collection Editor and click OK to commit your entries.

- Black
- Blue
- Gold
- Green
- Red
- Yellow

Press F5 to run the project. Click the arrow at the right side of the combo box and a drop-down list appears (see Figure 7.18).

FIGURE 7.18

Combo boxes conserve space.

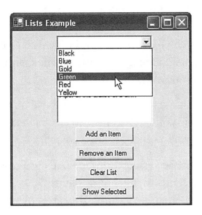

Next, try typing in the text **Magenta**. Visual Basic .NET lets you do this. Indeed, you can type any text that you want. You'll often want to restrict a user to entering only values that appear in the list. To do this, you change the DropDownStyle property of the combo box. Close the form to stop the running project and change the DropDownStyle property of the combo box to **DropDownList**. Press F5 to run the project again and try to type text into the combo box. You can't. However, if you enter a character that's the start of a list item, Visual Basic .NET selects the closest matching entry.

When set as a DropDownList, a combo box won't allow any text entry, and therefore, the user is limited to selecting items from the list. As a matter of fact, clicking in the "text box" portion of the combo box opens the list the same as though you clicked the drop-down arrow.

Stop the running project now and save your work. As you can see, the combo box and list box offer similar functionality, and in fact, the coding of their lists is identical. Each one of these controls serves a slightly different purpose, however. Which one is better? That depends entirely on the situation. As you use professional applications, pay attention to their interfaces; you'll start to get a feel for which control is appropriate in a given situation.

Summary

In this hour, you learned how to present text to a user. You learned that the Label control is perfect for displaying static text (text the user can't enter) and that the text box is the control to use for displaying edited text. You can now create text boxes that contain many

7

lines of text, and you know how to add scrollbars when the text is greater than what can be displayed in the control.

I don't think I've ever seen a form without at least one button on it, and you've now learned how to add buttons to your forms and how to do some interesting things such as adding a picture to a button. For the most part, working with buttons is a simple matter of adding one to a form, setting its Name and Text properties, and adding some code to its Click event—all of which you now know how to do.

Check boxes and option buttons are used to present true/false and mutually exclusive options, respectively. In this hour, you learned how to use each of these controls and how to use group boxes to logically group sets of related controls.

Lastly, you learned how to use list boxes and combo boxes to present lists of items to a user. You now know how to add items to a list at design time as well as runtime, and you know how to sort items. The List Box and Combo Box are powerful controls, and I encourage you to dig deeper into the functionality they possess.

Without controls, users would have nothing to interact with on your forms. In this hour, you learned how to use the standard controls to begin building functional interfaces. The controls discussed in this hour have been around since the early days of Visual Basic .NET, and in fact, behave very much like they did years ago. Keep in mind that I only scratched the surface of each of these controls and that most do far more than I've hinted at here. Mastering these controls will be easy for you because you'll be using them a lot.

Q&A

Q Can I place radio buttons directly on a form?

A Yes. The form is a container, so all radio buttons placed on a form are mutually exclusive to one another. If you wanted to add a second set of mutually exclusive buttons, they'd have to be placed on a container control. In general, I think it's best to place radio buttons in a group box rather than on a form because the group box provides a border and a caption for the radio buttons and makes it much easier to move around the set of radio buttons (you simply move the group box) when you're designing the form.

Q I've seen what appear to be list boxes that have a check box next to each item in the list. Is this possible?

A Yes. In earlier versions of Visual Basic, this was functionality inherent in the standard list box. In Visual Basic .NET, this is accomplished using an entirely different control: the checked list box.

Workshop

The Workshop is designed to help you anticipate possible questions, review what you've learned, and get you thinking about how to put your knowledge into practice. The answers to the quiz are in Appendix B, "Answers to the Quizzes."

Quiz

1. Which control would you use to display text that the user can't edit?
2. What common property is shared by the Label control and text box and whose value determines what the user sees in the control?
3. In order to change the Height of a text box, you must set what property?
4. What is the default event of a Button control?
5. A button whose Click event is triggered when the user presses Enter, regardless of the control that has the focus, is called an...?
6. Which control would you use to display a yes/no value to a user?
7. How would you create two distinct sets of mutually exclusive option buttons?
8. To manipulate items in a list, you use what collection?
9. What method adds an item to a list in a specific location?

Exercises

1. Create a form with a text box and a combo box. Add a button that, when clicked, adds the contents of the text box to the combo box.
2. Create a form with two list boxes. Add a number of items to one list box at design time using the Properties window. Create a button that, when clicked, removes the selected item in the first list and adds it to the second list.

7

HOUR 8

Using Advanced Controls

The standard controls presented in the previous hour enable you to build many types of functional forms. However, to create truly robust and interactive applications, you've got to use the more advanced controls. As a Windows user, you've encountered many of these controls, such as the Tab control, which presents data on tabs, and the Tree View control, which displays hierarchical lists such as the one in Explorer. In this hour, you'll learn about these advanced controls and learn how to use them to make professional interfaces like those you're accustomed to seeing in commercial products.

The highlights of this hour include

- Creating timers
- Creating tabbed dialog boxes
- Storing pictures in an Image List control
- Building enhanced lists using the List View control
- Creating hierarchical lists with the Tree View control

In many of the examples in this hour, I show how to add items to collections at design time. Keep in mind that everything you can do at design time can also be accomplished using Visual Basic code.

Creating Timers

All the controls you used in Hour 7, "Working with Traditional Controls," had in common the fact that the user can interact with them. Not all controls have this capability— or restriction—depending on how you look at it. Some controls are designed for use only by the developer. One such control is the Open File Dialog control you used in your Picture Viewer application in Hour 1, "Jumping In with Both Feet: A Visual Basic .NET Programming Tour." Another control that's invisible at runtime is the Timer control. The Timer control's sole purpose is to trigger an event at a specified interval of time.

Create a new Windows Application titled **Timer Example**. Change the name of the default form to **fclsTimerExample** and then set its Text property to **Timer Example**. Next, be sure to set the Startup object property of the project to fclsTimerExample or the project won't run.

Add a new Timer control to your form by double-clicking the Timer item in the Toolbox. The Timer control is invisible at runtime, so it's added to the gray area at the bottom of the screen rather than placed on the form (see Figure 8.1). Set the properties of the Timer control as follows:

Property	Value
Name	**tmrClock**
Enabled	**True**
Interval	**1000**

You probably noticed that there are very few properties for the Timer control compared to the other controls you've worked with. The most important property of the Timer control is the Interval property. The Interval property determines how often the Timer control fires its Tick event (where you'll be placing code to do something when the designated time elapses). The Interval property is specified in milliseconds, so a setting of 1,000 is equal to 1 second. As with many controls, the best way to understand how the Timer control works is to use it in a project. Using the Timer control and a Label control, you're going to create a simple clock. The way the clock will work is that the Timer control will fire its Tick event once every second (because you've set the Interval property to 1000 milliseconds). Within the Tick event, you'll update the label's Text property to the current system time.

FIGURE 8.1
Invisible-at-runtime controls are shown at the bottom of the designer, not on a form.

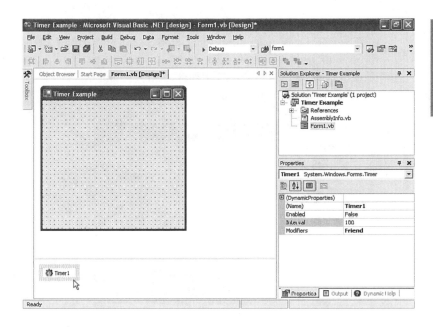

Add a new label to the form and set its properties as follows:

Property	Value
Name	**lblClock**
BorderStyle	**FixedSingle**
Location	**96,120**
Size	**100,23**
Text	*(make blank)*
TextAlign	**MiddleCenter**

Next, double-click the Timer control to access its Tick event. When a timer is first enabled, it starts counting (in milliseconds) from 0. When the amount of time specified in the Interval property passes, the Tick event fires and the timer starts counting from 0 once again. This cycle continues until the timer is disabled (its Enabled property is set to False). Because you've set the Enabled property of the timer to True at design time, it will start counting as soon as the form on which it's placed is loaded. Enter the following statement in the Tick event:

```
lblClock.Text = TimeOfDay
```

TimeOfDay is a very handy function of Visual Basic .NET that returns the current time of day, so all this statement does is set the Text property of the label to the current time of day. It's important to remember that it does this once per second. Press F5 to run the project now and you'll see the Label control acting as a clock, updating the time once every second (see Figure 8.2).

FIGURE 8.2

Timers make it easy to execute at specified intervals.

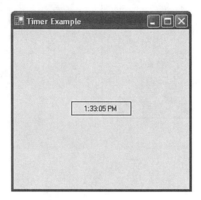

Stop the running project now and save your work.

Timers are powerful, but you must take care not to overuse them. For a timer to work, Windows must be aware of the timer and must constantly compare the current internal clock to the interval of the timer. It does all this so that it can notify the timer at the appropriate time to execute its Tick event. In other words, timers take system resources. This isn't a problem for an application that uses a few timers, but I wouldn't overload an application with a dozen timers unless I had no other choice (and there's almost always another choice) .

Creating Tabbed Dialog Boxes

Windows 95 was the first version of Windows to introduce a tabbed interface. Since then, tabs have been widely adopted as a primary interface element. Tabs provide two major benefits: a logical grouping of controls and a reduction of required screen space. Although tabs might look complicated, they are actually easy to build and use.

Create a new Windows Application named **Tabs Example**. Change the name of the default form to **fclsTabs**, set its Text property to **Tabs Example**, and change the Startup object property of the project to fclsTabs. Next, add a new Tab control to your form by double-clicking the TabControl item in the Toolbox. At first, the new control looks more like a panel than a set of tabs because it doesn't actually have any tabs. Set the Tab control's properties as follows:

8

Property	Value
Name	**tabMyTabs**
Location	**8,16**
Size	**272,208**

The tabs that appear on a Tab control are determined by the control's TabPages collection. Click the TabPages property of the Tab control in the Properties window and then click the small button that appears. Visual Basic shows the TabPage Collection Editor. As you can see, your Tab control has no tabs. Click Add now to create a new tab (see Figure 8.3).

FIGURE 8.3

New Tab controls have no tabs; you must create them.

Each tab in the collection is referred to as a *page*. Visual Basic names each new page TabPage*X*, where *x* is a unique number. Although you don't have to change the name of a page, it's sometimes easier to work with a Tab control if you give each tab a meaningful name, such as pgeGeneralPage, pgePreferencesPage, and so forth. Set the Name property of your new page to **pgeContacts** now. Each page has a number of properties, but the property you'll be concerned with most is the Text property because the value of the Text property determines the text the user will see on the tab. Change the Text property of your new tab page to **Contacts**. Next, click Add to create a second page. Change the Name of the new tab to **pgeAppointments**, set the Text property to **Appointments,** and then click OK to close the dialog box. Your Tab control now has two tabs (pages).

The properties on the editor are always in categorized mode, regardless of the way you choose to view properties in the Properties window.

A quick way to add or remove a tab is to use the shortcuts provided in the description pane at the bottom of the Properties window.

Each page on a Tab control acts as a container, much like a Panel or Group Box control. This is why you can't drag the Tab control by clicking in the middle of it. To drag a container control, you have to click and drag the dotted border around the control. Add a text box to the first tab now by dragging the TextBox item from the toolbox and dropping in on the tab page. After it's on the page, drag it to approximately the center of the page. Next, click the Appointments tab, just as if you were a user switching tabs. You might have to click it twice: once to select the Tab control and a second time to switch tabs. If so, click slowly to avoid double-clicking the Tab control and showing its default event.

As you can see, the Appointments tab comes to the front, and the text box is no longer visible. Visual Basic has hidden the first page and shown the second. Drag a check box from the toolbox and drop it on the Appointments page, and then click Contacts once more. Again, Visual Basic handles the details of showing and hiding the tab pages; you no longer see the check box, but you do see the text box (see Figure 8.4).

FIGURE 8.4

The Tab control makes it easy to create a tabbed interface.

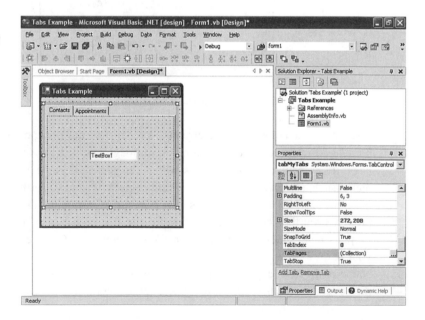

By understanding two simple programming elements, you'll be able to do 99% of what you need to with the Tab control. The first element is that you'll need to know which tab is selected at runtime. The SelectedIndex property of the control (not of the TabIndex property) sets and returns the index of the currently selected tab: 0 for the first tab, 1 for the second, and so forth. The second thing to know is how to tell when the user switches tabs. The Tab control has a SelectedIndexChanged event, which fires whenever the selected tab is changed. In this event, you can check the value of SelectedIndex to determine the tab that's been selected.

Perhaps the trickiest issue with the Tab control is that each tab page has its own set of events. If you double-click the tabs themselves, you'll get a set of global events for the Tab control (this is where you'll find the SelectedIndexChanged event). If you double-click a page on the tabs, you'll get a unique set of events for that page; each page has its own set of events.

Storing Pictures in an Image List

Many of the controls I discuss in this hour have the capability to attach pictures to different types of items. The Tree View control, which is used in Explorer for navigating folders, for example, displays images next to each folder node. Not all of these pictures are the same; the control uses specific pictures to denote information about each node. It would have been possible for Microsoft to make each control store its images internally, but that would be highly inefficient because it wouldn't allow controls to share the same pictures—you'd have to store the pictures in each control that needed them. This would also cause a maintenance headache. For example, say you had 10 Tree View controls and each displays a folder image for folder nodes. Now, it's time to update your application and you want to update the folder image to something a bit nicer. If the image were stored in each Tree View control, you'd have to update all 10 of them (and risk missing one). Instead, Microsoft created a control dedicated to storing pictures and serving them to other controls: the Image List. When you put images in an Image List control, it's easy to share them among other types of controls.

Create a new Windows Application named **Lists and Trees**. Change the name of the default form to **fclsListsAndTrees**, set its Text property to **Lists and Trees Example**, and set the Startup object of the project to fclsListsAndTrees. Next, add a new Image List control by double-clicking the ImageList item in the toolbox. As with the Timer control, the Image List is an invisible-at-runtime control, so it appears below the form, not on it. Change the name of the Image List to **imgMyImages**.

The sole purpose of an Image List control is to store pictures and make them available to other controls. The pictures are stored in the Images collection of the control. Click the Images property of the Image List control in the Properties window and then click the small button that appears. Visual Basic displays the Image Collection Editor. Notice that this editor is similar to other editors you've used in this hour. Click Add to display the Open dialog box and use this dialog box to locate and select a 16×16 pixel bitmap. If you don't have a 16×16 pixel bitmap, you can create one using Microsoft Paint, or download samples I've provided at http://www.samspublishing.com/ or http://www.jamesfoxall.com. After you've added an image, click OK to close the Image Collection Editor.

Take a look at the ImageSize property of the Image control. It should be 16,16. If it doesn't, the bitmap you selected isn't 16×16 pixels; this property is set to the dimensions of the first picture added to the Image List.

You can't always rely on the background where a picture will be displayed to be white—or any other color for that matter. Because of this, the Image List control has a TransparentColor property. By default, the TransparentColor property is set to Transparent. This isn't an intuitive setting, because in effect it means that no color is treated as transparent (unless the image is an icon that has a transparent area). If you designate a specific color for the TransparentColor property, when a picture is served from the Image List to another control, all occurrences of the specified color will appear transparent—the background will show through. This gives you the power to create pictures that can be served to controls without concern about the color on which the picture will appear.

That's all there is to adding images to an Image List control. The power of the Image List resides in its capability to be linked to by other controls, so that they can access the pictures the Image List stores.

Building Enhanced Lists Using the List View

The List View control is like a list box on steroids—and then some. The List View can be used to create simple lists, multicolumn grids, and icon trays. The right pane in Explorer is a List View. (You might not know it, but you can change the appearance of the List View in Explorer by right-clicking it and using the View submenu of the shortcut menu that appears.) The primary display options available for Explorer's List View are Large Icons, Small Icons, List, and Details. These correspond exactly to the display options available for a List View by way of its View property. You're now going to create a List View with a few items on it and experiment with the different views—including showing a picture for the items.

I can only scratch the surface of this great control here. After you've learned the basics in this hour, I highly recommend that you spend some time with the List View control, the help text, and whatever additional material you can find. I use the List View all the time, and it's a very powerful tool to have in your arsenal—displaying lists is *very* common.

8

Add a List View control to your form now by double-clicking the ListView item in the Toolbox. Set the properties of the List View as follows:

Property	Value
Name	**lstMyListView**
Location	**8,8**
Size	**275,97**
SmallImageList	**imgMyImages**
View	**Details**

As you can see, you can attach an Image List to a control via the Properties window (and with code as well, of course). Not all controls support the Image List, but those that do make it as simple as setting a property to link to an Image List control. The List View actually allows linking to two Image Lists: one for large icons (32×32 pixels) and one for small images. In this example, you're going to use only small pictures. If you wanted to use the large format, you could hook up a second Image List containing larger images to the List View's LargeImageList property.

Creating Columns

When you changed the View property to Details, an empty header was placed at the top of the control. The contents of this header are determined by the columns defined in the Columns collection.

Select the Columns property on the Properties window and click the small button that appears. Visual Basic then displays the ColumnHeader Collection Editor window. Click Add to create a new header and change its Text property to **Name** and its Width property to **120**. Click Add once more to create a second column and change its Text property to **State**. I haven't had you change the names of the columns in this example because you're not going to be referencing them by name.

Click OK to save your column settings and close the window. Your List View should now have two named columns (see Figure 8.5).

Adding List Items

Complete the following steps to add two items to the List View:

1. Click the Items property in the Properties window and then click the small button that appears, which displays the ListViewItem Collection Editor dialog box.

2. Click Add to create a new item, and change the item's Text property to **James Foxall**.

FIGURE 8.5

*Use List Views to pre-
sent multicolumn lists.*

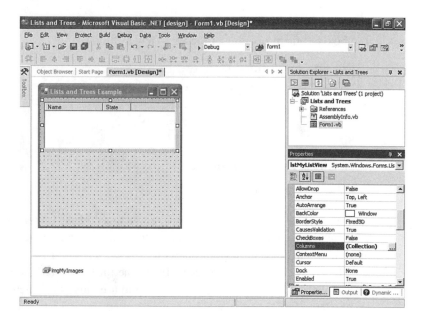

3. Next, open the drop-down list for the ImageIndex property. Notice how the list
   contains the picture in the linked Image List control (see Figure 8.6). Select the
   image.

FIGURE 8.6

*Pictures from a linked
Image List are readily
available to the
control.*

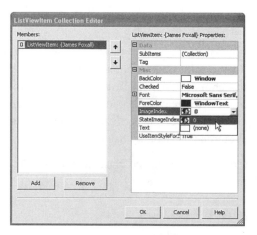

The Text property of an item determines the text displayed for the item in the list
view. If the View property is set to Details and multiple columns have been
defined, the value of the Text property appears in the first column. Subsequent
column values are determined by the SubItems collection.

4. Click the SubItems property and then click the small button that appears, which displays the ListViewSubItem Collection Editor. The item that appears in the list refers to the text of the item itself, which you don't want to change.

5. Click Add to create a new subitem and change its text to **Nebraska**.

6. Click OK to return to the ListViewItem Collection Editor.

7. Click the Add button to create another item. This time, change the Text property to your name and use the techniques you just learned to add a sub item. For the Text property of the subitem, enter your state of residence. Go ahead and give it an item just as you did for my name.

8. When you're finished, click OK to close the ListViewItem Collection Editor. Your List View should now contain two list items (see Figure 8.7).

FIGURE 8.7

List views offer much more functionality than a standard list box.

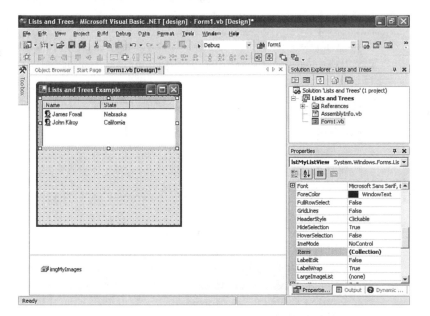

9. Next, experiment with the View property of the List View control to see how the various settings affect the appearance of the control. The Large Icons setting doesn't display an icon because you didn't link an Image List control to the LargeImageList property of the List View. Be sure to set the View property back to Details before continuing.

10. Press F5 to run the project and try selecting your name by clicking your state. You can't. The default behavior of the List View is to consider only the clicking of the first column as selecting an item.

11. Stop the project and change the FullRowSelect property to True; then run the project once more.

12. Click your state again and this time your name becomes selected (actually, the entire row becomes selected). Personally, I prefer to set up all my List Views with FullRowSelect set to True, but this is just a personal preference. Stop the project now and save your work.

Manipulating a List View Using Code

You've just learned the basics of working with a List View control. Even though you performed all the steps in Design view for this example, you'll probably manipulate your list items using code because you won't necessarily know ahead of time what to display in the list. Next, I'll show you how to work with the List View in code.

Adding List Items Using Code

Adding an item using Visual Basic code is very simple—if the item you're adding is simple. To add an item to your list view, you use the Add method of the Items collection, like this:

```
lstMyListView.Items.Add("Bob Benzel")
```

If the item is to have a picture, you can specify the index of the picture as a second parameter, like this:

```
lstMyListView.Items.Add("Jason Goss",0)
```

If the item has subitems, things get more complicated. The Add method enables you to specify only the text and image index. To access the additional properties of a list item, you need to get a reference to the item in code. Remember that new items have only one subitem by default; you have to create additional items. The Add method of the Items collection returns a reference to the newly added item. Knowing this, you can create a new variable to hold a reference to the item, create the item, and manipulate anything you choose to about the item using the variable (see Hour 11, "Using Constants, Data Types, Variables, and Arrays," for information about using variables). The following code creates a new item and appends a subitem to its SubItems collection:

```
Dim objListItem As ListViewItem
objListItem = lstMyListView.Items.Add("Jim White ", 0)
objListItem.SubItems.Add("Nebraska")
```

Determining the Selected Item in Code

The List View control has a collection that contains a reference to each selected item in the control: the SelectedItems collection. If the MultiSelect property of the List View is set to True (as it is by default), the user can select multiple items by holding down the

Ctrl or Shift key when clicking items. This is why the List View supports a SelectedItems collection rather than a SelectedItem property. To gather information about a selected item, you refer to it by its index. For example, to print the text of the first selected item (or the only selected item if just one is selected), you could use code like this:

```
If lstMyListView.SelectedItems.Count > 0 Then
    Debug.WriteLine(lstMyListView.SelectedItems(0).Text)
End If
```

The reason you check the Count property of the SelectedItems collection is that if no items are selected, a runtime error would occur if you attempted to reference element 0 in the SelectedItems collection.

Removing List Items Using Code

To remove a list item, use the Remove method of the Items collection. The Remove Item method accepts and expects a reference to a list item. To remove the currently selected item, for example, you could use a statement such as

```
lstMyListView.Items.Remove(lstMyListView.SelectedItems(0))
```

Again, you'd want to make sure that an item is actually selected before using this statement.

Removing All List Items

If you're filling a List View using code, you'll probably want to clear the contents of the List View first. That way, if the code to fill the List View is called a second time, duplicate entries won't be created. To clear the contents of a List View, use the Clear method of the Items collection, like this:

```
lstMyListView.Items.Clear()
```

The List View control is an amazingly versatile tool. As a matter of fact, I rarely use the standard List Box control; I prefer to use the List View because of its added functionality, such as displaying an image for an item. I've barely scratched the surface here, but you now know enough to begin using this awesome tool in your own development.

Creating Hierarchical Lists with the Tree View

The Tree View control is used to present hierarchical data. Perhaps the most commonly used Tree View control is found in Explorer, where you can use the Tree View to navigate the folders and drives on your computer. The Tree View is perfect for displaying hierarchical data, such as a departmental display of employees. In this section, I'll teach you the basics of the Tree View control so that you can use this powerful interface element in your applications.

The Tree View's items are contained in a Nodes collection, much like items in a List View are stored in an Items collection. To add items to the tree, you append them to the Nodes collection. As you can probably see by now, after you understand the basics of objects and collections, you can apply that knowledge to almost everything in Visual Basic. For instance, the skills you learned in working with the Items collection of the List View control are similar to the skills needed for working with the Nodes collection of the Tree View control. In fact, these concepts are very similar to working with list boxes and combo boxes.

Add a Tree View control to your form now by double-clicking the TreeView item in the toolbox. Set the Tree View control's properties as follows:

Property	Value
Name	**tvwLanguages**
ImageList	**imgMyImages**
Location	**8,128**
Size	**275,97**

Adding Nodes to a Tree View

Working with nodes at design time is very similar to working with a List View's Items collection. So, I'll show you how to work with nodes in code. To add a node you call the Add method of the Nodes collection (which you'll do in this example). Add a new button to your form and set its properties as follows:

Property	Value
Name	**btnAddNode**
Location	**8,240**
Size	**75,23**
Text	**Add Node**

Double-click the button to access its Click event and enter the following code:

```
tvwLanguages.Nodes.Add("James")
tvwLanguages.Nodes.Add("Visual Basic")
```

Press F5 to run the project, and then click the button. Two nodes will appear in the tree, one for each Add method call (see Figure 8.8).

FIGURE 8.8

Nodes are the items that appear in a tree.

Notice how both nodes appear at the same level in the hierarchy; neither node is a parent or child of the other. If all your nodes will be at the same level in the hierarchy, you should consider using a List View control instead because what you're creating is simply a list.

Stop the project and return to the button's Click event. Any given node can be both a parent to other nodes and a child of a single node (the parent node of any given node can be referenced via the Parent property of a node). For this to work, each node has its own Nodes collection. This can be confusing, but if you realize that children nodes belong to the parent node, it starts to make sense (it can still get confusing in practice, though).

You're now going to create a new button that adds the same two nodes as before but makes the second node a child of the first. Return to the Design view of the form and then create a new button and set its properties as shown:

Property	Value
Name	**btnCreateChild**
Location	**96,240**
Size	**80,23**
Text	**Create Child**

Double-click the new button to access its Click event and add the following code:

```
Dim objNode As TreeNode
objNode = tvwLanguages.Nodes.Add("James")
objNode.Nodes.Add("Visual Basic")
```

This code is similar to what you created in the List View example. The Add method of the Nodes collection returns a reference to the newly created node. Thus, this code creates a variable of type TreeNode (variables are discussed in detail in Hour 11), creates a new node whose reference is placed in the variable, and then adds a new node to the Nodes collection of the first node. To see the effect this has, press F5 to run the project and click the new button. You'll see a single item in the list, with a plus sign to the left of it. This plus sign indicates that child nodes exist. Click the plus sign, and the node is expanded to show its children (see Figure 8.9).

FIGURE 8.9

You can create as deep a hierarchy as you need using the Tree View control.

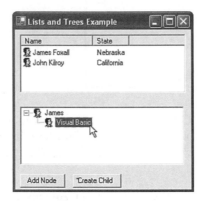

This example is a simple one—a single parent node having a single child node. However, the principles used here are the same as those used to build complex trees with dozens or hundreds of nodes.

Removing Nodes

To remove a node, you call the Remove method of the Nodes collection. The Remove method accepts and expects a valid node, so you must know which node to remove. Again, the Nodes collection works very much like the Items collection in the List View control, so the same ideas apply. For example, the currently selected node is returned in the SelectedNode property of the Tree View control. So, to remove the currently selected node you could use this statement:

```
tvwLanguages.Nodes.Remove(tvwLanguages.SelectedNode)
```

If this statement were called when no node is selected, an error would occur. In Hour 11, you'll learn all about data types and equalities, but here's a preview: If an object variable doesn't reference an object, it's equivalent to the Visual Basic keyword Nothing. Knowing this, you could validate whether an item is selected with a little bit of logic using code like the following. (Note that unlike with the List View control, only one node can be selected at a time in a Tree View control.)

```
If Not (tvwLanguages.SelectedNode Is Nothing) Then
    tvwLanguages.Nodes.Remove(tvwLanguages.SelectedNode)
End If
```

Removing a parent node causes all its children to be removed as well.

Clearing All Nodes

To clear all nodes in a Tree View, invoke the Clear method of the Nodes collection, like this:

```
tvwLanguages.Nodes.Clear()
```

As with the List View, I've only scratched the surface of the Tree View. Spend some time becoming familiar with the basics of the Tree View, as I've shown here, and then dig a bit deeper to discover the not-so-obvious power and flexibility of this control.

Summary

Visual Basic includes a number of controls that go beyond the standard functionality of the traditional controls discussed in Hour 7. In this hour, I discussed the most commonly used advanced controls. You learned how to use the Timer control to trigger events at predetermined intervals. You also learned how to use the Tab control to create the tabbed dialog boxes with which you're so familiar.

Also in this hour, you learned how to add pictures to an Image List control so that other controls can use them. The Image List makes it easy to share pictures among many controls, making it a very useful tool. Finally, I taught you the basics of the List View and Tree View controls—two controls you can use to build high-end interfaces that present structured data. The more time you spend with all these controls, the better you'll become at creating great interfaces.

Q&A

Q What if I need a lot of timers, but I'm concerned about system resources?

A When possible, use a single timer for multiple duties. This is extremely easy when two events occur at the same interval—why bother creating a second timer? When two events occur at different intervals, you can use some decision skills along with static variables (discussed in Hour 11) to share Timer events.

Q What else can I do with an Image List control?

A You can assign a unique picture to a node in a Tree View control when the node is selected. You can also display an image in the tab of a tab page in a Tab control. There are a lot of uses, and as you learn more about advanced controls, you'll see additional opportunities for using images from an Image List.

Workshop

The Workshop is designed to help you anticipate possible questions, review what you've learned, and get you thinking about how to put your knowledge into practice. The answers to the quiz are in Appendix B, "Answers to the Quizzes."

Quiz

1. What increment of time is applied to the Interval property of the Timer control?
2. What collection is used to add new tabs to a Tab control?
3. What property returns the index of the currently selected tab?
4. True or False: You should use different Image List controls for storing images of different sizes.
5. To see columns in a List View control, the View property must be set to what?
6. The additional columns of data that can be attached to an item in a List View are stored in what collection?
7. What property of what object would you use to determine how many items are in a List View?
8. Each item in a Tree View control is called what?
9. How do you make a node the child of another node?

Exercises

1. Add a second Image List control to your project with the List View. Place an icon (32×32 pixels) in this Image List and link the Image List to the LargeImageList property of the List View control. Change the View property to Large Icons. Does the icon appear next to a list item? If not, is there a property of an item you can set so that it does?
2. Create a new project and add a List View, a button, and a Text Box to the default form. Create a new item in the List View using the text entered into the Text Box when the button is clicked.

HOUR 9

Adding Menus and Toolbars to Forms

The use of a graphical user interface (GUI) for interacting with and navigating programs is one of the greatest features of Windows. Despite this, a fair number of Windows users still rely primarily on the keyboard, preferring to use a mouse only when absolutely necessary. Data-entry people in particular never take their hands off the keyboard. Many software companies receive support calls from angry customers because a commonly used function is accessible only by using a mouse. Menus are the easiest way to navigate your program for a user who relies on the keyboard, and Visual Basic .NET makes it easier than ever to create menus for your applications. In this hour, you'll learn how to build, manipulate, and program menus on a form. In addition, I'll teach you how to use the Toolbar control to create attractive and functional toolbars. Finally, you'll learn how to finish off a form with a status bar.

The highlights of this hour include the following:

- Adding, moving, and deleting menu items
- Creating checked menu items

- Programming menus
- Implementing context menus
- Assigning shortcut keys
- Creating toolbar items
- Defining toggle buttons and separators
- Creating a status bar

Building Menus

When I said that Visual Basic .NET makes building menus easier than ever, I wasn't kidding. The menu-building capabilities of Visual Basic .NET are far beyond those of previous versions of Visual Basic. Building menus is now an immediately gratifying process. I can't stress enough how important it is to have good menus, and now that it's so easy to do, there's no excuse for not putting menus in an application.

> When running an application for the first time, users will often scan the menus before opening a manual. (Most users never open the manual!) When you provide comprehensive menus, you make your program easier to learn and use.

Adding Menu Items

Adding menus to a form is accomplished by way of a control: the Main Menu control. The Main Menu control is a bit odd in that it's the only control I know of (besides the context menu control discussed later in this hour) that sits at the bottom of the form in the space reserved for controls without an interface (like a Timer control), yet actually has a visible interface on the form. Start by creating a new Windows Application project named **Menus and More**, and then follow these steps:

1. Change the name of the default form to **fclsMenusAndMore**, set its Text property to **Menus and More**, and change the Startup object of the project to fclsMenusAndMore.

2. Next, add a new Main Menu control to your form by double-clicking the MainMenu item in the toolbox. (Don't worry about changing its name at this time, because you won't be referencing it in code.) As you can see, the control is added to the pane at the bottom of the form designer. Take a look at the top of the form—you'll see the text Type Here (see Figure 9.1).

FIGURE 9.1

A menu has no items when first added to a form.

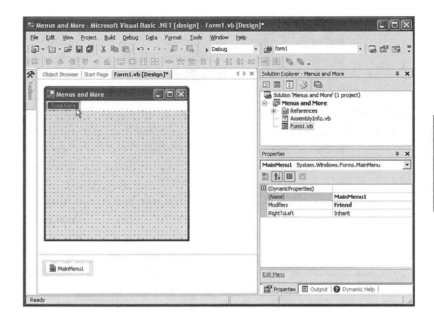

3. Click this text and type **&File**. As you begin typing, Visual Basic displays two new boxes that say Type Here (see Figure 9.2).

FIGURE 9.2

Creating a menu item automatically prepares the control for more items.

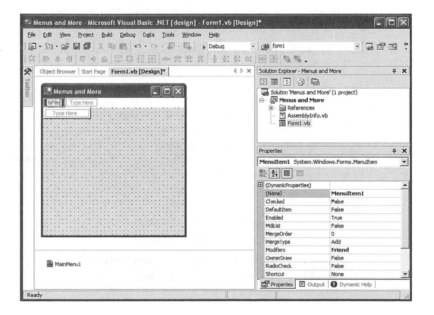

9

Notice the Properties window (if it's not visible, click F4 to show it). The text you just entered created a new menu item. Each menu item is an object, and therefore, the item has properties. MenuItem1 isn't very descriptive, so change the name of the item to **mnuFileMenu**. Notice that you're naming the File item you just created, not changing the name of the Main Menu control.

NEW TERM You might be wondering why I had you enter the ampersand (**&**) in front of the word File. Take a look at your menu now, and you'll see that Visual Basic doesn't display the ampersand; instead, it displays the text with the F underlined, as in File. The ampersand, when used in the Text property of a menu item, tells Visual Basic to underline the character immediately following it. For top-level menu items, such as the File item you just created, this underlined character is known as an *accelerator key*. Pressing Alt + an accelerator key opens the menu as if the user had clicked it. You should avoid assigning the same accelerator key to more than one top-level menu item on a given menu. When the menu item appears on a drop-down menu(as opposed to being a top-level item), the underlined character is called a *hotkey*. When a menu is visible (open), the user can press a hotkey to trigger the corresponding menu item the same as if it were clicked. Again, don't use the same hotkey for more than one item on the same menu.

4. Click the Type Here text that appears to the immediate right of the File item and enter the text **&Help**. Visual Basic gives you two more Type Here items—the same as when you entered the File item. Adding new menu items is a matter of clicking a Type Here box and entering the text for an item.

5. Change the name of your new menu item to **mnuHelpMenu**.

If you click a Type Here box *below* an existing menu item, you'll add a new item to the same menu as the item above the box. If you click the Type Here box to the right of a menu item, you'll create a submenu using the menu to the left of the box as the entry point for the submenu. As you've already seen, clicking the Type Here box along the top of the menu bar creates a top-level menu.

6. Click once more on the File item to display a Type Here box below it. Click this Type Here box and enter the text **&Quit**.

7. Change the name of the new item to **mnuQuit**. Now is a good time to save your work, so click Save All on the toolbar.

Moving and Deleting Menu Items

Deleting and moving menu items are even easier processes than adding new items. To delete a menu item, right-click it and choose Delete from the context menu that appears. To move an item, drag it from its current location and drop it in the location in which you want it placed.

Creating Checked Menu Items

A menu item that isn't used to open a submenu can display a check mark next to its text. Check marks are used to create menu items that have state—the item is either selected or it isn't. You're now going to create a checked menu item. Click the Type Here box below the Quit menu item and enter **Ask Before Closing** and then change the name of this new item to **mnuAskBeforeClosing**. Next, change the Checked property of the new item to True. Notice that the menu item now has a check mark next to it (see Figure 9.3).

FIGURE 9.3

Menu items can be used to indicate state.

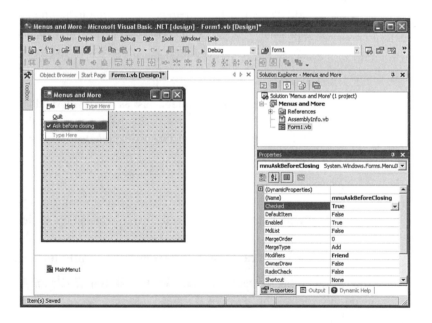

Press F5 to run the project. The menu will appear on your form, just as you designed it (see Figure 9.4). Click the File menu to open it and then click Quit; nothing happens. In fact, the checked state of your menu item doesn't even change. In the next section, I'll show you how to add code to menu items to make them actually do something (as well as change their checked state). Stop the project before continuing.

FIGURE 9.4

What you see (at design time) is what you get (at runtime).

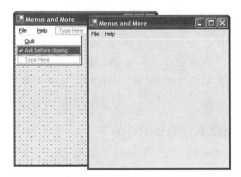

Programming Menus

As I've said before, every menu item is a unique object—that's why you were able to change the name for each item you created. Although individual menu items aren't controls per se, adding code behind them is very similar to adding code behind a control. You're now going to add code to the Exit and Ask Before Closing menu items.

Follow these steps to create the exit code:

1. Click the File menu now to open it.

2. Double-click the Quit menu item. Just as when you double-click a control, Visual Basic displays the code editor with the default event for the menu item you've clicked. For menu items, this is the Click event.

3. Enter the following code:

   ```
   Me.Close()
   ```

   As you know by now, this code closes the current form. This has the effect of stopping the project because this is the only form and it's designated as the Startup object.

4. Switch back to the form designer (click the Form1.vb [Design] tab).

You're now going to create the code for the Ask Before Closing button. This code will invert the Checked property of the menu item; if Checked = True, it will be set to False, and vice versa.

1. Double-click the Ask Before Closing item to access its Click event and enter the following code:

   ```
   mnuAskBeforeClosing.Checked = Not (mnuAskBeforeClosing.Checked)
   ```

   The function Not()is used to perform a negation of a Boolean (true or false) value. Don't worry; I discuss this in detail in Hour 12, "Performing Arithmetic, String

Manipulation, and Date/Time Adjustments." For now, realize that if the current value of the Checked property is True, Not returns False. If Checked is currently False, Not returns True. Therefore, the checked value will toggle between True and False each time the menu item is clicked.

2. Press F5 to run the project. Open the File menu by pressing Alt+F (remember, the F is the accelerator key).

3. Next, click the Ask Before Closing button—it becomes unchecked. Click the menu item once more and it becomes checked again.

4. Click it a third time to remove the check mark, and then click Quit to close the form.

Did you notice that you weren't asked whether you really wanted to quit? That's because the quit code hasn't been written to consider the checked state of the Ask Before Closing button.

Follow these steps to ensure the user is prompted accordingly:

1. Return to the Click event of the Quit button and change its code to look like this:

```
If mnuAskBeforeClosing.Checked Then
    MessageBox.Show("Do you really wish to exit?", "Menus", _
        MessageBoxButtons.YesNo) = DialogResult.No Then
        Exit Sub
    End If
End If
Me.Close()
```

Now when the user selects the Quit button, Visual Basic considers the checked state of the Ask Before Closing menu item. If the item is checked, Visual Basic asks users whether they really want to exit. If a user chooses No, the procedure quits and the form doesn't unload. This code might be a bit foreign to you now, but you'll learn the ins and outs of making decisions (executing code based on conditions) and message boxes in later hours.

2. Press F5 to run the project. Open the File menu, click the Ask Before Closing item to toggle its state. Make sure that it's selected when you're done and then click Quit.

3. This time, Visual Basic asks you to confirm your intentions rather than immediately closing the form. Go ahead and close the form, and then click Save All on the toolbar to save your work.

When designing your menus, look at some of the many popular Windows applications available and consider the similarities and differences between their menus and yours. Although your application might be quite unique and therefore have very different menus from other applications, there are probably similarities as well. When possible, make menu items in your application follow the same structure and design as similar items in the popular programs. This will shorten the learning curve of your application, reduce user frustration, and save you time.

Implementing Context Menus

Context menus are the pop-up menus that appear when you right-click an object on a form. Context menus get their name from the fact that they display context-sensitive choices—menu items that relate directly to the object that's right-clicked. Most Visual Basic controls have a default context menu (also called a *shortcut menu*), but you can assign custom context menus if you desire. Add a new text box to the form and set its properties as follows:

Property	Value
Name	**txtMyTextbox**
Location	**96,122**
Size	**100,20**
Text	*(make blank)*

Press F5 to run the project, and then right-click the text box to display its context menu (see Figure 9.5). This menu is the default context menu for the Text Box control; it's functional but limited. Stop the project now and return to Design view.

FIGURE 9.5

Most items have a default context menu.

Creating context menus is very much like creating regular menus. Context menus, however, are created using a different control: the Context Menu control. Follow these steps to implement a custom context menu in your project:

1. Add a new context menu to the form by double-clicking the ContextMenu item in the toolbox. Like the Main Menu control, the Context Menu control is placed in the pane below the form designer. When the control is selected, a Context Menu item appears at the top of the form. Change its name to **mnuContext**.

2. Clicking the Context Menu box at the top of the form opens the context menu, which is empty by default. Click the Type Here box and enter the text **Clear text box** (see Figure 9.6). You've just created a context menu with a single menu item.

FIGURE 9.6

Context menus are edited much like regular menus.

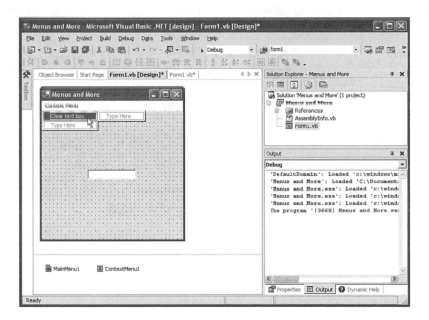

3. Change the name of the new menu item to **mnuClearTextbox**, and then double-click the item to access its Click event.

    Enter the code

    ```
    txtMyTextbox.Text = ""
    ```

4. Linking a control to a context menu is accomplished by setting a property. Display the form designer once more, and then click the Text Box control to select it and display its properties in the Properties window.

5. Change the ContextMenu property of the text box to **mnuContextMenu**; the context menu is now linked to the text box. Press F5 to run the project.

6. Enter some text into the text box and then right-click the text box; your custom context menu appears in place of the default context menu.

7. Choose Clear Text Box from the context menu, and the contents of the text box will clear. Stop the project and save your work.

Assigning Shortcut Keys

If you've spent any time learning a Microsoft application, you've most likely learned some keyboard shortcuts. For instance, pressing Alt+P in any application that prints has the same effect as opening the File menu and choosing Print. You can add the same type of shortcuts to your menus by following these steps:

1. Click the Main Menu control at the bottom of the form designer, click File on its menu, and then click Quit to select the Quit menu item.

2. Next, click the Shortcut property in the Properties window and then click the down arrow that appears. This list contains all the shortcut keys that can be assigned to a menu item.

3. Locate and select CtrlQ (for Quit) in the list (see Figure 9.7).

FIGURE 9.7

A shortcut key is assigned using the Shortcut property of a menu item.

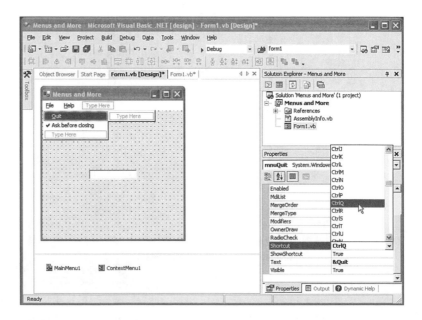

4. Press F5 to run the project once more. Next, press Ctrl+Q, and the application will behave just as though you opened the File menu and clicked the Quit item.

Although it isn't always possible, try to assign logical shortcut key combinations. The meaning of F6 is hardly intuitive, for example. But, when assigning modifiers such as Ctrl with another character, you have some flexibility. For instance, the key combination of Ctrl+Q might be a more intuitive shortcut key for Quit than Ctrl+T.

9

Using the Toolbar Control

Generally speaking, when a program has a menu (as most programs should), it should also have a toolbar. Toolbars are one of the easiest ways for a user to access program functions. Unlike menu items, toolbar items are always visible and therefore immediately available. In addition, toolbar items have ToolTips, which enable a user to discover a tool button's purpose simply by hovering the pointer over the button.

Toolbar items are really shortcuts for menu items; every item on a toolbar should have a corresponding menu item. Remember that some users prefer to use the keyboard, in which case they need to have keyboard access to functions via menus.

The actual items you place on a toolbar will depend on the features supported by the application. However, the mechanics of creating toolbars and toolbar items is the same regardless of the buttons you choose to use. Toolbars are created using the Toolbar control.

1. Add a new Toolbar control to your form now by double-clicking the ToolBar item in the toolbox. A new toolbar is then added to the top of your form (see Figure 9.8). Change the name of the toolbar to **tbrMainToolbar**.

   Every toolbar you've used displays pictures on buttons. The Toolbar control gets the pictures for its buttons from an Image List control.

2. Go ahead and add an Image List control to the form now and change its name to **imgMyPictures**.

3. Add a new 16×16 pixel bitmap to the Images collection of the Image List control. You can use a picture you created or use one from the samples I've made available on the Web site.

4. When you're finished adding the new button, close the Image Collection Editor and select the Toolbar control on the form.

5. Set the ImageList property of the toolbar to use the image list you've just created.

FIGURE 9.8

*New toolbars default
to the top of the form
and have no buttons.*

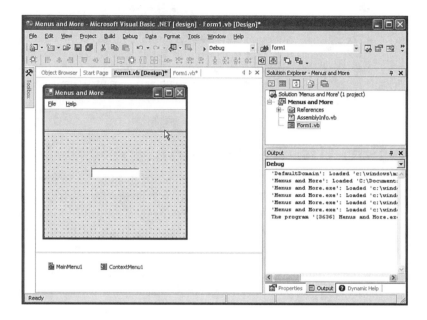

Adding Toolbar Buttons Using the Buttons Collection

Like many other controls you've already learned about, the Toolbar control supports a
special collection: the Buttons collection. The Buttons collection contains the buttons
that appear on the toolbar (ooh, tricky). Click the Buttons property in the Properties window, and then click the small button that appears; the ToolBarButton Collection Editor
displays. The list of button members is empty because new toolbars have no buttons.
Click Add to create a new button, and set its properties as follows:

Property	Value
Name	**tbbQuit**
ImageIndex	**0**
Text	**Quit**
ToolTipText	**Quit this application**

Click OK to close the ToolBarButton Collection Editor. Your new button is now visible
on the toolbar. As you can see, text appears below the picture in the button, but this is *not*
how most toolbars appear. Not a problem—access the Buttons collection once more and
clear the Text property of the button.

Programming Toolbars

Unlike menus, where each menu item receives its own Click event, the Toolbar control has one common Click event that fires when the user clicks any button on the toolbar. Double-click the Toolbar control on the form to access the toolbar's ButtonClick event (close the button editor first if it's open). Enter the following code:

```
If e.Button Is tbbQuit Then
   Me.Close()
End If
```

The Button property of the e object is an object property that holds a reference to the button that's clicked. (The e object is discussed in detail in Hour 10, "Creating and Calling Code Procedures.") This code uses an If statement to determine whether the clicked button is the Quit button. If the Quit button was clicked, the form closes. (Decision-making constructs such as If...Then and Select...Case are discussed in Hour 13, "Making Decisions in Visual Basic Code.")

Go ahead and Press F5 and run your project. Clicking the Close button should then close your application.

Creating Toggle Buttons

The button that you've created for your toolbar is a standard pushbutton. When the user clicks it with the mouse, the button will appear to be pressed while the user holds down the mouse button and will return to a normal state when the user releases the mouse button. Although this is the style you'll use for most of your toolbar buttons, the Toolbar control supports other styles as well. One such style is the toggle button. A toggle button, much like the check mark of a menu item, is used to denote state. When a toggle button is clicked, it appears in a pressed state and stays that way until clicked once more, in which case it returns to its normal appearance. Microsoft Word has a number of such buttons. The paragraph alignment buttons, for example, are all toggle buttons—the button that corresponds to the current paragraph's alignment appears pressed.

Add a new button to your toolbar now and set its properties as follows:

Property	Value
Name	**tbbInvisible**
Text	**Invisible**
Style	**ToggleButton**

Next, click OK to close the editor and the new button will appear on the toolbar. Take note that you didn't have to designate a picture for the toolbar item (but you usually should). Because you don't want the toolbar's height to be larger than necessary, change the TextAlign property of the Toolbar control to Right. Your toolbar should now look like the one in Figure 9.9.

FIGURE 9.9

Toolbar items can display a picture, text, or a combination of both.

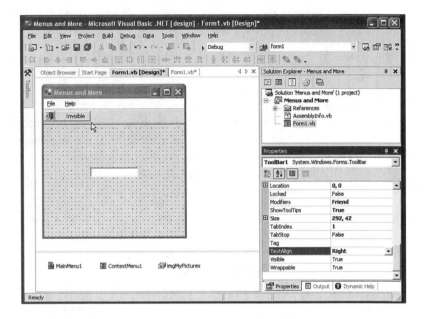

Again, double-click the toolbar to access its ButtonClick event. Now that there are two buttons, the simple If...Then statement is no longer suited to determining the button pushed. Change the code in your procedure to match the following:

```
If e.Button Is tbbQuit Then
    Me.Close()

ElseIf e.Button Is tbbInvisible Then
    txtMyTextbox.Visible = Not (tbbInvisible.Pushed)

End If
```

This code is a bit more complex than the previous code. The ElseIf statement is evaluated if the first If statement is False. In this case, only if e.Button is not the Quit button. The new statement that you're interested in here is where the Visible property of the text box is set. Remember, the Not function negates a value. Therefore, this statement sets the Visible property of the text box to the negation of the pushed state of the tbbInvisible button. In other words, when the button is pushed, the text box is hidden, and when the button is not pushed (depressed), the text box is visible.

Press F5 to run the project now and notice that the text box is visible. Click the Invisible button on the toolbar and note that its appearance changes to a pushed state and the text box becomes hidden (see Figure 9.10). Click the button once more to return the button's state to normal, and the text box reappears. When you're finished, stop the project and save your work.

FIGURE 9.10

Toggle-style buttons appear "pressed" when clicked.

9

Creating Separators

As you add more buttons to a toolbar, it becomes evident that you need a way to logically group them. Placing related buttons next to one another is a great start toward building a good toolbar. However, a toolbar can be a bit difficult to use even if its buttons are placed in a logical order, unless the buttons are separated into groups. Placing a space between sets of related buttons creates button groups. You're now going to add a separator space to your toolbar.

Add a new button to your toolbar using the Buttons collection in the Properties window. Change its name to tbbSeparator1 and change its Style to Separator. When you change the Style property of the button to Separator, it disappears from the toolbar (or at least it seems to). When a button is designated as a separator, it's simply an empty placeholder used to create a space between two buttons. Because this separator is at the end row of buttons, you can't see it. Move it to the second position by selecting it in the ToolBarButton Collection Editor and clicking the up arrow that appears to the right of the Members list; this arrow and the one below it are used to move a button up or down in the list. Click OK to save your changes and your toolbar will now have a space between the two buttons (see Figure 9.11).

FIGURE 9.11

Separators are used to create spaces between groups of buttons.

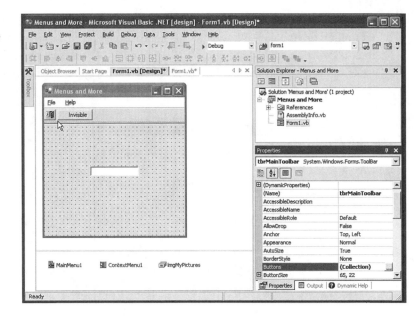

Creating Drop-Down Menus for Toolbar Buttons

You need to be familiar with one last type of toolbar button. Follow these steps:

1. Create a new button using the Buttons collection in the Properties window and set its name to **tbbDropdown**.

2. Set the button's Style property to DropDownButton.

3. Finally, set the DropDownMenu property to mnuContext and click OK to commit your changes.

Notice how the button has a drop-down arrow on it. Press F5 to run the project and click the drop-down arrow; the menu that you designated in the DropDownMenu property appears (see Figure 9.12). As you can see, the DropDownMenu property makes it easy to integrate drop-down menus with your toolbars.

FIGURE 9.12

Toolbar buttons can be used to display drop-down menus.

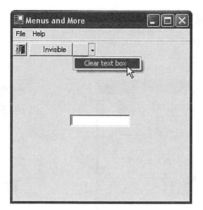

Creating a Status Bar

The last control I'm going to show you is the Status Bar control. The status bar isn't nearly as fancy, or even as useful, as other controls such as the Toolbar or the Main Menu (but it's also not as difficult to work with). Nevertheless, a status bar adds value to an application in that it makes available information, and users have come to expect it. In its simplest form, a status bar displays a text caption and *sizing grip*—the three diagonal lines to the right of the control that the user can drag with the mouse to change the size of the form.

Add a new status bar to the form now by double-clicking the StatusBar item in the toolbox. Change the name of the status bar to **sbrMyStatusBar**. The Text property determines the text displayed in the left side of the status bar. Notice that the Text is set to the default name of the control. Change the Text property to **Menus and Toolbars Example** and notice how the text in the status bar changes (see Figure 9.13).

If a form's border is sizable, the user can click and drag the sizing grip at the right side of the status bar to change the size of the form. The status bar isn't smart enough to realize when a form's border can't be resized; you'll have to change the SizingGrip property of the status bar to False to hide the grip.

The default behavior of the status bar is quite simple, consisting of text and a sizing grip. However, you can create more complex status bars using this control.

The Status Bar control contains a Panels collection. To see how a panel works, follow these steps:

1. Select the Panels property in the Properties window and click the small button that appears.

FIGURE 9.13

Status bars dress out a form.

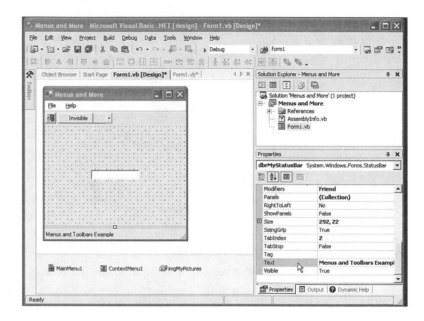

2. On the StatusBarPanel Collection Editor, click Add to create a new panel and set the Text of the panel to **Panel Text**.

3. Set the AutoSize property to Contents, and click OK to save your changes.

Nothing looks different, right? This is because one last thing is required to display the status bar panels. Change the ShowPanels property of the status bar to True now, and the status bar will display its panel (see Figure 9.14). You can add multiple panels to a Status Bar control, and even tailor the appearance of each panel by changing the border style or displaying an image from a linked Image List control. The Status Bar is such a simple control that you might overlook using it. However, I encourage you to use it when appropriate.

FIGURE 9.14

Status bars can display custom panels.

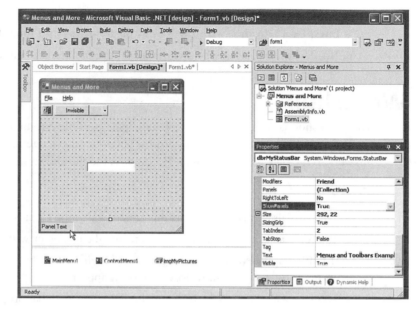

Summary

Menus, toolbars, and status bars add tremendous value to an application by greatly enhancing its usability. In this hour, you learned how to use the Main Menu control to build comprehensive menus for your applications. You learned how to add, move, and delete menu items and how to define accelerator and shortcut keys to facilitate better navigation via the keyboard. You also saw how toolbars provide shortcuts for accessing common menu items. You learned how to use the Toolbar control to create functional toolbars complete with bitmaps, drop-downs, and logical groupings. Finally, you discovered how to use a status bar to dress up the application. Implementing these items is an important part of the interface design process for an application, and you now have the skills necessary to start putting them into your own programs.

Q&A

Q I have a number of forms with nearly identical menus. Do I really need to take the time to create menus for all these forms?

A Not as much as you think. Create a Main Menu control that has the common items on it, and then copy and paste the control to other forms. You can then build on this menu structure, saving you a lot of time.

Q **I've seen applications that allow the end user to customize the menus and tool-bars. Can I do that with the Visual Basic menus and toolbars?**

A No. To accomplish this behavior, you'll have to purchase a third-party component.

Workshop

The Workshop is designed to help you anticipate possible questions, review what you've learned, and get you thinking about how to put your knowledge into practice. The answers to the quiz are in Appendix B, "Answers to the Quizzes."

Quiz

1. True or False: Form menu bars are created using the Context Menu control.

2. To create an accelerator, or hotkey, preface the character with a(n):

3. If you've designed a menu using a Main Menu control, but that menu isn't visible on the form designer, how do you make it appear?

4. To place a check mark next to a menu item, you set what property of the item?

5. How do you add code to a menu item?

6. Toolbar items are part of what collection?

7. To create a separator on a toolbar, you create a new button and set what property?

8. True or False: Every button on a toolbar has its own Click event.

9. What must you do to have panels appear on a status bar?

Exercises

1. Modify the code you created for the toolbar that closes the form to take into consideration the checked status of the Ask Before Closing menu item.

2. Implement a toggle button that works just like the Ask Before Closing menu item.

PART III

Making Things Happen—Programming

Hour

10 Creating and Calling Code Procedures

11 Using Constants, Data Types, Variables, and Arrays

12 Performing Arithmetic, String Manipulation, and Date/Time Adjustments

13 Making Decisions in Visual Basic Code

14 Looping for Efficiency

15 Debugging Your Code

16 Designing Objects Using Classes

17 Interacting with Users

18 Working with Graphics

HOUR 10

Creating and Calling Code Procedures

You've now spent about 9 hours building the basic skills necessary to navigate Visual Basic .NET and to create an application interface. Creating a good interface is extremely important, but it's only one step toward creating a Windows program. After you've created the basic interface of an application, you need to enable the program to do something. The program might perform an action all on its own, or it might perform actions based on a user interacting with the interface—either way, you write Visual Basic code to make your application perform tasks. In this hour, you'll learn how to create sets of code (called *modules*), how to create isolated code routines that can be executed (called *procedures*), and how to invoke procedures.

The highlights of this hour include

- Creating Visual Basic code modules
- Creating code procedures
- Calling procedures
- Exiting procedures

- Passing parameters
- Using Sub Main
- Avoiding recursive procedures
- Working with tasks

Creating Visual Basic Code Modules

NEW TERM A *module* is a place to store the code you write. Before you can begin writing
Visual Basic code, you must start with a module. You've already worked with
one type of module: a *class module* used to create a form (refer to Hour 5, "Building
Forms—The Basics," for more information). When you double-click an object on a form,
you access events that reside in the form's class module. In addition to class modules,
you can create *standard modules*. Code written in standard modules is always available;
it's not necessary to instantiate an object derived from the module to access the code. As
a matter of fact, you *can't* create an object based on a standard module.

> Class modules are used as templates for the instantiation of objects. I discuss
> the specifics of creating such objects in Hour 16, "Designing Objects Using
> Classes." Most of the techniques discussed in this hour apply to class mod-
> ules, but I'm going to focus this discussion on standard modules because
> they're easier to use.

Although you could place all your program's code in a single standard module or even in
a class module, it's best to create different modules to group related sets of code. In addition, it's best not to place code that isn't specifically related to a form within a form's
class module; place such code in a standard module or, preferably, in a specialized class
module.

> The current development trend centers on object-oriented programming
> (OOP), which revolves around class modules. I'll give you a primer on OOP in
> Hour 16, but it's a very advanced topic, so I don't cover it in detail. I highly
> recommend that you read a dedicated object-oriented programming book,
> such as *Sams Teach Yourself Object-Oriented Programming with Visual Basic
> .NET in 21 Days*, after you're comfortable with the material in this book.

The primary general rule for using standard modules is that you should create modules to group related sets of code. This isn't to say you should create dozens of modules. Rather, group related functions into a reasonably sized set of modules. For instance, you might want to create one module that contains all your printing routines and another that holds your data-access routines. In addition, I like to create a general-purpose module in which to place all the various routines that don't necessarily fit in more specialized modules.

> In general, it's preferable to create classes and instantiate objects rather than use standard modules, but no rules are set in stone. Some OOP purists suggest (strongly) that you never use a standard module. Remember that a standard module is simply a tool, and all tools have a purpose.

10

Start Visual Basic now and create a new Windows Application project named **Modules And Procedures**.

Rename the default form **fclsMain**, set its Text property to **Module Example**, and set the Startup object to fclsMain. Next, create a new standard module by choosing Add Module from the Project menu. Visual Basic then displays the Add New Item dialog box, as shown in Figure 10.1.

FIGURE 10.1

All new project items are added using this dialog box.

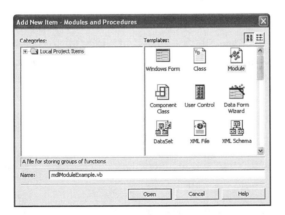

Note that this is the same dialog box used to add new forms. Visual Basic knows that you want to add a module, so the Module icon is selected for you. Change the name of the module to **mdlModuleExample.vb** and click Open to create the new module. Visual Basic creates the new module and positions you in the code window—ready to enter code (see Figure 10.2).

FIGURE 10.2

Modules have no graphical interface, so you always work with modules in the code editor.

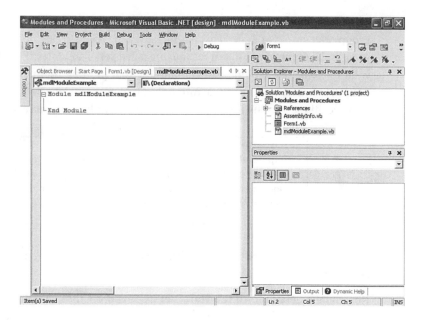

Save your project now by clicking Save All on the toolbar.

Writing Code Procedures

NEW TERM   After you've created the module(s) in which to store your code, you can begin to write Visual Basic .NET code procedures. A *procedure* is a discrete set of code that can be called from other code. Procedures are much like events, but rather than being executed by a user interacting with a form or control, procedures are executed when called by a code statement.

There are two types of procedures in Visual Basic:

- Procedures that return a value (called *functions*)
- Procedures that do not return a value

There are many reasons to create a procedure that returns a value. A function can return True or False, for example, depending on whether it was successful in completing its task. You could also write a procedure that accepts certain parameters (data passed to the procedure, in contrast to data returned by the procedure) and returns a value based on those parameters. For instance, you could write a procedure that enables you pass it a sentence, and in return it passes back the number of spaces within the sentence. The possibilities are limited only by your imagination. Just keep in mind that a procedure doesn't *have* to return a value.

Declaring Procedures That Don't Return Values

To create a procedure, whether it be a Sub (a procedure that doesn't return a value) or a Function (a procedure that returns a value), you first declare it within a module. In your new module, type the following and press the Enter key:

```
Public Sub TellTheUser(ByVal strMessage As String)
```

When you press Enter, Visual Basic automatically inserts a blank line and creates the text End Sub—you've just created a new procedure!

The declaration of a procedure (the statement used to define a procedure) has a number of parts. The first word, Public in this case, is a *keyword* (that is, a word with a special meaning in Visual Basic). Public defines the scope of this procedure (scope is discussed in detail in the next hour). Public designates that the procedure can be called from code contained in modules other than the one containing the defined procedure. You can use the keyword Private in place of Public to restrict access to the procedure only to code in the module in which the procedure resides.

The scope designator is optional, and if omitted, creates a Public procedure. You should always explicitly designate the scope of your procedures.

The word Sub (short for *subroutine*) is another Visual Basic keyword. Sub is used to declare a procedure that doesn't return a value. Later in this hour, you'll learn how to create procedures that return values.

The third word, TellTheUser, is the name of the procedure and can be just about any string of text you want it to be. Note, however, that you can't assign a name that's a keyword, nor can you use spaces within a name. In the example you're building, the procedure will simply display a specified message to the user, so we use the name TellTheUser. You should always give procedures strong names that reflect their purpose. You can have two procedures with the same name only if they have different scope (also discussed in the next hour).

Some programmers prefer the readability of spaces in names, but in many instances, such as when naming procedures, spaces can't be used. A common technique is to use an underscore (_) in place of a space, such as in Tell_The_User, but I recommend that you just use mixed case, as you have in this example.

10

NEW TERM Immediately following the name of the procedure is a set of parentheses surrounding some text. Within these parentheses you can define *parameters*— data to be passed to the procedure by the calling code. In this example, you've created a parameter that accepts a string of text. This routine will then display the text to the user.

> You must always supply parentheses, even when a procedure doesn't accept any parameters (in which case nothing is placed between the parentheses).

Add the following code to your TellTheUser procedure:

```
MessageBox.Show(strMessage, "Module Example", MessageBoxButtons.OK, _
                MessageBoxIcon.Information)
```

All this procedure does is use the MessageBox.Show method to display the text passed to it. I've kept this example simply so that you can focus on the mechanics of the procedure, rather than the sample code within the procedure. When you've finished entering your code, it should look like that in Figure 10.3.

FIGURE 10.3

All code for a procedure must reside between the procedure declaration and its corresponding End statement.

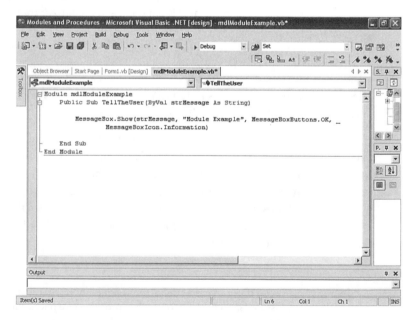

Declaring Procedures That Return Values

NEW TERM The procedure you've just created doesn't return a value. You're now going to declare a *function*—a procedure that returns a value. Here's the general syntax of a function declaration:

```
Public/Private Function functionname(parameters) As datatype
```

You'll notice two key differences between declaring a procedure that doesn't return a value and declaring one that does. First, you use the keyword Function in place of the keyword Sub. Second, you add additional text to the right of the parentheses. When declaring a function, you'll always enter two words to the right of the parentheses. The first word is always As, and the second word is a data type. Data types are discussed in detail in the next hour, so it's not important that you fully understand them now. It's important, however, that you understand what's happening.

As I've stated, functions return values. The data type entered after As denotes the type of data returned by the function. The function that you're about to enter returns a numeric value of type Integer. If the function were to return a string of text, it would be declared As String. It's very important that you declare the proper data type for your functions.

Position the cursor at the end of new End Sub statement and press Enter twice to create two blank lines. Enter the following procedure declaration:

```
Public Function ComputeLength(ByVal strText As String) As Integer
```

Note that Visual Basic created an End statement for you again, but this time the statement is End Function rather than End Sub. This behavior keeps the End statements consistent with their corresponding declaration statements. Add the following code to the new function:

```
Return strText.Length
```

The keyword Return accomplishes two tasks. First, it causes the procedure to immediately terminate—no further code is executed in the procedure. Second, it passes back as the return value whatever value you specify. In this example, you're returning the number of characters in the supplied string. Your module should now look like the one in Figure 10.4.

10

FIGURE **10.4**

*Modules often contain
many procedures.*

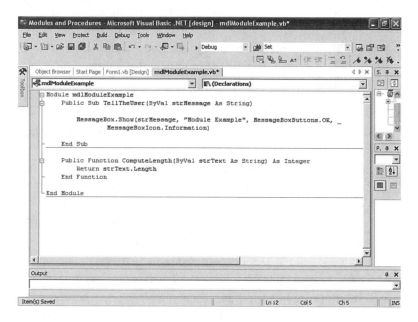

Creating the User Interface of Your Project

Now that you've written the procedures for this example, you now need to create the
interface for the project. Click the Form1.vb [Design] tab in the integrated development
environment (IDE) to display the form designer for the default form.

You'll need two buttons on this form—one to call each of your procedures. Add the first
button to the form by double-clicking the Button icon in the toolbox and then set its
properties as follows:

Property	*Value*
Name	**btnTellTheUser**
Location	**96,104**
Size	**96,23**
Text	**Tell The User**

Add a second button to the form and set its properties as follows:

Property	*Value*
Name	**btnComputeLength**
Location	**96,136**
Size	**96,23**
Text	**Compute Length**

The last control you need to add to your form is a text box. When the user clicks either of the two buttons, the contents of the text box will be passed to the associated procedure.

Add a text box to the form by double-clicking the Textbox icon in the toolbox. Set the new text box's properties as follows:

Property	Value
Name	**txtUserInput**
Location	**88,72**
Size	**112,20**
Text	*(make blank)*

Your form should now look like the one shown in Figure 10.5. You're now ready to write the Visual Basic code to call your procedures.

FIGURE 10.5

Not all that attractive, but functional enough for our purposes.

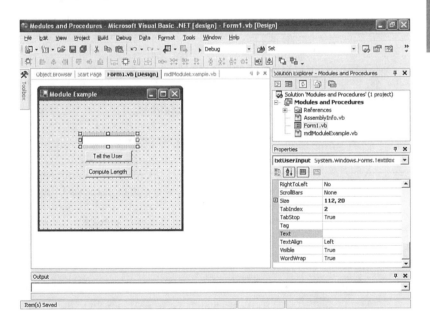

Calling Code Procedures

Calling a procedure is fairly simple. You're first going to write code to call the procedures you as *Sub* (a procedure that doesn't return a value). Double-click the Tell The User button to access its Click event and take a look at the event declaration:

```
Private Sub btnTellTheUser_Click(ByVal sender As System.Object, _
                        ByVal e As System.EventArgs) _
                        Handles btnDrawEllipse.Click
```

As you can see, events are procedures. The only real difference is that event procedures are called automatically in response to the user doing something, rather than being called by code you write. In this case, the btnTellTheUser_Click event is called when the user clicks the btnTellTheUser button. This procedure is declared as Private, so only procedures within this module can call this procedure (yes, you can call event procedures). Add the following statement to this Click event:

```
Call TellTheUser(txtUserInput.Text)
```

The Call keyword tells Visual Basic that you want to invoke a procedure that doesn't return a value (declared using Sub).

The procedure name and parentheses always follow the Call statement. If the procedure expects one or more parameters, place them within the parentheses. In this case, the DrawEllipse procedure expects a reference to a form. By specifying the keyword Me, you're passing a reference to the current form.

Using Call is a very common way of calling Sub procedures, but the proper .NET way leaves off the Call statement like this:

```
TellTheUser(txtUserInput.Text)
```

Go ahead and remove the word Call from you statement now. Visual Basic .NET won't complain because the word Call is optional.

> When you type in the name of a valid procedure and then the left paren-
> thesis, Visual Basic displays a small ToolTip showing the parameters expected
> by the procedure (see Figure 10.6). It can be difficult to remember the para-
> meters expected by all procedures (not to mention the proper order in
> which to pass them), so this little feature will save you a great deal of time
> and frustration.

All that's left to do is add code that computes the length of the string entered by the user. Again, display the form in Design view. Double-click the Compute Length button to access its Click event and enter the following statements:

```
MessageBox.Show(ComputeLength(txtUserInput.Text), _
                "Modules Example", MessageBoxButtons.OK, _
                MessageBoxIcon.Information)
```

The statement in this procedure illustrates how you can integrate a function call within another statement. When calling a function, think of the function in terms of the value it returns. For example, when you set a form's Height property, you set it with code like this:

```
MyForm.Height = 200
```

FIGURE 10.6

Visual Basic displays the parameters expected of a procedure when using the Call statement.

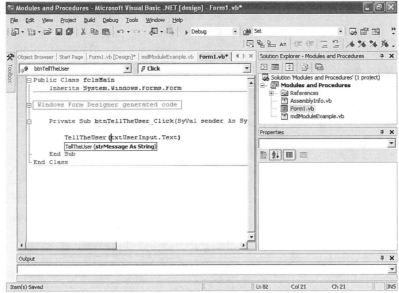

This statement sets a form's height to 200. Suppose that you have a procedure that returns a value that you want to use to set the form's Height property. Thinking of the procedure in terms of the value it returns, you could replace the literal value with the function, like the following:

```
MyForm.Height = MyProcedure()
```

Try to look at the statement you entered using this way of thinking. As you know by now, MessageBox.Show displays a message to the user. You also know that the function returns a number: the number of characters in the text entered by the user. When Visual Basic .NET executes this code, it calls the function, gets the return value, and then displays it to the user in a MessageBox.

> When calling function procedures, you must treat the function call as you would treat the literal value returned by the function. This often means placing a function call on the right side of an equal sign or embedding it in an expression.

The project is now complete. Click Save All on the toolbar to save your work, and then press F5 to run the project. Enter some text into the text box and click the Tell The User button and a message box will appear (see Figure 10.7).

FIGURE 10.7
*Clicking the button
calls the function that
displays the message
in the house that Jack
built.*

Here's what is happening when you click the Tell The User button:

1. The Tell The User button's Click event is triggered.
2. The statement within the Click event is executed.
3. Code execution jumps to the TellTheUser procedure.
4. The code within the TellTheUser procedure gets executed.
5. Execution returns to the Click event.

Click the Compute Length button now to display the number of characters in your text. Here's what happens:

1. The Compute Length button's Click event is triggered.
2. The reference to the ComputeLength function causes code execution to jump to that function.
3. The ComputeLength function determines the length of the string. This value is passed back (returned) as the result of the function.
4. Execution returns to the Click event.
5. The result of the function is displayed in the MessageBox (see Figure 10.8).

FIGURE 10.8
*debug.WriteLine()
sends text to the
Output window.*

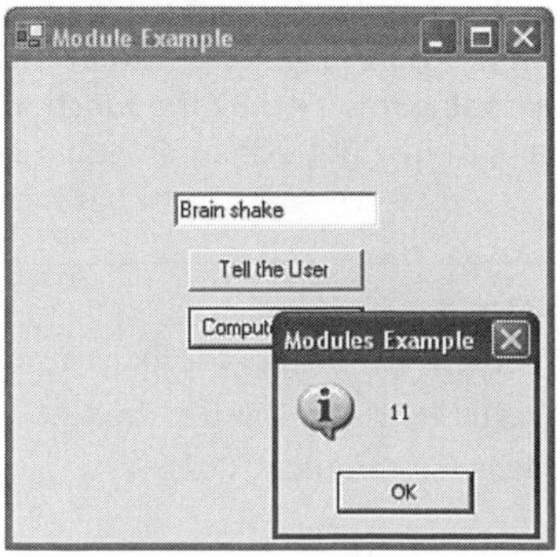

Passing Parameters

Parameters are used within a procedure to allow the calling code to pass data into the procedure. You've already seen how parameters work—parameters are created within the parentheses of a procedure declaration. A parameter definition consists of a name for the parameter, the word As, and a data type, as shown here:

```
Public Sub MyProcedure(strMyStringParameter As String)
```

> After you've read about variables in Hour 11, "Using Constants, Data Types, Variables, and Arrays," this structure will make much more sense. Here, I just want you to get the general idea of how to define and use parameters.

You can define multiple parameters for a procedure by separating them with a comma, like this:

```
Public Sub MyProcedure(strMyStringParameter As String, _
                       intMyIntegerParameter as Integer)
```

New Term A calling procedure passes data to the parameters by way of *arguments*. This is mostly a semantic issue; when defined in the declaration of a procedure, the item is called a *parameter*. When the item is part of the statement that calls the procedure, it's called an *argument*. Arguments are passed within parentheses—the same as how parameters are defined. If a procedure has multiple arguments, you separate them with commas. For example, you could pass values to the procedure just defined using a statement such as this:

```
Call MyProcedure("This is a string", 11)
```

The parameter acts like an ordinary variable within the procedure. Remember, variables are storage entities whose values can be changed. In the Call statement shown previously, we sent literal values to the procedure. We could have also sent the values of variables like this:

```
Call MyProcedure(strAString, intAnInteger)
```

New Term An important thing to note about passing variables in Visual Basic .NET is that parameters are passed *by value* rather than *by reference*. When passed by value, the procedure receives a copy of the data. Changes to the parameter don't affect the value of the original variable. When passed by reference, the parameter is actually a pointer to the original variable. Changes made to the parameter within the procedure propagate to the original variable. To pass a parameter by reference, you preface the parameter definition with the keyword ByRef as shown here:

```
Public Sub MyProcedure(ByRef strMyStringParameter As String, _
                       intMyIntegerParameter as Integer)
```

Parameters defined without ByRef are passed by value—this is the default behavior of parameters in Visual Basic .NET. Therefore, in this declaration, the first parameter is passed by reference, whereas the second parameter is passed by value.

> The default behavior in previous versions of Visual Basic was that parameters were passed by reference, not by value. To pass a parameter by value, you had to preface the parameter definition with ByVal.

Exiting Procedures

Code within a procedure ordinarily executes from beginning to end—literally. When an End Sub or End Function statement is reached, execution returns to the statement that made the procedure call. You can force execution to leave the procedure at any time by using an Exit Sub or Exit Function statement. Obviously, you use Exit Sub in procedures declared with the keyword Sub, and you use Exit Function in procedures declared with the keyword Function. If Visual Basic encounters such an exit statement, the procedure terminates immediately, and code returns to the statement that called the procedure.

Avoiding Infinite Recursion

It's possible to call procedures in such a way that a continuous loop occurs. Consider the following two procedures:

```
Public Sub DoSomething()
   Call DoSomethingElse()
End Function

Public Sub DoSomethingElse()
   Call DoSomething()
End Function
```

Calling either of these procedures produces an infinite loop of procedure calls and results in the error shown in Figure 10.9.

FIGURE **10.9**

Infinite recursion results in a stack overflow exception (error).

NEW TERM This endless loop is known as a *recursive* loop. Without getting too technical, Visual Basic .NET allocates some memory for each procedure call in an area known as the stack. Only a finite amount of space is on the stack, so infinite recursion eventually uses all the available stack space and an exception occurs. This is a serious error, and steps should be taken to avoid such recursion.

Legitimate uses exist for recursion, most notably in the use of algorithms such as those used in calculus. Deliberate recursion techniques don't create infinite recursion, however; there is always a point at which the recursion stops (hopefully, before the stack is consumed). If you have an interest in such algorithms, you should consider reading a book dedicated to the subject.

Using Sub Main

Although you haven't used the technique so far in this book, it's possible to use a code procedure rather than a form as an entry point to an application. In Hour 5, you learned how to designate a form as the startup object for a project. When a form is designated as the Startup object, it's the first thing loaded when the project runs. There will be times when you'd rather not load a form at startup, and some situations might occur in which you have no forms at all within a project. Visual Basic has a provision for this, enabling you to specify a procedure within a standard module as the entry point for an application.

To use a code procedure as the entry point of a project, you must follow two steps:

1. Change the Startup Object property of the project. To display the Project Properties dialog box (see Figure 10.10), right-click the project's name in the Solution Explorer and choose Properties from the context menu.

    The Startup Object drop-down list contains a list of all the forms in the project. In addition, the list contains an item titled Sub Main. Select this item to specify a code procedure as the entry point.

FIGURE **10.10**

The Startup Object property determines the entry point of the project.

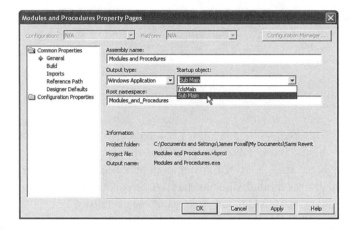

2. Create the procedure that will serve as the entry point to the project (that is, the Sub Main procedure). As you might expect, the entry point has to be a Sub procedure titled Main. Realize that Visual Basic doesn't create this procedure for you, however. You must create a Sub procedure titled Main in a standard module (not a class module), and this procedure can't have any parameters. Because of these restrictions, all Sub Main procedures look like this:

```
Public Sub Main()
End Sub
```

If you designate Sub Main as your Startup object but don't actually *create* a Sub procedure titled Main in a standard module, Visual Basic returns a build error. Whether or not you choose a form as the Startup object of a project or specify a Sub Main procedure depends entirely on the situation, as well as on your programming style. Personally, I like to use Sub Main because it gives me an easy-to-find starting point. I use Sub Main to set up conditions (load user preferences and so forth) and display any necessary forms—remember that you can use the techniques in Hour 5 to display a form in Sub Main, if you choose.

Working with Tasks

One of the most exciting IDE enhancements in Visual Basic .NET (in my opinion) is the new Task List. Tasks are really all about managing code. If your Task List window isn't displayed, show it now by choosing Show Tasks from the View menu and then choosing All. Tasks are used to keep track of critical spots in code or things that need to be done. Visual Basic automatically creates some tasks for you, and you can create your own as needed.

One instance in which Visual Basic creates tasks is when your code has compile (build) errors. Because Visual Basic knows the exact error and the offending statement, it creates an appropriate task. Figure 10.11 shows the Task List containing a build error. Notice how the task's description tells you the exact problem. Double-clicking a system-generated task takes you directly to the related statement (double-clicking a task that you created has a different effect, as we'll discuss shortly). If the task exists in a module that isn't loaded, Visual Basic loads the module and then takes you to the statement. This greatly simplifies the process of addressing compile errors in code; you can simply work through the list of tasks rather than compiling, fixing an error, compiling again, fixing the next error, and so on.

FIGURE 10.11

Tasks help you keep track of critical spots in code.

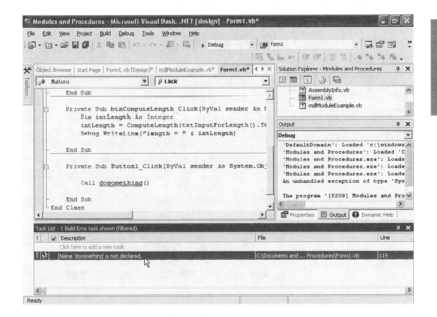

In addition to system-generated tasks, you can create your own tasks as often and wherever needed. In the past, it was common to place certain comments such as TODO: in code where you needed to come back and address something. When you wanted to address the issues, you had to perform a text search in your code. This was a highly inefficient process. Unfortunately, these comments were often missed or just plain forgotten.

Now you can create a task wherever you need to. Creating a task is easy. Ironically, the menu item used to create tasks has changed since the first edition of Visual Basic .NET (it was easier to get to before). Now, to create a task for a specific code statement you follow these steps:

1. Click anywhere on the code statement so the insertion point is on the code line.
2. Open the Edit menu, and then open the Bookmarks submenu.
3. Choose Add Task List Shortcut from the Bookmarks submenu.

Visual Basic creates a task shortcut at the statement (as indicated by a blue arrow in the left margin of the code window) and adds the task to the Task List window. The default description for the next task is the actual code statement you flagged (see Figure 10.12). To change this text, click the description in the Task List to put it in Edit mode and then change the text. To go directly to the statement to which a task is attached, double-click the shortcut arrow next to the task in the Task List (the arrow is the same one that appears in the left margin of the code window) .

FIGURE 10.12

Tasks make it easy to track issues that need to be addressed.

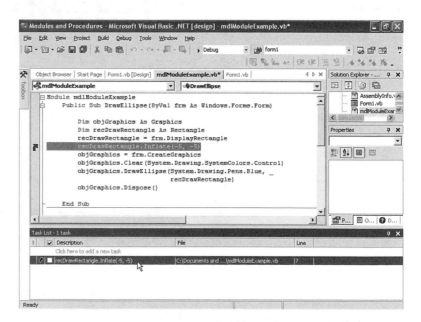

You don't have to attach a task to a code statement. To create a task that isn't attached to code, click the first row of the Task List. The default text Click here to add a new task goes away, and you're free to enter the description of your new task.

To delete a task you've created, click once on the task in the Task List to select it and then right-click the task and choose Delete from the context menu. You can't delete a task created by Visual Basic as a result of a build error—you must correct the error to make the task go away.

Tasks are an incredibly simple yet useful tool. I highly encourage you to use them in your development.

Summary

In this hour, you learned how a procedure is a discrete set of code designed to perform a task or related set of tasks. Procedures are where you write Visual Basic code. Some procedures might be as short as a single line of code, whereas others will be pages in length. You learned how to define procedures and how to call them; creating and calling procedures is critical to your success in programming with Visual Basic. Be sure to avoid creating recursive procedures! Because you use procedures so often, they'll become second nature to you in no time.

Keep in mind that every procedure should perform a specific function; you should avoid creating procedures that perform many different tasks. For example, suppose that you want to create a set of code that draws an ellipse on a form. Consider you also want to clear the form. If you placed both sets of code in the same procedure, the ellipse would be drawn and then immediately erased. By placing each set of code in its own procedure, you can draw the ellipse by calling one procedure and then erase it at any time by calling the other procedure. By placing these routines in a module rather than attaching them to a specific form, you also make the procedures available to any form that needs them.

10

Modules are used to group related procedures. In this hour, I focused on the standard module, which is little more than a container for procedures. Remember to group related procedures in the same module and to give each module a descriptive name. In Hour 16, you'll build on your experience with modules and work with class modules, which demands good segregation of discrete modules.

Typically, forms are used as the entry point for a program. However, you learned how to designate and create a Sub Main procedure to use a code procedure as the entry point of a project. This technique is easy to forget. If you run into a tricky startup situation, however, remember that Sub Main often provides for more flexibility than a form does at startup.

Finally, you learned about Visual Basic .NET's new Task List feature. You now know that Visual Basic creates some tasks for you but that you're free to create tasks as you see fit. You learned how to easily jump to a statement that's related to a task and how to create tasks that aren't related to a specific code statement. The Task List is a powerful weapon to have in your development arsenal, and I encourage you to use it.

Q&A

Q Do I need to pay much attention to scope when defining my procedures?

A It might be tempting to create all your procedures as Public, but this is bad coding practice for a number of reasons. For one thing, you'll find that in larger projects, you have procedures with the same name that do slightly different things. Usually, these routines are relevant only within a small scope. However, if you create all Public procedures, you'll run into conflicts when you create a procedure with the same name in the same scope. If the procedure isn't needed at the Public level, don't define it for public access.

Q How many modules is a reasonable amount?

A That's hard to say. In my largest application (which is a *very* large application), I have about 18 modules (and I'm reducing them over time as I replace them with class modules). Anything greater than that and the project might become difficult to manage.

Workshop

The Workshop is designed to help you anticipate possible questions, review what you've learned, and get you thinking about how to put your knowledge into practice. The answers to the quiz are in Appendix B, "Answers to the Quizzes."

Quiz

1. What are the entities called that are used to house procedures?

2. True or False: To access procedures in a class module, you must first create an object.

3. To declare a procedure that returns a value, do you use Sub or Function?

4. True or False: You use a Call statement to call a procedure that returns a value.

5. Data that has been passed into a procedure by a calling statement is called what?

6. To pass multiple arguments to a procedure, separate them with what?

7. The situation in which a procedure or set of procedures continue to call each other in a looping fashion is called what?

8. To create a procedure as an entry point in code, what must you name the procedure?

9. How do you attach a task to a code statement?

Exercises

1. Create a procedure as part of a form that accepts one string and outputs a different string. Add code to the TextChanged event of a text box to call the procedure, passing the contents of the text box as the argument. Pass back as the result of the procedure the uppercase version of string passed into it. (Hint: Use the Visual Basic UCase() function.)

2. Create a single procedure that calls itself. Call this procedure from the Click event of a button and observe the resulting error.

10

Hour 11

Using Constants, Data Types, Variables, and Arrays

NEW TERM As you write your Visual Basic procedures, you'll regularly need to store and retrieve various pieces of information. As a matter of fact, I can't think of a single application I've written that didn't need to store and retrieve data in code. For example, you might want to keep track of how many times a procedure has been called, or store a property value and use it at a later time. Such data can be stored as constants, variables, or arrays. *Constants* are named values that you define once at design time and cannot be changed after that, but can be referenced as often as needed. *Variables*, on the other hand, are like storage bins; you can retrieve or replace the data in a variable as often as you need to. *Arrays* act like grouped variables, enabling you to store many values in a single array variable.

NEW TERM Whenever you define one of these storage entities, you have to decide the type of data it will contain. For example, is a new variable going to hold a string value (text) or perhaps a number? If it will hold a number, is the number a whole number, an integer, or something else entirely? After you determine the type of data to store, you must choose the level of visibility that the data has to other procedures within the project (this visibility is known as *scope*). In this hour, you'll learn the ins and outs of Visual Basic .NET's new data types (they differ from those in Visual Basic 6, even though some share the same names), how to create and use these storage mechanisms, and how to minimize problems in your code by reducing scope.

The highlights of this hour include the following:

- Understanding data types
- Determining data type
- Converting data to different data types
- Defining and using constants
- Dimensioning and referencing variables
- Understanding explicit variable declaration and strict typing
- Working with arrays
- Determining scope
- Declaring static variables
- Using a naming convention

 I cover a lot of important material in this hour, but you'll notice a lack of hands-on examples. You're going to use variables throughout the rest of this book, and you've already used them in earlier hours. I've used the space in this hour to teach you the meat of the subject; you'll get experience with the material in other hours.

Understanding Data Types

In any programming language, the *compiler*, the part of the Visual Studio .NET Framework that interprets the code you write into a language the computer can understand, must fully understand the type of data you're manipulating in code. For example, if you asked the compiler to add the following values, it would get confused:

"Dog" + 659

When the compiler gets confused, it either refuses to compile the code (which is the preferred situation because you can address the problem before your users run the application), or it halts execution and displays an exception (error) when it reaches the confusing line of code. (These two types of errors are discussed in detail in Hour 15, "Debugging Your Code.") Obviously, you can't add the word *Dog* to the number 659 because these two values are different types of data. In Visual Basic, these two values are said to have two different *data types*. In Visual Basic, constants, variables, and arrays must always be defined to hold a specific type of information.

Determining Data Type

NEW TERM   *Data typing*—the act of defining a constant, variable, or array's data type—can be confusing. To Visual Basic, a number is not a number. A number that contains a decimal value is different from a number that doesn't. Visual Basic can perform arithmetic on numbers of different data types, but you can't store data of one type in a variable with an incompatible type. Because of this limitation, you must give careful consideration to the type of data you plan to store in a constant, a variable, or an array at the time you define it. Table 11.1 lists the Visual Basic data types and the range of values each one can contain.

TABLE 11.1   The Visual Basic Data Types

Data Type	Value Range
Boolean	True or False
Byte	0 to 255
Char	0 to 65535
Date	January 1,1 CE to December 31,9999
Decimal	+/–79,228,162,514,264,337,593,543,950,335 with no decimal point; +- –7.9228162514264337593543950335 with 28 places to the right of the decimal; use this data type for currency values
Double	–1.79769313486232E308 to –4.94065645841247E–324 for negative values; 4.94065645841247E-324 to 1.79769313486232E308 for positive values
Integer	–2,147,483,648 to 2,147,483,647
Long	–9,223,372,036,854,775,808 to 9,223,372,036,854,775,807
Object	Any type can be stored in a variable of type Object
Short	–32,768 to 32,767
Single	–3.402823E38 to –1.401198E–45 for negative values; 1.401198E–45 to 3.402823E38 for positive values
String	0 to approximately 2 billion characters

11

Tips for Determining Data Type

The list of data types might seem daunting at first, but you can follow some general guidelines for choosing among them. As you become more familiar with the different types, you'll be able to fine-tune your data type selection.

Following are some helpful guidelines for using data types:

- If you want to store text, use the String data type. The String data type can be used to store any valid keyboard character, including numbers and nonalphabetic characters.

- To store only the value True or False, use the Boolean data type.

- If you want to store a number that contains no decimal places and is greater than −32,768 and smaller than 32,767, use the Short data type.

- To store numbers with no decimal places, but with values larger or smaller than Short allows, use the Integer or Long (short for *long integer*) data types.

- If you need to store numbers that contain decimal places, use the Single data type. The Single data type should work for almost all your values containing decimals, unless you're writing incredibly complex mathematical applications or need to store very large numbers; in that case, use a Double.

- To store currency amounts, use the Decimal data type.

- If you need to store a date and/or a time value, use the Date data type. When you use the Date data type, Visual Basic recognizes common date and time formats. For example, if you store the value 7/22/2001, Visual Basic doesn't treat it as a simple text string; it knows that the text represents July 22, 2001.

The Object data type requires special attention. If you define a variable or array as an Object data type, you can store just about any value you care to in it; Visual Basic determines what data type to use when you set the variable's value.

Several drawbacks exist to using Object data types. First, Object data types take up more memory than the other data types. In addition, Visual Basic takes a little longer to perform calculations on Object data types. Unless you have a specific reason to do so—and there are valid reasons, such as when you don't know the type of data to be stored ahead of time—don't use the Object data type. Instead, become familiar with the explicit data types and use them appropriately.

Casting Data from One Data Type to Another

NEW TERM Under most circumstances, Visual Basic won't allow you to move data of one type into a variable of another type. The process of changing a value's data type is known as *casting*. Casting to a data type that holds a larger value or that has greater precision is called *casting upward* (a narrowing cast), whereas casting to a data type that holds a smaller value or has less precision is known as *casting downward* (a widening case). Visual Basic will generally cast downward but not upward. For instance, you can set the value of a variable declared as Double to the value of a variable declared as Single without an explicit cast because there's no risk of losing data—Double holds more than Single. However, you can't set a variable declared as Single to the value of a variable declared as Double without explicitly casting the type using a data type conversion function because you run the risk of losing data.

Table 11.2 lists the type conversion functions you can use to cast data to a different type (think of C as standing for *cast*). The use of these functions is pretty straightforward: Pass the data to be cast as the parameter, and the function returns the value with the return type. For example, to place the value of a variable declared as Double into a variable declared as Single, you could use a statement such as the following:

```
sngVariable = CSng(dblVariable)
```

TABLE 11.2 The Type Conversion Functions

Function	Converts To
CBool(*expression*)	Boolean
CByte(*expression*)	Byte
CChar(*expression*)	Char
CDate(*expression*)	Date
CDbl(*expression*)	Double
CDec(*expression*)	Decimal
CInt(*expression*)	Integer
CLng(*expression*)	Long
CObj(*expression*)	Object
CShort(*expression*)	Short
CSng(*expression*)	Single
CStr(*expression*)	String

11

A Boolean value holds only True or False. However, it's important to understand how Visual Basic works with Boolean values under the hood. In Visual Basic .NET, True is stored internally as –1 (negative 1), whereas False is stored as 0. In actuality, any nonzero number can represent True, but Visual Basic always treats True internally as –1. When casting a numeric value to a Boolean, Visual Basic casts a value of 0 as False and casts any nonzero number as True. This becomes important when you start evaluating numeric values using Boolean logic (discussed in Hour 12, "Performing Arithmetic, String Manipulation, and Date/Time Adjustments").

Defining and Using Constants

When you hard-code numbers in your procedures (such as in intVotingAge = 19), a myriad of things can go wrong. Hard-coded numbers are generally referred to as *magic numbers* because they're often shrouded in mystery; the meaning of such a number is obscure because the digits themselves give no indication of what the number represents. Constants are used to eliminate the problems of magic numbers.

You define a constant as having a specific value at design time, and that value never changes throughout the life of your program. Constants offer the following benefits:

- **Elimination or reduction of data entry problems**   It's much easier to remember to use a constant named c_pi than it is to enter 3.14159265358979 everywhere that pi is needed. The compiler will catch misspelled or undeclared constants, but it doesn't care one bit what you enter as a literal value.

- **Code is easier to update**   If you hard-coded a mortgage interest rate at 6.785, and rate changed to 7.00, you'd have to change every occurrence of 6.785 in code. In addition to the possibility of data entry problems, you'd run the risk of changing a value of 6.785 that had nothing to do with the interest rate—perhaps a value that represented a savings bond yield. With a constant, you change the value once at the constant declaration, and all code uses the new value.

- **Code is easier to read**   Magic numbers are often anything but intuitive. Well-named constants, on the other hand, add clarity to code. For example, which of the following statements makes the most sense to you?

```
decInterestAmount = CDec((decLoanAmount * 0.075) * 12)
```

or

```
decInterestAmount = CDec((decLoanAmount * c_sngInterestRate) * _
                    c_intMonthsInTerm)
```

Constant definitions have the following syntax:

```
Const name As datatype = value
```

To define a constant to hold the value of pi, for example, you could use a statement such as this:

```
Const c_pi As Single = 3.14159265358979
```

Note how I prefix the constant name with c_. I do this so that it's easier to determine what's a variable and what's a constant when reading code. See the "Naming Conventions" section later in this hour for more information.

After a constant is defined, you can use the constant's name in code in place of the constant's value. For example, to output the result of two times the value of pi, you could use a statement like this (the * character is used for multiplication and is covered in the next hour):

```
Debug.WriteLine(c_pi * 2)
```

Using the constant is much easier and less prone to error than typing this:

```
Debug.WriteLine(3.14159265358979 * 2)
```

Constants can be referenced only in the scope in which they are defined. I discuss scope in the section "Determining Scope."

Declaring and Referencing Variables

Variables are similar to constants in that when you reference a variable's name in code, Visual Basic substitutes the variable's value in place of the variable name when the code executes. This doesn't happen at compile time, though. Instead, it happens at runtime—the moment the variable is referenced. This is because variables, unlike constants, can have their values changed at any time.

Declaring Variables

NEW TERM The act of defining a variable is called *declaring* (and sometimes referred to as *dimensioning*), which is most commonly accomplished using the keyword Dim (short for *dimension*). (Variables with scope other than local are dimensioned in a slightly different way, as discussed in the section on scope later this hour.) You've already used the Dim statement in previous hours, so the basic Dim statement should look familiar to you:

```
Dim variablename As datatype = initialvalue
```

It's possible to declare multiple variables of the same type on a single line, as in

```
Dim I, J, K As Integer
```

However, this is often considered bad form because it tends to make the code harder to read when strong variable names are used.

You don't have to specify an initial value for a variable, although being able to do so in the Dim statement is a very cool and useful new feature of Visual Basic .NET. To create a new String variable and initialize it with a value, for example, you could use two statements like this:

```
Dim strName As String

strName = "Bob Benzel"
```

However, if you know the initial value of the variable at design time, you can include it on the Dim statement like this:

```
Dim strName As String = "Bob Benzel"
```

Note, however, that supplying an initial value doesn't make this a constant; it's still a variable and the value can be changed at any time. This method of creating an initial value eliminates a code statement and makes the code a bit easier to read because you don't have to go looking to see where the variable is initialized.

It's important to note that all data types have a default initial value. For the string data type, this is an empty string. An "empty string" might sound odd; it's essentially no value—a string with no text in it. Empty strings are written in code as `""`. For numeric data types, the value is 0; the output of the following statements would be 2:

```
Dim sngMyValue As Single

Debug.WriteLine (sngMyValue + 2)
```

You can't use a reserved word to name a constant or a variable. For instance, you couldn't use Sub or Public as a variable name. There is no master list of reserved words. You'll naturally pick up most of the common ones because you'll use them so often. For others, the compiler will tell you when something is a reserved word. If you use a naming convention for your variables, you'll greatly reduce the chance of running into reserved words.

Passing Literal Values to a Variable

The syntax of assigning a *literal* value (a hard-coded value such as 6 or "test") to a variable depends on the data type of the variable.

For strings, you must pass the value in quotes, like this:

```
strCollegeName = "Bellevue University"
```

For Date values (discussed in more detail in Hour 12), you enclose the value in # symbols, like this:

```
objBirthDate = #7/22/1969#
```

For numeric values, you don't enclose the value in anything:

```
IntAnswerToEverything = 42
```

Using Variables in Expressions

Variables can be used anywhere an expression is expected. The arithmetic functions, for example, operate on expressions. You could add two literal numbers and store the result in a variable like the following:

```
intMyVariable = 2 + 5
```

You could replace either or both literal numbers with numeric variables or constants, as shown next:

```
intMyVariable = intFirstValue + 5

intMyVariable = 2 + intSecondValue

intMyVariable = intFirstValue + intSecondValue
```

Variables are a fantastic way to store values during code execution, and you'll use variables all the time—from performing decisions and creating loops to using them as a temporary place to stick a value. Remember to use a constant when you know the value at design time and the value won't change. When you don't know the value ahead of time or the value might change, use a variable with a data type appropriate to the function of the variable.

11

> In Visual Basic .NET, variables are created as objects. Feel free to create a
> variable and explore the members (that is, the properties and methods) of
> the variable. You do this by entering the variable name and pressing a
> period (this works only after you've entered the statement that defines the
> variable). For example, to determine the length of the text within a string
> variable, you can use the Length property of a string variable like this:
>
> strMyVariable.Length
>
> There are some powerful features dangling off the data type objects.

Enforced Variable Declaration and Data Typing

NEW TERM By default, Visual Basic .NET forces you to declare variables before you can use
them. This is called *explicit variable declaration*. In addition to this behavior,
you can force Visual Basic .NET to strictly enforce data typing. *Strict typing* means that
Visual Basic .NET will perform widening conversions for you automatically if no data or
precision is lost, but for other conversions, you must explicitly cast the data from one
type to another.

Explicit Variable Declaration

In the past, Visual Basic's default behavior enabled you to create variables on-the-fly
(implicit variable declaration), and it didn't even have a provision for enforcing strict
data typing. Although you can turn both of these new features off, you shouldn't. In fact,
I recommend that you turn on string typing, which is off by default in new projects.

Take a look at the code following this paragraph now. No really, right NOW. There's a
problem with it and I want you to see if you can spot it. With Visual Basic .NET's
Option Explicit project property turned on, the following code would cause a compile
error because of the misspelling of the variable name on the WriteLine() statement. (Did
you notice it?) When you turn off explicit variable declaration, Visual Basic doesn't
check at compile time for such inconsistencies, and it would gladly run this code:

```
Dim intMyVariable As Integer
intMyVariable = 10
Debug.WriteLine(intMyVariabl)
```

So, would an error occur at runtime? If not, what do you think would be printed? 10?
Nope, nothing!

Notice that in WriteLine() statement, an e is missing from the intMyVariable name. As
Visual Basic compiles your code, it looks at each code entry and attempts to determine
whether it's a keyword, a function call, a variable, a constant, or another entity that it

understands. If the entry isn't determined to be something Visual Basic knows about, the default behavior is to generate a compile error.

With explicit variable declaration turned off (that is, the Option Explicit setting turned off), however, Visual Basic .NET alters this behavior. Instead, it creates a brand-new variable—of type Object, no less. As I stated earlier, all variables are initialized with some default value. New object variables are empty, which is a value of sorts. Therefore, nothing prints in this example and no error occurs. You want to talk about hard-to-find errors? This is one of the hardest I can come up with. If you're tired and it's late, it could take you hours to notice that a variable name is misspelled (I've been there, trust me). There is simply no valid reason to turn off explicit variable declaration. Since Option Explicit is turned on for all new projects by default, there's really no reason to mess with this setting.

Strict Typing

Strict typing is the process by which Visual Basic .NET enforces data typing; you can put a value in a variable only if the value is of the correct data type. If you want to cast a value of one type into a variable of another type that holds a smaller number of has less precision, you must use a type-conversion function. With this feature turned off (which it is for new projects by default), Visual Basic .NET lets you move any type of data into any variable, regardless of the data types involved. To do this, it has to make a best guess as to how the data should be cast, which can cause inaccuracies such as truncating a large number when moving it from a Double to a Single. There are rare circumstances in which you might need to turn off strict typing, but these only come up with advanced programming. Leaving strict typing on forces you to write better code, so I advocate that you turn it on in your projects. To turn on Option Strict within a project, follow these steps:

1. Right-click the project name in the Solution Explorer and choose Properties from the context menu.
2. On the Project Properties page, click the Build item in the three on the left.
3. Open the Option Strict drop-down list and choose On.

Working with Arrays

An array is a special type of variable—it's a variable with multiple dimensions. Think of an ordinary variable as a single mail slot. You can retrieve or change the contents of the mail slot by referencing the variable. An array is like having an entire row of mail slots (called *elements*). You can retrieve and set the contents of any of the individual mail slots at any time by referencing the single array variable. You do this by using an index that points to the appropriate slot.

11

Dimensioning Arrays

Arrays are dimensioned in much the same way as ordinary variables, with one notable exception. Consider this statement:

```
Dim strMyArray(10) As String
```

This code is very similar to the Dim statement of an ordinary String variable, with the difference being the number 10 surrounded by parentheses. The number in parentheses determines how many "mail slots" the array variable will contain, and it must be a literal value or a constant—it can't be another variable. The important point to remember is that the number you specify isn't the exact number of elements in the array—it's one less, as you'll see.

> It's possible to create arrays that can be resized at runtime. However, this is beyond the scope of this book.

Referencing Array Variables

To place a value in an array index, you specify the index number when referencing the variable. Most computer operations consider 0 to be the first value in a series, not 1, as you might expect. This is how array indexing behaves. For example, for an array dimensioned with 10 elements (declared using (9)), you would reference the elements sequentially using the indexes 0, 1, 2, 3, 4, 5, 6, 7, 8, and 9.

> Notice that the upper index is the number specified when the array was declared. Because 0 is a valid element, you end up with one more than the number you used to declare the array. This can be confusing. To simplify your development, you might just consider ignoring element 0 and using elements 1 through the declared upper value.

To place a value in the first element of the array variable, you would use 0 as the index, like this:

```
strMyArray(0) = "This value goes in the first element"
```

To reference the second element, you could use a statement like this:

```
StrMyVariable = strMyArray(1)
```

The data type specified for the array variable is used for all the elements in the array. You can use the Object type to hold any type of data in any element, but doing so isn't recommended for all the reasons I discussed earlier.

Creating Multidimensional Arrays

Array variables require only one declaration, yet they can store numerous pieces of data; this makes them perfect for storing sets of related information. The array example shown previously is a single-dimension array. Arrays can be much more complex than this example and can have multiple dimensions of data. For example, a single array variable could be defined to store the personal information shown previously for different people. Multidimensional arrays are declared with multiple parameters such as the following:

```
Dim intMeasurements(3,2) as Integer
```

This Dim statement creates a two-dimensional array. The first dimension (defined as having four elements: 0, 1, 2, 3, and 4) serves as an index to the second dimension (defined as having three elements: 0, 1, 2). Suppose that you want to store the height and weight of three people in this array. You reference the array as you would a single-dimension array, but you include the extra parameter index. The two indexes together specify an element, much like coordinates in Battleship relate to specific spots on the game board. Figure 11.1 illustrates how the elements are related.

FIGURE 11.1

Two-dimensional arrays are like a wall of mail slots.

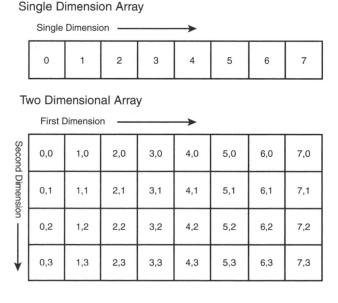

Single Dimension Array

Two Dimensional Array

11

Elements are grouped according to the first index specified; think of the first set of indexes as being a single-dimension array. For example, to store the height and weight of a person in the array's first dimension (remember, arrays are zero-based), you could use code such as the following:

```
intMeasurements(0,0) = FirstPersonsHeight
intMeasurements(0,1) = FirstPersonsWeight
```

I find it helpful to create constants for the array elements, which makes array references much easier to understand. Consider this:

```
Const c_Height As Integer = 0
Const c_Weight As Integer = 1
intMeasurements(0,c_Height) = FirstPersonsHeight
intMeasurements(0,c_Weight) = FirstPersonsWeight
```

You could then store the height and weight of the second and third person like this:

```
intMeasurements(1,c_Height) = SecondPersonsHeight
intMeasurements(1,c_Weight) = SecondPersonsWeight
intMeasurements(2,c_Height) = ThirdPersonsHeight
intMeasurements(2,c_Width) = ThirdPersonsWeight
```

In this array, I've used the first dimension to differentiate people. I've used the second dimension to store a height and weight for each element in the first dimension.

Because I've consistently stored heights in the first slot of the array's second dimension and weights in the second slot of the array's second dimension, it becomes easy to work with these pieces of data. For example, you can retrieve the height and weight of a single person as long as you know the first dimension index used to store the data. You could print out the total weight of all three people using the following code:

```
Debug.WriteLine(intMeasurements (0,c_Weight) + intMeasurements(1,c_Weight) + _
                intMeasurements(2,c_Weight))
```

When working with arrays, keep the following points in mind:

- The first element in any dimension of an array has an index of 0.
- Dimension an array to hold only as much data as you intend to put into it.
- Dimension an array with a data type appropriate to the values to be placed in the array's elements.

Arrays are a great way to store and work with related sets of data in Visual Basic .NET code. Arrays can make working with larger sets of data much simpler and more efficient than using other methods. To maximize your effectiveness with arrays, study the For...Next loop discussed in Hour 14, "Looping for Efficiency." Using a For...Next loop, you can quickly iterate (loop sequentially) through all the elements in an array.

Determining Scope

Constants, variables, and arrays are extremely useful ways to store and retrieve data in Visual Basic code. Hardly a program is written that doesn't use at least one of these elements. To properly use them, however, it's critical that you understand scope.

You had your first encounter with scope in Hour 10, "Creating and Calling Code Procedures," with the keywords Private and Public. You learned that code is written in procedures and that procedures are stored in modules. *Scope* refers to the level that a constant, a variable, an array, or a procedure can be "seen" in code. For a constant or variable, scope can be one of the following:

- Block level
- Procedure level (local)
- Module level
- Global

Scope has the same effect on array variables as it does on ordinary variables. For the sake of clarity, I'll reference variables in this discussion on scope, but understand that what I discuss applies equally to arrays (and constants, for that matter).

Understanding Block Scope

NEW TERM *Block scope*, also called *structure* scope, is new to Visual Basic .NET. Visual Basic considers whether a variable is dimensioned within a structure, and if so, it gives the variable block scope.

Structures are coding constructs that consist of two statements, in contrast to one. For example, you've already used If...Then decision structures in previous hours. Such a structure looks like this:

```
If expression Then
    <statements to execute when expression is True>
End If
```

The standard Do...Loop structure, which you'll learn about in Hour 14, is used to create a loop; it looks like this:

```
Do
    <statements to execute in the loop>
Loop
```

11

If a variable is declared within a structure, the variable's scope is confined to the structure; the variable isn't created until the Dim statement occurs, and it's destroyed when the structure completes. If a variable is needed only within a structure, contemplate declaring it in the structure to give it block scope. Consider the following example:

```
If blnCreateLoop Then
   Dim intCounter As Integer
   For intCounter = 1 to 100
      ' Do something
   Next intCounter
End if
```

By placing the Dim statement within the If structure, you ensure that the variable is created only if it's needed.

 The various structures, including looping and decision-making structures, are discussed in later hours.

Understanding Procedure-Level (Local) Scope

NEW TERM   When you declare a constant or variable within a procedure, that constant or variable has *procedure-level*, or *local scope*. Most of the variables you'll create will have procedure scope. As a matter of fact, almost all the variables you've created in previous hours have had procedure-level scope. You can reference a local constant or variable within the same procedure, but it isn't visible to other procedures. If you try to reference a local constant or variable from a procedure other than the one in which it's defined, Visual Basic returns a compile error. To the procedure making the reference, the variable or constant doesn't exist. It's generally considered best practice to declare all your local variables at the top of a procedure, but Visual Basic doesn't care where you place the Dim statements within the procedure. Note, however, that if you place a Dim statement within a structure, the corresponding variable will have block scope, not local scope.

Understanding Module-Level Scope

When a constant or variable has module-level scope, it can be viewed by all procedures within the module containing the declaration. To procedures in all other modules, however, the constant or variable doesn't exist. To create a constant or variable with module-level scope, you must place the declaration within a module but not within a procedure. There is a section for this—called the Declarations section—at the top of each module. Use module-level scope when many procedures must share the same variable and passing the value as a parameter is not a workable solution.

Although module variables declared using Dim are private to the module, best practice dictates that you use the Private keyword to declare private module level variables. That means it's possible to create public module variables, and you'll learn about them in the next section.

For all modules other than those used to generate forms, it's easy to add code to the Declarations section; simply add the Public/Private statements just after the module declaration line and prior to any procedure definitions, as shown in Figure 11.2.

FIGURE 11.2
The Declarations section exists above all declared procedures.

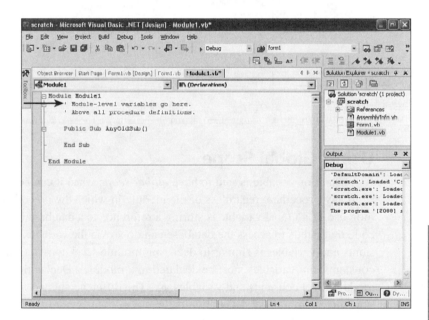

Modules used to generate forms have lots of system-generated code within them, so where to place module-level variables might not be so obvious. The important thing to remember is that you can't place code in front of any Inherits statements. Visual Basic inserts Inherits statements in modules used to build forms, so place module-level variables after any and all Inherits statements in such classes (see Figure 11.3).

A quick way to get to the Declarations section of any module is to choose (Declarations) from the procedure drop-down list in the upper-right corner of a module window.

FIGURE 11.3

The Declarations section includes the Inherits statements, but nothing can come before the Inherits statements.

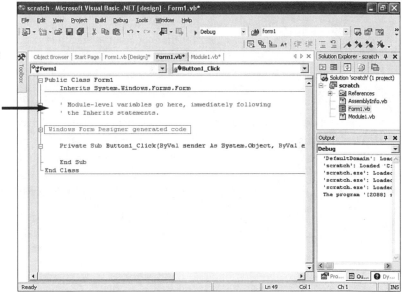

Using Global Scope

A constant or variable is said to have *global scope* when it can be seen and referenced from any procedure, regardless of the module in which the procedure exists. One common use of a global variable is storing a reference to a database connection so that all code that needs to access the database can do so via the variable. Creating global constants and variables is similar to declaring module-level constants and variables. Global constants and variables must be declared in a module's Declarations section, the same as module-level constants and variables are. The difference between a module-level declaration and a global-level declaration is the use of the keyword Public. (Restrictions exist that you must follow to create global variables and constants, and they'll be discussed in the following section.)

To declare a global constant, begin the constant declaration with the word Public, like this:

```
Public Const MyConstant As Integer = 1
```

To dimension a variable as a global variable, replace the keyword Dim or Private with the word Public, like this:

```
Public strMyVariable as String
```

> If Visual Basic gives you the compile error `The name 'variablename' is not declared`, first verify that you spelled the variable or constant reference correctly, and then verify that the variable or constant you're trying to reference is visible in the current scope.

To create a constant or variable of global scope, you must declare the constant or variable in a standard module—not a class-based module. If you declare a public variable or constant in a class module, the variable or constant behaves like a property of the class. This is a very useful technique, and I discuss it in Hour 16, "Designing Objects Using Classes." Regardless, such a constant or variable does not have global scope; it has module-level scope.

Scope Name Conflicts

You can't have two variables of the same name in the same scope, but you can use the same variable name for variables with different scope. For example, if you create two public variables of the same name in standard modules (not class modules), you've created two global variables with the same name. This will cause a compile error everywhere you attempt to access the variable. All variable references are ambiguous; which one should Visual Basic use? You could, however, create a local variable with the same name as a global variable (or even a module variable). Visual Basic always uses the variable with the closest scope. Therefore, when referencing the variable name in the procedure containing the local variable, Visual Basic would use the local variable. When accessing the variable from another procedure, on the other hand, the local variable is invisible, so the code would reference the global variable.

> In general, the smaller (more limited) the scope the better. When possible, make your variables block or local variables. If you have to increase scope, attempt to make the variable a module-level variable. You should use global variables only when there are no other options (and there are usually other options). The larger the scope, the more possibilities exist for problems and the more difficult it is to debug those problems. In general, when considering a global variable, attempt to wrap the data in a class as discussed in Hour 16.

11

Declaring Variables of Static Scope

When you create a variable within a procedure (local or block scope), the variable exists only during the lifetime of the procedure or block (the scope of the variable). When a variable goes out of scope, it's destroyed and whatever value was stored in the old variable is gone. The next time the procedure is called, Visual Basic .NET creates a brand-new variable. Consider the following procedure:

```
Public Sub MyProcedure()
   Dim intMyInteger As Integer
   intMyInteger = intMyInteger + 10
End Sub
```

If you call this procedure, it creates a new variable called intMyInteger, sets its value to its current value, + 10, and then the procedure ends. Numeric variables have an initial value of 0, so when End Sub is encountered in this example, the value of intMyInteger = 10. When the procedure ends, the variable goes out of scope and is therefore destroyed. If you were to call the procedure again, it would create a new variable called intMyInteger (which again would default to 0) and increase its value by 10. Again, the procedure would end and the variable would be destroyed. You can create variables that persist between procedure calls by using the keyword Static.

To create a static variable, use the keyword Static in place of the keyword Dim. The following code is similar to the last example, except that the variable created here is a static variable; it stays in existence and retains its value between calls to the procedure in which it resides:

```
Public Sub MyProcedure()
   Static intMyInteger As Integer
   intMyInteger = intMyInteger + 10
End Sub
```

The first time this procedure is called, the variable intMyInteger is created with a default value of 0, and then the variable is increased by 10. When the procedure ends, the variable isn't destroyed; instead, it persists in memory and retains its value. The next time the procedure is called, Visual Basic has no need to create a new variable, so the previous variable would be used and 10 would be added to its value. The variable would have a value of 20 at the conclusion of the second procedure call. Each subsequent call to the procedure would increase the value in intMyInteger by 10.

Static variables aren't nearly as common as ordinary variables, but they have their uses. For one thing, static variables enable you to minimize scope (which is a good thing). Why create a module-level variable when only one procedure uses it? As you create your Visual Basic projects, keep static variables in mind. If you ever have a need to create a variable that retains its value between calls but whose scope is only procedure or block level, you can do so by creating a static variable.

Naming Conventions

To make code more self-documenting (always an important goal) and to reduce the chance of programming errors, you need an easy way to determine the exact data type of a variable or the exact type of a referenced control in Visual Basic code.

Using Prefixes to Denote Data Type

Table 11.3 lists the prefixes of the common data types. Although you don't have to use prefixes, there are many advantages to be gained by doing so.

TABLE 11.3   Prefixes for Common Data Types

Data Type	Prefix	Sample Value
Boolean	bln	blnLoggedIn
Byte	byt	bytAge
Char	chr	chrQuantity
Date	dte	dteBirthday
Decimal	dec	decSalary
Double	dbl	dblCalculatedResult
Integer	int	intLoopCounter
Long	lng	lngCustomerID
Object	obj	objWord
Short	sho	shoTotalParts
Single	sng	sngMortgageRate
String	str	strFirstName

The prefix of obj should be reserved for when a specific prefix isn't available. The most common use of this prefix is when referencing automation libraries of other applications. For instance, when automating Microsoft Word, you create an instance of Word's Application object. Because no prefix exists specifically for Word objects, obj works just fine. That is,

```
Dim objWord As Word.Application
```

You can hover the pointer over any variable in code and a tooltip will show you the declaration of the variable.

Denoting Scope Using Variable Prefixes

Prefixes are useful not only to denote data type, they also can be used to denote scope (see Table 11.4). In particularly large applications, a scope designator is almost a necessity. Again, Visual Basic doesn't care whether you use prefixes, but consistently using prefixes benefits you as well as others who have to review your code.

TABLE 11.4   Prefixes for Variable Scope

Prefix	Description	Example
g	Global	g_strSavePath
m	Module-level	m_blnDataChanged
st	Static variable	st_blnInHere
(no prefix)	Nonstatic variable, local to procedure	

Other Prefixes

Prefixes aren't just for variables. All standard objects (including forms and controls) can use a three-character prefix. There are simply too many controls and objects to list all the prefixes here, although you'll find that I use control prefixes throughout this book. If you're interested in learning more about naming conventions and coding standards in general, I recommend that you take a look at my book, *Practical Standards for Microsoft Visual Basic* (MS Press).

Summary

In this hour, you learned how to eliminate magic numbers by creating constants. By using constants in place of literal values, you increase code readability, reduce the possibilities of coding errors, and make it much easier to change a value in the future.

In addition, you learned how to create variables for data elements in which the initial value isn't known at design time or for elements whose values will be changed at run-time. You learned how arrays add dimensions to variables and how to declare and reference them in your code.

Visual Basic enforces strict data typing, and in this hour you learned about the various data types and how they're used, as well as tips for choosing data types and functions for converting data from one type to another. Finally, you learned about scope—a very important programming concept—and how to manage scope within your projects.

Writing code that can be clearly understood even by those who didn't write it is a worth-while goal. Naming prefixes go a long way toward accomplishing this goal. In this hour, you learned the naming prefixes for the common data types, and you learned to use prefixes to denote scope.

Q&A

Q Are any performance tricks related to the many data types?

A One trick when using whole numbers (values with no decimal places) is to use the data type that matches your processor. For instance, most current home and office computers have 32-bit processors. The Visual Basic .NET Integer data type is made up of 32 bits. Believe it or not, Visual Basic can process an Integer variable faster than it can process a Short variable, even though the Short variable is smaller. This has to do with the architecture of the CPU, memory, and bus. The explanation is complicated, but the end result is that you should usually use Integer rather than Short, even when working with values that don't require the larger size of the Integer.

Q Are arrays limited to two dimensions?

A Although I only showed two dimensions (that is, intMeasurements(3,1)), arrays can have many dimensions, such as intMeasurements(3,3,3,4). The technical maximum is 60 dimensions, but you probably won't use more than three.

Workshop

The Workshop is designed to help you anticipate possible questions, review what you've learned, and get you thinking about how to put your knowledge into practice. The answers to the quiz are in Appendix B, "Answers to the Quizzes."

Quiz

1. What data type would you use to hold currency values?

2. Which data type can be used to hold any kind of data and essentially serves as a generic data type?

3. What numeric values does Visual Basic internally equate to True and False?

4. What can you create to eliminate magic numbers by defining a literal value in one place?

5. What type of data element can you create in code that can have its value changed as many times as necessary?

11

6. What are the first and last indexes of an array dimensioned using `Dim` `a_strMyArray(5) As String`?

7. What word is given to describe the visibility of a constant or variable?

8. In general, is it best to limit the scope of a variable or to use the widest scope possible?

9. What type of local variable persists data between procedure calls?

Exercises

1. Create a project with a text box, a button, and a label control. When the user clicks the button, move the contents of the text box to a variable, and then move the contents of the variable to the Text property of the label. (Hint: A String variable will do the trick.)

2. Rewrite the following code so that a single array variable is used rather than two standard variables. (Hint: Do not use a multidimensional array.)

```
Dim strGameTitleOne As String
Dim strGameTitleTwo As String
strGameTitleOne = "Splinter Cell"
strGameTitleTwo = "No One Lives Forever"
```

Hour **12**

Performing Arithmetic, String Manipulation, and Date/Time Adjustments

NEW TERM Just as arithmetic is a necessary part of everyday life, it's also vital to developing Windows programs. You probably won't write an application that doesn't add, subtract, multiply, or divide some numbers. In this hour, you learn how to perform arithmetic in code. You also learn about order of operator precedence, which determines how Visual Basic .NET evaluates complicated expressions (equations). After you understand operator precedence, you'll learn how to compare equalities—something you'll do all the time.

Boolean logic is the logic Visual Basic .NET itself uses to evaluate expressions in decision-making constructs. If you've never programmed before, Boolean logic might be a new concept to you. In this hour, I explain what you need to know about Boolean logic to create efficient code that performs as expected. Finally, I show you how to manipulate strings and work with dates and times.

The highlights of this hour include

- Performing arithmetic
- Understanding the order of operator precedence
- Comparing equalities
- Understanding Boolean logic
- Manipulating strings
- Working with dates and times

Performing Basic Arithmetic Operations with Visual Basic .NET

To be a programmer, you have to have solid math skills; you'll be performing a lot of basic arithmetic when writing Visual Basic .NET applications. To get the results you're looking for in any given calculation, you must

- Know the mathematical operator that performs the desired arithmetic function
- Understand and correctly use order of precedence

Using the correct mathematical operator is simple. Most are easy to commit to memory, and you can always look up the ones you're not quite sure of. I'm not going to go into great detail on any of the math functions (if you've made it this far, I'm sure that you have a working grasp of math), but I'll cover them all.

In Hour 10, "Creating and Calling Code Procedures," I mentioned how the Debug.WriteLine() method prints text to the Output window. I use this method in the examples throughout this hour. For more specific information on the Debug object, see Hour 15, "Debugging Your Code."

Performing Addition

Simple addition is performed using the standard addition symbol, the + character. The following line prints the sum of 4, 5, and 6:

```
debug.WriteLine(4 + 5 + 6)
```

You don't have to use a hard-coded value with arithmetic operators. You can use any of the arithmetic operators on numeric variables and constants. For example:

```
Const c_FirstValue As Integer = 4
```

```
Const c_SecondValue As Integer = 5
debug.WriteLine(c_FirstValue + c_SecondValue)
```

This bit of code prints the sum of the constants c_FirstValue and c_SecondValue, which is 9.

Performing Subtraction and Negation

Like the addition operator, you're probably familiar with the subtraction operator because it's the same one you would use on a calculator or when writing an equation: the – character. The following line of code prints 2 (the total of 6–4):

```
debug.WriteLine(6 - 4)
```

As with written math, the – character is also used to denote a negative number. For example, to print the value –6, you would use a statement such as the following:

```
debug.WriteLine(-6)
```

Performing Multiplication

If you work with adding machines, you already know the multiplication operator. The multiplication character is the * character. You can enter this character using Shift+8 or by pressing the * key located in the upper row of the keypad section of the keyboard. Although you would ordinarily use a × when writing multiplication equations such as $6 = 3 \times 2$ on paper, you'll receive an error if you try this in code; you have to use the * character. The following statement prints 20 (5 multiplied by 4):

```
debug.WriteLine(5 * 4)
```

Performing Division

Division is accomplished using the / operator. This operator is easy to remember if you think of division as fractions. For example, one-eighth is written as 1/8, which literally means one divided by eight. The following statement prints 8 (32 divided by 4):

```
debug.WriteLine(32 / 4)
```

Be sure not to confuse the division character, /, with the backslash character, \. If you use the backslash character, Visual Basic .NET will perform the division, but it will return only the integer portion (the remainder is discarded).

12

Performing Exponentiation

NEW TERM *Exponentiation* is the process of raising a number to a certain power. An equation example is 10^2, which is 10 to the 2nd power, or 100. The same equation in Visual Basic .NET code looks like this:

```
debug.WriteLine(10 ^ 2)
```

The number placed to the left of the ^ operator is the base, whereas the number to the right is the power/exponent.

Performing Modulus Arithmetic

Modulus arithmetic is the process of performing division on two numbers but keeping only the remainder. Modulus arithmetic is performed using the Mod keyword, in contrast to using a / operator symbol. The following are examples of Mod statements and the values they would print:

```
debug.WriteLine(10 Mod 5)         ' Prints 0

debug.WriteLine(10 Mod 3)         ' Prints 1

debug.WriteLine(12 Mod 4.3)       ' Prints 3.4

debug.WriteLine(13.6 Mod 5)       ' Prints 3.6
```

The first two statements are relatively easy to understand: 5 goes into 10 twice with no remainder, and 3 goes into 10 three times with a remainder of 1. Visual Basic .NET processes the third statement as 4.3 going into 12 two times with a remainder of 3.4. In the last statement, Visual Basic .NET performs the Mod operation as 5 going into 13.6 twice with a remainder of 3.6.

Determining the Order of Operator Precedence

NEW TERM When several arithmetic operations occur within a single equation (called an *expression*), Visual Basic .NET has to resolve the expression in pieces. The order in which these pieces are evaluated is known as *operator precedence*. To fully understand operator precedence, you have to brush up a bit on your algebra skills (most of the math you perform in code is algebraic).

Consider the following expression:

```
debug.WriteLine(6 + 4 * 5)
```

Two arithmetic operations occur in this single expression. To evaluate the expression, Visual Basic .NET must perform both operations: multiplication and addition. Which operation does Visual Basic .NET perform first? Does it matter? Absolutely. If Visual

Basic .NET performs the addition before the multiplication, you end up with the following:

Step 1: 6 + 4 = 10

Step 2: 10 * 5 = 50

The final result would be that of Visual Basic .NET printing 50. Now look at the same equation with the multiplication performed prior to addition:

Step 1: 4 * 5 = 20

Step 2: 20 + 6 = 26

In this case, Visual Basic .NET would print 26—a dramatically different number from the one computed when the multiplication is performed first. To prevent these types of problems, Visual Basic .NET consistently performs arithmetic operations in the same order—the order of operator precedence. Table 12.1 lists the order of operator precedence for arithmetic and Boolean operators. (Boolean operators are discussed later in this hour.) If you're familiar with algebra, you'll note that the order of precedence used by Visual Basic .NET is the same as that used in algebraic formulas.

TABLE 12.1   Visual Basic .NET's Order of Operator Precedence

Arithmetic	Logical
Exponentiation (^)	Not
Negation (-)	And
Multiplication and division (*, /)	Or
Modulus arithmetic (**Mod**)	
Addition and subtraction (**+**, **-**)	
String concatenation (**&**)	

12

All comparison operators such as >, <, and = (discussed in the next section) have an equal precedence. When operators have an equal precedence, Visual Basic .NET evaluates them from left to right. Notice that multiplication and division operators have an equal precedence, so in an expression that has both, the operators would be evaluated from left to right. The same holds true for addition and subtraction. When expressions contain operators from more than one category (arithmetic, comparison, or logical), arithmetic operators are evaluated first, comparison operators are evaluated next, and logical operators are evaluated last.

Just as when writing an equation on paper, you can use parentheses to override the order of operator precedence. Operations placed within parentheses are always evaluated first. Consider the previous example:

```
debug.WriteLine(6 * 5 + 4)
```

Using the order of operator precedence, Visual Basic .NET evaluates the equation like this:

```
debug.WriteLine((6 * 5) + 4)
```

The multiplication is performed first, and then the addition. If you want the addition performed prior to the multiplication, you could write the statement like this:

```
debug.WriteLine(6 * (5 + 4))
```

 When writing complex expressions, you absolutely must keep in mind the order of operator precedence and use parentheses to override the default operator precedence when necessary. Personally, I try to always use parentheses so that I'm sure of what's happening and my code is easier to read.

Comparing Equalities

Comparing values, particularly variables, is even more common than performing arithmetic (but you need to know how Visual Basic .NET arithmetic works before you can understand the evaluation of equalities). Table 12.2 (column 2) shows the Visual Basic .NET comparison operators.

Comparison operators are most often used in decision-making structures, as explained in the next hour. Indeed, these operators are best understood using a simple If…Then decision structure. In an If…Then construct, Visual Basic .NET considers the expression on the If statement, and if the expression equates to True, the code between the If and End If statements is executed. For example, the following is an If…Then operation (a silly one at that) expressed in English, not in Visual Basic .NET code:

IF DOGS BARK, THEN SMILE.

If this were in Visual Basic .NET code format, Visual Basic .NET would evaluate the If condition, which in this case is *dogs bark*. If the condition is found to be True, the code following Then is performed. Because dogs bark, you'd smile. Notice how these two things (dogs barking and you smiling) are relatively unrelated. This doesn't matter; the point is that if the condition evaluates to True, certain actions (statements) occur.

You'll often compare the value of one variable to that of another variable or to a specific value when making decisions. The following are some basic comparisons and how Visual Basic .NET evaluates them:

```
debug.WriteLine(6 > 3)        ' Evaluates to True

debug.WriteLine(3 = 4)        ' Evaluates to False

debug.WriteLine(3 >= 3)       ' Evaluates to True

debug.WriteLine(5 <= 4)       ' Evaluates to False
```

Performing comparisons is pretty straightforward. If you get stuck writing a particular comparison, attempt to write it in English before creating it in code.

Understanding Boolean Logic

Boolean logic is a special type of arithmetic/comparison. Boolean logic is used to evaluate expressions to either True or False. This might be a new concept to you, but don't worry; it's not difficult to understand. Boolean logic is performed using a logical operator. Consider the following sentence:

If black is a color and wood comes from trees then print "ice cream".

At first glance, it might seem that this is nonsensical. However, Visual Basic .NET could make sense of this statement using Boolean logic. First, notice that three expressions are actually being evaluated within this single sentence. I've added parentheses in the following sentence to clarify two of the expressions.

If (black is a color) and (wood comes from trees) then print "ice cream".

Boolean logic evaluates every expression to either True or False. Therefore, substituting True or False for each of these expressions yields the following:

If (True) and (True) then print "ice cream".

Now, for the sake of clarity, here's the same sentence with parentheses placed around the final expression to be evaluated:

If (True And True) then print "ice cream".

This is the point where the logical operators come into play. The And operator returns True if the expressions on each side of the And operator are true (see Table 12.2 for a complete list of logical operators). In the sentence we're considering, the expressions on both sides of the And operator are True, so the expression evaluates to True. Replacing the expression with True yields:

If True then print "ice cream".

12

This would result in the word "ice cream" being printed. If the expression had evaluated to False, nothing would be printed. As you'll see in the next hour, the decision constructs always fully evaluate their expressions to either True or False, and statements execute according to the results.

 As you work with Boolean logic, keep in mind that Visual Basic .NET uses −1 to represent True and 0 to represent False, as described in Hour 11, "Using Constants, Data Types, Variables, and Arrays."

TABLE 12.2   Logical (Boolean) Operators

Operator	Description
And	Evaluates to True when the expressions on both sides are True.
Not	Returns the opposite of the expression it operates on. It evaluates to True when the expression is False, and False when the expression is True.
Or	Evaluates to True if an expression on either side evaluates to True.
Xor	Evaluates to True if one, and only one, expression on either side evaluates to True.

Using the And Operator

The And operator is used to perform a logical conjunction. If the expressions on both sides of the And operator evaluate to True, the And operation evaluates to True. If either expression is False, the And operation evaluates to False, as illustrated in the following examples:

```
debug.WriteLine(True And True)        ' Prints True

debug.WriteLine(True And False)       ' Prints False

debug.WriteLine(False And True)       ' Prints False

debug.WriteLine(False And False)      ' Prints False

debug.WriteLine((32 > 4) And (6 = 6))   ' Prints True
```

Using the Not Operator

The Not operator performs a logical negation. That is, it returns the opposite of the expression. Consider the following examples:

```
debug.WriteLine(Not (True))      ' Prints False

debug.WriteLine(Not (False))     ' Prints True
```

```
debug.WriteLine(Not (5 = 5))      ' Prints False

debug.WriteLine(Not((4 < 2)))     ' Prints True
```

The first two statements are easy enough; the opposite of True is False and vice versa. For the third statement, remember that Visual Basic .NET 's operator precedence dictates that arithmetic operators are evaluated first (even if no parentheses are used), so the first step of the evaluation would look like this:

```
debug.WriteLine(Not (True))
```

The opposite of True is False, of course, so Visual Basic .NET prints False.

The fourth statement would evaluate to

```
debug.WriteLine(Not (False))
```

This happens because 4 is *not* less than 2, which is the expression Visual Basic .NET evaluates first. Because the opposite of False is True, this statement would print True.

Using the Or Operator

The Or operator is used to perform a logical disjunction. If the expression to the left *or* right of the Or operator evaluates to True, the Or operation evaluates to True. The following are examples using Or operations, and their results:

```
debug.WriteLine(True Or True)          ' Prints True

debug.WriteLine(True Or False)         ' Prints True

debug.WriteLine(False Or True)         ' Prints True

debug.WriteLine(False Or False)        ' Prints False

debug.WriteLine((32 < 4) Or (6 = 6))   ' Prints True
```

Using the Xor Operator

The Xor operator performs a nifty little function. I personally haven't had to use it much, but it's great for those times when its functionality is required. If one—and only one—of the expressions on either side of the Xor operator is True, the Xor operation evaluates to True. Take a close look at the following statement examples to see how this works:

```
debug.WriteLine(True Xor True)          ' Prints False

debug.WriteLine(True Xor False)         ' Prints True

debug.WriteLine(False Xor True)         ' Prints True

debug.WriteLine(False Xor False)        ' Prints False

debug.WriteLine((32 < 4) Xor (6 = 6))   ' Prints True
```

12

Manipulating Strings

Recall from the previous hour that a string is text. Visual Basic .NET provides many functions for working with strings. Although string manipulation isn't technically arithmetic, the things that you do with strings are very similar to things you do with numbers, such as adding two strings together; string manipulation is much like creating equations. Chances are you'll be working with strings a lot in your applications. Visual Basic .NET includes a number of functions that enable you to do things with strings, such as retrieve a portion of string or find one string within another. In the following sections, you'll learn the basics of string manipulation.

Concatenating Strings of Text

NEW TERM Visual Basic .NET makes it possible to "add" two strings of text together to form one string. Although purists will say it's not truly a form of arithmetic, it's very much like performing arithmetic on strings, so this hour was the logical place in which to present this material. The process of adding two strings together is called *concatenation*. Concatenation is very common. For example, you might want to concatenate variables with hard-coded strings to display meaningful messages to the user, such as Are you sure you wish to delete the user XXX?, where XXX is the contents of a variable.

To concatenate two strings, you use the & operator as shown in this line of code:

```
debug.WriteLine("This is" & "a test.")
```

This statement would print

```
This isa test.
```

Notice that there is no space between the words *is* and *a*. You could easily add a space by including one after the word *is* in the first string or before the *a* in the second string, or you could concatenate the space as a separate string, like this:

```
debug.WriteLine("This is" & " " & "a test.")
```

NEW TERM Text placed directly within quotes is called a *literal*. Variables are concatenated in the same way as literals, and can even be concatenated with literals. The following code creates two variables, sets the value of the first variable to "James", and sets the value of the second variable to the result of concatenating the variable with a space and the literal "Foxall":

```
Dim strFirstName as String
Dim strFullName as String
strFirstName = "James"
strFullName = strFirstName & " " & "Foxall"
```

The final result is that the variable strFullName contains the string James Foxall. Get comfortable concatenating strings of text—you'll do this often.

> In addition to the ampersand, Visual Basic .NET will let you use the + sign to concatenate strings—*don't do this*. It makes the code harder to read and might yield incorrect results when you don't use Option Strict.

Using the Basic String Functions

Visual Basic .NET includes a number of functions that make working with strings of text considerably easier than it might be otherwise. These functions enable you to easily retrieve a piece of text from a string, compute the number of characters in a string, and even determine whether one string contains another. The following is a summary of the basic string functions.

Determining the Number of Characters Using Len()

The Len() function accepts a string (variable or literal) and returns the number of characters in the string. The following statement prints 26, the total number of characters in the literal string "Pink Floyd reigns supreme." Remember, the quotes surrounding the string tell Visual Basic .NET that the text within them is a literal; they aren't part of the string. Len() is often used in support of the other string functions, which you'll learn next.

```
debug.WriteLine(Len("Pink Floyd reigns supreme."))      ' Prints 26
```

12

> Another way to get the number of characters in a string variable is to use the variable's Length property, as in
>
> ```
> debug.WriteLine(strMyStringVariable.Length())
> ```

Retrieving Text from the Left Side of a String Using Microsoft.VisualBasic.Left()

The Microsoft.VisualBasic.Left() function returns a portion of the left side of the string passed to it. The Microsoft.VisualBasic.Left() function accepts two parameters:

- The string from which to retrieve a portion of the left side
- The number of characters to retrieve

The Microsoft.VisualBasic.Left() function always retrieves text starting with the leftmost character. For example, the following statement prints Queen, the first five characters of the string.

```
debug.WriteLine(Microsoft.VisualBasic.Left("Queen to Queen's Level Three.", 5))
```

Microsoft.VisualBasic.Left() is commonly used with the InStr() function (discussed shortly) to retrieve the path portion of a variable containing a filename and path combination, such as c:\Myfile.txt. If you know where the \ character is, you can use Microsoft.VisualBasic.Left() to get the path.

 If the number of characters requested is greater than the number of characters in the string, the entire string is returned. If you're unsure about the number of characters in the string, use the Len() function.

Retrieving Text from the Right Side of a String Using Microsoft.VisualBasic.Right()

The Microsoft.VisualBasic.Right() function is the sister to the Microsoft.VisualBasic.Left() function; instead of returning text from the left side of the string, Microsoft.VisualBasic.Right() returns text from the right side of the string. Note, however, that the returned characters are always in the same order in which they appear within the original string. Microsoft.VisualBasic.Right() doesn't retrieve the characters from right to left. Instead, it starts at the rightmost character, counts back the number of characters you specify, and returns that many characters from the right side of the string. The following statement prints hing., the last five characters in the string.

```
debug.WriteLine(Microsoft.VisualBasic.Right("Duck tape fixes everything.", 5))
```

Retrieving Text Within a String Using Microsoft.VisualBasic.Mid()

When you need to retrieve a portion of text from within a string (from neither the left side nor the right side), use the Microsoft.VisualBasic.Mid() function. The Microsoft.VisualBasic.Mid() function enables you to specify where in the string to begin retrieving text, as well as how many characters to retrieve. The Microsoft.VisualBasic.Mid() function accepts the following three parameters:

- The string from which to retrieve a portion of text
- The character at which to begin retrieving text
- The number of characters to retrieve

The following statement prints the text look li. This occurs because the Microsoft.VisualBasic.Mid() function begins at the fifth character (the *l* in *look*) and retrieves seven characters.

```
debug.WriteLine(Microsoft.VisualBasic.Mid("You look like you could _
 use a monkey.", 5, 7))
```

Not many people realize this, but it's possible to omit the last parameter. When you omit the last parameter, the Microsoft.VisualBasic.Mid() function returns everything from the starting character to the end of the string. The following statement prints the text ter crows at midnight.; it returns everything beginning with the ninth character.

```
debug.WriteLine(Microsoft.VisualBasic.Mid("The rooster crows at midnight.", 9))
```

Determining Whether One String Contains Another Using InStr()

At times you'll need to determine whether one string exists within another. For example, suppose that you let users enter their full name into a text box, and that you want to separate the first and last names before saving them into individual fields in a database. The easiest way to do this is to look for the space in the string that separates the first name from the last. You could use a loop to examine each character in the string until you find the space, but Visual Basic .NET includes a native function that does this for you, faster and easier than you could do it yourself: the InStr() function. The basic InStr() function has the following syntax:

```
InStr([start, ] stringtosearch, stringbeingsought)          ' Returns a long
```

> The InStr() function has always been an enigma to me. For one thing, it's the only function I've ever seen in which the first parameter is optional but the following parameters are required. Secondly, it's documented with the second parameter called *string1* and the third parameter called *string2*. This makes it difficult to remember which parameter is used for what and will probably force you to reference the help when you use it.

The InStr() function searches one string for the occurrence of another. If the string is found, the character location of the start of the search string is returned. If the search string is not found within the other string, 0 is returned. The following code searches a variable containing the text "James Foxall", locates the space, and uses Left() and Mid() to place the first and last names in separate variables:

```
Dim strFullName As String = "James Foxall"
Dim strFirstName As String
Dim strLastName As String
```

12

```
Dim intLocation As Integer

intLocation = InStr(strFullName, " ")

strFirstName = Left(strFullName, intLocation - 1)
strLastName = Mid(strFullName, intLocation + 1)
```

> This code assumes that a space will be found and that it won't be the first or last character in the string. In your applications, your code might need to be more robust, checking to see whether InStr() returned 0, indicating that no match was found.

When this code runs, InStr() returns 6, the location in which the first space is found. Notice how I subtracted 1 from intLocation when using Microsoft.VisualBasic.Left(). If I didn't, the space would be part of the text returned by Microsoft.VisualBasic.Left(). The same holds true with adding 1 to intLocation in the Microsoft.VisualBasic.Mid() statement.

I omitted the first parameter in this example because it's not necessary when you want to search from the first character in the string. To search from a different location, supply the number of characters to begin searching from as the first parameter.

Trimming Beginning and Trailing Spaces from a String

In the previous example, I showed how you need to add 1 or subtract 1 from the value returned by the InStr() function to avoid getting the space that was found as part of your first or last names. As you work with strings, you'll often encounter situations in which spaces exist at the beginning or ending of strings. Visual Basic .NET includes three functions for automatically removing spaces from the beginning or end of a string (none of these functions removes spaces that exist *between* characters in a string).

Function	Description
Trim()	Removes all leading and trailing spaces from the supplied string
LTrim()	Removes only the leading spaces from the supplied string
RTrim()	Removes only the trailing spaces from the supplied string

For example, consider that you didn't subtract 1 from the value of intLocation in the previous example. That is, you used a statement such as the following:

```
strFirstName = Microsoft.VisualBasic.Left(strFullName, intLocation)
```

strFirstName would contain the text "James ". Notice the space at the end of the name. To remove the space, you could use Trim() or LTrim(), like this:

```
strFirstName = Trim(Left(strFullName))
```

> Use Trim() in place of RTrim() or LTrim() unless you specifically want to keep spaces at one end of the string.

Replacing Text Within a String

It's not uncommon to have to replace a piece of text within a string to some other text. For example, some people still put two spaces at the end of a sentence, even though this is no longer necessary because of proportional fonts. You could replace all double spaces with a single space using a loop and the string manipulation functions discussed so far, but there's an easier way: the Replace function. A basic Replace function call has the following syntax:

```
Replace(expression, findtext, replacetext)
```

The *expression* argument is the text to search, such as a string variable. The *findtext* argument is used to specify the text to look for within *expression*. The *replacetext* argument is used to specify the text used to replace the *findtext*. Consider the following code:

```
Dim strText As String = "Give a man a fish"
strText = Replace(strText, "fish", "sandwich")
```

When this code completes, strText contains the string "Give a man a sandwich". Replace is a powerful function that can save many lines of code, and you should use it in place of a home-grown replace function whenever possible.

Working with Dates and Times

Dates are a unique beast. In some ways, they act like strings, where you can concatenate and parse pieces. In other ways, dates seem more like numbers in that you can add to or subtract from them. Although you'll often perform math-type functions on dates (such as adding a number of days to a date or determining the number of months between two dates), you don't use the typical arithmetic operations. Instead, you use functions specifically designed for working with dates.

12

Understanding the Date Data Type

Working with dates is very common. No matter the application, you'll need to create a variable to hold a date, using the Date data type. You can get a date into a Date variable in several ways. Recall that when setting a string variable to a literal value, the literal is enclosed in quotes. When setting a numeric variable to a literal number, the number is not closed in quotes:

```
Dim strMyString As String = "This is a string literal"
Dim intMyInteger As Integer = 69
```

When setting a Date variable to a literal date, you enclose the literal in # signs, like this:

```
Dim dteMyBirthday As Date = #7/22/1969#
```

When using Option Strict, you cannot assign a string directly to a Date variable. For instance, if you let the user enter a date into a text box and you want to move the entry to a Date variable, you would have to do something like

```
objMyDateVariable = CDate(txtBirthDay.Text)
```

You'd also have to convert a date to a string when moving it from a Date variable to a text box (again, only when Option Strict is on). For more information on the data type conversion functions, refer to Hour 11.

It's important to note that Date variables store a date and a time—always. For example, the following code:

```
Dim dteBirthday As Date = #7/22/1969#
debug.WriteLine(dteBirthday)
```

Produces this output:

```
7/21/1969 12:00:00 AM
```

Notice that the previous example output the time 12:00:00 AM, even though no time was specified for the variable. This is the default time placed in a Date variable when only a date is specified. Although a Date variable always holds a date and a time, on occasion, you'll be concerned only with either the date or the time. Later, I'll show you how to use the Format() function to retrieve just a date or a time.

Visual Basic .NET includes a new structure called DateTime. This structure has members that enable you to do many things similar to the functions I discuss here. According to Microsoft, neither method is preferred over the other. The DateTime structure can be a bit more complicated, so I've chosen to teach you about the Date variable.

Adding to or Subtracting from a Date or Time

To add a specific amount of time (such as one day or three months) to a specific date or time, use the DateAdd() function. The DateAdd function has the following syntax:

```
DateAdd(interval, number, date) As Date
```

Note that all three parameters are required. The first parameter is an enumeration and determines *what* you're adding (month, day, hour, minute, and so on). Table 12.3 lists the possible values for *interval*. The second parameter is how much of the interval to add. The final parameter is a date. Supplying a negative value for *number* subtracts that much of the *interval* from the date. For instance, to add 6 months to the date 7/22/69, you could use the following statements:

```
Dim objMyBirthday As Date = #7/22/1969#
objMyBirthday = DateAdd(DateInterval.Month, 6, objMyBirthday)
```

After this second statement executes, objMyBirthday contains the date 1/22/1970 12:00:00 AM.

> You can use the literal string that corresponds to the enumeration (see Table 12.3), rather than using the enumerated name. For example, the previous statement could be written as
>
> ```
> objMyBirthday = DateAdd("m", 6, objMyBirthday)
> ```

TABLE 12.3 Allowable Values for the Interval Parameter of DateAdd()

Enumeration Value	String	Unit of Time Interval to Add
DateInterval.Day	d	Day; truncated to integral value
DateInterval.DayOfYear	y	Day; truncated to integral value
DateInterval.Hour	h	Hour; rounded to nearest millisecond
DateInterval.Minute	n	Minute; rounded to nearest millisecond
DateInterval.Month	m	Month; truncated to integral value
DateInterval.Quarter	q	Quarter; truncated to integral value
DateInterval.Second	s	Second; rounded to nearest millisecond
DateInterval.Weekday	w	Day; truncated to integral value
DateInterval.WeekOfYear	ww	Week; truncated to integral value
DateInterval.Year	yyyy	Year; truncated to integral value

12

The following code shows sample DateAdd() function calls and the date they would return:

```
DateAdd(DateInterval.Year, 2, #3/3/1968#)      ' Returns 3/3/70

DateAdd(DateInterval.Month, 5, #5/14/1998#)    ' Returns 10/14/1998

DateAdd(DateInterval.Month, -1, #3/6/2000#)    ' Returns 2/6/2000

DateAdd(DateInterval.Hour, -1, #6/28/1996 8:00:00 PM#)  _
          ' Returns 6/28/1996 7:00:00 PM
```

> Visual Basic .NET will never advance more calendar months than specified when adding months. For example, DateAdd("m", 1, #1/31/1969#) produces the date 2/28/1969. Because February doesn't have 31 days, Visual Basic .NET uses the last day of the month.

Determining the Interval Between Two Dates or Times

The DateAdd() function enables you to easily add time to or subtract time from a date or time. You can just as easily retrieve the interval between two existing dates or times by using the DateDiff() function. The basic DateDiff() function has the following syntax:

DateDiff(interval, Date1, Date2**)** As Long

The *interval* parameter accepts the same values as the interval parameter of the DateAdd() function (refer to Table 12.3). The DateDiff() function returns a number—the number indicating the number of the specified intervals between the two supplied dates. For example, this code prints 9, the number of weeks between the two dates:

```
Dim dteStartDate As Date = #10/10/2001#
Dim objEndDate As Date = #12/10/2001#
debug.WriteLine(DateDiff(DateInterval.WeekOfYear, dteStartDate, objEndDate))
```

If the second date comes before the first, the number returned is negative. The following statements should help illustrate how DateDiff() works by showing you some function calls and the values they return:

```
DateDiff(DateInterval.Year, #7/22/1969#, #10/22/2001#)    ' Returns 32

DateDiff(DateInterval.Month, #3/3/1992#, #3/3/1990#)      ' Returns -24

DateDiff(DateInterval.Day, #3/3/1997#, #7/2/1997#)        ' Returns 121
```

Notice that the second function call returns –24. Whenever the first date passed to the DateDiff()function comes after the second date, a negative number is returned. This is useful in determining the order of two dates; you can simply compare them using

DateDiff() and determine which is the later date by whether DateDiff() returns a positive or negative number.

Retrieving Parts of a Date

Sometimes, it can be extremely useful to know just a part of a date. For example, you might have let a user enter his birth date, and you want to perform an action based on the month in which he was born. To retrieve part of a date, use the DatePart() function. The basic DatePart() function has the following syntax:

DatePart(*interval*, *date*) As Integer

Again, the possible values for *interval* are the same as used for both DateAdd() and DateDiff(). The following should illustrate the use of DatePart():

```
DatePart(DateInterval.Month, #7/22/1969#)   ' Returns 7

DatePart(DateInterval.Hour, #3:00:00 PM#)   ' Returns 15 (military format)

DatePart(DateInterval.Quarter,  #6/9/2001#) ' Returns 2
```

Formatting Dates and Times

As I stated earlier, at times you'll want to work with only the date or a time within a Date variable. In addition, you'll probably want to control the format in which a date or time is displayed. All this is accomplished with the Format() function. The Format() function is capable of powerful formatting of all sorts of items in addition to dates and times, such as monetary figures and strings. I can't possibly show you everything about the Format() function here, but I do want to show you how to use Format() to output either the date portion or the time portion of a Date variable.

The basic Format() function has the following syntax:

```
Format(expression, style)
```

The parameter *expression* is the expression to format, and *style* is a string containing information specifying the formatting. For example, to display the month portion of a date, you use M in the style. Actually, specifying a single M displays the month as a single digit for 1–9 and a double digit for 10–12. Specifying two Ms always shows the month in double digits. Three Ms produce a three-digit abbreviated month, and four Ms return the entire month name, regardless of how many characters are in the name. (Note: lowercase m is used to return minutes, not months.) The following examples illustrate this:

```
Format(#1/22/2002#, "M")    ' Returns 1

Format(#1/22/2002#, "MM")   ' Returns 01
```

12

```
Format(#1/22/2002#, "MMM")      ' Returns Jan

Format(#1/22/2002#, "MMMM")     ' Returns January
```

There are formatting characters for years, days, hours, minutes, and even a.m. and p.m. The list of allowable formatting characters is huge, and I encourage you to explore them in the Visual Basic .NET help text. Because my goal here is to show you how to extract a date or a time, I'll show you some common formatting:

```
Format(#7/22/2001#, "MMM. d,  yyyy")    ' Returns Jul. 22, 2001

Format(#7/22/2001#, "MMMM yyyy")        ' Returns July 2001

Format(#9:37:00 PM#, "h:mm am/pm")      ' Returns 9:37 pm"

Format(#5/14/1998 9:37:00 PM#, "MM/dd/yyyy h:mm am/pm") _
       ' Returns 05/14/1998 9:37 pm
```

As you can see, the comma, the colon, and the period characters are not symbolic but appear in the formatted string in the location in which they are placed within *style*. This information should be enough to get you going, but I highly encourage you to explore the `Format()` function on your own—it's a very powerful and useful function.

Retrieving the Current System Date and Time

Visual Basic .NET gives you the capability to retrieve the current system date and time. This is accomplished by way of the DateTime structure. The DateTime structure has a number of members that mimic the functionality of many of the date functions I've discussed, as well as some additional members. One member, Today, returns the current system date. For example, to place the current system date in a new Date variable, you could use a statement such as this:

```
Dim objToday As Date = DateTime.Today
```

To retrieve the current system date *and* time, use the Now property of DateTime like this:

```
Dim objToday As Date = DateTime.Now
```

Commit DateTime.Today and DateTime.Now to memory. You'll need to retrieve the system date and/or time in an application, and this is by far the easiest way to get that information.

If you just want to get the current time without the date, call DateTime.TimeOfDate.

Determining Whether a Value Is a Date

At times, it might be necessary to determine whether a value is a date. For instance, if you enable users enter their birthday into a text box, you'll want to ensure that they enter a date before attempting to perform any date functions on the value. Visual Basic .NET includes a function just for this purpose: the IsDate() function. IsDate() accepts an expression, and returns True if the expression is a date and False if not. For instance, the following statement would print True if the content of the text box is a date; otherwise, it would print False:

```
Debug.WriteLine(IsDate(txtBirthday.Text))
```

Summary

Being able to work with all sorts of data is crucial to your success as a Visual Basic .NET developer. Just as you need to understand basic math to function in society, you need to be able to perform basic math in code to write even the simplest of applications. Knowing the arithmetic operators, as well as understanding the order of operator precedence, will take you a long way in performing math using Visual Basic .NET code.

Boolean logic is a special form of evaluation used by Visual Basic .NET to evaluate simple and complex expressions alike down to a value of True or False. In the following hours, you'll learn how to create loops and how to perform decisions in code. What you learned here about Boolean logic is critical to your success with loops and decision structures; you'll use Boolean logic perhaps even more often than you'll perform arithmetic.

Manipulating strings and dates each takes special considerations. In this hour, you learned how to work with both types of data to extract portions of values and to add pieces of data together to form a new whole. String manipulation is pretty straightforward, and you'll get the hang of it soon enough as you start to use some of the string functions. Date manipulation, on the other hand, can be a bit tricky. Even experienced developers need to refer to the online help at times. You learned the basics in this hour, but don't be afraid to experiment on your own.

Q&A

Q Should I always specify parentheses to ensure that operators are evaluated as I expect them to be?

A Visual Basic .NET never fails to evaluate expressions according to the order of operator precedence, so using parentheses isn't necessary when the order of precedence is correct for an expression. However, using parentheses assures *you* that the

12

expression is being evaluated, and might make the expression easier to read by other people. This really is your choice.

Q I would like to use the same custom date format whenever I work with dates. Any advice on how to best accomplish this?

A I'd create a global constant that represents the formatting you want to use, and use that constant in your Format() calls as shown here. This way, if you want to change your format, you have to change only the constant value, and all Format() calls that use the constant will use the new value.

```
Const gc_MyUSDateFormat As String = "MMM. d, yyyy"
debug.WriteLine(Format(objStartDate, gc_MyUSDateFormat))
```

Workshop

The Workshop is designed to help you anticipate possible questions, review what you've learned, and get you thinking about how to put your knowledge into practice. The answers to the quiz are in Appendix B, "Answers to the Quizzes."

Quiz

1. Which character is used to perform exponentiation?

2. To get only the remainder of a division operation, you use which operator?

3. Which operation is performed in the following expression—the addition or the multiplication?

   ```
   x = 6 + 5 * 4
   ```

4. Does this expression evaluate to True or to False?

   ```
   ((True Or True) And False) = Not True
   ```

5. Which Boolean operator performs a logical negation?

6. The process of appending one string to another is called?

7. What function can be used to return the month of a given date?

8. What function returns the interval between two dates?

Exercises

1. Create a project that has a single text box on a form. Assume that the user enters a first name, a middle initial, and a last name into the text box. Parse the contents into three variables—one for each part of the name.

2. Create a project that has a single text box on a form. Assume that the user enters a valid birthday into the text box. Use the date functions to tell the user exactly how many days old he is.

Hour **13**

Making Decisions in Visual Basic Code

In Hour 10, "Creating and Calling Code Procedures," you learned to separate code into multiple procedures so that they can be called in any order required. This goes a long way in organizing code, but you still need a way to selectively execute code procedures or groups of statements within a procedure. You can use decision-making techniques to accomplish this. Decision-making constructs are coding structures enable you to execute or omit code based on the current situation, such as the value of a variable. Visual Basic includes two constructs that enable you to make any type of branching decision you can think of: If…Then…Else and Select Case.

In this hour, you'll learn how to use the decision constructs provided by Visual Basic to perform robust yet efficient decisions in Visual Basic code. In addition, you'll learn how to use the GoTo statement to redirect code within a procedure. You'll probably create decision constructs in every application you build, so the quicker you master these skills, the easier it will be to create robust applications.

The highlights of this hour include

- Making decisions using If...Then
- Expanding the capability of If...Then using Else and ElseIf
- Evaluating an expression for multiple values using Select Case
- Redirecting code flow using GoTo

Making Decisions Using If...Then

By far the most common decision-making construct used is the If...Then construct. A simple If...Then construct looks like this:

```
If expression Then

    ...    ' code to execute when expression is True.

End If
```

The If...Then construct uses Boolean logic, as discussed in Hour 12, "Performing Arithmetic, String Manipulation, and Date/Time Adjustments," to evaluate an expression to either True or False. The expression might be simple (If x = 6 Then) or complicated (If x=6 And Y>10 Then). If the expression evaluates to True, the code placed between the If statement and the End If statement executes. If the expression evaluates to False, Visual Basic jumps to the End If statement and continues execution, bypassing all the code between the If and End If statements.

You're going to create a simple If...Then construct in a Visual Basic project. Create a new Windows Application named **Decisions Example**, and follow these steps:

1. Rename the default form **fclsDecisions**, set the Text property of the form to **Decisions Example**, and change the Startup object to fclsDecisions.

2. Add a new text box to the form by double-clicking the TextBox icon in the toolbox. Set the properties of the text box as follows:

Property	Value
Name	**txtInput**
Location	**44,44**
Text	*(make blank)*

3. Add a new button to the form by double-clicking the Button icon in the toolbox. Set the button's properties as follows:

Property	Value
Name	**btnIsNumeric**
Location	**156,42**
Size	**100,23**
Text	**Is text numeric?**

Your form should now look like the one in Figure 13.1.

FIGURE 13.1

You'll use If...Then to determine whether text entered in the text box is a number.

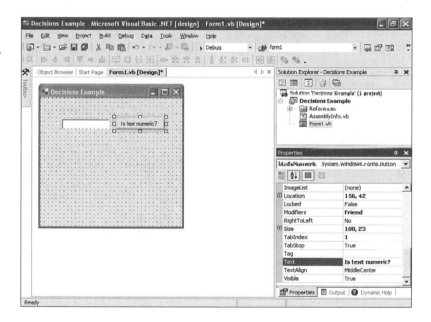

You're now going to add code to the button's Click event. This code will use a simple If...Then construct and the Visual Basic function IsNumeric() to determine whether the text entered in the text box is numeric. Double-click the button now to access its Click event, and enter the following code:

```
If IsNumeric(txtInput().Text) Then
    MessageBox.Show("The text is a number.")
End If
```

This code is simple when examined one statement at a time. Look closely at the first statement and recall that a simple If...Then statement looks like this:

```
If expression Then
```

13

In the code you entered, *expression* is

```
IsNumeric(txtInput().Text)
```

IsNumeric() is a Visual Basic function that evaluates a given string and returns True if the string is a number and False if it isn't. Here, you're passing the contents of the text box to the IsNumeric() function and instructing Visual Basic to make a decision based on the result. If IsNumeric() returns True, execution proceeds with the line immediately following the If statement and a message is displayed. If IsNumeric() returns False, execution jumps to the End If statement and no message is displayed.

If you have only a single line of code to execute in a simple If...Then construct, you can place the single statement of code immediately after the word Then and omit the End If statement. For example, the code you entered could have been entered like this:

```
If IsNumeric(txtInput().Text) Then MessageBox.Show("The text is a number.")
```

Although this code works, it's considered a better practice to use an End If statement, and I highly recommend that you do so.

Executing Code When *Expression* Is False

If you want to execute some code when *expression* evaluates to False, include an Else statement between If and End If like this:

```
If expression Then
    ...     ' code to execute when expression is True.
Else
    ...     ' code to execute when expression is False.
End If
```

> If you want to execute code only when *expression* equates to False, not when True, use the Not operator on the expression as in
>
> `If Not(expression) Then`
>
> Refer to Hour 12 for more information on Boolean logic.

By including an Else clause, you can have one set of statements execute when *expression* is True and another set of statements execute when *expression* is False. In the example you've built, if users enter a number, they'll get a message. However, if they don't enter a number, they'll receive no feedback. Modify your code to look like the following, which ensures that the user always gets a message:

```
If IsNumeric(txtInput().Text) Then
    MessageBox.Show("The text is a number.")
```

```
Else
    MessageBox.Show("The text is not a number.")
End If
```

If the user enters a number now, the message The text is a number is displayed, but nothing more. When Visual Basic encounters the Else statement, execution jumps to the End If statement because code within an Else statement executes only when *expression* is False. Likewise, if the user enters text that isn't a number, the message The text is not a number is displayed, but nothing more; when *expression* evaluates to False, execution immediately jumps to the Else statement.

Click Save All on the toolbar to save your work and then press F5 to run the project. Enter some text into the text box and click the button. A message box appears, telling you whether the text you entered is numeric or not (see Figure 13.2).

FIGURE 13.2

If...Then gives you great flexibility in making decisions.

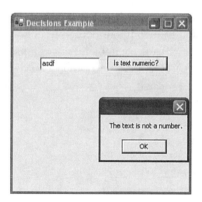

Feel free to enter other strings of text and click the button as often as you like. When you're satisfied the code is working, choose Stop Debugging from the Debug menu.

 Get comfortable with If...Then. Chances are good that you'll include at least one in every project you create.

13

Using ElseIf for Advanced Decision Making

If...Then...Else gives you lots of flexibility in making decisions. Visual Basic has a statement that even further expands the power of this construct and can reduce code that might otherwise be needed to nest If...Then statements (*nesting* involves placing one If...Then construct within another). Specifically, the ElseIf statement enables your program to evaluate a second expression when an If...Then statement equates to False.

The following shows a basic ElseIf structure:

```
If expression Then
   ...
ElseIf expression2 Then
   ...
End If
```

This code performs the same function as the following nested If...Then statements:

```
If expression Then
   ...
Else
   If expression2 Then
      ...
   End If
End If
```

The ElseIf statement not only reduces code, it also makes complex If...Then decision structures much easier to read and follow. It's important to note that you can use multiple ElseIf statements and even use an Else as a catchall. For example:

```
If optSendToPrinter.Value Then
   ' Code to print document goes here.
ElseIf optSendToScreen.Value Then
   ' Code to perform a print preview goes here.
ElseIf optSendEmail.Value Then
   ' Code to email the document goes here.
Else
   ...
End If
```

Be aware that the primary If statement and all its ElseIf statements are mutually exclusive; only one will ever execute its code.

Nesting If...Then Constructs

As mentioned earlier, you can nest If...Then statements to further refine your decision-making process. The format you use can be something like this:

```
If optSendToPrinter.Value Then
   If blnDriverSelected Then
      ' Print the document
   Else
      ' Prompt for a printer driver.
   End If
Else
   ...
End If
```

One thing to keep in mind when nesting If…Then constructs is that you must have a corresponding End If statement for every If…Then statement, unless the If…Then statement executes only one statement and that statement appears on the same line as If…Then.

Evaluating an Expression for Multiple Values Using Select Case

At times, the If…Then construct isn't capable of handling a decision situation without a lot of extra work. One such situation is when you need to perform different actions based on numerous possible values of an expression, not just True or False. For instance, suppose that you want to perform actions based on the age of the user. The following shows what you might create using If…Then:

```
If lngAge < 10  Then
   ...
ElseIf lngAge < 18 Then
   ...
ElseIf lngAge < 21 Then
   ...
Else
   ...
End If
```

As you can see, this structure can be a bit hard to read. If you don't analyze it from top to bottom (as the compiler does), you might not get the whole picture. For instance, if you looked at the last ElseIf, you might think that the code for that ElseIf would execute if the user is under the age of 21. However, when you realize that the previous ElseIf statements caught all ages up to 18, it becomes apparent that the last ElseIf runs only when the user is between 18 and 20.

The important thing to realize here is that each ElseIf is really evaluating the same expression (lngAge) but considering different values for the expression. Visual Basic includes a much better decision construct for evaluating a single expression for multiple possible values: Select Case.

A typical Select Case construct looks like this:

```
Select Case expression
   Case value1
      ...
   Case value2
      ...
   Case value3
      ...
   Case Else
      ...
End Select
```

13

Case Else is used to define code that executes only when *expression* doesn't evaluate to any of the values in the Case statements. Use of Case Else is optional.

Evaluating More Than One Possible Value in a Case Statement

The Select Case statement enables you to create some pretty advanced expression comparisons. For example, you can specify multiple comparisons in a single Case statement by separating the comparisons with a comma (,). Consider the following:

```
Select Case strColor
    Case "Red","Purple","Orange"
        ' Color is a warm color.
    Case "Blue","Green","Blue Violet"
        ' Color is a cool color.
End Select
```

When Visual Basic .NET encounters a comma within a Case statement, it evaluates the expression against each item in the comma-separated list. If *expression* matches any one of the items, the code for the Case statement executes. This can considerably reduce the number of Case statements in a complicated construct.

Another advanced comparison is the keyword To. When To is used, Visual Basic looks at the expression to determine whether the value is within a range designated by To. When using To, you can't include Is = as you can with a simple expression. Here's an example:

```
Select Case lngAge
    Case 1 To 7
        ' Code placed here executes if lngAge is 1, 7 or any number in between.
End Select
```

The keyword To can be used with strings as well. For example:

```
Select Case strName
    Case "Hartman" To "White"
        ' Code placed here executes if the string is Hartman, White,
        ' or if the string falls alphabetically between these two names.
End Select
```

Here's the Age example shown earlier, but this time Select Case is used:

```
Select Case lngAge
    Case Is < 10
        ...
    Case 11 To 18
        ...
    Case 19 To 21
        ...
    Case Else
    ...
End Select
```

The Select Case makes this decision much easier to follow. Again, the key with Select Case is that it's used to evaluate a single expression for more than one possible value.

Building a Select Case Example

You're now going to build a project that uses advanced expression evaluation in a Select Case structure. This simple application will display a list of animals to the user in a combo box. When the user clicks a button, the application will display the number of legs of the animal chosen in the list (if an animal is selected). Create a new Windows Application named **Select Case Example**. Rename the default form to **fclsSelectCaseExample**. Set the form's Text property to **Select Case Example** and set the Startup object to fclsSelectCaseExample. Add a new combo box to the form by double-clicking the ComboBox item on the toolbox. Set the combo box's properties as follows:

Property	Value
Name	**cboAnimals**
Location	**80,100**
Text	*(make blank)*

Next, you'll add some items to the list. Click the Items property of the combo box, and then click the Build button that appears in the property to access the String Collection Editor for the combo box. Enter the text as shown in Figure 13.3; be sure to press Enter at the end of each list item to make the next item appear on its own line.

FIGURE 13.3

Each line you enter here becomes an item in the combo box at runtime.

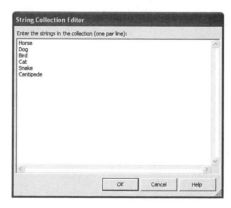

13

Next you'll add a Button control. When the button is clicked, a Select Case construct will be used to determine which animal the user has selected and tell the user how many legs the selected animal has. Add a new button to the form by double-clicking the Button tool in the toolbox. Set the button's properties as follows:

Property	Value
Name	**btnShowLegs**
Location	**102,130**
Text	**Show Legs**

Your form should now look like the one in Figure 13.4. Click Save All on the toolbar to save your work before continuing.

FIGURE 13.4

This example uses only a combo box and a Button control.

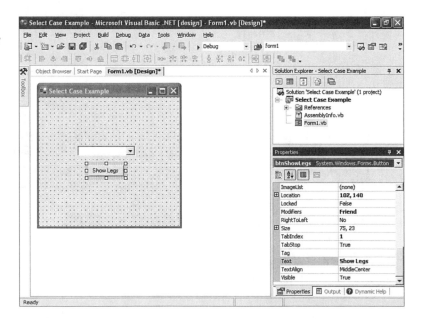

All that's left to do is add the code. Double-click the Button control to access its Click event, and then enter the following code:

```
Select Case cboAnimals().Text
   Case Is = "Bird"
      MessageBox.Show("The animal has 2 legs.")
   Case Is = "Horse", "Dog", "Cat"
      MessageBox.Show ("The animal has 4 legs.")
   Case Is = "Snake"
      MessageBox.Show ("The animal has no legs.")
```

```
    Case Is = "Centipede"
        MessageBox.Show ("The animal has 100 legs.")
    Case Else
        MessageBox.Show ("You did not select from the list!")
End Select
```

Here's what's happening: The Select Case construct compares the content of the cboAnimals combo box to a set of predetermined values. Each Case statement is evaluated in the order in which it appears in the list. Therefore, the expression is first compared to "Bird". If the content of the combo box is Bird, the MessageBox.Show statement immediately following the Case statement is called and code execution then jumps to the End Select statement. If the combo box doesn't contain Bird, Visual Basic looks to see whether the content is "Horse", "Dog", or "Cat". If the combo box contains any of these values, the MessageBox.Show statement following the Case statement is called, and execution then jumps to the End Select statement. Each successive Case statement is evaluated the same way. If no matches are found for any of the Case statements, the MsgBox in the Case Else statement is called. If there were no matches and no Case Else statement, no code would execute.

As you can see, the capability to place multiple possible values for the expression on a single Case statement reduced the number of Case statements as well as redundant code (code that would have to be duplicated for each Case statement in which animals had the same number of legs). Also, adding a new animal to the list can be as simple as adding the animal's name to an existing Case statement.

Try it now by pressing F5 to run your project and then follow these steps:

1. Select an animal from the list and click the button.

2. Try clearing the contents of the combo box and click the button.

3. When you're finished, choose Stop Debugging from the Debug menu to stop the project and click Save All on the toolbar.

Creative Uses of Select Case

You might be surprised at what you can do with a Select Case statement when you give it some thought. One of the coolest tricks I know uses Select Case to determine which radio button in a group is selected.

When a radio button is selected, its Checked property returns True. Essentially, this means you have to look at the Checked property of each radio button in a group until you find the one that's set to True. The Visual Basic documentation recommends using an If...Then construct like this:

```
Dim strMessage As String = "You selected "
```

13

```
If radioButton1.Checked = True Then
   strMessage = strMessage & radioButton1.Text
ElseIf radiobutton2.Checked = True Then
   strMessage = strMessage & radioButton2.Text
ElseIf radiobutton3.Checked = True Then
   strMessage = strMessage & radioButton3.Text
End If
MessageBox.Show(strMessage)
```

Personally, I think all those ElseIf statements are messy. Consider this: Although you're looking at the Checked property of a number of radio button controls, you're comparing them all to a single value—the value True.

Now, if you look at True as the expression and the Checked properties of the controls as the possible values, you can replace the If...Then construct with a Select Case construct such as the following:

```
Dim strMessage As String
Select Case True
   Case Is = radioButton1.Checked
      strMessage = strMessage & radioButton1.Text
   Case Is = radioButton2.Checked
      strMessage = strMessage& radioButton2.Text
   Case Is = radioButton3.Checked
      strMessage = strMessage & radioButton3.Text
End Select
MessageBox.Show(strMessage)
```

This seems much tidier to me. You can pretty much accomplish any decision-making task you can think of using If...Then or Select Case. The skill comes in creating the cleanest and most readable decision structure possible.

> You can nest Select Case constructs within one another. In addition, you can nest Select Case constructs within If...Then constructs, and vice versa; you can pretty much nest decision constructs in any way you see fit.

Branching Within a Procedure Using GoTo

NEW TERM Decision structures are used to selectively execute code. When a decision statement is encountered, Visual Basic evaluates an expression and diverts code according to the result. However, you don't have to use a decision structure to divert code because Visual Basic includes a statement that can be used to jump code execution to a predetermined location within the current procedure: the GoTo statement.

Before I talk about how to use GoTo, I want to say that under most circumstances, it's considered bad coding practice to use a GoTo. Code that's heavily laden with GoTos is difficult to read and debug because the execution path is so convoluted. Such code is often called *spaghetti code*, and should be avoided at all costs. I'd say that in 99% of the situations in which GoTo is used, there's a better approach to the problem, and I'll show an example of just such a case shortly. Nevertheless, GoTo, like all other statements, is a tool. Although it's not needed as often as some of the other Visual Basic statements, it's still a useful tool to have at your disposal—when used judiciously.

NEW TERM   To jump to a specific location in a procedure, you must first define the jump location using a *code label*. A code label is not the same as a label control that you place on a form. You create a code label by positioning the cursor on a new line in a procedure, typing in a name for the label followed by a colon, and pressing Enter. Code labels can't contain spaces and they can't be a Visual Basic reserved word. For instance, you can't create a code label called Print because Print is a reserved word in Visual Basic. However, you could create a label called PrintAll because PrintAll isn't a reserved word. Code labels act as pointers that you can jump to using GoTo. The following shows an example using GoTo to jump code execution to a label:

```
Private Sub GotoExample()
    Dim intCounter As Integer
    intCounter = 0
IncrementCounter:
    intCounter = intCounter + 1
    If intCounter < 5000 Then GoTo IncrementCounter
End Sub
```

This procedure does the following:

- Dimensions an Integer variable called intCounter.
- Sets the new variable to 0.
- Defines a code label titled IncrementCounter. One or more GoTo statements can be used to jump code execution to this label at any time.
- Increments intCounter by 1.
- Uses an If…Then statement to determine whether intCounter has exceeded 5000. If it hasn't, a GoTo statement forces code execution back to the IncrementCounter label, where intCounter is incremented and tested again, creating a loop.

This code works, and you're welcome to try it. However, this is *terrible* code. Remember how I said that the use of a GoTo can often be replaced by a better coding approach? In this case, Visual Basic has specific looping constructs that you'll learn about in the next hour. These looping constructs are far superior to building your own loop under most conditions, so you should avoid building a loop using a GoTo statement. As a matter of fact, one of the biggest misuses of GoTo is using it in place of one of Visual Basic's

13

internal looping constructs. In case you're interested, here's the loop that would replace the use of GoTo in this example:

```
Dim intCounter As Integer
For intCounter = 1 To 5000
   ...
Next intCounter
```

This discussion might leave you wondering why you would ever use GoTo. One situation in which I commonly use GoTo statements is to create single exit points. As you know, you can force execution to leave a procedure at any time using Exit Sub or Exit Function. Cleanup code is often required before a procedure exits. In a long procedure, you might have many exit statements. However, such a procedure can be a problem to debug because cleanup code might not be run under all circumstances. All procedures have a single entry point, and it makes sense to give them all a single exit point. With a single exit point, you use a GoTo statement to go to the exit point, rather than an Exit statement. The following procedure illustrates using GoTo to create a single exit point:

```
Private Sub DoSomething()
   ' If it is necessary to exit the procedure, perform a GoTo to
   ' the PROC_EXIT label, rather than using an Exit statement.
PROC_EXIT:
   Exit Sub
End Sub
```

An even better approach to creating a single exit point is to wrap the contents of a procedure in a Try...Catch...Finally block as discussed in Hour 15, "Debugging Your Code."

Summary

In this hour you learned how to use Visual Basic's decision constructs to make decisions in Visual Basic code. You learned how to use If…Then statements to execute code when an expression evaluates to True and to use Else to run code when the expression evaluates to False. For more complicated decisions, you learned how to use ElseIf statements to add further comparisons to the decision construct. You even learned how you can nest If…Then structures for more flexibility.

In addition to If…Then, you learned how to use Select…Case to create powerful decision constructs to evaluate a single expression for many possible values. You learned how you can check for multiple possible values using a single Case statement, which can greatly increase legibility and reduce redundancy. Finally, you learned that mixing creativity with Select Case can yield some very useful results.

Decision-making constructs are often the backbone of applications. Without the capability to run specific sets of code based on changing situations, your code would be very linear and hence very limited. Become comfortable with the decision constructs and make a conscious effort to use the best construct for any given situation. The better you are at writing decision constructs, the faster you'll be able to produce solid and understandable code.

Q&A

Q **What if I want to execute code only when an expression in an If...Then statement is False, not True? Do I need to place the code in an Else clause, and no code after the Then?**

A This is where Boolean logic helps. What you need to do is make the expression evaluate to True for the code you want to run. This is accomplished using the Not operator, like this:

```
If Not expression Then
```

Q **How important is the order in which Case statements are created?**

A This all depends on the situation. In the earlier example in which the selected animal was considered and the number of legs it has was displayed, the order has no effect. If you're going to perform numeric comparisons, such as the Age example shown in the text, the order is critical; it's possible to prevent a Case statement from ever being evaluated if you're not careful. For instance, comparing a variable to <12 before comparing it to =6 would mean that the first comparison would evaluate to True if the variable was 6, so the second comparison would never take place.

Workshop

The Workshop is designed to help you anticipate possible questions, review what you've learned, and get you thinking about how to put your knowledge into practice. The answers to the quiz are in Appendix B, "Answers to the Quizzes."

Quiz

1. Which decision construct should you use to evaluate a single expression to either True or False?

2. Evaluating expressions to True or False for both types of decision constructs is accomplished using _____ logic.

13

3. If you want code to execute when the expression of an If...Then statement evaluates to False, include an _____ clause.

4. True or False: You don't need an End If statement when only one statement is to execute when an expression in an If...Then statement evaluates to True.

5. Which decision construct should you use when evaluating the result of an expression that might equate to one of many possible values?

6. To place multiple possible values on a single Case statement, separate them using a _____.

7. Is it possible that more than one Case statement might have its code execute?

8. True or False: You can use GoTo to jump code execution to a different procedure.

9. To use GoTo to jump execution to a new location in code, what must you create as a pointer to jump to?

Exercises

1. Create a project that enables the user to enter text into a text box. Use an If...Then construct to determine whether the text entered is a circle, triangle, square, or pentagon, and display the number of sides the entered shape has. If the text doesn't match one of these shapes, let the users know that they must enter a shape.

2. Rewrite the following code using only an If...Then structure; the new code should *not* contain a GoTo:

```
...
If Not(blnAddToAge) Then GoTo SkipAddToAge
intAge = intAge + 1
SkipAddToAge:
...
```

Hour 14

Looping for Efficiency

NEW TERM As you develop your Visual Basic .NET programs, you'll encounter situations in which you need to execute the same code statement or statements repeatedly. You'll often need to execute these statements a specific number of times, but you might need to execute them as long as a certain condition persists (an expression is True) or until a condition occurs (an expression becomes True). Visual Basic .NET includes constructs that enable you to easily define and execute these repetitive code routines: *loops*. This hour shows you how to use the two major looping constructs to make your code smaller, faster, and more efficient.

The highlights of this hour include

- Looping a specific number of times using For…Next
- Looping based on a condition using Do…Loop

Looping a Specific Number of Times Using For...Next

The simplest type of loop to create is the For...Next loop, which has been around since the earliest forms of the BASIC language. With a For...Next loop, you instruct Visual Basic .NET to begin a loop by starting a counter at a specific value. Visual Basic .NET then executes the code within the loop, increments the counter by a defined incremental value, and repeats the loop until the counter reaches an upper limit you've set. The following is the syntax for the basic For...Next loop:

```
For countervariable = start To end [Step step]
    ... [statements to execute in loop]
[Exit For]
    ... [statements to execute in loop]
Next [countervariable]
```

Initiating the Loop Using For

The For statement both sets up and starts the loop. The For statement has the component shown in Table 14.1.

TABLE 14.1 Components of the For Statement

Part	Description
countervariable	A previously declared variable of a numeric data type (Integer, Long, and so on). This variable is incremented each time the loop occurs.
start	The number you want to start counting from.
end	The number you want to count to. When *countervariable* reaches the *end* number, the statements within the For...Next loop are executed one final time and execution continues with the line following the Next statement.
step	The amount you want *countervariable* incremented each time the loop is performed. *step* is an optional parameter; if you omit the *step* parameter, *countervariable* is incremented by 1.
Exit For	A statement that can be used to exit the loop at any time. When Exit For is encountered, execution jumps to the statement following Next.

Closing the Loop with the Next Statement

Every For statement must have a corresponding Next statement. You don't have to specify the *countervariable* name with the Next statement, but you should because it makes the code easier to read. The following are examples of simple For...Next loops, along with explanations of what they do:

```
Dim intCounter As Integer
For intCounter = 1 To 100
   debug.WriteLine(intCounter)
Next intCounter
```

This routine declares an Integer variable named intCounter, and then starts a loop with a For statement. The Loop initializes intCounter at 1, prints the value of intCounter, increments intCounter, and continues looping. Because *Step* has been omitted, the variable intCounter is increased by 1 every time the loop is performed. This loop would execute 100 times, printing the numbers 1 through 100 to the Output debug window.

This next routine performs the same as the previous example:

```
Dim intCounter As Integer
For intCounter = 1 To 100
   debug.WriteLine(intCounter)
Next
```

Note that the Next statement doesn't specify the name of the counter whose loop is to be executed. This is perfectly legal, but it's not good coding practice. Consider the following example:

```
Dim intCounter As Integer
Dim intSecondCounter as Integer
For intCounter = 1 To 100
   For intSecondCounter = 1 to 100
      debug.WriteLine(intSecondCounter)
   Next intSecondCounter
Next intCounter
```

This code executes a loop within a loop. If you omitted the variable names on the Next statements, the code would run, but from a programmer's standpoint, it would be difficult to read and understand.

Specifying an Increment Value Using Step

Step is used in a For...Next statement to designate the value to increment the counter variable each time the loop occurs. As you've seen, when Step is omitted, the counter variable is incremented by one—always. If you want the counter variable incremented by one, you don't need to use Step (it doesn't make the code any easier to read). However, if you need to increment the counter variable by a value other than one, you have to use Step.

Here's an example of a simple For...Next loop that uses Step:

```
Dim intCounter As Integer
For intCounter = 1 To 100 Step 4
 debug.WriteLine(intCounter)
Next intCounter
```

14

This code works much like the first example, except that each time Next is reached, intCounter is incremented by 4 rather than by 1. This loop would execute a total of 25 times (not 100 times). To create a For…Next loop that counts backward, specify a negative value for Step, as shown here:

```
Dim intCounter As Long
For intCounter = 100 To 1 Step -1
 debug.WriteLine(intCounter)
Next intCounter
```

This loop initializes intCounter at a value of 100 and decrements intCounter by 1 each time Next is reached. The loop executes until intCounter is reduced to 1 (the End value).

Although you'll know the start and end of a For…Next loop when you initialize it (you have to specify a start and end or you can't create the loop), at times you'll need to exit a loop before you reach the end value. To exit a For…Next loop at any time, use the Exit For statement as shown in the following example:

```
Dim intCounter As Integer
For intCounter = 1 To 100
  If <condition> Then Exit For
 debug.WriteLine(intCounter)
Next intCounter
```

When Visual Basic .NET encounters an Exit For statement, code execution jumps immediately to the statement following the Next statement of the current loop—the loop stops. In this example, *<condition>* could be a variable or any expression. *<condition>* is usually something that changes during the lifetime of the loop; if *<condition>* doesn't change, there's no point in evaluating it.

Creating a For…Next Example

You're now going to create a procedure containing two For…Next loops, one nested within the other. The first loop counts from 1 to 100 and sets the Width property of a Label control to the current counter value—this emulates a Windows progress meter. The second loop is used to slow the execution of the first loop—an old programmer's trick using a For…Next loop.

Create a new Windows Application named **For Next Example**. Change the name of the default form to **fclsForNextExample**, set the form's Text property to **For…Next Example**, and change the Startup object to fclsForNextExample. Add a Label control to the form by double-clicking the Label tool in the toolbox. Set the label's properties as follows:

Property	Value
Name	**lblMeter**
BackColor	*(Set to a light blue or any color you like)*
Location	**100,100**
Size	**100,17**
Text	*(Make blank)*

Next, add a button to the form by double-clicking the Button item in the toolbox. Set the button's properties as follows:

Property	Value
Name	**btnForNext**
Location	**88,125**
Size	**125,23**
Text	**Run a For...Next loop**

Your form should look like the one shown in Figure 14.1.

FIGURE 14.1

This simple project emulates a status bar.

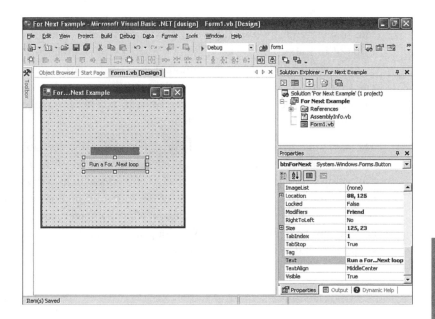

14

All that's left to do is to write the code. Double-click the button to access its Click event and enter the following:

```
Dim intLabelWidth As Integer
Dim intPauseCounter As Integer
For intLabelWidth = 1 To 100
   lblMeter.Width = intLabelWidth
   lblMeter.Refresh()
   For intPauseCounter = 1 To 600000
   Next intPauseCounter
Next intLabelWidth
```

This code should make some sense to you by now. The first two lines simply create variables for the loops. The third line starts the first For...Next loop using the variable intLabelWidth, initializes the variable to 1, and sets the upper limit of the loop to 100. Because the Step argument is omitted, the loop will increment the counter by 1 each time the loop completes.

> Using a loop to create a delay is actually a very poor and outdated coding technique. There are other options for creating a delay, such as calling System.Threading.Thread.Sleep(). This example is designed to illustrate nested loops—which it does—not to show the best way to create a delay.

The first statement within this For...Next loop sets the width of the Label control to the value of intLabelWidth. The width of the label will be updated 100 times. The next statement simply calls the Refresh method of the Label control to ensure that it paints itself. Painting often catches up when the CPU has idle time. Because you want the transition from a small label to a large one to be smooth, you need to make sure the label paints itself after each update to its Width property.

The next statement starts a second For...Next loop using the intPauseCounter variable, initializes intPauseCounter to 1, and sets the upper limit of the loop to 600,000. Following this line is the Next statement for this new loop. Why is there no code between the For and Next statements of the intPauseCounter loop? This loop is used simply to create a delay within the processor. Most computers are so fast that if you didn't add a delay here, the first For...Next loop would update the label's width from 1 to 100 so quickly that you might not even see it update!

I wrote this code on a 2.4GHz machine; you might have to alter this value if your processor speed is much different. If you have a slower CPU, reduce this value. If you have a much faster processor (and let me say WOW!), increase this value. Wait until you test this code before making changes to the upper limit of intPauseCounter, however. Again, using another method, such as calling System.Threading.Thread.Sleep(), would allow precise control over the delay regardless of the speed of the machine.

Click Save All on the toolbar and press F5 to run the project. The label starts with a width of 100. Click the button, and you'll see the label's width change to 1 and then increment to 100. If the speed is too slow or too fast, stop the project and adjust the upper limit of the inner For...Next loop.

If you were to forgo a loop and write each and every line of code necessary to draw the label with a width from 1 to 100, it would take 100 lines of code. Using a simple For...Next loop, you performed the same task in just a few lines.

Use a For...Next loop when you know the number of times you want the loop to execute. This doesn't mean that you have to actually know the number of times you want the loop to execute at design time; it simply means that you must know the number of times you want the loop to execute when you first start the loop. You can use a variable to define any of the parameters for the For...Next loop, as illustrated in the following code:

```
Dim intCounter As Integer
Dim intUpperLimit as Integer
intUpperLimit = 100
For intCounter = 1 To intUpperLimit
    debug.WriteLine(intCounter)
Next intCounter
```

One of the keys to writing efficient code is to eliminate redundancy. If you find yourself typing the same (or a similar) line of code repeatedly, chances are it's a good candidate for a loop.

Using Do...Loop to Loop an Indeterminate Number of Times

14

In some situations, you won't know the exact number of times a loop must be performed—not even when the loop begins. You could start a For...Next loop specifying an upper limit that you know is larger than the number of loops needed, check for a terminating condition within the loop, and exit the loop using an Exit For statement when the condition is met. However, this approach is extremely inefficient and usually impractical. When you need to create such a loop, using Do…Loop is the answer.

Creating a Do…Loop

Do…Loop comes in a number of flavors. Its most basic form has the following syntax:

```
Do
    [Statements]
Loop
```

Ending a Do…Loop

A Do…Loop without some sort of exit mechanism or defined condition is an endless loop. In its most basic form (shown previously), nothing is present to tell the loop when to stop looping. At times you might need an endless loop (game programming is an example), but most often, you'll need to exit the loop when a certain condition is met. Like the For…Next loop, the Do…Loop has a statement you can use to exit the loop at any time: the Exit Do statement. For example, you could expand the Do…Loop we're discussing to include an Exit Do statement such as the following:

```
Do
    [Statements]
    If expression Then Exit Do
Loop
```

In this code, the loop would execute until *expression* evaluates to True. Generally, the expression is based on a variable that's modified somewhere within the loop. Obviously, if the expression never changes, the loop never ends.

You can build an expression into the Do…Loop structure itself using one of two keywords: While or Until. The following is a simple Do…Loop using the While keyword:

```
Do While expression
    [Statements]
Loop
```

As long as *expression* evaluates to True, this loop continues to occur. If *expression* evaluates to False when the loop first starts, the code between the Do and Loop statements doesn't execute—not even once.

Here's a similar Do…Loop that uses the Until keyword:

```
Do Until expression
    [Statements]
Loop
```

This loop behaves differently from the loop that uses While. When you define a loop using the keyword Until, the loop executes repeatedly until *expression* evaluates to True. As long as *expression* is False, the loop occurs. This is essentially the opposite behavior of While. If *expression* is True when the loop begins, the code between the Do and Loop statements doesn't execute—not even once.

Notice how both While and Until can prevent the loop from executing at all. This occurs because when *expression* is placed on the Do statement, it's evaluated before entering the loop and again after each occurrence of the loop. You can put a While or Until on the Loop statement rather than on the Do statement. When you do so, the loop executes once before *expression* is evaluated. Therefore, such loops always occur at least once. You need to be aware of how this changes the behavior of the loop. Here's the previous example with the While keyword placed on the Loop statement:

```
Do
    [Statements]
Loop While expression
```

Again, this loop executes as long as *expression* evaluates to True. The difference between this Do...Loop and the Do...Loop with While on the Do statement is that the code between the Do and Loop statements always executes at least once; *expression* isn't evaluated until the loop has completed its first cycle. Therefore, such a loop always executes *at least once*, regardless of the value of expression. Here's the same code that was shown previously, this time with the Until keyword placed on the Loop statement rather than on the Do statement:

```
Do
    [Statements]
Loop Until expression
```

Again, this loop executes until *expression* evaluates to True. However, the code within this loop always executes at least once; *expression* isn't evaluated until the loop completes its first cycle.

Creating a Do...Loop Example

You're now going to create an example using a Do...Loop that updates a label to once again simulate a progress meter. This loop performs the same function as the For...Next loop you created in the previous example, but its structure is quite different.

If your For...Next example is currently running, choose Stop Debugging from the Debug menu. Add another button to the form by double-clicking the Button item in the Toolbox. Set the new button's properties as follows:

14

Property	Value
Name	**btnDoLoop**
Location	**88,160**
Size	**125,23**
Text	**Run a Do Loop**

Your form should now look like the one shown in Figure 14.2.

FIGURE 14.2

You'll use the same form for both loop examples.

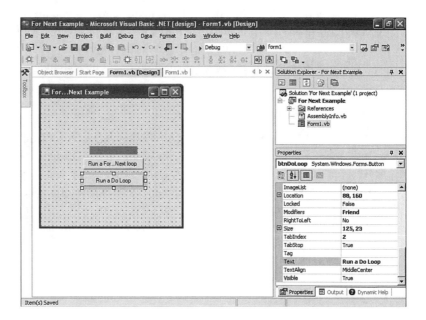

Double-click the new button to access its Click event and then enter the following code:

```
Dim intLabelWidth As Integer
Dim intPauseCounter As Integer
intLabelWidth = 1
Do Until intLabelWidth = 100
   lblMeter.Width = intLabelWidth
   intLabelWidth = intLabelWidth + 1
   lblMeter.Refresh()
   For intPauseCounter = 1 To 600000
   Next intPauseCounter
Loop
```

Again, this code is more easily understood when broken down:

- The first two lines create two variables: one for the Do...Loop and one for the For...Next loop, which is still used to slow down the procedure.

- The variable intLabelWidth is set to 1.

- A Do...Loop is started using the Until keyword. This loop will execute until intLabelWidth has the value 100.

- The label's Width property is set to the value of intLabelWidth.

- The label is forced to refresh its appearance.

- The intLabelWidth variable is incremented by 1.

- A For...Next loop is used to slow down the procedure, just as in the previous example.

- When the Loop statement is encountered, code execution jumps back to the Do statement and intLabelWidth is evaluated again. If it's not 100, the code within the loop occurs.

Click Save All on the toolbar to save the project and then press F5 to run it. Click the Run a Do Loop button to see the progress meter set itself to 1 pixel and then update itself by 1 until it reaches 100 pixels.

You've now seen how to perform the same function with two entirely different coding techniques. This is fairly common when creating programs; multiple approaches usually exist to solve to a given problem. Simply being aware of your options makes writing code that much easier. When you hear of people optimizing their code, they're usually looking for a different, faster approach to a problem they've already solved.

> Visual Basic .NET supports one more loop type: the While...End While loop. All I want to say about this loop is that it's almost the same as the Do...Loop (While...End While does the same thing as the Do...Loop, but uses different syntax), but the Do...Loop is more widely accepted (the While...End While is a hold-over from earlier versions of Visual Basic). I highly recommend that you don't use the While...End While loop; instead, use the Do...Loop.

Summary

Looping is a powerful technique that enables you to write tighter code. *Tighter* code is smaller, more efficient, and usually—but not always—more readable. In this hour, you learned to write For...Next loops for situations in which you know the precise number of times you want a loop executed. Remember, it's not necessary to know the number of iterations at design time, but you must know the number at runtime to use a For...Next loop. You learned how to use Step to increment the counter of a For...Next loop, and even how to exit a loop prematurely using Exit For.

14

In this hour, you also learned how to use the very powerful Do...Loop. Do...Loop enables you to create very flexible loops that can handle almost any looping scenario. Depending on your needs, you can evaluate an expression in a Do...Loop using While or Until. You learned how evaluating *expression* on the Do statement makes the loop behave differently than when evaluating on the Loop statement. If a For...Next loop can't do the job, some form of the Do...Loop will.

In addition to learning the specifics about loops, you've seen firsthand how multiple solutions to a problem can exist. Often, one approach is clearly superior to all other approaches, although you might not always find it. Other times, one approach might be only marginally superior or multiple approaches might all be equally applicable. Expert programmers are able to consistently find the best approaches to any given problem. With time, you'll be able to do the same.

Q&A

Q Are there any specific cases in which one loop is appropriate over another?

A Usually, when you have to walk an index or sequential set of elements (such as referencing all elements in an array), the For...Next loop is the best choice.

Q Should I be concerned about the performance differences between the two types of loops?

A With today's fast processors, chances are good that the performance difference between the two loop types in any given situation will be overshadowed by the readability and functionality of the best choice of loop. If you have a situation in which performance is critical, write the loop using all the ways you can think of, benchmark the results, and choose the fastest loop.

Workshop

The Workshop is designed to help you anticipate possible questions, review what you've learned, and get you thinking about how to put your knowledge into practice. The answers to the quiz are in Appendix B, "Answers to the Quizzes."

Quiz

1. To increment the counter variable in a For...Next loop by a value other than 1, you use what keyword?

2. True or False: You have to know the start and end values of a For...Next loop at design time to use this type of loop.

3. What statement is used to close a loop started with a For statement?

4. Is it possible to nest loops?

5. What type of loop do you most likely need to create if you don't have any idea how many times the loop must occur?

6. If you evaluate the expression in a Do...Loop on the Loop statement, is it possible that the code within the loop might never execute?

7. What statement do you use to terminate a Do...Loop without evaluating the expression on the Do or Loop statement?

Exercises

1. The status meter example using Do...Loop has a deliberate bug. The meter will display only to 99 (the label's width will adjust only to 99 pixels, not 100). The problem has to do with how the expression is evaluated. Find and correct this problem.

2. Use two For...Next loops nested within each other to size a label in two dimensions. Have the outer loop change the Width property of the label from 1 to 100, and have the inner loop change the Height property from 1 to 100. Don't be surprised by the result—the end result is rather odd.

14

HOUR 15

Debugging Your Code

No one writes perfect code. You're most certainly familiar with those problems that prevent code from executing properly—they're called *bugs*. Being new to Visual Basic .NET, your code will probably contain a fair number of bugs. As you gain proficiency, the number of bugs in your code will decrease, but bugs will never disappear entirely. Debugging is a skill and an art. This book can't teach you how to debug every possible build or runtime error you might encounter; however, in this hour, you'll learn the basic skills necessary to trace and correct most bugs in your code.

The highlights of this hour include the following:

- Adding comments to your code
- Identifying the two basic types of errors
- Working with break points
- Using the Command window
- Using the Output window
- Creating a structured error handler

The Task List window is useful for addressing build errors in code. Because its use goes beyond this simple debugging application, however, I discuss the Task List in Hour 10, "Creating and Calling Code Procedures."

Before proceeding, create a new Windows Application project named **Debugging Example**. Change the name of the default form to **fclsDebuggingExample**, set its Text property to **Debugging Example**, and change the Startup object of the project to fclsDebuggingExample.

Add a new text box to the form by double-clicking the TextBox item in the toolbox. Set the text box's properties as follows:

Property	Value
Name	**txtInput**
Location	**88,112**
Size	**120,20**
Text	(*make blank*)

Next, add a new button to the form by double-clicking the Button item in the toolbox, and set its properties as follows:

Property	Value
Name	**btnPerformDivision**
Location	**96,144**
Size	**104,23**
Text	**Perform Division**

Your form should now look like the one shown in Figure 15.1.

All this little project does is divide 100 by whatever is entered into the text box. As you write the code to accomplish this, various bugs will be introduced (on purpose), and you'll learn to correct them. Save your project now by clicking the Save All button on the toolbar.

FIGURE 15.1

This simple interface will help you learn debugging techniques.

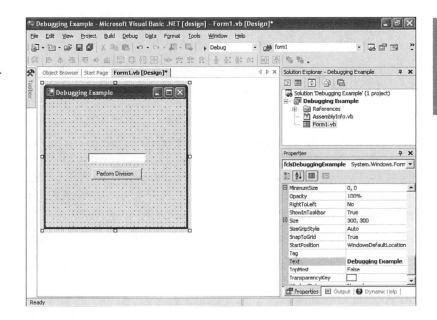

15

Adding Comments to Your Code

One of the simplest things you can do to reduce bugs from the start—and make tracking down existing bugs easier—is to add comments to your code. A code comment is simply a line of text that Visual Basic .NET knows isn't actual code. Comment lines are stripped from the code when the project is compiled to create a distributable component, so comments don't affect performance. Visual Basic .NET's code window shows comments as green text. This makes it easier to read and understand procedures. You should consider adding comments to the top of each procedure stating the procedure's purpose. In addition, you should add liberal comments throughout all procedures, detailing what's occurring in the code.

Comments are meant to be read by humans, not by computers. Strive to make your comments intelligible. Keep in mind that a comment that's hard to understand isn't much better than no comment at all. Also remember that comments serve as a form of documentation. Just as documentation for an application must be clearly written, code comments should also follow good writing principles.

To create a comment, precede the comment text with the apostrophe character ('). For example, a simple comment might look like this:

```
' This is a comment because it is preceded with an apostrophe.
```

Comments can also be placed at the end of a line of code, like this:

```
Dim intAge as Integer        ' Used to store the user's age in years.
```

Everything to the right of and including the apostrophe in this statement is a comment. By adding comments to your code procedures, you don't have to rely on memory to decipher a procedure's purpose or mechanics. If you've ever had to go back and work with code you haven't looked at in a while or had to work with someone else's code, you probably already have a great appreciation for comments.

Double-click the button now to access its `Click` event and add the following two lines of code (comments, actually):

```
' This procedure divides 100 by the value entered in
' the text box txtInput.
```

Notice that after you press Enter to create a new line, the comment text turns green.

When creating code comments, strive to do the following:

- Document the purpose of the code (the *why,* not the *how*).
- Clearly indicate the thinking and logic behind the code.
- Call attention to important turning points in code.
- Reduce the need for readers to run a simulation of code execution in their heads.

Identifying the Two Basic Types of Errors

NEW TERM Essentially, two types of errors can occur in code: compile errors and runtime errors. A *compile error* (commonly called a *build error*) is code that prevents Visual Basic .NET's compiler from being able to process the code. Visual Basic .NET won't compile a project that has a build error in it. A Call statement with incorrect parameters, for example, will generate a build error. *Runtime errors* are those that don't occur at compile time but are encountered when the project is being run. Runtime errors are usually a result of trying to perform an invalid operation on a variable.

For example, the following code won't generate a compile error:

```
intResult = 10 / intSomeOtherVariable
```

NEW TERM Under most circumstances, this code won't even generate a runtime error. However, what happens if the value of intSomeOtherVariable is 0? Ten divided

15

by zero is undefined, which won't fit into intResult (intResult is an Integer variable). Attempting to run the code with the intSomeOtherVariable variable having a value of 0 causes Visual Basic .NET to return a runtime error. A runtime error is called an *exception*, and when an exception occurs, it's said to be *thrown* (that is, Visual Basic .NET throws an exception when a runtime error occurs). When an exception is thrown, code execution stops at the offending statement and Visual Basic .NET displays an error message. You can prevent Visual Basic .NET from stopping execution when an exception is thrown by writing special code to handle the exception (writing error handlers is discussed later in this hour) .

Add the following statements to the Click event, right below the two comment lines:

```
Dim lngAnswer As Long
lngAnswer = 100 / CLng(txtInput.Text)
MessageRox.Show("100/" & txtInput.Text & " is " & lngAnswer)
```

The misspelling of the function name MessageBox is intentional; type in the preceding line of code exactly as it appears. Although you've spelled the function name incorrectly, Visual Basic .NET doesn't return an immediate error. Notice, however, that Visual Basic .NET displays a wavy blue line under the function name. Move the pointer over the underlined text and leave it there for a second; Visual Basic .NET displays a tip explaining the nature of the error (see Figure 15.2).

FIGURE 15.2
Visual Basic .NET highlights build errors in the code window using wavy lines.

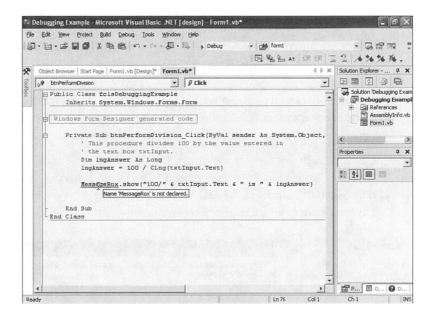

Press F5 to run the project. When you do, Visual Basic .NET displays a message that a build error was found and asks whether you want to continue. Because the code won't run, there's no point in continuing, so click No to return to the code editor. Take a look at the Task List (if it's not displayed, use the View menu to show it). All build errors in the current project appear in the Task List (see Figure 15.3). To view a particular offending line of code, double-click an item in the Task List.

FIGURE 15.3

Build errors are easy to find using the Task List.

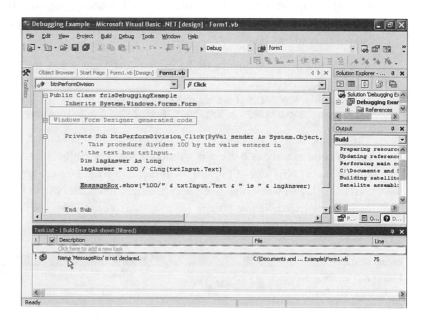

Build errors are very serious in that they prevent code from being compiled; they completely prevent execution. Build errors must be corrected before you can run the project. Double-click the build error in the Task List to go directly to the error.

Correct the problem by changing the R to a B so that the function name is MessageBox. After you've made this change, press F5 to run the project. Visual Basic .NET no longer returns a build error; you've just successfully debugged a problem! Click the Perform Division button now, and you'll receive another error (see Figure 15.4).

FIGURE 15.4

A runtime exception halts code execution at the offending line.

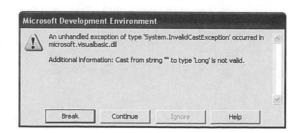

15

This time the error is a runtime error, or exception. If an exception occurs, you know that the code compiled without a problem because build errors prevent code from compiling and executing. This particular exception is an Invalid Cast exception. Invalid cast exceptions generally occur when you attempt to perform a function using a variable, and the variable is of an incompatible data type for the specified operation. Click Break to view the offending line of code. Visual Basic .NET denotes the offending statement with a yellow arrow (the arrow indicates the current statement). At this point, you know that the statement has a bug, and you know it's related to data typing. Choose Stop Debugging from the Debug menu now to stop the running project and return to the code editor.

Using Visual Basic .NET 's Debugging Tools

Visual Basic .NET includes a number of debugging tools to help you track down and eliminate bugs. In this section, you'll learn to use break points, the Command window, and the Output window—three tools that form the foundation of any debugging arsenal.

Working with Break Points

NEW TERM Just as an exception halts the execution of a procedure, you can deliberately stop execution at any statement of code by creating a *break point*. When Visual Basic .NET encounters a break point while executing code, execution is halted at the break statement, prior to it being executed. Break points enable you to query or change the value of variables at a specific instance in time, and they let you step through code execution one line at a time.

You're going to create a break point to help troubleshoot the exception in your MessageBox statement.

Adding a break point is simple. Just click in the gray area to the left of the statement at which you want to break code execution. When you do so, Visual Basic .NET displays a red circle, denoting a break point at that statement (see Figure 15.5). To clear a break point, click the red circle.

> Break points are saved with the project. This is new to Visual Basic. NET and makes it much easier to suspend a debugging session; you don't have to reset all your break points each time you open the project.

Figure 15.5

Break points give you control over code execution.

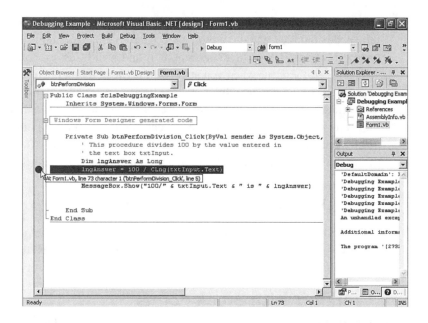

Stop the running project by clicking the Stop button on the toolbar, and then set a new break point on the statement shown in Figure 15.5 (the statement in which lngAnswer is set). Do this by clicking in the gray area to the left of the statement. After you've set the break point, press F5 to run the program. Click the Perform Division button again. When Visual Basic .NET encounters the break point, code execution is halted (before the statement with the break point executes) and the procedure with the break point is shown. In addition, the cursor is conveniently placed at the statement with the current break point. Notice the yellow arrow overlaying the red circle of the break point (see Figure 15.6). This yellow arrow marks the next statement to be executed. It just so happens that the statement has a break point, so the yellow arrow appears over the red circle (the yellow arrow won't always be over a red circle, but it will always appear in the gray area aligned with the next statement to execute).

When code execution is halted at a break point, you can do a number of things. See Table 15.1 for a list of the most common actions. For now, press F5 to continue program execution. Again, you get an overflow exception. Click Break to access the code procedure with the error.

FIGURE 15.6

A yellow arrow denotes the next statement to be executed.

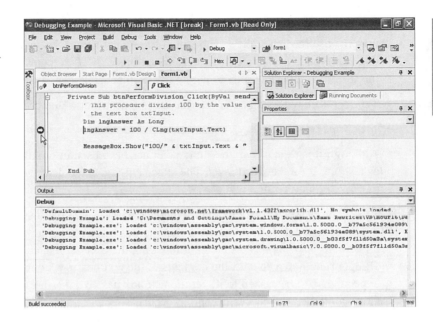

TABLE 15.1 Actions That Can Be Taken at a Break Point

Action	Keystroke	Description
Continue Code Execution	F5	Continues execution at the current break statement.
Step Into	F11	Executes the statement at the break point and then stops at the next statement. If the current statement is a function call, F11 enters the function and stops at the first statement in the function.
Step Over	F10	Executes the statement at the break point and then stops at the next statement. If the current statement is a function call, the function is run in its entirety; execution stops at the statement following the function call.
Step Out	Shift+F11	Runs all the statements in the current procedure and halts execution at the statement following the one that called the current procedure.

Using the Command Window

Break points themselves aren't usually sufficient to debug a procedure. In addition to break points, you'll often use the Command window to debug code. The Command window is a Visual Studio .NET IDE window that generally appears only when your project is in Run mode. If the Command window isn't displayed, press Ctrl+Alt+A to display it now (or use the Other Views submenu of the View menu). Using the Command window, you can type in code statements that Visual Basic .NET executes immediately. You'll use the Command window now to debug our problem statement example.

Type the following statement into the Command window and press Enter:

```
? txtinput.text
```

Although it isn't intuitive, the ? character has been used in programming for many years as a shortcut for the word *print*. The statement you entered simply prints the contents of the Text property of the text box.

NEW TERM   Notice how the command window displays "" on the line below the statement you entered. This indicates that the text box contains an empty string (also called a *zero-length string*). The statement throwing the exception is attempting to use the CLng() function to convert the contents of the text box to a Long. The CLng() function expects data to be passed to it, yet the text box has no data (the Text property is empty). Consequently, an overflow exception occurs.

> Generally, when you receive an overflow exception, you should look at any variables or properties being referenced to ensure that the data they contain is appropriate data for the statement. You'll often find that the code is trying to perform an operation that's inappropriate for the data being supplied.

You can do a number of things to prevent this error. The most obvious is to ensure that the text box contains a value before attempting to use CLng(). Do this now. Visual Basic .NET doesn't allow you to modify code when in Break mode, so choose Stop Debugging from the Debug menu before continuing.

> Previous versions of Visual Basic enabled you to modify code on-the-fly in Break mode. This was a very powerful feature of the language. Unfortunately, Visual Basic .NET doesn't support this feature; you'll have to stop a running project before making code changes.

Add the following statements to your procedure, right above the statement that throws the exception (the one with the break point) :

```
If txtInput.Text = "" Then
   Exit Sub
End If
```

15

Press F5 to run the project once more, and click the Perform Division button. This time, Visual Basic .NET won't throw an exception and it won't halt execution at your break point; the test you just created causes code execution to leave the procedure before the statement with the break point is reached.

Next, follow these steps:

1. Type your name into the text box and click the Perform Division button again. Now that the text box is no longer empty, execution passes the statement with the exit test and stops at the break point.

2. Press F5 to continue executing the code, and again you'll receive an exception. This time, however, the exception is an invalid cast exception; this is different from the exception thrown previously.

3. Click Break to enter Break mode, and type the following into the Command window (be sure to press Enter when you're done):

```
? txtinput.text
```

The Command window prints your name.

Well, you eliminated the problem of not supplying any data to the CLng() function, but something else is wrong.

Press F5 to continue executing the code and take a closer look at the exception text. The last statement in the text says Cast from String ("your name") to Long is not valid. It apparently still doesn't like what's being passed to the CLng() function.

By now, it might have occurred to you that no logical way exists to convert alphanumeric text to a number; CLng() needs a number to work with. You can easily test this by following these steps:

1. Click Break and choose Stop Debugging from the Debug menu.

2. Press F5 to run the project.

3. Enter a number into the text box and click the button. Code execution again stops at the break point.

4. Press F11 to execute the statement. No errors this time! Press F5 to continue execution and Visual Basic .NET will display the message box (finally). Click OK to dismiss the message box and then close the form to stop the project.

You can use the Command window to change the value of a variable, in addition to printing the value.

Because the CLng() function expects a number, but the text box contains no intrinsic way to force numeric input, you have to accommodate this situation in your code. Visual Basic .NET includes a handy function called IsNumeric(), which returns True if the supplied argument is a number, or False if not. You can use this function to ensure that only a number is passed to the CLng() function. Add the following statement immediately below the last If...Then statement you entered:

```
If Not (IsNumeric(txtInput.Text)) Then Exit Sub
```

This statement simply passes the contents of the text box to the IsNumeric() function. If the function returns False (the text is not a number), the procedure is exited. Your procedure should now look similar to the one shown in Figure 15.7. Realize that the first If...End If statement is redundant; this new statement will catch when a user hasn't entered anything into the text box.

FIGURE 15.7

The final code, complete with data verification.

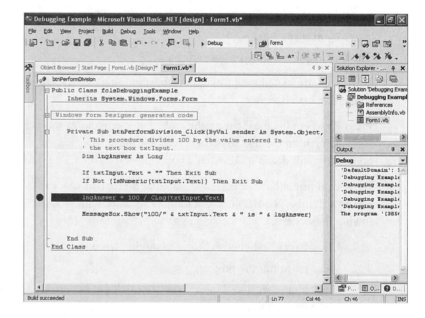

Go ahead and press F5 to run the project, enter some nonnumeric text into the text box, and click the button. If you entered the code correctly, no exception will occur; the data validation tests you've created prevent inappropriate data from being passed to the CLng() function. You just debugged the procedure!

The Command window is a powerful debugging tool. You can use it to get and set variables as well as view the value in a property. You can even use the Command window to call functions. For instance, while in Break mode, you could enter the following into the Command window, and Visual Basic .NET would print the result of the function call:

```
? IsNumeric(txtInput.Text)
```

Get comfortable using the Command window; it'll help you through many tough debugging sessions.

Using the Output Window

The Output window (see Figure 15.8) is used by Visual Basic .NET to display various status messages and build errors. The most useful feature of the Output window, for general use, is the capability to send data to it from a running application. This is especially handy when debugging applications.

FIGURE 15.8

The Output window displays a lot of information—some of which is useful.

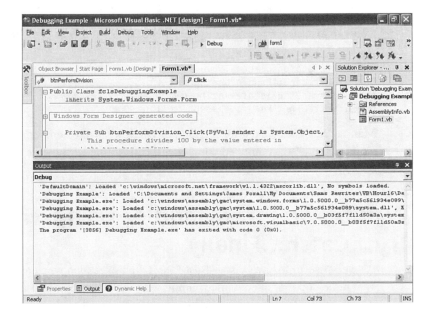

You've already used the Output window in previous hours, but you might not have seriously considered its application to debugging. As you can see from Figure 15.8, some data sent to the Output window by Visual Basic .NET isn't that intuitive—in fact, you can ignore much of what is automatically sent to the Output window. What you'll want to use the Output window for is printing data for debugging (as you've done and will continue to do throughout this book). Therefore, it's no coincidence that printing to the Output window is accomplished via the Debug object.

To print data to the Output window, use the WriteLine() method of the Debug object, like this:

```
Debug.WriteLine(lngInteger1 + lngInteger2)
```

Whatever you place within the parentheses of the WriteLine() method is printed to the Output window. Note that you can print literal text, numbers, variables, and expressions. WriteLine() is most useful in cases where you want to know the value of a variable, but you don't want to halt code execution using a break point. For example, suppose that you have a number of statements that manipulate a variable. You can sprinkle WriteLine() statements into the code to print the variable's contents at strategic points. When you do this, you'll want to print some text along with the variable's value so that the output makes sense to you. For example:

```
Debug.WriteLine("Results of area calculation = " & sngArea)
```

You can also use WriteLine() to create checkpoints in your code, like this:

```
Debug.WriteLine("Passed Checkpoint 1")
' Execute statement here
Debug.WriteLine("Passed Checkpoint 4")
' Execute another statement here
Debug.WriteLine("Passed Checkpoint 3")
```

Many creative uses exist for the Output window. Just remember that the Output window isn't available to a compiled component; calls to the Debug object are ignored by the compiler when creating distributable components.

Writing an Error Handler Using Try…Catch…Finally

It's very useful to have Visual Basic .NET halt execution when an exception occurs. When the code is halted while running with the IDE, you receive an error message and you're shown the offending line of code. However, when your project is run as a compiled program, an unhandled exception causes the program to terminate (crash to the desktop). This is one of the most undesirable things an application can do. Fortunately, you can prevent exceptions from stopping code execution (and terminating compiled programs) by writing code specifically designed to deal with exceptions. Exception-handling code is used to instruct Visual Basic .NET on how to deal with an exception, rather than relying on Visual Basic .NET 's default behavior.

NEW TERM   Visual Basic .NET supports *structured error handling* (a formal way of dealing with errors) in the form of the Try…Catch…Finally structure. Creating structured error-handling code can be a bit confusing at first, and like most coding principles, it's best understood by doing it.

15

Create a new Windows Application called **Structured Exception Handling**. Change the name of the default form to **fclsExceptionHandlingExample**, set its Text property to **Try...Catch...Finally**, and change the Startup object of the project to fclsExceptionHandlingExample. Add a new button to the form and set its properties as follows:

Property	Value
Name	**btnCatchException**
Location	**104,128**
Size	**96,23**
Text	**Catch Exception**

Double-click the button and add the following code. Be aware that when you enter the Try statement, Visual Basic .NET automatically creates the End Try statement.

```
Try
   Debug.WriteLine("Try")
Catch
   Debug.WriteLine("Catch")
Finally
   Debug.WriteLine("Finally")
End Try
Debug.WriteLine("Done Trying")
```

As you can see, the Try...End Try structure has starting and ending statements, much like loops and decision constructs. The Try...End Try structure is used to wrap code that might cause an exception and provides you the means of dealing with thrown exceptions. Table 15.2 explains the sections of this structure.

TABLE 15.2 Sections of the Try...End Try Structure

Section	Description
Try	The Try section is where you place code that might cause an exception. You can place all of a procedure's code within the Try section, or just a few lines.
Catch	Code within the Catch section executes only when an exception occurs; it's the code you write to catch the exception.
Finally	Code within the Finally section occurs when the code within the Try and/or code within the Catch sections completes. This section is where you place your *cleanup code*—code that you want always executed regardless of whether an exception occurs.

Press F5 to run the project and then click the button. Next, take a look at the contents of the Output window. The Output window should contain the following lines of text:

```
Try
Finally
Done Trying
```

Here's what happened:

1. The Try block begins, and code within the Try section executes.
2. No exception occurs, so code within the Catch section doesn't execute.
3. When all statements within the Try section finish executing, the code within the Finally section executes.
4. When all statements within the Finally section finish executing, execution jumps to the statement immediately following End Try.

Stop the project now by choosing Stop Debugging from the Debug menu. Now that you understand the basic mechanics of the Try…End Try structure, you're going to add statements within the structure so that an exception occurs and is handled.

Change the contents of the procedure to match this code:

```
Dim lngNumerator As Long = 10
Dim lngDenominator As Long = 0
Dim lngResult As Long

Try
   Debug.WriteLine("Try")
   lngResult = lngNumerator / lngDenominator
Catch
   Debug.WriteLine("Catch")
Finally
   Debug.WriteLine("Finally")
End Try

Debug.WriteLine("Done Trying")
```

Again, press F5 to run the project. Click the button and take a look at the Output window. This time, the text in the Output window should read

```
Try
Catch
Finally
Done Trying
```

Notice that this time the code within the Catch section executes. That's because the statement that sets lngResult causes an overflow exception. Had this statement not been placed within a Try block, Visual Basic .NET would've raised the exception and an error dialog box would've appeared. However, because the statement is placed within the Try block, the exception is caught. *Caught* means that when the exception occurred, Visual Basic

15

.NET directed execution to the Catch section. (You do not have to use a Catch section; in which case, caught exceptions are simply ignored.) Notice also how the code within the Finally section executes after the code within the Catch section. Remember that code within the Finally section always executes, regardless of whether an exception occurs.

Dealing with an Exception

Catching exceptions so that they don't crash your application is a noble thing to do, but it's only part of the error-handling process. You'll usually want to tell the user (in a friendly way) that an exception has occurred. You'll probably also want to tell the user what type of exception occurred. To do this, you must have a way of knowing what exception was thrown. This is also important if you intend to write code to deal with specific exceptions. The Catch statement enables you to specify a variable to hold a reference to an exception object. Using that exception object, you can get information about the exception. The following is the syntax used to place the exception in an exception object:

```
Catch variablename As Exception
```

Modify your Catch section to match the following:

```
Catch objException As Exception
    Debug.WriteLine("Catch")
    MsgBox("An error has occurred: " & objException.Message)
```

The Message property of the exception object contains the text that describes the specific exception that occurs. Run the project and click the button, and Visual Basic .NET displays your custom error message (see Figure 15.9) .

Like other code structures, Visual Basic .NET has a statement that can be used to exit a Try...End Try structure at any time: Exit Try. Note, however, that if you use Exit Try, code jumps to the statement immediately following the End Try statement; the code in the Finally section won't execute.

Handling an Anticipated Exception

At times, you'll anticipate a specific exception being thrown. For example, you might write code that attempts to open a file when the file does not exist. In such an instance, you'll probably want the program to perform certain actions when this exception is thrown. When you anticipate a specific exception, you can create a Catch section designed specifically to deal with that one exception.

Recall from the previous section that you can retrieve information about the current exception using a Catch statement, such as

```
Catch objException As Exception
```

By creating a generic Exception variable, this Catch statement will catch any and all exceptions thrown by statements within the Try section. To catch a specific exception, change the data type of the exception variable to a specific exception type. Remember the code you wrote earlier that caused an System.InvalidCastException when an attempt was made to pass an empty string to the CLng() function? You could have used a Try...End Try structure to deal with the exception, using code such as this:

```
Dim lngAnswer As Long
Try
    lngAnswer = 100 / CLng(txtInput.Text)
    MsgBox("100/" & txtInput.Text & " is " & lngAnswer)
Catch objException As System.InvalidCastException
    MsgBox("You must enter something in the text box.")
Catch objException As Exception
    MsgBox("Caught an exception that wasn't an invalid cast.")
End Try
```

Notice that there are two Catch statements in this structure. The first Catch statement is designed to catch only an overflow exception; it won't catch exceptions of any other type. The second Catch statement doesn't care what type of exception is thrown, it catches all of them. The second Catch statement acts as a catch-all for any exceptions that aren't overflow exceptions because Catch sections are evaluated from top to bottom, much like Case statements in the Select...Case structure. You could add more Catch sections to catch other specific exceptions if the situation calls for it.

Visual Basic .NET supports unstructured error handling in the way of On Error statements. This method of handling errors, although still supported by Visual Basic .NET, is now considered antiquated. You might encounter procedures that use this form of error handling in legacy or sample code, but Microsoft strongly recommends that you use the Try...Catch ...Finally structure for dealing with exceptions in all new code.

Summary

In this hour, you learned the basics for debugging applications. You learned how adding useful and plentiful comments to your procedures makes debugging easier. However, no matter how good your comments are, you'll still have bugs.

You learned about the two basic types of errors: build errors and runtime errors (exceptions). Build errors are easier to troubleshoot because the compiler tells you exactly what line contains a build error and generally provides useful information about the error. Exceptions, on the other hand, can crash your application if not handled properly. You learned how to track down exceptions using break points, the Command window, and the Output window. Finally, you learned to how to make your applications more robust by creating structured error handlers using the Try…End Try structure.

No book can teach you everything you need to know to write bug-free code. However, this hour taught you the basic skills you need to track down and eliminate many types of errors in your programs. As your skills as a programmer improve, so will your debugging abilities.

Q&A

Q Should I alert the user that an exception has occurred to just let the code keep running?

A If you've written code to handle the specific exception, there's probably no need to tell the user about it. However, if an exception occurs that the code doesn't know how to address, you should provide the user with the exception information so that she can report the problem and you can fix it.

Q Should I comment every statement in my application?

A Probably not. However, you should consider commenting every decision-making and looping construct in your program. Such sections of code are usually pivotal to the success of the procedure, and what they do isn't always obvious.

Workshop

The Workshop is designed to help you anticipate possible questions, review what you've learned, and get you thinking about how to put your knowledge into practice. The answers to the quiz are in Appendix B, "Answers to the Quizzes."

Quiz

1. What type of error prevents Visual Basic .NET from compiling and running code?

2. What is another name for a runtime error?

3. What character is used to denote a comment?

4. To halt execution at a specific statement in code, you set a

5. Explain the yellow arrow and red circles that can appear in the gray area in the code editor.

6. What IDE window would you use to poll the contents of a variable in break mode?

7. True or False: You must always specify a Catch section in a Try...End Try structure.

Exercises

1. In the code example that sets lngAnswer to the result of a division expression, change lngAnswer from a long to a single (call it sngAnswer). Next, remove the two If statements that test contents of the text box before performing the division. Do you get the same two exceptions that you did when the variable was a long? Why or why not?

2. Rewrite the code that sets lngAnswer to the result of a division expression so that the code is wrapped in a Try...End Try structure. Remove the If statements that perform data validation, and create a Catch sections for the exception that might be thrown.

HOUR **16**

Designing Objects Using Classes

You learned about what makes an object an object in Hour 3, "Understanding Objects and Collections." Since that hour, you've learned how to manipulate objects such as forms and controls. The real power of leveraging objects comes from being able to design and implement custom objects of your own design. In this hour, you'll learn how to create your own objects by using classes (in contrast to using standard modules). You'll learn how to define the template for an object and how to create your own custom properties and methods.

The highlights of this hour include the following:

- Encapsulating data and code using classes
- Comparing classes with standard modules
- Creating an object interface
- Exposing object attributes as properties
- Exposing functions as methods

- Instantiating objects from classes
- Binding an object reference to a variable
- Understanding object lifetime
- Releasing object references

There is simply no way to become an expert on programming classes in a single hour. However, when you've finished with this hour, you'll have a working knowledge of creating classes and deriving custom objects from those classes; consider this hour a primer on object-oriented programming. I strongly encourage you to seek other texts that focus on object-oriented programming after you feel comfortable with the material presented throughout this book.

Understanding Classes

Classes enable you to develop applications using object-oriented programming (OOP) techniques (recall that I discussed OOP briefly in Hour 3). Classes are templates that define objects. Although you might not have known it, you've been programming with classes throughout this book. When you create a new form in a Visual Basic .NET project, you're actually creating a class that defines a form; forms instantiated at runtime are derived from the class. Using objects derived from predefined classes (such as a Visual Basic .NET Form class), is just the start of enjoying the benefits of object-oriented programming—to truly realize the benefits of OOP, you must create your own classes.

The philosophy of programming with classes is considerably different from that of traditional programming. Proper class-programming techniques can make your programs better, both in structure and in reliability. Class programming forces you to consider the logistics of your code and data more thoroughly, causing you to create more reusable and extensible object-based code.

Encapsulating Data and Code Using Classes

An object derived from a class is an encapsulation of data and code; that is, the object comprises its code *and* all the data it uses. For example, suppose that you need to keep track of employees in an organization and that you must store many pieces of information for each employee, such as name, date hired, and title. In addition, suppose that you need methods for adding and removing employees, and you want all this information and functionality available to many functions within your application. You could use standard modules to manipulate the data, but doing so would most likely require many variable arrays as well as code to manage those arrays.

NEW TERM   A better approach is to encapsulate all the employee data and functionality (adding and deleting routines and so forth) into a single, reusable object. *Encapsulation* is the process of integrating data and code into one entity: an object. Your application, as well as external applications, could then work with the employee data through a consistent interface—the Employee object's interface. (An *interface* is a set of exposed functionality—essentially, code routines that define methods, properties, and events.)

> Creating objects for use outside of your application is beyond the scope of this book. However, the techniques you'll learn in this hour are directly applicable to creating externally creatable objects.

The encapsulation of data and code is the key detail of classes. By encapsulating the data and the routines to manipulate the data into a single object by way of a class, you free up application code that needs to manipulate the data from the intricacies of data maintenance. For example, suppose that company policy has changed so that when a new employee is added to the system, a special tax record must be generated and a form must be printed. If the data and code routines weren't encapsulated in a common object but were written in various places throughout your code, you would have to modify each and every module that contained code to create a new employee record. By using a class to create an object, you need to change the code in only one location: within the object. As long as you don't modify the interface of the object (discussed shortly), all the routines that use the object to create a new employee will instantly have the policy change in effect.

Comparing Classes with Standard Modules

Classes are similar to standard modules in how they appear in the Visual Studio .NET design environment and in the way in which you write code within them. However, the behavior of classes at runtime differs greatly from that of standard modules. With a standard module, all module-level data (static and module-level variables) is shared by all procedures within the module. In addition, there are never multiple instances of the module data. With classes, objects are instantiated from a class and each object receives its own set of module data.

As you learned in Hour 11, "Using Constants, Data Types, Variables, and Arrays," module-level variables in a standard module exist for the lifetime of the application. However, module variables for a class exist only for the duration of the object's lifetime. Objects can be created and destroyed at will, and when an object is destroyed, all its data is destroyed as well.

NEW TERM Classes differ from standard modules in more ways than just in how their data behaves. When you define a standard module, its public functions and procedures are instantly available to other modules within your application. However, public functions and procedures of classes aren't immediately available to your program. Classes are templates for objects. At runtime, your code doesn't interact with the code in the class module per se, but it instantiates objects derived from the class. Each object acts as its own class "module," and thus it has its own set of module data. When classes are exposed externally to other applications, the application containing the class's code is called the *server*. Applications that create and use instances of objects are called *clients*. When you use instances of classes in the application that contains those classes, the application itself acts as both a client and a server. In this hour, I'll refer to the code instantiating an object derived from a class as *client code*.

Begin by creating a new Windows Application titled **Class Programming Example**. Change the name of the default form to **fclsClassExample** and set its Text property to **Class Example**. Next, change the Startup object of the project to fclsClassExample. Add a new class to the project by choosing Add Class from the Project menu. Save the class with the name **clsMyClass.vb** (see Figure 16.1) .

FIGURE 16.1

Classes are added to a project just as other object files are added.

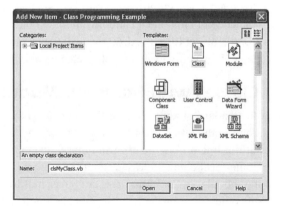

Creating an Object Interface

For an object to be created from a class, the class must expose an interface. As I mentioned earlier, an interface is a set of exposed functionality (properties, methods, and events). An interface is the means by which client code communicates with the object derived from the class. Some classes expose a limited interface, whereas some expose complex interfaces. The content and quantity of your class's interface is entirely up to you.

The interface of a class consists of one or more of the following members:

16

- Properties
- Methods
- Events

For example, assume that you're creating an Employee object (that is, a class used to derive employee objects). You must first decide how you want client code to interact with your object. You'll want to consider both the data contained within the object and the functions that the object can perform. You might want client code to be able to retrieve the name of an employee and other information such as sex, age, and the date of hire. For client code to get these values from the object, the object must expose an interface member for each of the items. You'll recall from Hour 3 that values exposed by an object are called *properties*. Therefore, each piece of data discussed here would have to be exposed as a property of the Employee object.

In addition to properties, you can expose functions—such as a Delete or AddNew function. These functions may be simple in nature or very complex. The Delete function of the Employee object, for example, might be quite complex. It might need to perform all the actions necessary to delete an employee, including such things as removing the employee from an assigned department, notifying the accounting department to remove the employee from the payroll, notifying the security area to revoke the employee's security access, and so on. Publicly exposed functions of an object, as you should again remember from Hour 3, are called *methods*.

Properties and methods are the most commonly used interface members. Although designing properties and methods might be new to you, by now using them isn't—you've been using properties and methods in almost every hour so far. Here, you're going to learn the techniques for creating properties and methods for your own objects.

For even more interaction between the client and the object, you can expose custom events. Custom object events are similar to the events of a form or a text box. However, with custom events you have complete control over the following:

- The name of the event
- The parameters passed to the event
- When the event occurs

 Creating custom events is complicated, and I'll cover only custom properties and methods in this hour.

Properties, methods, and events together make up an object's interface. This interface acts as a contract between the client application and the object. Any and all communication between the client and the object must transpire through this interface (see Figure 16.2).

FIGURE 16.2

Clients interact with an object via the object's interface.

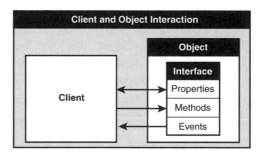

The technical details of the interaction between the client and the object by way of the interface are, mercifully, handled by Visual Basic .NET. Your responsibility is to define the properties, methods, and events of an object so that its interface is logical, consistent, and exposes all the functionality a client must have to use the object.

Exposing Object Attributes as Properties

Properties are the attributes of objects. Properties can be read-only, or they can allow both reading and writing of their values. For example, you might want to let a client retrieve the value of a property containing the path of the component, but not let the client change it because the path of a running component can't be changed.

You can add properties to a class in two ways. The first is to declare public variables. Any variable declared as public instantly becomes a property of the class (actually, it acts like a property but it isn't technically a property). For example, suppose that you have the following statement in the Declarations section of a class:

```
Public Quantity as Integer
```

Clients could read from and write to the property using code like the following:

```
objMyObject.Quantity = 139
```

This works, but significant limitations exist that make this approach less than desirable:

- You can't execute code when a property value changes. For example, what if you wanted to write the quantity change to a database? Because the client application can access the variable directly, you have no way of knowing when the value of the variable changes.
- You can't prevent client code from changing a property because the client code accesses the variable directly.
- Perhaps the biggest problem is this: How do you control data validation? For instance, how could you ensure that Quantity was never set to a negative value?

You simply can't work around these issues using a public variable. Instead of exposing public variables, you should create class properties using property procedures.

Property procedures enable you to execute code when a property is changed, to validate property values, and to dictate whether a property is read-only, write-only, or both readable and writable. Declaring a property procedure is similar to declaring a standard Function or Sub procedure, but with some important differences. The basic structure of a property procedure looks like this:

```
Public Property propertyname() As Long
    Get
        ' Code to return the property's value goes here.
    End Get

    Set(ByVal Value As Long)
        ' Code that accepts a new value goes here.
    End Set
End Property
```

The first word in the property declaration simply designates the scope of the property (Public or Private). Properties declared with Public are available to code outside of the class (they can be accessed by client code). Properties declared as Private are available only to code within the class. Immediately following Public or Private is the word Property. This word tells Visual Basic .NET that you're creating a property procedure rather than a Sub or Function procedure. Next comes the property name and data type.

Type the following two statements into your class:

```
Private m_intHeight As Integer
```

```
Public Property Height() As Integer
```

After entering the statements, press Enter to commit the statements, and Visual Basic .NET will fill in the rest of the procedure template for you (see Figure 16.3).

FIGURE 16.3

Visual Basic.NET creates property procedure templates.

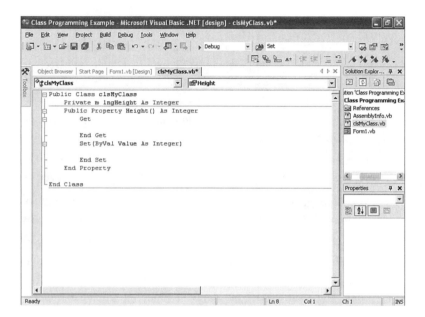

You might be wondering why you just created a module-level variable of the same name as your property procedure (with a naming prefix, of course). After all, I just finished preaching about the problems of using a module-level variable as a property. The reason is that a property has to get its value from somewhere, and a module-level variable is usually the best place to store it. The property procedure will act as a wrapper for this variable. Notice that here the variable is private rather than public. This means that no code outside the class can view or modify the contents of this variable; as far as client code is concerned, this variable doesn't exist.

Between the property declaration statement and the End Property statement are two constructs: the Get construct and a Set construct. Each of these constructs is discussed in its own section.

Creating Readable Properties Using the Get Construct

The Get construct is used to place code that returns a value for the property when read by a client. If you remove the Get and End Get statements, clients won't be able to read the value of the property. It's rare that you'll want to create such a property, but you can.

Think of the Get construct as a function; whatever you return as the result of the function becomes the property value. Add the following statement between the Get and End Get statements:

```
Return m_intHeight
```

Just as you dictate the result of a function by setting the function name to a value, you return the value of the property by setting the property's name (the name of the Property procedure) to a value.

16

Creating Writable Properties Using the Set Construct

The Set construct is where you place code that accepts a new property value from client code. If you remove the Set and End Set statements, clients won't be able to change the value of the property. Leaving the Get construct and removing the Set construct creates a read-only property; clients can retrieve the value of the property but they cannot change it.

Add the following statement between the Set and End Set statements:

```
m_intHeight = Value
```

If you look closely at the Set statement, you'll see that it's similar to a Sub declaration and that Value is a parameter. Value contains the value being passed to the property by the client code. The statement you just entered assigns the new value to the module-level variable.

As you can see, the property procedure is a wrapper around the module-level variable. When the client code sets the property, the Set construct stores the new value in the variable. When the client retrieves the value of the property, the Get construct returns the value in the module-level variable.

So far, the property procedure, with its Get and Set constructs, doesn't do anything differently from what it would do if you were to simply declare a public variable (only the property procedure requires more code). However, look at this variation of the same Set construct:

```
Set(ByVal Value As Long)
    If m_intHeight < 10 Then Exit Property
    m_intHeight = Value
End Set
```

This Set construct restricts the client to setting the Height property to a value greater than 10. If a value less than 10 is passed to the property, the property procedure terminates without setting m_intHeight. You're not limited to performing only data validation; you can pretty much add whatever code you desire and even call other procedures. Go ahead and add the verification statement to your procedure so that the Set construct looks like this one. Your code should now look like the procedure shown in Figure 16.4.

FIGURE 16.4

This is a property procedure, complete with data validation.

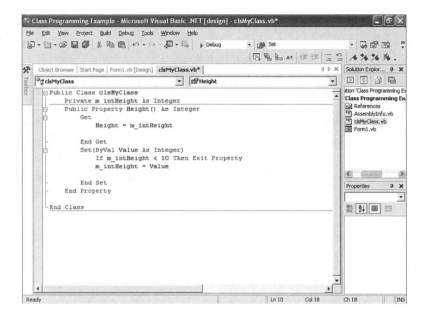

Exposing Functions as Methods

Unlike a property that acts as an object attribute, a method is a function exposed by an object. Methods are nothing more than exposed code routines. A method can return a value, but it doesn't have to. Methods are easier to create than properties because they're defined just like ordinary Sub and Function procedures. To create a method within a class, create a public Sub or Function procedure. Create the following procedure in your class now (enter this code on the line following the End Property statement):

```
Public Function AddTwoNumbers(ByVal intNumber1 As Integer, _
                              ByVal intNumber2 As Integer) As Long
   AddTwoNumbers = intNumber1 + intNumber2
End Function
```

Like normal Sub and Function procedures, methods defined with Function return values, whereas methods defined with Sub don't. To make a procedure private to the class and therefore invisible to client code, declare the procedure as Private rather than Public.

Instantiating Objects from Classes

After you obtain a reference to an object and assign it to a variable, you can manipulate the object using an object variable. Let's do so now.

Click the Form1.vb Design tab to view the form designer and add a button to the form by double-clicking the Button item in the toolbox. Set the button's properties as follows:

Property	Value
Name	**btnCreateObject**
Location	**104,120**
Size	**88,23**
Text	**Create Object**

Next, double-click the button to access its Click event and enter the following code:

```
Dim objMyObject As clsMyClass
objMyObject = New clsMyClass()
MessageBox.Show(objMyObject.AddTwoNumbers(1, 2))
```

The first statement creates a variable of type Object (dimension variables were discussed in Hour 11). The second statement needs an explanation. Because the variable appears on the left side of the equal sign, you can deduce that the variable is being set to some value.

However, what appears on the right side of the equal sign might look foreign to you. You want to place a reference to an object in the variable, but no object has yet been created. The New keyword tells Visual Basic .NET to create a new object, and the text following New is the name of the class to use to derive the object (remember, classes are object templates). The last statement calls the AddTwoNumbers method of your class and displays the result in a message box.

Go ahead and run the project by pressing F5 and then click the button to make sure everything is working correctly. When finished, stop the project and save your work.

Binding an Object Reference to a Variable

An object can contain any number of properties, methods, and events; every object is different. When you write code to manipulate an object, Visual Basic .NET has to understand the interface of the object or your code won't work. Resolving the interface members (the properties, methods, and events of the object) occurs when an object variable is bound to an object. There are two forms of binding: early binding (which occurs at compile time) and late binding (which occurs at runtime). It's important that you have at least a working understanding of binding if you're to create code based on classes. Although I can't explain the intricacies and technical details of early binding versus late binding in this hour, I'll teach you what you need to know to perform each type of binding.

16

Benefits exist to both types of binding, but early binding is generally superior to late binding because code that uses late-bound objects requires more work (time and resources) by Visual Basic .NET than code that uses early-bound objects.

Late Binding an Object Variable

When you dimension a variable as data type Object, as shown in the following code sample, you're late binding to the object.

```
Dim objMyObject As Object
objMyObject = New clsMyClass()
MessageBox.Show(objMyObject.AddTwoNumbers(1, 2))
```

When you late bind an object, the binding occurs at runtime when the variable is set to reference an object. For a member of the object to be referenced, Visual Basic .NET must determine and use the internal ID of the specified member. Fortunately, because Visual Basic .NET handles all the details, you don't need to know the ID of a member. Just be aware that Visual Basic .NET needs to know the ID of a member in order to use it. When you late bind an object variable (dimension the variable As Object), the following occurs behind the scenes:

1. Visual Basic .NET obtains a special ID (the Dispatch ID) of the property, method, or event that you want to call. This takes time and resources.

2. An internal array containing the parameters of the member, if any, is created.

3. The member is invoked using the ID obtained in step 1.

The preceding steps require a great deal of overhead and adversely affect the performance of an application. Therefore, late binding isn't the preferred method of binding. Late binding does have some attractive uses, but most of them are related to using objects outside your application, not to using objects derived from classes within the project.

One of the main drawbacks of late binding is the inability for the compiler to check the syntax of the code manipulating an object. Because the ID of a member and the parameters it uses aren't determined until runtime, the compiler has no way of knowing whether you're using a member correctly—or even if the member you're referencing exists. This can result in a runtime exception or some other unexpected behavior. Change the third statement in your code to look like the following (deliberately misspell the AddTwoNumbers method):

```
MessageBox.Show(objMyObject.AddtoNumbers(1, 2))
```

Press F5 to run the project. No problems—well, so far, at least. Even though the method name is spelled incorrectly, Visual Basic .NET compiles the project without raising a build error. This happens because the variable is declared As Object, and Visual Basic .NET has no idea what will eventually be placed in the variable. Therefore, it can't perform any syntax checking at compile time and just assumes that whatever action you perform with the variable is correct. Click the button now to create the object and call the method. When you do, you'll get the exception shown in Figure 16.5.

FIGURE 16.5

Exceptions such as this are a risk of late binding.

As explained in the previous hour, runtime exceptions are more problematic than build errors because they're usually encountered by end users and under varying circumstances. When you late bind objects, it's easy to introduce these types of problems; therefore, a real risk of throwing exceptions exists with late binding. As you'll see in the next section, early binding reduces a lot of these risks.

Go ahead and click Break, and then choose Stop Debugging from the Debug menu before continuing.

Early Binding an Object Variable

If Visual Basic .NET can determine a Dispatch ID for a member at compile time, there's no need to look up the ID when the member is referenced at runtime. This results in considerably faster calls to object members. Not only that, but Visual Basic .NET can also validate the member call at compile time, reducing the chance of errors in your code.

Early binding occurs when you dimension a variable as a specific type of object, rather than just As Object. When a variable is early bound, Visual Basic .NET looks up the Dispatch IDs of the object's members at compile time.

The following are important reasons to use early binding:

- Speed.
- More speed.
- Objects, their properties, and their methods appear in IntelliSense drop-down lists.
- The compiler can check for syntax and reference errors in your code so that many problems are found at compile time, rather than at runtime.

For early binding to take place, an object variable must be declared as a specific object type (that is, not As Object). Change the Dim statement in the code you've entered to read:

```
Dim objMyObject As clsMyClass
```

As soon as you commit this statement, Visual Basic .NET displays a wavy blue line under the bad method call (see Figure 16.6). This occurs because Visual Basic .NET now knows the exact type of object the variable will contain; therefore, it can and does perform syntax checking on all member references. Because it can't find a member with the name AddToNumbers, it flags this as a build error. Try running the project by pressing F5 and you'll see that Visual Basic .NET does indeed recognize this as a build problem.

FIGURE 16.6

With early-bound objects, Visual Basic .NET performs syntax checking for you.

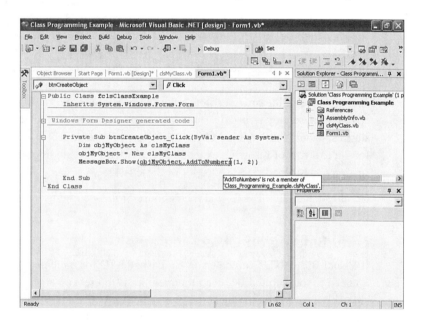

Place your cursor at the period between the words objMyObject and AddToNumbers. Delete the period and then type a period once more. This time, Visual Basic .NET displays an IntelliSense drop-down list with all the members of the class (see Figure 16.7). Go ahead and select the AddTwoNumbers member to fix your code.

Creating a New Object When Dimensioning a Variable

You can instantiate a new object on the declaration statement by including the keyword New, like this:

```
Dim objMyObject As New clsMyClass()
```

FIGURE 16.7

Visual Basic .NET displays IntelliSense drop-down lists of members for early-bound objects.

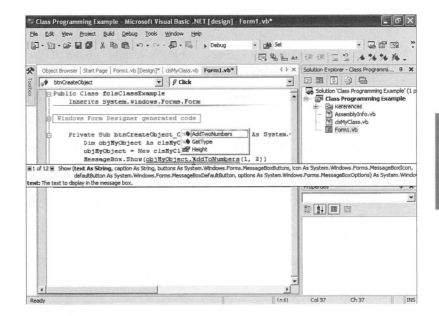

This approach alleviates the need for a second statement to create a new instance of the object. However, if you do this, the variable will always contain a reference to an object. If a chance exists that you might not need the object, you should probably avoid using the New keyword on the Dim statement. Consider the following:

```
Dim objMyObject As clsMyClass
If condition Then
    objMyObject = New clsMyObject
    ' Code to use the custom object would go here.
End If
```

Remember that instantiating an object takes resources. In this code, no object is created if *condition* is False. If you were to place the word New on the Dim statement, a new object would be instantiated whenever this code was executed, regardless of the value of *condition*.

Releasing Object References

When an object is no longer needed, it should be destroyed so that all the resources used by the object can be reclaimed. Objects are destroyed automatically when the last reference to the object is released. Although two primary ways exist to release an object reference, one is clearly better than the other.

One way to release a reference to an object is simply to let the object variable holding the reference go out of scope. As you might recall from Hour 11, variables are destroyed when they go out of scope. This is no less true for object variables. However, you can't necessarily be assured that an object is fully released and that all the memory being used by an object is freed by letting an object's variable go out of scope. Therefore, relying on scope to release objects isn't a good idea.

To explicitly release an object, set the object variable equal to Nothing, like this:

```
objMyObject = Nothing
```

When you set an object variable equal to Nothing, you're assured that the object reference is fully released. The object won't be destroyed, however, if other variables are referencing it. After the last reference is released, the garbage collector will eventually destroy the object (I talk about the garbage collector in Appendix A, "The 10,000-Foot View"). Go ahead and add the statement shown previously to your procedure—right after the statement that shows the message box.

If you don't correctly release object references, your application might experience resource leaks, become sluggish, and consume more resources than it should.

Understanding the Lifetime of an Object

An object created from a class exists as long as a variable holds a reference to it. Fortunately, Visual Basic .NET (or more specifically, the .NET Framework as discussed in Appendix A) handles the details of keeping track of the references to a given object; you don't have to worry about this when creating or using objects. When all the references to an object are released, the object is flagged and eventually destroyed by the garbage collector.

The following are key points to remember about an object's lifetime, and what they mean to your application:

- An object is created (and hence referenced) when an object variable is declared using the keyword New. For example,

  ```
  Dim objMyObject = New clsMyClass()
  ```

- An object is created (and hence referenced) when an object variable is assigned an object using the keyword New. For example,

  ```
  objMyObject = New clsMyClass()
  ```

- An object is referenced when an object variable is assigned an existing object. For example,

  ```
  objThisObject = objThatObject
  ```

- An object reference is released when an object variable is set to Nothing (refer to the section "Releasing Object References" earlier in this hour).

- An object is destroyed sometime after the last reference to it is released. This handled by the garbage collector, which is discussed in Appendix A.

Understanding the lifetime of objects is very important. You've now seen how and when object references are created, but you also need to know how to explicitly release an object reference. Only when all references to an object are released is the object flagged for destruction and the resources it uses reclaimed.

Summary

Object-oriented programming is an advanced methodology that enables you to create more robust applications; programming classes is the foundation of OOP. In this hour, you learned how to create classes, which are the templates used to instantiate objects. You also earned how to create a custom interface consisting of properties and methods, and how to use the classes you've defined to instantiate and manipulate objects by way of object variables.

Although previous versions of Visual Basic support objects to some extent, it's worth noting that Visual Basic .NET is the first *true* object-oriented version of Visual Basic. Visual Basic .NET is now on par with languages such as C++ for OOP capabilities. In this hour, you learned the basic mechanics of programming objects with classes. Object-oriented programming takes considerable skill, and you'll need to master the concepts in this book before you can really begin to take advantage of what OOP has to offer. Nevertheless, what you learned in this hour will take you further than you might think. Using an OOP methodology is as much a way of thinking as it is a way of programming; consider how things in your projects might work as objects, and before you know it, you'll be creating robust classes.

Q&A

Q Should I always try to place code into classes rather than standard modules?

A Not necessarily. As with most things, there are no hard-and-fast rules. Correctly programming classes takes some skill and experience, and programming standard modules is easier for the beginner. If you want to experiment with classes, I encourage you to do so. However, don't feel as though you have to place everything into a class.

Q I want to create a general class with a lot of miscellaneous procedures—sort of a catch-all class. What's the best way to do this?

A If you want to create some sort of utility class, I recommend calling the class something like clsUtility. Create a global variable to hold a reference to an object

16

instantiated from this class. In the Sub Main of your program, set the global variable to a new instance of the class. Then you can use the global variable throughout your application to access the utility functions, rather than having to instantiate a new object each time you want to use the functions.

Workshop

The Workshop is designed to help you anticipate possible questions, review what you've learned, and get you thinking about how to put your knowledge into practice. The answers to the quiz are in Appendix B, "Answers to the Quizzes."

Quiz

1. To create objects, you must first create a template. This template is called a:
2. One of the primary benefits of object-oriented programming is that objects contain both their data and their code. This is called:
3. With standard modules, public variables and routines are always available to code in other modules. Is this true with public variables and routines in classes?
4. True or False: Each object derived from a class has its own set of module-level data.
5. What must you do to create a property that can be read but not changed by client code?
6. What's the best way to store the internal value of a property within a class?
7. Which is generally superior, early binding or late binding?
8. If an object variable is declared As Object, is it early bound or late bound?
9. What's the best way to destroy an object reference?

Exercises

1. Add a new property to your class called DropsInABucket. Make this property a Long, and set it up so that client code can read the property value but not set it. Finally, add a button to the form that, when clicked, prints the value of the property to the Output window (it will be 0 by default). When this is working, modify the code so that the property always returns 1,000,000.
2. Add a button to your form that creates two object variables of type clsMyClass(). Use the New keyword to instantiate a new instance of the class in one of the variables. Then set the second variable to reference the same object and print the contents of the Height property to the Output window.

Hour **17**

Interacting with Users

Forms and controls are the primary means by which users interact with an application and vice versa. However, program interaction can and often does go deeper than that. For example, a program can display customized messages to a user, and it can be finely tuned to deal with certain keystrokes or mouse clicks. In this hour, you'll learn how to create functional and cohesive interaction between your application and the user. In addition, you'll learn how to program the keyboard and the mouse so that you can expand the interactivity of your program beyond what's natively supported by a form and its controls.

The highlights of this hour include the following:

- Displaying messages using the MessageBox.Show() function
- Creating custom dialog boxes
- Using InputBox() to get information from a user
- Interacting with the keyboard
- Using the common mouse events

Displaying Messages Using the MessageBox.Show() Function

A message box is a small dialog box that displays a message to the user (just in case that wasn't obvious enough). Message boxes are often used to tell the user the result of some action, such as `The file has been copied` or `The file could not be found`. A message box is dismissed when the user clicks one of the message box's available buttons. Most applications have *many* message boxes, but developers don't often display messages correctly. It's important to remember that when you display a message to a user, you're communicating with the user. In this section, I'm going to teach you not only how to use the MessageBox.Show function to display messages, but how to use the statement effectively.

The MessageBox.Show function can be used to tell a user something or ask the user a question. In addition to text, which is its primary function, you can also use this function to display an icon or display one or more buttons that the user can click. Although you're free to display whatever text you want, you must choose from a predefined list of icons and buttons.

The MessageBox.Show method is an overloaded method. This means that the method was written with numerous constructs supporting various options. While coding in Visual Studio .NET, IntelliSense displays a drop-down scrolling list displaying any of the twelve overloaded MessageBox.Show method calls to aid in coding. Following are a few ways to call MessageBox.Show:

To display a message box with specified text, a caption in the title bar, and an OK button, use this syntax:

```
MessageBox.Show(MessageText, Caption)
```

To display a message box with specified text, caption, and one or more specific buttons, use this syntax:

```
MessageBox.Show(MessageText, Caption, Buttons)
```

To display a message box with specified text, caption, buttons, and icon, use this syntax:

```
MessageBox.Show(MessageText, Caption, Buttons, Icon)
```

In all these statements, *MessageText* is the text to display in the message box, *Caption* determines what appears in the title bar, *Buttons* determines which buttons the user sees, and *Icon* determines what icon (if any) appears in the message box. Consider the following statement, which produces the message box shown in Figure 17.1.

```
MessageBox.Show("This is a message.", "Hello There")
```

FIGURE 17.1

A message box in its simplest form.

As you can see, if you omit *Buttons*, Visual Basic .NET displays only an OK button. You should always ensure that the buttons displayed are appropriate for the message.

> The older-style basic MsgBox() function (which is still supported, although not recommended) defaults the caption for the message box to the name of the project. There is no default for MessageBox.Show, so you should always specify a caption or you'll get an empty title bar for the dialog box.

Specifying Buttons and an Icon

Using the *Buttons* parameter, you can display one or more buttons in the message box. The *Buttons* parameter type is *MessageBoxButtons*, and the allowable values are shown in Table 17.1.

TABLE 17.1 Allowable Enumerators for MessageBoxButtons

Member	Description
AbortRetryIgnore	Displays Abort, Retry, and Ignore buttons
OK	Displays OK button only
OKCancel	Displays OK and Cancel buttons
YesNoCancel	Displays Yes, No, and Cancel buttons
YesNo	Displays Yes and No buttons
RetryCancel	Displays Retry and Cancel buttons

Because the *Buttons* parameter is an enumerated type, Visual Basic .NET gives you an IntelliSense drop-down list when specifying a value for this parameter. Therefore,

17

committing these values to memory isn't all that important; you'll commit the ones you use most often to memory fairly quickly

The *Icon* parameter determines the symbol displayed in the message box. The Icon parameter is an enumeration from the MessageBoxIcon type. Table 17.2 shows the most commonly used values of MessageBoxIcon.

TABLE 17.2 Enumerators for MessageBoxIcon

Members	Description
Exclamation	Displays a symbol consisting of an exclamation point in a triangle with a yellow background
Information	Displays a symbol consisting of a lowercase letter i in a circle
None	Displays no symbol
Question	Displays a symbol consisting of a question mark in a circle
Stop	Displays a symbol consisting of a white X in a circle with a red background
Warning	Displays a symbol consisting of an exclamation point in a triangle with a yellow background

The *Icon* parameter is also an enumerated type; therefore, C# gives you an IntelliSense drop-down list when specifying a value for this parameter.

The message box in Figure 17.2 was created with the following statement:

```
MessageBox.Show("I'm about to do something...","MessageBox sample", _
    MessageBoxButtons.OKCancel,MessageBoxIcon.Information)
```

FIGURE 17.2

Assign the Information icon to general messages.

The message box in Figure 17.3 was created with a statement almost identical to the previous one, except that the second button is designated as the default button. If a user presses the Enter key with a message box displayed, the message box acts as though the user clicked the default button. You'll want to give careful consideration to the default button in each message box. For example, if the application is about to do something that the user probably doesn't want to do, it's best to make the Cancel button the default button—in case the user is a bit quick when pressing the Enter key. Following is the statement used to generate the message box in Figure 17.3:

```
MessageBox.Show("I'm about to do something irreversible...", _
    "MessageBox sample", _
    MessageBoxButtons.OKCancel,MessageBoxIcon.Information, _
    MessageBoxDefaultButton.Button2)
```

FIGURE 17.3

The default button has a dark border.

The Error icon is shown in Figure 17.4. The Error icon is best used in rare circumstances, such as when an exception has occurred. Overusing the Error icon is like crying wolf—when a real problem emerges, the user might not take notice. Notice here how I've displayed only the OK button. If something has already happened and there's nothing the user can do about it, don't bother giving the user a Cancel button. The following statement generates the message box shown in Figure 17.4:

```
MessageBox.Show("Something bad has happened!","MessageBox sample", _
    MessageBoxButtons.OK,MessageBoxIcon.Error)
```

FIGURE 17.4

If users have no control over what has occurred, don't give them a Cancel button.

In Figure 17.5, a question has been posed to the user, so I displayed the Question icon. Also note how I assumed that the user would probably choose No, so I made the second button the default. In the next section, you'll learn how to determine which button the user clicks. Here's the statement used to generate the message box shown in Figure 17.5:

```
MessageBox.Show("Would you like to format your hard drive now?", _
    "MessageBox sample",MessageBoxButtons.YesNo,MessageBoxIcon.Question, _
    MessageBoxDefaultButton.Button2)
```

FIGURE 17.5

A message box can be used to ask a question.

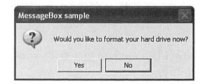

17

As you can see, designating buttons and icons isn't all that difficult. The real effort comes in determining which buttons and icons are appropriate for a given situation.

Determining Which Button Is Clicked

You'll probably find that many of your message boxes are simple, containing only an OK button. For other message boxes, however, you must determine which button a user clicks. Why give the user a choice if you're not going to act on it?

The MessageBox.Show() method returns the button clicked as a DialogResult enumeration. The DialogResult has the values shown in Table 17.3.

TABLE 17.3   Enumerators for DialogResult

Members	Description
Abort	Return value Abort; usually sent from a button labeled Abort.
Cancel	Return value Cancel; usually sent from a button labeled Cancel.
Ignore	Return value Ignore; usually sent from a button labeled Ignore.
No	Return value No; usually sent from a button labeled No.
None	Nothing is returned from the dialog box. The model dialog continues running.
OK	Return value OK; usually sent from a button labeled OK.
Retry	Return value Retry; usually sent from a button labeled Retry.
Yes	Return value Yes; usually sent from a button labeled Yes.

Note the text "usually sent from" in the descriptions of the DialogResult values. When you create custom dialog boxes (as shown later in this hour), you can assign a DialogResult to any button of your choosing.

Performing actions based on the button clicked is a matter of using one of the decision constructs. For example:

```
If (MessageBox.Show("Would you like to do X?","MessageBox sample", _
    MessageBoxButtons.YesNo,MessageBoxIcon.Question) = DialogResult.Yes) Then
    ' Code to do X would go here.
End If
```

As you can see, MessageBox.Show() is a method that gives you a lot of bang for your buck; it offers considerable flexibility.

Creating Good Messages

The MessageBox.Show method is surprisingly simple to use, considering all the different forms of messages it enables you to create. The real trick is in providing appropriate messages to users at appropriate times. In addition to considering the icon and buttons to display in a message, you should follow these guidelines for crafting message text:

- Use a formal tone. Don't use large words, and avoid using contractions. Strive to make the text immediately understandable and not overly fancy; a message box is not a place to show off your literary skills.

- Limit messages to two or three lines. Lengthy messages are not only harder for users to read, but they can also be intimidating. When a message box is used to ask a question, make the question as succinct as possible.

- Never make users feel as though they've done something wrong. Users will, and do, make mistakes, but you should craft messages that take the sting out of the situation.

- Spell check all message text. The Visual Basic .NET code editor doesn't spell check for you, so you should type your messages in a program such as Word and spell check the text before pasting it into your code. Spelling errors have an adverse effect on a user's perception of a program.

- Avoid technical jargon. Just because someone uses software doesn't mean that he's a technical person; explain things in plain English (or whatever the native language of the GUI happens to be).

- Be sure that the buttons match the text! For example, don't show the Yes/No buttons if the text doesn't present a question to the user.

Creating Custom Dialog Boxes

Most of the time, the MessageBox.Show method should be a sufficient means to display messages to a user. At times, however, the MessageBox.Show method is too limited for a given purpose. For example, suppose that you want to display a lot of text to a user (such as a log file of some sort) and therefore want a message box that is sizable by the user.

Custom dialog boxes are nothing more than standard modal forms with one notable exception: One or more buttons are designated to return a dialog result, just as the buttons on a message box shown with the MessageBox.Show method return a dialog result.

You're now going to create a custom dialog box. Create a new Windows Application titled **Custom Dialog Example**. Change the name of the default form to **fclsMain**, set its

Text property to **Custom Dialog Box Example**, and set the Startup object of the project to fclsMain. Add a new button to the form and set its properties as follows:

Property	Value
Name	**btnShowCustomDialogBox**
Location	**72,180**
Size	**152,23**
Text	**Show Custom Dialog Box**

Next, you're going to create the custom dialog box. Add a new form to the project by choosing Add Windows Form from the Project menu. Save the new form with the name **fclsCustomDialogBox.vb**. Change the Text property of the new form to **This is a custom dialog box**, and set its FormBorderStyle to FixedSingle. Add a new text box to the form and set its properties as follows:

Property	Value
Name	**txtCustomMessage**
Location	**8,8**
Locked	**True**
Multiline	**True**
Size	**275,220**
Text	**Custom message goes here**

For a custom dialog box to return a result like a standard message box does, it must have buttons that are designated to return a dialog result. This is accomplished by setting the DialogResult property of a button (see Figure 17.6).

Add a new button to the form and set its properties as shown in the following table. This button will act as the custom dialog box's Cancel button.

Property	Value
Name	**btnCancel**
DialogResult	**Cancel**
Location	**216,240**
Size	**75,23**
Text	**Cancel**

FIGURE 17.6

The DialogResult property determines the return value of the button.

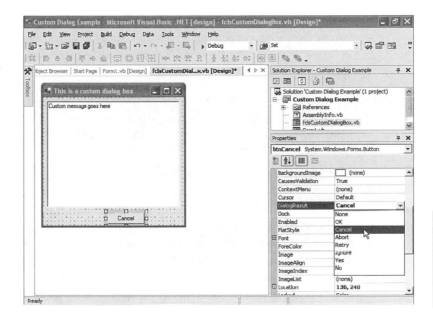

Lastly, you need to create an OK button for the custom dialog box. Create another button and set its properties as shown in the following table:

Property	Value
Name	**btnOK**
DialogResult	**OK**
Location	**136,240**
Size	**75,23**
Text	**OK**

Specifying a dialog result for one or more buttons is the first step in making a form a custom dialog box. The second part of the process is in how the form is shown. As you learned in Hour 5, "Building Forms—The Basics," forms are displayed by calling the Show property of a form variable. However, to show a form as a custom dialog box, you call the ShowDialog method instead. When a form is displayed using ShowDialog, the following occurs:

- The form is shown modally.
- If the user clicks a button that has its DialogResult property set to return a value, the form is immediately closed and that value is returned as the result of the ShowDialog method call.

17

Notice how you don't have to write code to close the form; clicking a button with a dialog result closes the form automatically. This simplifies the process of creating custom
dialog boxes. Return to the first form in the form designer by clicking the Form1.vb
[Design] tab.

Double-click the button you created and add the following code:

```
Dim objCustomDialogBox As New fclsCustomDialogBox()
If objCustomDialogBox.ShowDialog = DialogResult.OK Then
   MessageBox.Show("You clicked OK.")
Else
   MessageBox.Show("You clicked Cancel.")
End If
objCustomDialogBox = Nothing
```

When you typed the equal sign after the word ShowDialog, did you notice that Visual
Basic .NET gave you an IntelliSense drop-down list with the possible dialog results?
These results correspond directly with the values you can assign a button using the
DialogResult property. Press F5 to run the project, click the button to display your custom
dialog box (see Figure 17.7), and then click one of the available dialog box buttons. When
you're satisfied that the project is working correctly, stop the project and save your work.

If you click the Close (X) button in the upper-right corner of the form, the
form is closed and the code behaves as if you've clicked Cancel because the
Else code occurs.

FIGURE 17.7
*The ShowDialog
method enables you to
create custom message
boxes.*

The capability to create custom dialog boxes is a powerful feature. A call to
MessageBox.Show is usually sufficient, but when you need more control over the appearance and contents of a message box, creating a custom dialog box is the way to go.

Using InputBox() to Get Information from a User

The MessageBox.Show method enables you to ask the user simple Yes/No, OK/Cancel–type questions, but it doesn't enable you to get specific input from a user, such as text or a number. When you need input from a user, you have two choices:

- Create a form with one or more controls to capture the data
- Use the InputBox() function to gather data from the user

The InputBox() function is capable of capturing only one piece of data, so it's not appropriate for most data entry. However, in some situations, you might find that you need only one piece of data and creating a custom form in such a situation would be overkill. For example, suppose that you have a simple application, and you want the user to enter a name when she first starts the application. You could use the InputBox() function to have the user enter her name rather than design a special form.

The basic syntax of the InputBox() function looks like this:

```
InputBox(prompt, [title], [defaultresponse])
```

The first two parameters are similar to the corresponding parameters in MsgBox(). The first parameter is the prompt to display to the user. This is where you specify the instructions or question that you want posed to the user. The *title* parameter determines the text that appears in the title bar. Again, if you omit *title*, the name of the project is shown. The following statement creates the input box shown in Figure 17.8:

```
strResult = InputBox("What is your favorite color?", "Enter Color")
```

FIGURE 17.8

The input box enables a user to enter a single piece of information.

The last parameter, *defaultresponse*, enables you to specify text that appears by default in the text box portion of the input box. For example, the following statement produces the input box shown in Figure 17.9:

```
strResult = InputBox("How many eggs do you want to order?", "Order Eggs", "12")
```

17

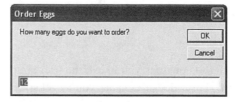

You should remember two things about the return value of InputBox(). The first is that the result is always a string. The second is that an empty string is returned if the user clicks Cancel. The fact that InputBox() can return only a string and not a number is a limitation, but it's one that you can work around.

You're now going to create a project that uses an InputBox() to get the age of the user. If the user clicks Cancel or enters something other than a number, the program behaves accordingly. Create a new Windows Application titled **InputBox Example**. Change the name of the default form to **fclsInputBoxExample**, set its Text property to **InputBox Example**, and set the Startup Object property of the project to fclsInputBoxExample. Add a new button to the form and set its properties as follows:

Property	Value
Name	**btnGetAge**
Location	**112,120**
Size	**75,23**
Text	**Enter Age**

Double-click the button to access its Click event and enter the following code:

```
Dim strResult As String
Dim intAge As Integer

strResult = InputBox("Please enter your age.", "Enter Age")

If strResult = "" Then
   MsgBox("You clicked cancel!")
ElseIf IsNumeric(strResult) Then
   ' The user entered a number, store the age as a number.
   intAge = CInt(strResult)
   MsgBox("You entered " & intAge & ".")
Else
   MsgBox("You did not enter a number.")
End If
```

Nothing in this procedure, short of the call to InputBox(), should be new to you. What happens here is that the InputBox() function is used to ask the user to enter the user's age. Because InputBox() always returns a string, you used a string variable to hold the result. Next, an If…Else If…Else …End If construct is used to evaluate the result of the InputBox() call. The first test looks to see whether the result is a zero-length string. If so, it assumes that the user clicked Cancel. Next, the result is evaluated to see whether it is a number. If it is a number, the result is converted to an integer and displayed back to the user. Go ahead and Press F5 and test the project.

If the user doesn't enter anything, an empty string is returned just as though the user clicked Cancel. There's no way to know the difference between clicking Cancel and not entering any text when using the InputBox.

17

InputBox() is a handy function for gathering a single piece of information. As you can see, it's possible to work around the limitation of the function returning only a string. Keep the InputBox() function in mind; at times, it will come in handy.

Interacting with the Keyboard

Although most every control on a form handles its own keyboard input, on occasion you'll want to handle keyboard input directly. For example, you might want to perform an action when the user presses a specific key or releases a specific key. Most controls support three events that you can use to work directly with keyboard input. These are listed in Table 17.4.

TABLE 17.4   Events That Handle Keyboard Input

Event Name	Description
KeyDown	Occurs when a key is pressed down while the control has the focus
KeyPress	Occurs when a key is pressed (the key has been pushed down and then released) while the control has the focus
KeyUp	Occurs when a key is released while the control has the focus

These events fire in the same order in which they appear in Table 17.4. Suppose, for example, that the user presses a key while a text box has the focus. The following list shows how the events would fire for the text box:

1. When the user presses a key, the KeyDown event fires.

2. When the user releases a key, the KeyPress event fires.

3. After the KeyPress event fires, the KeyUp event fires, completing the cycle of keystroke events.

You're now going to create a project that illustrates handling keystrokes. This project has a text box that will refuse to accept any character that isn't a number; you'll be creating a numeric text box. Start by creating a new Windows Application titled **Keyboard Example**. Change the name of the default form to **fclsKeyboardExample**, set its Text property to **Keyboard Example**, and set the Startup Object property of the project to fclsKeyboardExample. Add a new text box to the form and set its properties as shown in the following table:

Property	Value
Name	**txtInput**
Multiline	**True**
Location	**24,80**
Size	**240,120**
Text	(*make blank*)

You're going to add code to the KeyPress event of the text box to "eat" keystrokes that aren't numbers. Double-click the text box now to access its default event. We're not interested in the TextChanged event, so choose KeyPress from the event list in the upper right of the code window. Next, go ahead and delete the TextChanged event because you're not going to be using it. Your code editor should look now look like Figure 17.10.

FIGURE 17.10

The KeyPress event is a good place to handle keyboard entry.

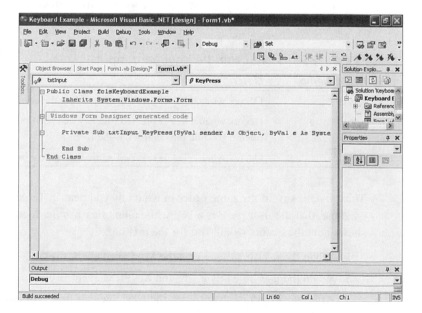

As you learned in Hour 4, "Understanding Events," the e parameter contains information specific to the occurrence of this event. In the keyboard-related events, the e parameter contains information about the key being pressed; it's what you'll be using to work with the keystroke made by the user.

The key being pressed is available as the KeyChar property of the e parameter. You're going to write code that handles the keystroke when the pressed key is anything other than a number. Add the following code to the KeyPress event:

```
If Not (IsNumeric(e.KeyChar)) Then
    e.Handled = True
End If
```

I imagine that you're curious about the Handled property of the e object. When you set this property to True, you're telling Visual Basic .NET that you handled the keystroke, and Visual Basic .NET should ignore it (that is, not add it to the text box). To see the effect this has, press F5 to run the project and enter text into the text box. Try entering both numbers and letters, and you'll find that only the numbers appear in the text box (see Figure 17.11) .

FIGURE 17.11

The keyboard events enable you to handle keystrokes as you see fit.

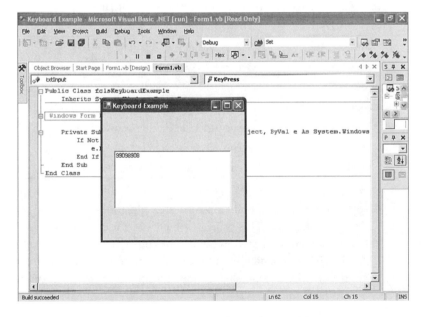

When you paste data from the clipboard, the KeyPress event isn't fired for each keystroke. It's therefore possible that a non-numeric character could appear in the text box. If you absolutely needed to keep non-numeric characters out of the text box, you'd need to make use of the TextChanged event.

It's not often that I need to catch a key press, but every now and then I do. The three keystroke events I've listed in Table 17.4 have always made it easy to do what I need to do, but if there's one caveat I've discovered, it's that you need to give careful consideration to which event you choose (such as KeyPress or KeyUp, for example). Different events work best in different situations, and the best thing to do is to start with what seems like the most logical event, test the code, and change the event if necessary.

Using the Common Mouse Events

As with keyboard input, most controls support mouse input natively; you don't have to write code to deal with mouse input. At times, you might need more control than that offered by the native functionality of a control, however. Visual Basic .NET supports six events that enable you to deal with mouse input directly. These events are listed in Table 17.5 in the order in which they occur.

TABLE 17.5 Events Used to Handle Mouse Input

Event Name	Description
MouseEnter	Occurs when the pointer enters a control
MouseMove	Occurs when the pointer moves over a control
MouseHover	Occurs when the pointer hovers over a control
MouseDown	Occurs when the pointer is over a control and a button is pressed
MouseUp	Occurs when the pointer is over a control and a button is released
MouseLeave	Occurs when the pointer leaves a control
Click	Occurs between the MouseDown and MouseUp events

You're now going to build a project that illustrates interacting with the mouse using the MouseMove event. This project will enable a user to draw on a form, much like you can draw in a paint program. Begin by creating a new Windows Application titled **Mouse Paint**. Change the name of the default form to **fclsMousePaint**, set its Text property to **Paint with the Mouse**, and set the Startup Object property of the project to fclsMousePaint.

Next, double-click the form to access its default event, the Load event. Enter the following statement into the load event:

```
m_objGraphics = Me.CreateGraphics
```

You've already used a graphics object a few times. What you're doing here is setting a graphics object to the client area of the form; any drawing performed on the object appears on the form. Because you're going to draw to this graphics object each time the mouse moves over the form, there's no point in creating a new graphics object each time you need to draw to it. Therefore, you're going to make m_objGraphics a module-level variable, which is instantiated only once—in the Load event of the form. Enter this statement into the Declarations section of your form class, immediately below the Inherits statement:

```
Private m_objGraphics As Graphics
```

As I've said previously, you should always destroy objects when you're done with them. In this case, you want the object to remain in existence for the life of the form. Therefore, you'll destroy it in the Closed event of the form, which occurs when the form is unloaded. Open the object drop-down list (the upper-left drop-down list) and choose (fclsMousePaint Events). Next, open the procedure drop-down list (the drop-down list in the upper right), and select Closed. Enter the following statement in the Closed event:

```
m_objGraphics.Dispose()
```

Your form should now look like the one shown in Figure 17.12.

FIGURE 17.12

Code in many places often works together to achieve one goal.

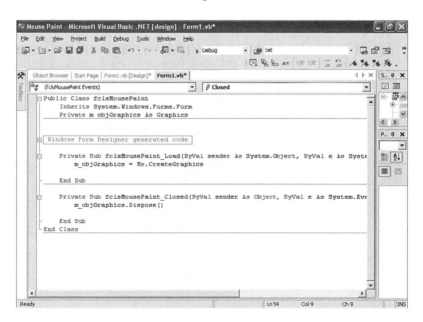

The last bit of code you need to add is the code that will draw on the form. You're going to place code in the MouseMove event of the form to do this. First, the code will make sure that the left mouse button is held down. If it isn't, no drawing takes place; the user must hold down the mouse button to draw. Next, a rectangle will be created. The coordinates of the mouse pointer will be used to create a very small rectangle that will be passed to the DrawEllipse method of the graphics object. This has the effect of drawing a tiny circle where the mouse pointer is positioned. Again, select (fclsMousePoint Events) from the object drop-down list, and this time select MouseMove from the list of event procedures. Add the following code to the MouseMove event:

```
Dim rectEllipse As Rectangle

If e.Button <> MouseButtons.Left Then Exit Sub

With rectEllipse
    .X = e.X - 1
    .Y = e.Y - 1
    .Width = 2
    .Height = 2
End With

m_objGraphics.DrawEllipse(System.Drawing.Pens.Blue, rectEllipse)
```

Like all events, the e object contains information related to the event. In this example, you're using the X and Y properties of the e object, which are the coordinates of the pointer when the event fires. In addition, you're checking the Button property of the object to make sure that the user is pressing the left button.

Your project is now complete! Save your work by clicking Save All on the toolbar, and then press F5 to run the project. Move your mouse over the form—nothing happens. Now, hold down the left mouse button and move the mouse. This time, you'll be drawing on the form (see Figure 17.13).

FIGURE 17.13

Capturing mouse events opens many exciting possibilities.

Notice that the faster you move the mouse, the more space appears between circles. This shows you that the user is able to move the mouse faster than the MouseMove event can fire, so you can't get every single movement of the mouse. This is important to remember.

Summary

Forms and controls allow for a lot of flexibility in the way a user interacts with an application. However, solid interactivity goes beyond just what is placed on a form. In this hour, you learned how to use the MessageBox.Show function to create informational dialog boxes. You learned how to specify an icon, buttons, and even how to designate a specific button as the default button. You also learned some valuable tips to help you create the best messages possible. You'll create message boxes frequently, so mastering this skill is important.

At times, a simple OK/Cancel or Yes/No question isn't applicable—you need more data from the user. In this hour, you learned how to use the InputBox() function to get a single piece of data from the user, and how to create custom dialog boxes. Although InputBox() always returns a string, you learned how to use it to gather numeric input as well.

Finally, you learned how to interact with the keyboard and the mouse directly through numerous events. The mouse or keyboard capabilities of a control sometimes fall short of what you want to accomplish. By understanding the concepts presented in this hour, you can go beyond the native capabilities of controls to create a rich, interactive experience for your users.

Q&A

Q Is it possible to capture keystrokes at the form level, rather than capturing them in control events?

A Yes. For the form's keyboard-related events to fire when a control has the focus, however, you must set the form's KeyPreview property to True. The control's keyboard events will still fire, unless you set KeyPressEventArgs.Handled to True in the control's KeyPress event.

Q If I need to gather two or three pieces of information from the user, is it okay to use multiple InputBox statements?

A Probably not. In this case, a form or custom dialog box is probably a better choice.

Workshop

The Workshop is designed to help you anticipate possible questions, review what you've learned, and get you thinking about how to put your knowledge into practice. The answers to the quiz are in Appendix B, "Answers to the Quizzes."

Quiz

1. What argument must you always supply a value for when calling MessageBox.Show?

2. If you don't supply a value for the *caption* parameter of MessageBox.Show, what is displayed in the title bar of the message?

3. How many icons can you show in a message box at once?

4. What type of data is always returned by the InputBox() function?

5. What's returned by InputBox() when the user clicks Cancel?

6. Which event fires first, the KeyUp or KeyPress event?

7. How do you determine which button is being pressed in a mouse-related event?

Exercises

1. Modify your custom dialog box project so that the OK button is the Accept button of the form. That way, the user must only press Enter to dismiss the dialog box. Next, make the Cancel button the Cancel button of the form so that the user can also press the Esc key to dismiss the form.

2. Modify your mouse paint project so that the form clears each time the user starts drawing. Hint: Clear the graphics object in the MouseDown event.

Hour 18

Working with Graphics

Visual Basic .NET provides an amazingly powerful array of drawing capabilities—much more than what was available in any previous version of Visual Basic. This power comes at the price of a steeper learning curve, however. Drawing isn't intuitive; you can't sit down for a few minutes with the online Help text and start drawing graphics. However, after you learn the basic principles involved, you'll find that drawing isn't that complicated. In this hour, you'll learn the basic skills for drawing shapes and text to a form or other graphical surface. You'll learn about pens, colors, and brushes (objects that help define graphics that you draw). In addition, you'll learn how to persist graphics on a form—and even how to create bitmaps that exist solely in memory.

The highlights of this hour include the following:

- Understanding the Graphics object
- Working with pens
- Using system colors
- Working with rectangles
- Drawing shapes

- Drawing text
- Persisting graphics on a form

Understanding the Graphics Object

NEW TERM At first, you might not come up with many reasons to draw to the screen, preferring to use the many advanced controls found within Visual Basic .NET to build your interfaces. However, as your applications grow in size and complexity, you'll find more and more occasion to draw your own interfaces directly to the screen. You might even choose to design your own controls (which you can do with Visual Basic .NET). In this hour, you'll learn the basics of drawing and printing to the screen; when you need this functionality, you *really* need this functionality. Using the skills you acquire in this hour, you'll be able to build incredibly detailed interfaces that look exactly the way you want them to look.

The code within the Windows operating system that handles drawing everything to the screen, including text, lines, and shapes, is called the *Graphics Device Interface* (*GDI*). The GDI processes all drawing instructions from applications as well as from Windows itself, and generates the output for the current display. Because the GDI generates what you see onscreen, it has the responsibility of dealing with the particular display driver installed on the computer and the settings of the driver, such as resolution and color depth. That means applications (and their developers) don't have to worry about these details; you write code that tells the GDI what to output and the GDI does whatever is necessary to produce that output. This behavior is called *device independence* because applications can instruct the GDI to display text and graphics using code that's independent of the particular display device.

Visual Basic .NET code communicates with the GDI primarily via a Graphics object. The basic process is the following:

- An object variable is created to hold a reference to a Graphics object.
- The object variable is set to a valid Graphics object (new or existing).
- To draw or print, you call methods of the Graphics object.

Creating a Graphics Object for a Form or Control

If you want to draw directly to a form or control, you can easily get a reference to the drawing surface by calling the CreateGraphics method of the object in question. For example, to create a Graphics object that draws to a text box, you could use code such as this:

```
Dim objGraphics As Graphics
objGraphics = TextBox1.CreateGraphics
```

When you call CreateGraphics, you're setting the object variable to hold a reference to the Graphics object of the form or control's client area. The client area of a form is the gray area within the borders and title bar of the form, whereas the client area of a control is usually the entire control. All drawing and printing done using the Graphics object is sent to the client area. In the code shown previously, the Graphics object references the client area of a text box, so all drawing methods executed on the Graphics object would draw directly to the text box.

 When you draw directly to a form or control, the object in question doesn't persist what's drawn on it. If the form is obscured in any way, such as by a window covering it or by minimizing the form, the next time the form is painted, it won't contain anything that was drawn on it. Later in this hour, I'll teach you how to persist graphics on a form.

Creating a Graphics Object for a New Bitmap

You don't have to set a Graphics object to the client area of a form or control; you can also set a Graphics object to a bitmap that exists only in memory. For performance reasons, you might want to use a memory bitmap to store temporary images or as a place to build complex graphics before sending them to a visible element (like a form or control). To do this, you first have to create a new bitmap.

To create a new bitmap, you dimension a variable to hold a reference to the new bitmap using the following syntax:

```
variable = New Bitmap(width, height, pixelformat)
```

The *width* and *height* arguments are exactly what they appear to be: the width and height of the new bitmap. The *pixelformat* argument, however, is less intuitive. This argument determines the color depth of the bitmap and might also specify whether the bitmap has an alpha layer (used for transparent portions of bitmaps). Table 18.1 lists a few of the common values for *pixelformat* (see Visual Basic's online Help for the complete list of values and their meanings).

TABLE 18.1 Common Values for *pixelformat*

Value	Description
Format16bppGrayScale	The pixel format is 16 bits per pixel. The color information specifies 65,536 shades of gray.
Format16bppRgb555	The pixel format is 16 bits per pixel. The color information specifies 32,768 shades of color, of which 5 bits are red, 5 bits are green, and 5 bits are blue.

TABLE 18.1   Continued

Value	Description
Format24bppRgb	The pixel format is 24 bits per pixel. The color information specifies 16,777,216 shades of color, of which 8 bits are red, 8 bits are green, and 8 bits are blue.

To create a new bitmap that's 640 pixels wide by 480 pixels tall and has a pixel depth of 24 bits, for example, you could use this statement:

```
objMyBitMap = New Bitmap(640, 480, Drawing.Imaging.PixelFormat.Format24bppRgb)
```

After the bitmap is created, you can create a Graphics object that references the bitmap using the FromImage() method, like this:

```
objGraphics = Graphics.FromImage(objMyBitMap)
```

Now any drawing or printing done using objGraphics would be performed on the memory bitmap. For the user to see the bitmap, you'd have to send the bitmap to a form or control. You'll do this later in this hour in the section "Persisting Graphics on a Form."

 When you're finished with a Graphics object, you should call its Dispose() method to ensure that all resources used by the Graphics object are freed.

Working with Pens

NEW TERM   A *pen* is an object that defines characteristics of a line. Pens are used to define color, line width, and line style (solid, dashed, and so on). Pens are used with almost all the drawing methods you'll learn about in this hour.

Visual Basic .NET supplies a number of predefined pens, and you can also create your own. To create your own pen, use the following syntax:

```
variable = New Pen(color, width)
```

After a pen is created, you can set its properties to adjust its appearance. For example, all Pen objects have a DashStyle property that determines the appearance of lines drawn with the pen. Table 18.2 lists the possible values for DashStyle.

TABLE 18.2 Possible Values for DashStyle

Value	Description
Dash	Specifies a line consisting of dashes.
DashDot	Specifies a line consisting of a pattern of dashes and dots.
DashDotDot	Specifies a line consisting of alternating dashes and double dots.
Solid	Specifies a solid line.
Custom	Specifies a custom dash style. The Pen object contains properties that can be used to define the custom line.

The enumeration for DashStyle is part of the Drawing.Drawing2D namespace. Therefore, to create a new, dark blue pen which draws a dotted line, you would use code like the following:

```
Dim objMyPen As Pen
objMyPen = New Pen(Drawing.Color.DarkBlue, 3)
objMyPen.DashStyle = Drawing.Drawing2D.DashStyle.Dot
```

The 3 passed as the second argument to create the new Pen defines the width of the pen in pixels.

Visual Basic includes many standard pens, which are available via the System.Drawing.Pens class, as in

```
objPen = System.Drawing.Pens.DarkBlue
```

When drawing using the techniques discussed shortly, you can use custom pens or system-defined pens—it's your choice.

Using System Colors

At some point, you might have changed your Windows theme, or perhaps you changed the image or color of your desktop. What you might not be aware of is that Windows enables you to customize the colors of almost all Windows interface elements. The colors that Windows allows you to change are called *system colors*. To change your system colors, right-click the desktop, choose Properties from the shortcut menu to display the Display Properties dialog box, and then click the Appearance tab (see Figure 18.1). To change the color for a specific item, you click the Advanced button, select the color attribute to change, and then choose a new color (if you're running a version of Windows other than Windows XP, your dialog box might be slightly different).

18

FIGURE **18.1**

*The Display Properties
dialog box enables you
to select the colors of
most Windows inter-
face elements.*

When you change a system color using the Display Properties dialog box, all loaded
applications should change their appearance to match your selection. In addition, when
you start any new applications, they should also match their appearance to your selection. If you had to write code to manage this behavior, you'd have to write a *lot* of code,
and you'd be justified in avoiding the whole mess. However, making an application
adjust its appearance to match the user's system color selections is actually quite trivial;
therefore, there's no reason not to do it. For the most part, it's automatic with controls
that you add to a form.

To designate that an interface color should stay in sync with a user's system colors, you
assign a system color to a color property of the item in question (see Figure 18.2). If you
wanted to ensure that the color of a button matches the user's system color, for example,
you would assign the System Color control to the BackColor property of the Button control. Table 18.3 lists the most common system colors you can use. For a complete list,
consult the online Help.

When a user changes a system color using the Display Properties dialog box, Visual
Basic automatically updates the appearance of objects that use system colors; you don't
have to write a single line of code to do this. Fortunately, when you create new forms
and when you add controls to forms, Visual Basic automatically assigns the proper system color to the appropriate properties so you don't usually have to muck with them.

FIGURE 18.2

*System colors are
assigned using the
System palette tab.*

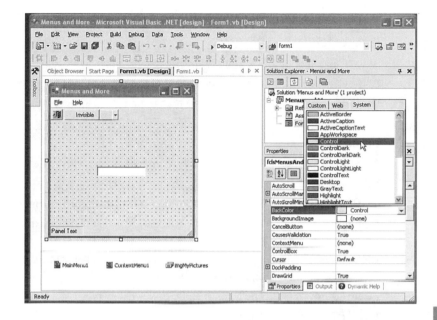

Be aware that you aren't limited to assigning system colors to their logically associated properties. You can assign system colors to any color property you want, and you can also use system colors when drawing. This enables you to draw custom interface elements that match the user's system colors, for example. Be aware, however, that if you do draw with system colors, Visual Basic won't update the colors automatically when the user changes system colors; you would have to redraw the elements with the new system color. In addition, if you apply system colors to properties that aren't usually assigned system colors, you run the risk of displaying odd color combinations, such as black on black, depending on the user's color settings.

Users don't just change their system colors for aesthetic purposes. I work with a programmer who is colorblind. He's modified his system colors so that he can see things better on the screen. If you don't allow your applications to adjust to the color preferences of the user, you might make using your program unnecessarily difficult, or even impossible, for someone with color blindness or visual acuity issues.

18

TABLE 18.3   System Colors

Enumeration	Description
ActiveCaption	The color of the background of an active caption bar (title bar).
ActiveCaptionText	The color of the text of the active caption bar (title bar).
Control	The color of the background of push buttons and other 3D elements.
ControlDark	The color of shadows on a 3D element.
ControlLight	The color of highlights on a 3D element.
ControlText	The color of the text on buttons and other 3D elements.
Desktop	The color of the Windows desktop.
GrayText	The color of the text on a user interface element when it's unavailable.
Highlight	The color of the background of highlighted text. This includes selected menu items as well as selected text.
HighlightText	The color of the foreground of highlighted text. This includes selected menu items as well as selected text.
InactiveBorder	The color of an inactive window border.
InactiveCaption	The color of the background of an inactive caption bar.
InactiveCaptionText	The color of the text of an inactive caption bar.
Menu	The color of the menu background.
MenuText	The color of the menu text.
Window	The color of the background in the client area of a window.

Working with Rectangles

Before learning how to draw shapes, you need to understand the concept of a rectangle as it relates to Visual Basic programming. A rectangle is a structure used to hold bounding coordinates used to draw a shape. A rectangle isn't necessarily used to draw a rectangle (although it can be). Obviously, a square can fit within a rectangle. However, so can circles and ellipses. Figure 18.3 illustrates how most shapes can be bound by a rectangle.

To draw most shapes, you must have a rectangle. The rectangle you pass to a drawing method is used as a bounding rectangle; the proper shape (circle, ellipse, and so on) is always drawn. Creating a rectangle is easy. First, you dimension a variable as Rectangle, and then you set the X, Y, Width, and Height properties of the object variable. The X, Y value is the coordinate of the upper-left corner of the rectangle—the Height and Width properties are self-explanatory. For example, the following code creates a rectangle that has its upper-left corner at coordinate 0,0, has a width of 100, and height of 50:

FIGURE **18.3**

Rectangles are used to define the bounds of most shapes.

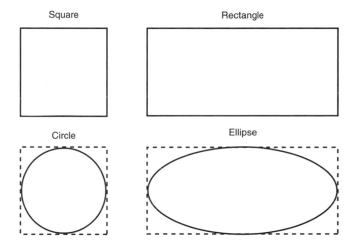

```
Dim rectBounding As New Rectangle()
rectBounding.X = 0
rectBounding.Y = 0
rectBounding.Width = 100
rectBounding.Height = 50
```

18

The Rectangle object enables you to send the X, Y, Height, and Width values as part of its initialize construct. Using this technique, you could create the same rectangle with only a single line of code:

```
Dim rectBounding as New Rectangle(0,0,100,50)
```

You can do a number of things with a rectangle after it's defined. Perhaps the most useful is the ability to enlarge or shrink the rectangle with a single statement. You enlarge or shrink a rectangle using the Inflate() method. The most common syntax of Inflate() is the following:

```
object.Inflate(changeinwidth, changeinheight)
```

When called this way, the rectangle width is enlarged (the left side of the rectangle remains in place) and the height is enlarged (the top of the rectangle stays in place). To leave the size of the height or width unchanged, pass 0 as the appropriate argument. To shrink a side, specify a negative number.

If you're going to do much with drawing, you'll use a lot of Rectangle objects, and I strongly suggest that you learn as much about them as you can.

Drawing Shapes

Now that you've learned about the Graphics object, pens, and rectangles, you'll probably find drawing shapes to be fairly simple. Shapes are drawn by calling methods of a Graphics object. Most methods require a rectangle, which is used as the bounding rectangle for the shape, as well as a pen. In this section, I'll show you what you need to do to draw different shapes.

> I've chosen to discuss only the most commonly drawn shapes. The Graphics object contains many methods for drawing additional shapes.

Drawing Lines

Drawing lines is accomplished with the DrawLine() method of the Graphics object. DrawLine() is one of the few drawing methods that doesn't require a rectangle. The syntax for DrawLine() is

```
object.DrawLine(pen, x1, y1, x2, y2)
```

Object refers to a Graphics object and *pen* refers to a Pen object, both of which have already been discussed. X1, Y1 is the coordinate of the starting point of the line, whereas X2, Y2 is the coordinate of the ending point; Visual Basic draws a line between the two points using the specified pen.

Drawing Rectangles

Drawing rectangles (and squares, for that matter) is accomplished using the DrawRectangle() method of a Graphics object. As you might expect, DrawRectangle() accepts a pen and a rectangle. Here's the syntax for calling DrawRectangle() in this way:

```
object.DrawRectangle(pen, rectangle)
```

If you don't have a Rectangle object (and you don't want to create one), you can call DrawRectangle() using the following format:

```
object.DrawRectangle(pen, X, Y, width, height)
```

Drawing Circles and Ellipses

Drawing circles and ellipses is accomplished by calling the DrawEllipse() method. If you're familiar with geometry, you'll know that a circle is simply an ellipse that has the same height as it does width. This is why no specific method exists for drawing circles: DrawEllipse() works perfectly. Like the DrawRectangle() method, DrawEllipse() accepts a pen and a rectangle. The rectangle is used as a bounding rectangle—the width of the rectangle is the width of the ellipse, whereas the height of the rectangle is the height of the ellipse. DrawEllipse() has the following syntax:

```
object.DrawEllipse(pen, rectangle)
```

In the event that you don't have a Rectangle object defined (and you don't want to create one), you can call DrawEllipse() with this syntax:

```
object.DrawEllipse(pen, X, Y, Width, Height)
```

Clearing a Drawing Surface

To clear the surface of a Graphics object, call the Clear() method, passing it the color to paint the surface like this:

```
objGraphics.Clear(Drawing.SystemColors.Control)
```

Drawing Text

Printing text on a Graphics object is very similar to drawing a shape, and the method name even contains the word *Draw*, in contrast to *Print*. To draw text on a Graphics object, call the DrawString() method. The basic format for DrawString() looks like this:

```
object.DrawString(stringoftext, font, brush, topX, leftY)
```

A few of these items are probably new to you. The argument *stringoftext* is fairly self-explanatory: it's the string you want to draw on the Graphics object. The *topX* and *leftY* arguments represent the coordinate at which drawing will take place; they represent the upper-left corner of the string, as illustrated in Figure 18.4.

The arguments *brush* and *font* aren't so obvious. Both arguments accept objects. A brush is similar to a pen, but whereas a pen describes the characteristics of a line, a brush describes the characteristics of a fill. For example, both pens and brushes have a color, but where pens have an attribute for defining a line style such as dashed or solid, a brush has an attribute for a fill pattern such as solid, hatched, weave, or trellis. When drawing text, a solid brush is usually sufficient. You can create brushes in much the same way as you create pens, or you can use one of the standard brushes available from the System.Drawing.Brushes class.

A Font object defines characteristics used to format text, including the character set (Times New Roman, Courier, and so on), size (point size), and style (bold, italic, normal, underlined, and so on). To create a new Font object, you could use code such as the following:

```
Dim objFont As Font
objFont = New System.Drawing.Font("Arial", 30)
```

18

FIGURE 18.4
The coordinate speci-fied in DrawString() represents the upper-left corner of the printed text.

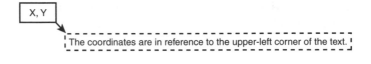

The text Arial in this code is the name of a font installed on my computer. In fact, Arial is one of the few fonts installed on all Windows computers. If you supply the name of a font that doesn't exist on the machine at runtime, Visual Basic will use a default font. The second parameter is the point size of the text. If you want to use a style other than normal, you can provide a style value as a third parameter, like this (note the logical Or, as discussed in Hour 12, "Performing Arithmetic, String Manipulation, and Date/Time Adjustments"):

```
objFont = New System.Drawing.Font("Arial Black", 30, _
                              FontStyle.Bold or FontStyle.Italic)
```

In addition to creating a Font object, you can also use the font of an existing object, such as a form. For example, the following statement prints text to a Graphics object using the font of the current form:

```
objGraphics.DrawString("This is the text that prints!", Me.Font, _
                    System.Drawing.Brushes.Azure, 0, 0)
```

Persisting Graphics on a Form

You'll often use the techniques discussed in this hour to draw to a form. However, you might recall from earlier hours that when you draw to a form (actually, you draw to a Graphics object that references a form), the things that you draw aren't persisted; the next time the form paints itself, the drawn elements will disappear. If the user minimizes the form or obscures the form with another window, for example, the next time the form is painted it will be missing all drawn elements that were obscured. You can use a couple of approaches to deal with this behavior:

- Place all code that draws to the form in the form's Paint event.
- Draw to a memory bitmap and copy the contents of the memory bitmap to the form in the form's Paint event.

If you're drawing only a few items, placing the drawing code in the Paint event might be a good approach. However, consider a situation in which you've got a lot of drawing code. Perhaps the graphics are drawn in response to user input, so you can't re-create them all at once. In these situations, the second approach is clearly better.

Building a Graphics Project Example

You're now going to build a project that uses the skills you've learned to draw to a form. In this project, you'll use the technique of drawing to a memory bitmap to persist the graphics each time the form paints itself.

> The project you're about to build is perhaps the most difficult yet. I'll explain each step of the process of creating this project, but I won't spend any time explaining the objects and methods that I've already discussed.

To make things interesting, I've used random numbers to determine font size as well as the X, Y coordinate of the text you're going to draw to the form. By far the easiest way to create a random number in Visual Basic. NET is to use the System.Random class. To generate a random number within a specific range (such as a random number between 1 and 10), you follow these three steps:

1. Create a new object variable of type System.Random.

2. Create a new instance of the Random class, passing a value to be used as the seed to generate random numbers. I use Now.Millisecond, which causes a pseudo-random number to be used as the seed, because this value changes every millisecond and probably won't be the same across repeated runs of the application.

3. Call the Next method of the Random object, passing it minimum and maximum values. The Random object will return a random number that falls within the specified range.

Start by creating a new Windows Application titled **Persisting Graphics**.

Change the name of the default form to **fclsMain**, set the form's Text property to **Persisting Graphics Example**, and change the Startup object of the project properties to **fclsMain**. The interface of your form will consist of a text box and a button. When the user clicks the button, the contents of the text box will be drawn on the form in a random location and with a random font size. Add a new text box to your form and set its properties as follows:

Property	Value
Name	**txtInput**
Location	**56,184**
Size	**100,20**
Text	*(make blank)*

18

Add a new button to the form and set its properties as follows:

Property	Value
Name	**btnDrawText**
Location	**160,184**
Text	**Draw Text**

Time to let the code fly!

As I mentioned earlier, all drawing will be performed using a memory bitmap, which will then be copied to the form. You'll reference this bitmap in multiple places, so you're going to make it a module-level variable. Double-click the form to access its Load event. Then add the following statement *immediately following the* Inherits *statement*; do not place this in the Load event of the form!

```
Private m_objDrawingSurface As Bitmap
```

For the bitmap variable to be used, it must reference a Bitmap object. A good place to initialize things is in the form's Load event, so put your cursor back in the Load event now and enter the following code:

```
Randomize()
' Create a drawing surface with the same dimensions as the client
' area of the form.
m_objDrawingSurface = New Bitmap(Me.ClientRectangle.Width, _
                      Me.ClientRectangle.Height, _
                      Drawing.Imaging.PixelFormat.Format24bppRgb)
InitializeSurface()
```

Your procedure should now look like the one shown in Figure 18.5.

The first statement in this procedure initializes the random number generator (you'll be using random numbers in another procedure). The next statement creates a new bitmap in memory. Because the contents of the bitmap are to be sent to the form, it makes sense to use the dimensions of the client area of the form as the size of the new bitmap—which is exactly what you've done. The final statement calls a procedure that you haven't yet created.

Position the cursor at the end of the End Sub statement and press Enter a few times to create a few new lines. You're now going to write code to initialize the bitmap. The code will clear the bitmap to the System Color control and then draw an ellipse that has the dimensions of the bitmap. (I've added comments to the code so that you can follow along with what's happening; all the concepts in this procedure have been discussed already.) Enter the following procedure in its entirety:

```
Private Sub InitializeSurface()
    Dim objGraphics As Graphics
    Dim rectBounds As Rectangle

    ' Create a Graphics object that references the bitmap and clear it.
    objGraphics = Graphics.FromImage(m_objDrawingSurface)
    objGraphics.Clear(System.Drawing.SystemColors.Control)

    ' Create a rectangle the same size as the bitmap.
    rectBounds = New Rectangle(0, 0, m_objDrawingSurface.Width, _
                        m_objDrawingSurface.Height)
    ' Reduce the rectangle slightly so the ellipse won't appear on the border.
    rectBounds.Inflate(-1, -1)

    ' Draw an ellipse that fills the form.
    objGraphics.DrawEllipse(System.Drawing.Pens.Orange, rectBounds)
End Sub
```

FIGURE 18.5

Make sure that your code appears exactly as it does here.

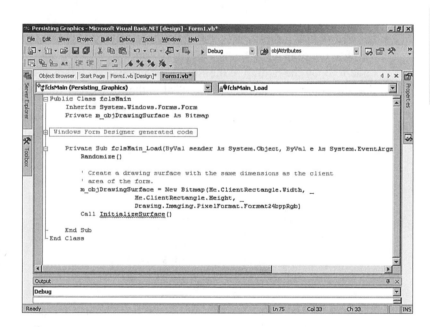

Your procedure should now look like the one shown in Figure 18.6.

FIGURE 18.6

Verify that your code is entered correctly.

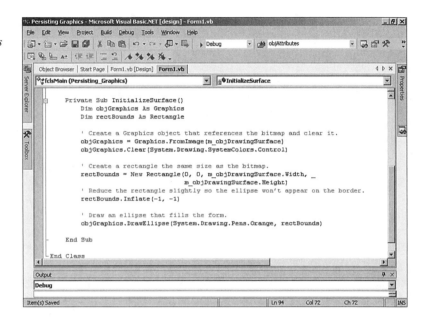

If you run your project now, you'll find that nothing is drawn to the form. This is because the drawing is being done to a bitmap in memory, and you haven't yet added the code to copy the bitmap to the form. The place to do this is in the form's Paint event so that the contents of the bitmap are sent to the form every time the form paints itself. This ensures that the items you draw always appear on the form.

Create an event handler for the form's Paint event by first choosing (fclsMain Events) from the object drop-down list in the upper-left corner of the code editor and then selecting Paint from the event drop-down list in the upper-right corner. Add the following code to the Paint event:

```
Dim objGraphics As Graphics
' You can't modify e.Graphics directly.
objGraphics = e.Graphics
' Draw the contents of the bitmap on the form.
objGraphics.DrawImage(m_objDrawingSurface, 0, 0, _
                      m_objDrawingSurface.Width, _
                      m_objDrawingSurface.Height)
```

The e parameter of the Paint event has a property that references the Graphics object of the form. You can't, however, modify the Graphics object using the e parameter (it's read-only), which is why you've created a new Graphics object to work with and then set the object to reference the form's Graphics object. The method DrawImage() draws the image in a bitmap to the surface of a Graphics object, so the last statement is simply sending the contents of the bitmap that exists in memory to the form.

If you run the project now, you'll find that the ellipse appears on the form. Furthermore, you can cover the form with another window, or even minimize it, and the ellipse will always appear on the form when it's displayed again—the graphics persist.

The last thing you're going to do is write code that draws the contents entered into the text box on the form. The text will be drawn with a random size and location. Return to the form designer and double-click the button to access its Click event. Add the following code:

```
Dim objGraphics As Graphics
Dim objFont As Font
Dim intFontSize As Integer
Dim intTextX As Integer
Dim intTextY As Integer
Dim objRandom As System.Random

' If no text has been entered, get out.
If txtInput.Text = "" Then Exit Sub

' Create a graphics object using the memory bitmap.
objGraphics = Graphics.FromImage(m_objDrawingSurface)

' Initialize the Random object.
objRandom = New Random(Now.Millisecond)

' Create a random number for the font size. Keep it between 8 and 48.
intFontSize = objRandom.Next(8, 48)
' Create a random number for X coordinate of the text.
intTextX = objRandom.Next(0, Me.ClientRectangle.Width - 20)
' Create a random number for Y coordinate of the text.
intTextY = objRandom.Next(0, Me.ClientRectangle.Height - 20)
' Create a new font object.
objFont = New System.Drawing.Font("Arial", intFontSize, _
                                FontStyle.Bold Or FontStyle.Italic)
' Draw the user's text.
objGraphics.DrawString(txtInput.Text, objFont, _
                        System.Drawing.Brushes.Red, intTextX, intTextY)
' Clean up.
objGraphics.Dispose()
' Force the form to paint itself. This triggers the Paint event.
Me.Invalidate()
```

18

The comments I've included should make the code fairly self-explanatory. However, the last statement bears discussing. The Invalidate() method of a form invalidates the client rectangle. This operation tells Windows that the appearance of the form is no longer accurate and that the form needs to be repainted. This, in turn, triggers the Paint event of the form. Because the Paint event contains the code that copies the contents of the memory bitmap to the form, invalidating the form causes the text to appear. If you don't call Invalidate() here, the text won't appear on the form (but it is still drawn on the memory bitmap).

 If you draw elements that are based on the size of the form, you'll need to call Invalidate()in the Resize event of the form; resizing a form doesn't trigger the form's Paint event.

Your project is now complete! Click Save All on the toolbar to save your work, and then press F5 to run the project. You'll notice immediately that the ellipse is drawn on the form. Type something into the text box and click the button. Click it again. Each time you click the button, the text is drawn on the form using the same brush, but with a different size and location (see Figure 18.7).

FIGURE **18.7**

Text is drawn on a form, much like ordinary shapes.

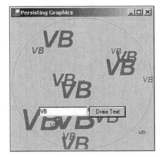

Summary

You won't need to add drawing capabilities to every project you create. However, when you need the capabilities, *you need the capabilities*. In this hour, you learned the basic skills for drawing to a graphics surface, which can be a form, control, memory bitmap, or one of many other types of surfaces. You learned that all drawing is done using a Graphics object, and you now know how to create a Graphics object for a form or control, and even how to create a Graphics object for a bitmap that exists in memory.

Most drawing methods require a pen and a rectangle, and you can now create rectangles and pens using the techniques you learned in this hour. After learning about pens and rectangles, you've found that the drawing methods themselves are pretty easy to use. Even drawing text is a fairly simple process when you've got a Graphics object to work with.

Persisting graphics on a form can be a bit complicated, and I suspect this will confuse a lot of new Visual Basic .NET programmers who try to figure it out on their own. However, you've now built an example that persists graphics on a form, and you'll be able to leverage the techniques involved when you have to do this in your own projects.

I don't expect you to be able to sit down for an hour and create an Adobe Photoshop knock-off. However, you now have a solid foundation on which to build. If you're going to attempt a project that performs a lot of drawing, you'll want to dig deeper into the Graphics object.

Q&A

Q **What if I need to draw a lot of lines, one starting where another ends? Do I need to call DrawLine() for each line?**

A The Graphics object has a method called DrawLines(), which accepts a series of points. The method draws lines connecting the sequence of points.

Q **Is there a way to fill a shape?**

A The Graphics object includes methods that draw filled shapes, such as FillEllipse() and FillRectangle().

Workshop

The Workshop is designed to help you anticipate possible questions, review what you've learned, and get you thinking about how to put your knowledge into practice. The answers to the quiz are in Appendix B, "Answers to the Quizzes."

Quiz

1. What object is used to draw to a surface?
2. To set a Graphics object to draw to a form directly, you call what method of the form?
3. What object defines the characteristics of a line? A fill pattern?
4. How do you make a color property adjust with the user's Windows settings?

18

5. What object is used to define the bounds of a shape to be drawn?

6. What method do you call to draw an irregular ellipse? A circle?

7. What method do you call to print text on a Graphics surface?

8. To ensure that graphics persist on a form, the graphics must be drawn on the form in what event?

Exercises

1. Modify the example in this hour to use a font other than Arial. If you're not sure what fonts are installed on your computer, open the Start menu and choose Settings and then Control Panel. You'll have an option on the Control Panel for viewing your system fonts.

2. Create a project that draws an ellipse that fills the form, much like the one you created in this hour. However, draw the ellipse directly to the form in the Paint event. Make sure that the ellipse is redrawn when the form is sized. (Hint: Invalidate the form in the form's Resize() event.)

PART IV
Working with Data

Hour

19 Performing File Operations

20 Controlling Other Applications Using Automation

21 Working with a Database

HOUR 19

Performing File Operations

It's very difficult to imagine any application other than a tiny utility program that doesn't make use of the file system. In this hour, you'll learn how to use the controls to make it easy for a user to browse and select files. In addition, you'll learn how to use the System.IO.File and System.IO.Directory objects to manipulate the file system more easily than ever before possible. Using these objects, you can delete files and directories, move them, rename them, and more. These objects are powerful, but please remember: Play nice!

The highlights of this hour include the following:

- Using the Open File Dialog and Save File Dialog controls
- Manipulating files with System.IO.File
- Manipulating directories with System.IO.Directory

Using the Open File Dialog and Save File Dialog Controls

In Hour 1, "Jumping In with Both Feet: A Visual Basic .NET Programming Tour," you used the Open File Dialog control to enable a user to browse for pictures to display in your Picture Viewer program. In this section, you'll move beyond those basics to learn important details about working with the Open File Dialog, as well as its sister control, the Save File Dialog.

You're going to build a project to illustrate most of the file-manipulation concepts discussed in this hour. Before continuing, create a new Windows Application titled **Manipulating Files**. Change the name of the default form to **fclsManipulatingFiles**, set its Text property to **Manipulating Files**, and then set the Startup object of the project to fclsManipulatingFiles. Add a new text box to the form and set its properties as shown in the following table:

Property	Value
Name	**txtSource**
Location	**95,8**
Size	**184,20**
Text	(*make blank*)

Using the Open File Dialog Control

The Open File Dialog control is used to display a dialog box that enables the user to browse and select a file (see Figure 19.1). It's important to note that usually the Open File Dialog doesn't actually open a file, but it enables a user to select a file that's then opened by code within the application.

Add a new Open File Dialog to your project now by double-clicking the OpenFileDialog item in the toolbox. The Open File Dialog doesn't have an interface per se, so it appears in the area below the form rather than on it. For the user to browse for files, you have to manipulate the Open File Dialog using its properties and methods.

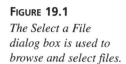

FIGURE 19.1

The Select a File dialog box is used to browse and select files.

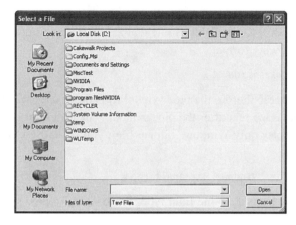

You're going to add a button to the form that, when clicked, enables a user to locate and select a file. If a user selects a file, the filename is placed in the text box you've created. Go ahead and add a button to the form now, and set its properties as follows:

Property	Value
Name	**btnOpenFile**
Location	**8,8**
Size	**80,23**
Text	**Source:**

Next, double-click the button and add the following code to its Click event:

```
OpenFileDialog1.InitialDirectory = "C:\"
OpenFileDialog1.Title = "Select a File"
```

The first statement specifies the directory to display when the dialog box is first shown. If you don't specify a directory for the InitialDirectory property, the active system directory is used (for example, the last directory browsed to with a different Open File dialog box).

The Title property of the Open File Dialog determines the text displayed in the title bar of the Select a File dialog box. If you don't specify text for the Title property, Visual Basic displays the word Open in the title bar.

19

Different types of files have different extensions. The Filter property determines what types of files appear in the Select a File dialog box (refer to Figure 19.1). A filter is specified in the following format:

```
Description|*.extension
```

The text that appears before the pipe symbol (|) is the descriptive text of the file type to filter on, whereas the text after the pipe symbol is the pattern used to filter files. For example, to display only Windows bitmap files, you could use a filter such as the following:

```
control.Filter = "Windows Bitmaps|*.bmp"
```

You can specify more than one filter type. To do so, add a pipe symbol between the filters, like this:

```
control.Filter = "Windows Bitmaps|*.bmp|JPEG Files|*.jpg"
```

You're going to restrict your Select a File dialog box to show only text files, so enter this statement in your procedure:

```
OpenFileDialog1.Filter = "Text Files|*.txt"
```

When you have more than one filter, you can specify which filter appears selected by default using the FilterIndex property. Although you've specified only one filter type in this example, it's still a good idea to designate the default filter, so add this statement to your procedure:

```
OpenFileDialog1.FilterIndex = 1
```

> The FilterIndex property is 1-based, not 0-based as most other properties and collections are.

Finally, you need to show the Select a File dialog box and take action based on whether the user selects a file. The ShowDialog() method of the Open File Dialog control acts much like the method of forms by the same name, returning a result that indicates the user's selection on the dialog box. Enter the following statements into your procedure:

```
If OpenFileDialog1.ShowDialog() <> DialogResult.Cancel Then
    txtSource.Text = OpenFileDialog1.FileName
else
    txtSource.Text = ""
End If
```

This code just places the selected filename into the text box txtSource. If the user clicks Cancel, the contents of the text box are cleared.

Press F5 to run the project and click the button. You'll get the same dialog box shown in Figure 19.1 (with different files and directories, of course). Select a text file and click Open, and Visual Basic places the name of the file into the text box.

By default, the Open File Dialog won't allow the user to enter a filename that doesn't exist. You can override this behavior by setting the CheckFileExists property of the Open File Dialog to False.

The Open File Dialog control has the capability to allow the user to select multiple files. It's rare that you need to do this (I don't recall ever needing this capability in one of my projects), so I won't go into the details here. If you're interested, take a look at the Multiselect property of the Open File Dialog in the Help text.

The Open File Dialog control makes enabling a user to browse and select a file almost trivial. Without this code, you'd have to write an astounding amount of very difficult code and probably still wouldn't come up with all the functionality supported by this control.

Using the Save File Dialog Control

The Save File Dialog control is very similar to the Open File Dialog control, but it's used to enable a user to browse directories and specify a file to save, rather than open. It's important to note that the Save File Dialog control doesn't actually save a file; it's used to enable a user to specify a filename to save. You'll have to write code to do something with the filename returned by the control.

You're going to use the Save File Dialog control to let the user specify a filename. This filename will be the target of various file operations you'll learn about later in this hour. Create a new text box on your form and set its properties as follows:

Property	Value
Name	**txtDestination**
Location	**95,40**
Size	**184,20**
Text	(*make blank*)

19

You're now going to create a button that, when clicked, enables the user to specify a filename to save a file. Add a new button to the form and set its properties as shown in the following table:

Property	Value
Name	**btnSaveFile**
Location	**8,40**
Size	**80,23**
Text	**Destination:**

Of course, none of this will work without adding a Save File dialog box. Double-click the SaveFileDialog item in the toolbox to add a new control to the project.

Next, double-click the new button you just created (btnSaveFile) and add the following code to its Click event:

```
SaveFileDialog1.Title = "Specify Destination Filename"
SaveFileDialog1.Filter = "Text Files|*.txt"
SaveFileDialog1.FilterIndex = 1

SaveFileDialog1.OverwritePrompt = True
```

The first three statements set properties that are identical to those of the Open File Dialog. The OverwritePrompt property, however, is unique to the Save File Dialog. When this property is set to True, Visual Basic asks users to confirm their selections when they choose a file that already exists, as shown in Figure 19.2. I highly recommend that you prompt the user about replacing files by ensuring that the OverwritePrompt property is set to True.

FIGURE 19.2

It's a good idea to get confirmation before replacing an existing file.

 If you want the Save File dialog box to prompt users when the file they specify *doesn't* exist, set the CreatePrompt property of the Save File Dialog control to True.

The last bit of code you need to add places the selected filename in the txtDestination text box. Enter the code as shown here:

```
If SaveFileDialog1.ShowDialog() <> DialogResult.Cancel Then
   txtDestination.Text = SaveFileDialog1.FileName
End If
```

Press F5 to run the project, and then click each of the buttons and select a file. When you're satisfied that your selections are being sent to the appropriate text box, stop the project and save your work. If your selected filenames aren't being sent to the proper text box, verify that your code is correct.

The Open File Dialog and Save File Dialog controls are very similar in their design and appearance, but each serves a specific purpose. You'll be using the interface you've just created throughout the rest of this hour.

Manipulating Files with the File Object

Visual Basic .NET includes a powerful namespace called System.IO (the IO object acts like an object property of the System namespace). Using various properties, methods, and object properties of System.IO, you can do just about anything you can imagine with the file system. In particular, the System.IO.File and System.IO.Directory objects provide you with extensive file and directory (folder) manipulation.

In the following sections, you'll continue to expand the project that you've created. You'll write code that manipulates the selected filenames by using the Open File Dialog and Save File Dialog controls.

19

> The code you'll write in the following sections is the real thing. For instance, the code for deleting a file really deletes a file. Don't forget this as you test your project; the files selected as the source and as the destination *will* be affected by your actions. I provide the cannon, and it's up to you not to shoot yourself in the foot.

Determining Whether a File Exists

Before attempting any operation on a file, such as copying or deleting it, it's a good idea to make certain the file exists. For example, if the user doesn't click the Source button to select a file, but instead types the name and path of a file into the text box, the user could type an incorrect filename. Attempting to manipulate a nonexistent file could result in an exception—which you don't want to happen. Because you're going to work with the source file selected by the user in many routines, you're going to create a central function that can be called to determine whether the source file exists. The function uses the Exists() method of the System.IO.File object to determine whether the file exists.

Add the following function to your form class:

```
Private Function SourceFileExists() As Boolean
    If Not (System.IO.File.Exists(txtSource.Text)) Then
        MessageBox.Show("The source file does not exist!")
    Else
        SourceFileExists = True
    End If
End Function
```

The Exists() method accepts a string containing the filename (with path) of the file to verify. If the file exists, Exists() returns True; otherwise, it returns False. Notice that you don't have to explicitly return False as the result of the function if the file isn't found; Boolean variables default to False when they're created.

Copying a File

Copying files is a common task. For instance, you might want to create an application that backs up important data files by copying them to another location. For the most part, copying is pretty safe—as long as you use a destination filename that doesn't already exist. Copying files is accomplished using the Copy() method of the System.IO.File class.

You're now going to add a button to your form. When the user clicks this button, the file specified in the source text box will be copied to a new file with the name given in the destination text box. Add a button to your form now and set its properties as shown in the following table:

Property	Value
Name	**btnCopyFile**
Location	**96,80**
Size	**75,23**
Text	**Copy**

Double-click the Copy button and add the following code:

```
If Not (SourceFileExists()) Then Exit Sub

System.IO.File.Copy(txtSource.Text, txtDestination.Text)
MessageBox.Show("The file has been successfully copied.")
```

The Copy() method has two arguments. The first is the file that you want to copy, and the second is the name and path of the new copy of the file. In this example, you're using the filenames in the two text boxes.

Press F5 to run the project and test your copy code now by following these steps:

1. Click the Source button and select a text file.
2. Click the Destination button to display the Save File dialog box. Don't select an existing file. Instead, type a new filename into the File Name text box and click Save. If you're asked whether you want to replace a file, click No and change your filename; don't use the name of an existing file.
3. Click Copy to copy the file.

After you get the message box telling you the file was copied, you can use Explorer to locate the new file and open it. Stop the project and save your work before continuing.

Moving a File

When you move a file, it's taken out of its current directory and placed in a new one. You can specify a new name for the file or use its original name. Moving a file is accomplished with the Move() method of the System.IO.File object. You're now going to create a button on your form that moves the file selected as the source to the path and the filename selected as the destination.

 I recommend that you use Notepad to create a text file, and use this temporary text file when testing from this point forward. This code, as well as the rest of the examples presented in this hour, can permanently alter or destroy a file.

19

Add a new button to the form and set its properties as follows:

Property	Value
Name	**btnMove**
Location	**96,112**
Size	**75,23**
Text	**Move**

Double-click the Move button and add the following code to its Click event:

```
If Not (SourceFileExists()) Then Exit Sub

System.IO.File.Move(txtSource.Text, txtDestination.Text)
MessageBox.Show("The file has been successfully moved.")
```

Go ahead and press F5 to test your project. Select a file to move (I recommend you create a dummy file in Notepad) and supply a destination file name. When you click Move, the file will be moved to the new location and be given the new name. Remember, if you specify a name for the destination that isn't the same as that of the source, the file will be given the new name when it's copied.

Deleting a File

Deleting a file can be a risky proposition. The Delete() method of System.IO.File deletes a file permanently—it doesn't send the file to the Recycle Bin. For this reason, you should take great care when deleting files. First and foremost, this means testing your code. When you write a routine to delete a file, be sure to test it under various conditions. For example, if you reference the wrong text box in this code, you would inadvertently delete the wrong file! Users aren't forgiving of such mistakes.

You're now going to add a button to your project that deletes the source file when clicked. Remember: Be careful when testing this code. Add a button to the form now and set its properties as follows:

Property	Value
Name	**btnDelete**
Location	**96,144**
Size	**75,23**
Text	**Delete**

Next, double-click the button and add the following code to its Click event:

```
If Not (SourceFileExists()) Then Exit Sub

If MessageBox.Show("Are you sure you want to delete the source file?", _
     "MyApp", MessageBoxButtons.YesNo , MessageBoxIcon.Question) = _
     DialogResult.Yes Then
   System.IO.File.Delete(txtSource.Text)
   MessageBox.Show("The file has been successfully deleted.")
End If
```

Notice that you've included a message box to confirm the user's intentions. It's a good idea to do this whenever you're about to perform a serious action that can't be undone. In fact, the more information you can give, the better. For example, I suggest that if this was production code (code meant for end users), you should include the name of the file in the message box so that the user knows without a doubt what the program intends to do. If you're feeling brave, press F5 to run the project, and then select a file and delete it. Again, I highly recommend that you use a dummy text file created in Notepad for these experiments.

Renaming a File

When you rename a file, it remains in the same directory and nothing materially happens to the contents of the file—the name is changed to something else. Because the original file isn't altered, renaming a file isn't as risky as performing an action such as deleting the file. Nevertheless, it's frustrating trying to determine what happened to a file when it was mistakenly renamed. To rename a file, use the Move() method of System.IO.File, specifying a new filename but keeping the same path.

Retrieving a File's Properties

Although many people don't realize it, files have a number of properties—such as the date the file was last modified. The easiest way to see these properties is to use Explorer. View the attributes of a file now by starting Explorer, right-clicking any file displayed in Explorer, and choosing Properties. Explorer shows the File Properties window with information about the file (see Figure 19.3).

FIGURE 19.3

Visual Basic provides a means to easily obtain most file properties.

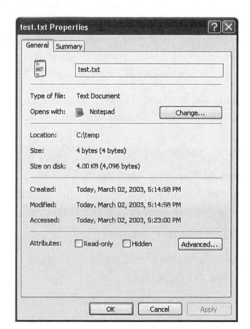

19

The System.IO.File object provides ways to get at most of the data displayed on the General tab of the File Properties dialog box shown in Figure 19.3. Some of this data is available directly from the File object, whereas other data is accessed using a FileAttributes object.

Getting Date and Time Information About a File

Getting the last created, last accessed, and last modified dates of a file is easy; the System.IO.File object supports a method for each of these dates. Table 19.1 lists the applicable properties and what they return.

TABLE 19.1   File Object Properties to Retrieve Data Information

Property	Description
GetCreationTime	Returns the date and time the file was created
GetLastAccessTime	Returns the date and time the file was last accessed
GetLastWriteTime	Returns the date and time the file was last modified

Getting the Attributes of a File

The attributes of a file (refer to the bottom of the dialog box shown in Figure 19.3) aren't available as properties of the System.IO.File object. How you determine an attribute is a bit complicated. The GetAttributes() method of System.IO.File returns a Long. This Long, in turn, acts as a set of flags for the various attributes. The method used to store these values is called *bit packing*. Bit packing is pretty complicated and has to do with the binary method in which values are stored in memory and on disk. Teaching bit packing is beyond the scope of this book—what I want to show you is how to determine whether a certain flag is set in a value that is bit packed.

The first step in determining the attributes is to get the Long containing the flags for the file attributes. To do this, create a Long variable and call GetAttributes(), like this:

```
Dim lngAttributes As Long
lngAttributes = System.IO.File.GetAttributes("c:\test.txt")
```

After you have the flags in the Long, by ANDing the variable with one of the flags shown in Table 19.2, you can determine whether a particular attribute is set. For example, to determine whether a file's ReadOnly flag is set, you use a statement like this:

```
lngAttributes And IO.FileAttributes.ReadOnly
```

When you logically AND a flag value with a variable, you get True if the variable contains the flag; otherwise, you get False.

TABLE 19.2   File Attribute Flags

Attribute	Meaning
Archive	The file's archive status. Applications use this attribute to mark files for backup and removal.
Directory	The file is a directory.
Hidden	The file is hidden and therefore isn't included in an ordinary directory listing.
Normal	The file is normal and has no other attributes set.
ReadOnly	The file is a read-only file.
System	The file is part of the operating system or is used exclusively by the operating system.
Temporary	The file is a temporary file.

Writing Code to Retrieve a File's Properties

Now that you know how to retrieve the properties of an object, you're going to use that knowledge to display the properties of the file specified in the source text box on your form. Begin by adding a new button to your form and setting its properties as shown in the following table:

Property	Value
Name	**btnGetFileProperties**
Location	**8,176**
Size	**80,56**
Text	**Get Properties of Source File**

Next, add a text box to the form and set its properties as follows:

Property	Value
Name	**txtProperties**
Location	**96,176**
Multiline	**True**
ScrollBars	**Vertical**
Size	**184,88**
Text	(*make blank*)

The code you enter into the Click event of this button will be a bit longer than most of the code you've entered so far. Therefore, I'll show the code in its entirety, and then I'll

19

explain what the code does. Double-click the button and add the following code to the button's Click event:

```
Dim strProperties As String
Dim lngAttributes As Long

If Not (SourceFileExists()) Then Exit Sub

'* Get the dates.
strProperties = "Created: " & System.IO.File.GetCreationTime(txtSource.Text)
strProperties = strProperties & vbCrLf
strProperties = strProperties & "Accessed: " & _
                System.IO.File.GetLastAccessTime(txtSource.Text)
strProperties = strProperties & vbCrLf
strProperties = strProperties & "Modified: " & _
                System.IO.File.GetLastWriteTime(txtSource.Text)

lngAttributes = System.IO.File.GetAttributes(txtSource.Text)

strProperties = strProperties & vbCrLf
strProperties = strProperties & "Normal: " & _
                CBool(lngAttributes And IO.FileAttributes.Normal)

strProperties = strProperties & vbCrLf
strProperties = strProperties & "Hidden: " & _
                CBool(lngAttributes And IO.FileAttributes.Hidden)

strProperties = strProperties & vbCrLf
strProperties = strProperties & "ReadOnly: " & _
                CBool(lngAttributes And IO.FileAttributes.ReadOnly)

strProperties = strProperties & vbCrLf
strProperties = strProperties & "System: " & _
                CBool(lngAttributes And IO.FileAttributes.System)

strProperties = strProperties & vbCrLf
strProperties = strProperties & "Temporary File: " & _
                CBool(lngAttributes And IO.FileAttributes.Temporary)

strProperties = strProperties & vbCrLf
strProperties = strProperties & "Archive: " & _
                CBool(lngAttributes And IO.FileAttributes.Archive)

txtProperties.Text = strProperties
```

All the various properties of the file are concatenated with the strProperties variable. The system constant vbCrLf denotes a carriage return and a linefeed, and concatenating this into the string ensures that each property appears on its own line.

The first set of statements simply calls the GetCreateTime(), GetLastAccessTime(), and GetLastWriteTime() methods to get the values of the date-related properties. Next, the attributes are placed in a variable by way of the GetAttributes() method and the state of each attribute is determined. The CBool() functions are used so that the words True and False appear, rather than the numeric results of the And operations.

Press F5 to run the project, click Source to select a file, and then click the button to get and display the attributes. If you entered the code exactly as shown, the attributes of the file should appear in the text box as they do in Figure 19.4.

FIGURE 19.4

The System.IO.File object enables you to look at the properties of a file.

Manipulating Directories with the Directory Object

Manipulating directories (folders) is very similar to manipulating files. However, rather than using System.IO.File, you use System.IO.Directory. If any of these method calls confuse you, refer to the previous section on System.IO.File for more detailed information. The following are the method calls:

- To create a directory, call the CreateDirectory() method of System.IO.Directory and pass the name of the new folder, like this:

```
System.IO.Directory.CreateDirectory("c:\my new directory")
```

- To determine whether a directory exists, call the Exists() method of System.IO.Directory and pass it the directory name in question, like this:

```
MsgBox(System.IO.Directory.Exists("c:\temp"))
```

- To move a directory, call the Move() method of System.IO.Directory. The Move() method takes two arguments. The first is the current name of the directory, and the second is the new name and path of the directory. When you move a directory, the contents of it are moved as well. The following illustrates a call to Move():

```
System.IO.Directory.Move("c:\current directory name", _
    "d:\new directory name")
```

19

- Deleting directories is even more perilous than deleting files because when you delete a directory, you also delete all files and subdirectories within the directory. To delete a directory, call the Delete() method of System.IO.Directory and pass it the directory to delete. I can't tell you enough that you have to be careful when calling this method; it can you get you in a lot of trouble. The following statement illustrates deleting a directory:

```
System.IO.Directory.Delete("c:\temp")
```

Summary

The Open File Dialog and Save File Dialog controls, coupled with System.IO, enable you to do many powerful things with a user's file system. In this hour, you learned how to let a user browse and select a file for opening and how to let a user browse and select a file for saving. Determining a user's file selection is only the first part of the process, however. You also learned how to manipulate files and directories, including renaming, moving, and deleting, by using System.IO. Finally, you learned how to retrieve the properties and attributes of a file.

With the techniques shown in this hour, you should be able to do most of what you'll need to do with files and directories. None of this material is very difficult, but don't be fooled by the simplicity; use care whenever manipulating a user's file system.

Q&A

Q What if I want to perform an operation on a file, but something is preventing the operation, such as the file might be open or I don't have rights to the file?

A All the method calls have one or more exceptions that can be thrown in the event that the method fails. These method calls are listed in the online help. You can use the techniques discussed in Hour 15, "Debugging Your Code," to trap the exceptions.

Q What if a user types a filename into one of the file dialog boxes, but the user doesn't include the extension?

A By default, both file dialog controls have their AddExtension properties set to True. When this property is set to True, Visual Basic automatically appends the extension of the currently selected filter.

Workshop

The Workshop is designed to help you anticipate possible questions, review what you've learned, and get you thinking about how to put your knowledge into practice. The answers to the quiz are in Appendix B, "Answers to the Quizzes."

Quiz

1. True or False: The Select a File dialog box automatically opens a file.
2. What symbol is used to separate a filter description from its extension?
3. What object is used to manipulate files?
4. What arguments are expected by System.IO.File.Copy()?
5. How would you rename a file?
6. True or False: Files deleted with System.IO.File.Delete() are sent to the Recycle Bin.
7. What object is used to manipulate folders?

Exercises

1. Create a project that enables a user to select a file with the Open File Dialog control. Store the filename in a text box. Provide another button that, when clicked, creates a backup of the file by making a copy of it with the extension .bak.
2. Create a project with a text box on a form in which the user can type in a three-digit file extension. Include a button that shows a Select a File dialog box when clicked, with the filter set to the extension entered by the user.

19

Hour **20**

Controlling Other Applications Using Automation

In Hour 16, "Designing Objects Using Classes," you learned how to use classes to create objects. In that hour, I mentioned that objects could be exposed to outside applications. Excel, for example, exposes most of its functionality as a set of objects. The process of using objects from another application is called *automation*. The externally accessible objects of an application compose its *object model*. Using automation to manipulate a program's object model enables you to reuse components. For instance, you can use automation with Excel to perform complex mathematical functions using the code that's been written and tested within Excel, rather writing and debugging the complex code yourself.

Programs that expose objects are called *servers*, and the programs that consume those objects are called *clients*. Creating automation servers requires advanced skills, including a very thorough understanding of programming classes. On the other hand, creating clients to use objects from other applications is relatively simple. In this hour, you'll learn how to create a client application that uses objects of an external server application. The highlights of this hour include the following:

- Creating a reference to an automation library
- Creating an instance of an automation server
- Manipulating the objects of an automation server

To understand automation, you're going to build a Microsoft Excel client—a program that automates Excel via Excel's object model.

> This exercise is designed to work with Excel 97, Excel 2000, or Excel 2002.

Create a new Windows Application named **Automate Excel**. Change the name of the default form to **fclsMain** and set its Text property to **Automate Excel**. Next, set the Startup object to fclsMain.

Add a button to the form by double-clicking the Button item in the toolbox and set the button's properties as follows:

Property	Value
Name	**btnAutomateExcel**
Location	**96,128**
Size	**104,23**
Text	**Automate Excel**

Creating a Reference to an Automation Library

NEW TERM To use the objects of a program that supports automation (a server), you have to reference the program's type library. A program's *type library* (also called its *object library*) is a file containing a description of the program's object model. After you've referenced the type library of an automation server (also called a *component*), you can access the objects of the server as though they were internal Visual Basic .NET objects.

To create a reference to a type library, follow these steps:

1. Display the Add Reference dialog box by choosing Add Reference from the Project menu (do this now). Many types of components support automation. Of course, .NET is the latest technology, but in the case of Excel, we're interested in the *COM* components. COM stands for Component Object Model, and it's been *the* technology for working with objects within Windows for many years. Microsoft's .NET platform is designed to replace COM, but this isn't going to happen overnight. There are literally thousands of objects are built on COM technology. In fact, all the Microsoft Office products up to and including Office XP are based on COM.

2. Click the COM tab now to display the available COM components (programs that have a type library) on your computer.

3. Scroll the list and locate the Microsoft Excel *X* Object Library (where *X* is the version of Excel installed on your computer). Double-click the Excel item to add it to the list of selected components at the bottom of the Add Reference dialog box (see Figure 20.1).

FIGURE 20.1

To use an object library, you need to reference it first.

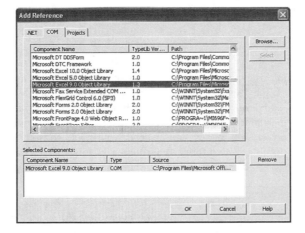

If you don't see an entry for Microsoft Excel, you probably don't have Excel installed on your computer; therefore, this code won't work. If you have multiple Excel entries, choose version 9 if it's listed.

Click OK now to add the reference to your project.

20

Visual Basic. NET doesn't work directly with COM components (as did previous versions of Visual Basic). Instead, it interacts through a *wrapper*, a set of code and objects that works as an intermediary between Visual Basic .NET and a COM component. When you add the reference to a COM component, .NET automatically creates this wrapper for you.

Creating an Instance of an Automation Server

Referencing a type library allows Visual Basic .NET to integrate the available objects of the type library with its own internal objects. After this is done, you can create object variables based on object types found in the type library. Excel has an object called Application, which acts as the primary object in the Excel object model. In fact, most Office programs have an Application object. How do you know what objects an automation server supports? The only sure way is to consult the documentation of the program in question or use the Object Browser discussed in Hour 3, "Understanding Objects and Collections."

In this example, you'll be using about a half-dozen members of an Excel object. This doesn't even begin to scratch the surface of Excel's object model, nor is it intended to. What you should learn from this example is the mechanics of working with an automation server. If you choose to automate a program in your own projects, you should consult the program's developer documentation to learn as much about its object model as you can—you're sure to be surprised at the functionality available to you.

Double-click the button to access its Click event, and then enter the following code, which creates a new Excel Application object:

```
Dim objExcel As New Excel.Application
```

Notice that Visual Basic .NET included Excel in its IntelliSense drop-down list of available objects. It was able to do this because you referenced Excel's type library. Excel is the reference to the server and Application is an object supported by the server. This statement creates a new Application object based on the Excel object model.

Manipulating the Server

After you have an instance of an object from an automation server, manipulating the server (creating objects, setting properties, calling methods, and so forth) is accomplished by manipulating the object. In the following sections, you'll manipulate the new Excel object by setting properties and calling methods, and in so doing will be manipulating Excel itself.

Forcing Excel to Show Itself

When Excel is started using automation, it's loaded but not shown. Remaining hidden enables the developer to use Excel's functionality and then close it without the user knowing what happened. For instance, you could create an instance of an Excel object, perform a complicated formula to obtain a result, close Excel, and return the result to the user—all without the user seeing Excel. In this example, you want to see Excel so that you can see what your code is doing. Fortunately, showing Excel couldn't be any easier. Add the following statement to make Excel visible:

```
ObjExcel.Visible = True
```

Creating an Excel Workbook

In Excel, a workbook is the file in which you work and store your data; you can't manipulate data without a workbook. When you first start Excel from the Start menu, an empty workbook is created for you. When you start Excel via automation, however, Excel doesn't create a workbook; you have to do it yourself. To create a new workbook, you use the Add method of the Workbooks collection. Enter the following statement to create a new workbook:

```
objExcel.Workbooks.Add()
```

Working with Data in an Excel Workbook

Workbooks contain a single worksheet by default. In this section, you're going to manipulate data in the worksheet. The following describes what you'll do:

1. Add data to four cells in the worksheet
2. Select the four cells
3. Total the selected cells and place the sum into a fifth cell
4. Bold all five cells

To manipulate cells in the worksheet, you manipulate the ActiveCell object, which is an object property of the Application object. Entering data into a cell involves first selecting a cell and then passing data to it. Selecting a cell is accomplished by calling the Select

20

method of the Range object; the Range object is used to select one or more cells. The Select method accepts a starting column and row and an ending column and row. If you want to select only a single cell, as we do here, you can omit the ending column and row. After the range is set, you pass data to the FormulaR1C1 property of the ActiveCell object (which references the cell specified by the Range object). Setting the FormulaR1C1 property has the effect of sending data to the cell. Sound confusing? Well, it is to some extent. Programs that support automation are often vast and complex, and programming them is usually far from intuitive.

If the program you want to automate has a macro builder (as most Microsoft products do), you can save yourself a lot of time and headache by creating macros of the tasks you want to automate. The macros are actually code, and in the case of Microsoft products, they're VBA code. VBA code is similar to Visual Basic 6 code. Although this code won't port directly to Visual Basic .NET, it's usually rather easy to migrate, and the macro builder does all or most of the work of determining objects and members for you.

The following section of code uses the techniques just described to add data to four cells. Enter this code into your procedure:

```
objExcel.Range("A1").Select()
objExcel.ActiveCell.FormulaR1C1 = "75"
objExcel.Range("B1").Select()
objExcel.ActiveCell.FormulaR1C1 = "125"
objExcel.Range("C1").Select()
objExcel.ActiveCell.FormulaR1C1 = "255"
objExcel.Range("D1").Select()
objExcel.ActiveCell.FormulaR1C1 = "295"
```

The next step is to have Excel total the four cells. You'll do this by using the Range object to select the cells, activating a new cell in which to place the total, and then using FormulaR1C1 again to create the total by passing it a formula, rather than literal value. Enter this code into your procedure:

```
objExcel.Range("A1:D1").Select()
objExcel.Range("E1").Activate()
objExcel.ActiveCell.FormulaR1C1 = "=SUM(RC[-4]:RC[-1])"
```

Next, you'll select all five cells and bold them. Enter the following statements to accomplish this:

```
objExcel.Range("A1:E1").Select()
objExcel.Selection.Font.Bold = True
```

The last thing you need to do is destroy the object reference by setting the object variable to Nothing. Excel remains open even though you've destroyed the automation instance (not all servers do this). Add this last statement to your procedure:

```
objExcel = Nothing
```

To help you ensure that everything is entered correctly, Listing 20.1 shows the procedure in its entirety.

LISTING 20.1 Code to Automate Excel

```
Private Sub btnAutomateExcel_Click(ByVal sender As System.Object, _
                                   ByVal e As System.EventArgs) _
                                   Handles btnAutomateExcel.Click
    Dim objExcel As New Excel.Application()
    objExcel.Visible = True
    objExcel.Workbooks.Add()
    objExcel.Range("A1").Select()
    objExcel.ActiveCell.FormulaR1C1 = "75"
    objExcel.Range("B1").Select()
    objExcel.ActiveCell.FormulaR1C1 = "125"
    objExcel.Range("C1").Select()
    objExcel.ActiveCell.FormulaR1C1 = "255"
    objExcel.Range("D1").Select()
    objExcel.ActiveCell.FormulaR1C1 = "295"
    objExcel.Range("A1:D1").Select()
    objExcel.Range("E1").Activate()
    objExcel.ActiveCell.FormulaR1C1 = "=SUM(RC[-4]:RC[-1])"
    objExcel.Range("A1:E1").Select()
    objExcel.Selection.Font.Bold = True
    objExcel = Nothing
End Sub
```

Testing Your Client Application

Now that your project is complete, press F5 to run it and click the button to automate Excel. If you entered the code correctly, Excel will start, data will be placed into four cells, the total of the four cells will be placed into a fifth cell, and all cells will be made bold (see Figure 20.2).

20

Automating applications, particularly Office products such as Excel and Word, requires a lot of system resources. If you intend to perform a lot of automation, you should use the fastest machine with the most memory that you can afford. Also, be aware that in order for automation to work, the client application (Excel is this case) has to be installed on the user's computer in addition to your application.

FIGURE 20.2

You can control almost every aspect of Excel using its object model.

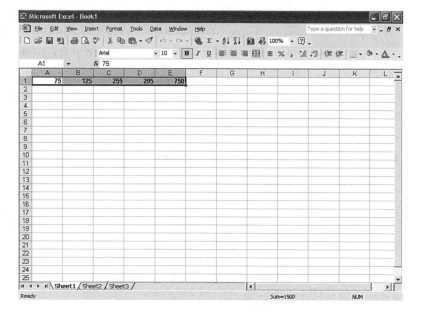

Summary

In this hour, you learned how a program can make available an object model that client applications can use to manipulate the program. You learned that the first step in automating a program (server) is to reference the type library of the server. After the type library is referenced, the objects of the server are available as though they're internal Visual Basic .NET objects. As you've seen, the mechanics of automating a program aren't that difficult—they build on the object-programming skills you've already learned in this book. The real challenge comes in learning the object model of a given server and in making the most productive use of the objects available.

Q&A

Q What are some applications that support automation?

A All the Microsoft Office products, as well as Microsoft Visio, support automation. You can create a robust application by building a client that makes use of multiple automation servers. For instance, you could calculate data in Excel and then format and print the data in Word.

Q **Can you automate a component without creating a reference to a type library?**

A Yes, but this is considerably more complicated than when using a type library. First of all, you can't early bind to objects because Visual Basic .NET knows nothing about the objects without a type library. This means you have no IntelliSense drop-down list to help you navigate the object model, and Visual Basic .NET won't perform any syntax checking on your automation code; the chances for bugs in this situation are almost unbearably large. To create a reference to a server using late binding, you use Visual Basic .NET 's CreateObject function.

Workshop

The Workshop is designed to help you anticipate possible questions, review what you've learned, and get you thinking about how to put your knowledge into practice. The answers to the quiz are in Appendix B, "Answers to the Quizzes."

Quiz

1. Before you can early bind objects in an automation server, you must do what?

2. What is the most likely cause of not seeing a type library listed in the Add References dialog box?

3. For Visual Basic .NET to use a COM library, it must create a:

4. To manipulate a server via automation, you manipulate:

5. To learn about the object library of a component, you should:

Exercises

1. Modify the Excel example to save the workbook. Hint: Consider the SaveAs() method of the Workbooks collection.

2. If you have Word installed, add the Word type library to a new project, create an object variable that holds a reference to Word's Application object, create a new document, and send some text to the document. You'll probably need to reference the VBA help file that ships with Word.

20

Hour 21

Working with a Database

You've heard it so many times that it's almost a cliché: This is the Information Age. Information is data, and managing information means working with databases. Database design is a skill unto itself, and entire books are devoted to database design and management. In this hour, you'll learn the basics of working with a database using ADO.NET, Microsoft's newest database technology. Although high-end solutions are built around advanced database technologies such as Microsoft's SQL Server, the Microsoft Jet database used by Microsoft Access is more readily available and easier to learn, so you'll build working examples that use a Jet database. Be aware, however, that 95% of what you learn here is directly applicable to working with SQL Server as well.

The highlights of this hour include the following:

- Introduction to ADO.NET
- Connecting to a database
- Understanding DataTables

- Creating a DataAdapter

- Referencing fields in a DataRow

- Navigating records

- Adding, editing, and deleting records

- Building an ADO.NET example

 You'll learn a lot in this hour, but realize that this material is really the tip of the iceberg. Database programming can be, and often is, very complex. This hour is intended to get you writing database code as quickly as possible, but if you plan to do a lot of database programming, you'll want to consult a dedicated book (or two) on the subject.

Start by creating a new Windows Application named **Database Example**. Change the name of the default form to **fclsMain** and set its Text property to **Database Example**. Next, right-click the project name in the Solution Explorer and change the Startup object to **fclsMain**.

Introducing ADO.NET

ADO.NET is the .NET platform's new database technology, and it builds on ADO (Active Data Objects). ADO.NET provides DataSet and DataTable objects that are optimized for moving disconnected sets of data across the Internet and intranets, including through firewalls. At the same time, ADO.NET includes the traditional connection and command objects, as well as an object called a DataReader, (which resembles a forward-only, read-only ADO RecordSet, in case you're familiar with ADO). Together, these objects provide the very best performance and throughput for retrieving data from a database.

In short, you'll learn about the following objects as you progress though this hour:

- OleDBConnection—Used to establish a connection to an OLEDB data source.

- SqlConnection—Used to establish a connection to a SQL Server data source.

- DataSet—A memory-resident representation of data. There are many ways of working with a DataSet, such as through DataTables.

- DataTable—Holds a result set of data for manipulation and navigation.

- DataAdapter—Used to populate a DataReader.

Connecting to a Database

To access data in a database, you must first establish a connection using an ADO.NET connection object. There are actually two connection objects included in the .NET Framework: the OleDbConnection object (for working with the same OLE DB data providers you would access through traditional ADO) and the SqlConnection object (for optimized access to Microsoft SQL Server). Because these examples connect to the Microsoft Jet Database, you'll be using the OleDbConnection object. To create an object variable of type OleDbConnection and initialize the variable to a new connection, you could use a statement like this:

```
Dim cnADONetConnection As New OleDb.OleDbConnection()
```

You're going to create a module-level variable to hold the connection, so double-click the form now to access its events and place the cursor below the Inherits statement at the top of the module. Enter the following statement:

```
Private m_cnADONetConnection As New OleDb.OleDbConnection()
```

Before using this connection, you must specify the data source to which you want to connect. This is done through the ConnectionString property of the ADO.NET connection object. The ConnectionString contains connection information such as the name of the provider, username, and password. The ConnectionString might contain many connection parameters; the set of parameters available varies depending on the source of data that you're connecting to. Some of the parameters used in the OLE DB ConnectionString are listed in Table 21.1. If you specify multiple parameters, separate them with a semicolon.

TABLE 21.1 Possible Parameters for ConnectionString

Parameter	Description
Provider	The name of the data provider (Jet, SQL, and so on) to use.
Data Source	The name of the data source (database) to connect to.
UID	A valid username to use when connecting to the data source.
PWD	A password to use when connecting to the data source.
DRIVER	The name of the database driver to use. This isn't required if a DSN is specified.
SERVER	The network name of the data source server.

The Provider= parameter is one of the most important at this point, and is governed by the type of database you're accessing. For example, when accessing a SQL Server database, you specify the provider information for SQL Server; and when accessing a Jet database, you specify the provider for Jet. In this example, you'll be accessing a Jet (Microsoft Access) database, so you'll use the provider information for Jet.

21

In addition to specifying the provider, you're also going to specify the database. I've provided a sample database at the Web site for this book. This code assumes that you've placed the database in a folder called C:\Temp. If you're using a different folder, you'll need to change the code accordingly.

To specify the ConnectionString property of your ADO.NET connection, place the following statement in the Load event of your form:

```
m_cnADONetConnection.ConnectionString = _
"Provider=Microsoft.Jet.OLEDB.4.0;Data Source=C:\temp\contacts.mdb"
```

When the connection string is defined, a connection to a data source is established by using the Open() method of the connection object.

Add the following statement to the Load event, right after the statement that sets the connection string:

```
m_cnADONetConnection.Open()
```

 Refer to the online documentation for information on the connection strings for providers other than Jet.

When you attach to an unsecured Jet database it isn't necessary to provide a username and password. When attaching to a secured Jet database, however, you must to provide a username and a password. This is done by passing the username and password as parameters in the ConnectionString property. The sample database I've provided isn't secured, so it isn't necessary to provide a username and password.

Closing a Connection to a Data Source

You should always *explicitly* close a connection to a data source. That means you shouldn't rely on a variable going out of scope to close a connection. Instead, you should force an explicit disconnect via code. This is accomplished by calling the Close() method of the connection object.

You're now going to write code to explicitly close the connection when the form is closed. Start by opening the object drop-down list in the code window and selecting (fclsMain Events) if it isn't already selected. Next, choose Closed from the event drop-down list to create an event handler for the Closed event. Enter the following statement in the Closed event:

```
m_cnADONetConnection.Close()
```

Manipulating Data

The easiest way to manipulate data using ADO.NET is to create a DataTable object containing the resultset of a table, query, or stored procedure. Using a DataTable object, you can add, edit, delete, find, and navigate records. The following sections explain how to use DataTables.

Understanding DataTables

NEW TERM DataTables contain a snapshot of data in the data source. You generally start by filling a DataTable, manipulating its results, and finally sending the changes back to the data source. The DataTable is populated using the Fill() method of a DataAdapter object, and changes are sent back to the database using the Update() method of a DataAdapter. *Any changes made to the DataTable appear only in the local copy of the data until you call the Update method.* Having a local copy of the data reduces contention by preventing users from blocking others from reading the data while it's being viewed. If you're familiar with ADO, you'll note that this is similar to the Optimistic Batch Client Cursor in ADO.

Creating a DataAdapter

To populate a DataTable, you must create a DataAdapter. The DataAdapter you're going to create will use the connection you've already defined to connect to the data source, and then execute a query you'll provide. The results of that query will be pushed into a DataTable.

Just as there are two ADO.NET connection objects in the .NET Framework, there are two ADO.NET DataAdapter objects as well: the OleDbDataAdapter and the SqlDataAdapter. Again, you'll be using the OleDbDataAdapter because you aren't connecting to Microsoft SQL Server.

The constructor for a DataAdapter optionally takes the command to execute when filling a DataTable or DataSet, as well as a connection specifying the data source (you could have multiple connections open in a single project). This constructor has the following syntax:

```
Dim cnADONetAdapter As New OleDb.OleDbDataAdapter([CommandText],[Connection]);
```

To add a DataAdapter to your project, first add the following statement immediately below the statement you entered to declare the m_cnADONewConnection object (in the class header, not in the Load event) to create a module-level variable:

```
Private m_daDataAdapter As New OleDb.OleDbDataAdapter
```

Next add the following statement at the bottom of the Load event of the form (immediately following the statement that opens the connection):

```
m_daDataAdapter = _
    New OleDb.OleDbDataAdapter("Select * From Contacts",m_cnADONetConnection)
```

21

Because you're going to use the DataAdapter to update the original data source, you must specify the insert, update, and delete statements to use to submit changes from the DataTable to the data source. ADO.NET lets you customize how updates are submitted by enabling you to manually specify these statements as database commands or stored procedures. In this case, you're going to have ADO.NET automatically generate these statements for you by creating a CommandBuilder object. Enter this statement in the class header to create the CommandBuilder module-level variable:

```
Private m_cbCommandBuilder As OleDb.OleDbCommandBuilder
```

The CommandBuilder is an interesting object in that after you initialize it, you no longer work with it directly: It works behind the scenes to handle the updating, inserting, and deleting of data. To make this work, you have to attach the CommandBuilder to a DataAdapter. You do so by passing a DataAdapter to the CommandBuilder. The CommandBuilder then registers for update events on the DataAdapter and provides the insert, update, and delete commands as needed. Add the following statement to the Form_Load event to initialize the CommandBuilder object:

```
m_cbCommandBuilder = New OleDb.OleDbCommandBuilder(m_daDataAdapter)
```

When using a Jet database, the CommandBuilder object can create the dynamic SQL code only if the table in question has a primary key defined.

Creating and Populating DataTables

You're going to create a module-level DataTable in your project. First create the DataTable variable by adding the following statement on the class header to create another module-level variable:

```
Private m_dtContacts As New DataTable
```

You're going to use an integer variable to keep track of the user's current position (row) within the DataTable. To do this, add the following statement immediately below the statement you just entered to declare the new DataTable object:

```
Private m_rowPosition As Integer = 0
```

You now have a DataAdapter that allows access to a data source via the connection. You've declared a DataTable that will hold a reference to data. Next add the following statement to the Load event of the form, after the existing code, to fill the DataTable with data:

```
m_daDataAdapter.Fill(m_dtContacts)
```

Because the DataTable doesn't hold a connection to the data source, it isn't necessary to close it when you're finished. Your class should now look like the one in Figure 21.1.

FIGURE 21.1

This code accesses a database and creates a DataTable that can be used anywhere in the class.

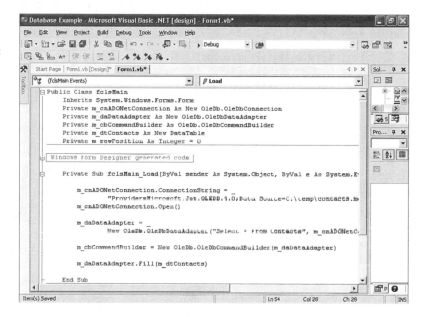

Referencing Fields in a DataRow

DataTables contain a collection of DataRows. To access a row within the DataTable, you specify the ordinal (index) of that DataRow. For example, you could access the first row of your DataTable like this:

```
Dim m_rwContact As DataRow = m_dtContacts.Rows(0)
```

Data elements in a DataRow are called *columns*. In the Contacts table I've created, for example, there are two columns: ContactName and State. To reference the value of a column, you can pass the column name to the DataRow like this

```
m_rwContact("ContactName") = "Bob Brown"
```

or

```
Debug.WriteLine(m_rwContact("ContactName"))
```

If you spell a column name incorrectly, an exception occurs when the statement executes at runtime; no errors are raised at compile time.

21

You're now going to create a procedure that's used to display the current record in the data table. Position the cursor *after* the right bracket that ends the fclsMain_Closed event (after its End Sub statement) and press Enter a few times to create some blank lines. Next, enter the following procedure in its entirety:

```
Private Sub ShowCurrentRecord()
    If m_dtContacts.Rows.Count = 0 Then
        txtContactName.Text = ""
        txtState.Text = ""
        Exit Sub
    End If

    txtContactName.Text = _
        m_dtContacts.Rows(m_rowPosition)("ContactName").ToString()
    txtState.Text = _
        m_dtContacts.Rows(m_rowPosition)("State").ToString()
End Sub
```

Make sure that the first record is shown when the form loads by adding this statement to the Form_Load event, *after* the existing statements:

```
Me.ShowCurrentRecord()
```

You've now ensured that the first record in the DataTable is shown when the form first loads. To display the data, you must add a few controls to the form. Create a new text box and set its properties as follows:

Property	Value
Name	**txtContactName**
Location	**48,112**
Size	**112,20**
Text	*(make blank)*

Add a second text box to the form and set its properties according to the following table:

Property	Value
Name	**txtState**
Location	**168,112**
Size	**80,20**
Text	*(make blank)*

Press F5 to run the project, and you'll see the first contact in the Contacts table displayed in the text box (see Figure 21.2) .

FIGURE 21.2
It takes quite a bit of prep work to display data.

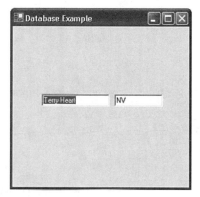

Navigating Records

The ADO.NET DataTable object supports a number of methods that can be used to access its DataRows. The simplest of these is the ordinal accessor that you used in your ShowCurrentRecord() method. Because the DataTable has no dependency on the source of the data, this same functionality is available regardless of where the data comes from.

You're now going to create buttons that the user can click to navigate the DataTable. The first button will be used to move to the first record in the DataTable. Add a new button to the form and set its properties as follows:

Property	Value
Name	**btnMoveFirst**
Location	**16,152**
Size	**32,23**
Text	**<<**

Double-click the button and add the following code to its Click event:

```
' Move to the first row and show the data.
m_rowPosition = 0
Me.ShowCurrentRecord()
```

A second button will be used to move to the previous record in the DataTable. Add another button to the form and set its properties as shown in the following table:

Property	Value
Name	**btnMovePrevious**
Location	**56,152**

21

Property	Value
Size	**32,23**
Text	**<**

Double-click the button and add the following code to its Click event:

```
' If not at the first row, go back one row and show the record.
If m_rowPosition <> 0 Then
    m_rowPosition = m_rowPosition - 1
    Me.ShowCurrentRecord()
End If
```

A third button will be used to move to the next record in the DataTable. Add a third button to the form and set its properties as shown in the following table:

Property	Value
Name	**btnMoveNext**
Location	**96,152**
Size	**32,23**
Text	**>**

Double-click the button and add the following code to its Click event:

```
' If not on the last row, advance one row and show the record.
If m_rowPosition <> (m_dtContacts.Rows.Count - 1) Then
    m_rowPosition = m_rowPosition + 1
    Me.ShowCurrentRecord()
End If
```

A fourth button will be used to move to the last record in the DataTable. Add yet another button to the form and set its properties as shown in the following table:

Property	Value
Name	**btnMoveLast**
Location	**136,152**
Size	**32,23**
Text	**>>**

Double-click the button and add the following code to its Click event:

```
' If there are any rows in the data table, move to the last and show the record.
If m_dtContacts.Rows.Count <> 0 Then
    m_rowPosition = m_dtContacts.Rows.Count - 1
```

```
    Me.ShowCurrentRecord()
End If
```

Editing Records

To edit records in a DataTable, you change the value of a particular column in the desired DataRow. Remember, though, that changes aren't made to the original data source until you call Update() on the DataAdapter, passing in the DataTable containing the changes.

You're now going to add a button that the user can click to update the current record. Add a new button to the form now and set its properties as follows:

Property	Value
Name	**btnSave**
Location	**176,152**
Size	**40,23**
Text	**Save**

Double-click the Save button and add the following code to its Click event:

```
' If there is existing data, update it.
If m_dtContacts.Rows.Count <> 0 Then
    m_dtContacts.Rows(m_rowPosition)("ContactName") = txtContactName.Text
    m_dtContacts.Rows(m_rowPosition)("State") = txtState.Text
    m_daDataAdapter.Update(m_dtContacts)
End If
```

Creating New Records

Adding records to a DataTable is performed very much like editing records. However, to create a new row in the DataTable, you must first call the NewRow method. After creating the new row, you can set its column values. The row isn't actually added to the DataTable, however, until you call the Add() method on the DataTable's RowCollection.

You're now going to modify your interface so that the user can add new records. You'll use one text box for the contact name and a second text box for the state. When the user clicks the button you'll provide, the values in these text boxes will be written to the Contacts table as a new record.

Start by adding a group box to the form and setting its properties as shown in the following table:

21

Property	Value
Name	**grpNewRecord**
Location	**16,192**
Size	**264,64**
Text	**New Contact**

Next, add a new text box *to the group box* and set its properties as follows:

Property	Value
Name	**txtNewContactName**
Location	**8,24**
Size	**112,20**
Text	*(make blank)*

Add a second text box to the group box and set its properties as shown:

Property	Value
Name	**txtNewState**
Location	**126,24**
Size	**80,20**
Text	*(make blank)*

Finally, add a button to the group box and set its properties as follows:

Property	Value
Name	**btnAddNew**
Location	**214,24**
Size	**40,23**
Text	**Add**

Double-click the Add button and add the following code to its Click event:

```
Dim drNewRow As DataRow = m_dtContacts.NewRow()

drNewRow("ContactName") = txtNewContactName.Text
drNewRow("State") = txtNewState.Text
m_dtContacts.Rows.Add(drNewRow)
m_daDataAdapter.Update(m_dtContacts)
```

```
m_rowPosition = m_dtContacts.Rows.Count - 1
Me.ShowCurrentRecord()
```

Notice that after the new record is added, the position is set to the last row and the ShowCurrentRecord() procedure is called. This causes the new record to appear in the text boxes you created earlier.

Deleting Records

To delete a record from a DataTable, you call the Delete() method on the DataRow to be deleted. Add a new button to your form (*not to the group box*) and set its properties as shown in the following table:

Property	Value
Name	**btnDelete**
Location	**224,152**
Size	**56,23**
Text	**Delete**

Double-click the Delete button and add the following code to its Click event:

```
' If there is data, delete the current row.
If m_dtContacts.Rows.Count <> 0 Then
    m_dtContacts.Rows(m_rowPosition).Delete()
    m_daDataAdapter.Update(m_dtContacts)
    m_rowPosition = 0
    Me.ShowCurrentRecord()
End If
```

Your form should now look like that in Figure 21.3.

FIGURE 21.3

A basic data-entry form.

Running the Database Example

Press F5 to run the project. If you entered all the code correctly and you placed the Contacts database into the C:\Temp folder (or modified the path used in code), the form should display without errors and the first record in the database will appear. Click the navigation buttons to move forward and backward. Feel free to change the information of a contact; click the Save button, and your changes will be made to the underlying database. Next, enter your name and state into the New Contact section of the form and click Add. Your name will be added to the database and displayed in the appropriate text boxes.

Using the Data Form Wizard

Visual Basic.NET includes a tool to help introduce you to ADO.NET: the Data Form Wizard. In this section, you're going to use the Data Form Wizard to create a form that's bound to the same database you used in the previous example. This form will show the records in the database, and provide for updating the underlying data as well.

Start by creating a new Windows Application titled **Data Form Example**. The Data Form Wizard is run by adding it to your project as a form template. Follow these steps to start the wizard:

1. Choose Add Windows Form from the Project menu to display the Add New Item dialog box.

2. Click the Data Form Wizard icon.

3. Change the name to **fclsDataForm.vb** (see Figure 21.4), and click Open to start the wizard.

FIGURE 21.4

The Data Form Wizard as a form template.

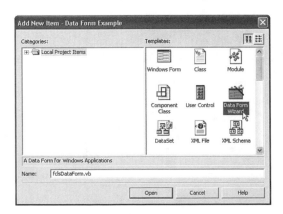

The first page of the wizard is simply an introduction. Click Next to get to the first real page. This next page is used to choose the dataset you want to bind to the form. ADO.NET datasets hold a collection of DataTables. (In case you're familiar with ADO, DataTables are similar to ADO recordsets.) Enter **AllContacts** into the text box (see Figure 21.5) and click Next to continue.

FIGURE 21.5

A DataTable is similar to an ADO recordset.

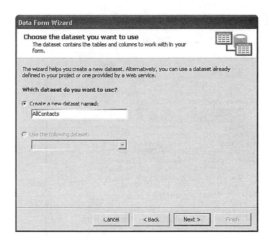

The next page of the wizard is used to specify a connection to a data source (see Figure 21.6). Note: Because you haven't previously defined a connection to the Contacts database, your drop-down list will be empty.

FIGURE 21.6

Use this page to specify a data source.

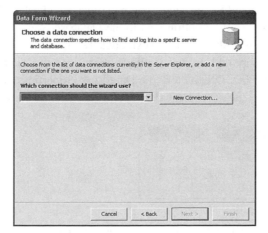

21

Click the New Connection button to display the Data Link Properties dialog box. Notice that this dialog box opens with the Connection page visible. Now click the Provider tab to see the list of installed providers on your computer (see Figure 21.7). Select Microsoft Jet 4.0 OLE DB Provider, and then click the Connection tab to return once again to the connection information.

FIGURE 21.7

You must specify the appropriate provider for the type of data source to which you're connecting.

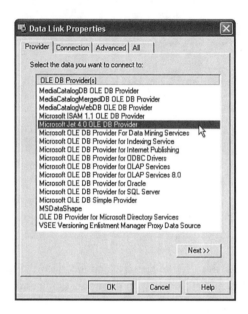

Now that you've selected the provider, you must locate and select the data source (your Jet database). Click the Build button next to the Database Name text box, and then locate and select the contacts.mdb database. Next, click Test Connection to make sure that the information you've supplied creates a valid connection to the database (see Figure 21.8). If the test succeeds, click OK to close the Data Link Properties dialog box. The database should now appear in the connection drop-down list. Click Next to continue.

FIGURE 21.8

Make sure that the connection is valid before starting your code.

The next step to completing the wizard is to choose the table or tables you want to use (see Figure 21.9). The tables you choose here will be used to supply the data that's bound to your form. Double-click the Contacts table to add it to the Selected Items list, and click Next to continue.

FIGURE 21.9

Use this page to choose the data to bind to the form.

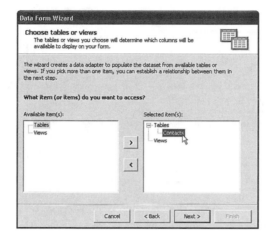

The page shown in Figure 21.10 is used to specify the columns that you want bound on the form. The two columns in your Contacts table are already selected by default, so click Next to continue.

FIGURE 21.10

You can choose which fields you want from the table.

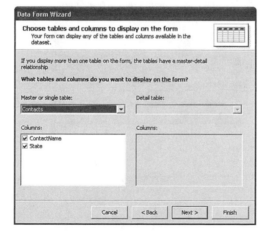

The last step of the wizard is specifying the style in which you want the data to appear (see Figure 21.11). Because the previous example had you work with individual controls for each column, leave the radio button All Records in a Grid selected (this will create a data grid). Click Finish to create your new data form, which will appear in the designer (see Figure 21.12). Visual Basic.NET might ask you if you want the password included in the connection string. If so, choose to include it (you haven't supplied a password anyway, so this isn't important at this time).

21

FIGURE 21.11
The Data Form Wizard gives you a number of choices for displaying your data.

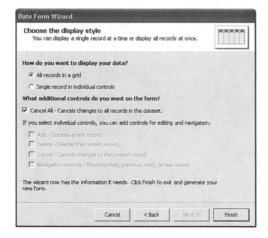

FIGURE 21.12
This bound grid was created by the Data Form Wizard.

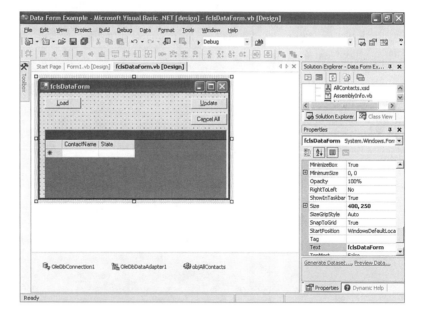

To test your form, you'll have to display it so follow these steps:

1. Click Form1.vb to display the designer for the default form in your project, and add a new button to the form. Set the button's properties as follows:

Property	Value
Name	**btnShowDataForm**
Location	**96,120**
Size	**104,23**

Property	Value
Text	**Show Data Form**

2. Double-click the button to access its Click event and add the following code:

```
Dim objDataForm = New fclsDataForm
objDataForm.Show()
```

3. Press F5 to run the project, and then click the button—your bound form will appear. To load the grid with records, click the Load button (see Figure 21.13) .

FIGURE 21.13

This grid is bound to the record source.

Stop the running project, click fclsDataForm.vb in the Solution Explorer, and then click the View Code button on the Solution Explorer to view the class. Notice that the Data Form Wizard created all the ADO.NET code for you (see Figure 21.14) and even included rudimentary error handling.

FIGURE 21.14

Every bit of this code was created automatically by the wizard.

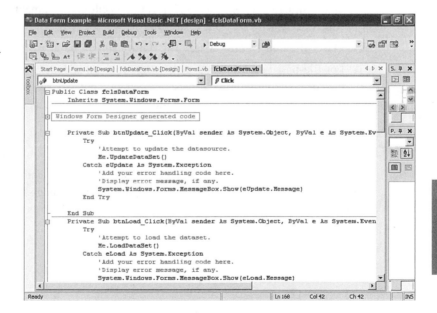

21

The Data Form Wizard is a great way to get started with ADO.NET, but it'll take you only so far. To create robust ADO.NET applications, you'll need to find one or more dedicated resources that focus on the intricacies of ADO.NET.

Summary

Most commercial applications use some sort of database. Becoming a good database programmer requires extending your skills beyond being just a good programmer. There's so much to know about optimizing databases and database code, creating usable database interfaces, creating a database schema—the list goes on and on. Writing any database application, however, begins with the basic skills you learned in this hour. You learned how to connect to a database, create and populate a DataTable, and navigate the records in the DataTable. In addition, you learned how to edit records and how to add and delete records. Finally, you learned how to use the Data Form Wizard to create a basic ADO.NET bound form. You're now prepared to write simple, yet functional, database applications.

Q&A

Q If I want to connect to a data source other than Jet, how do I know what connection string to use?

A Not only is different connection information available for different types of data sources, but also for different versions of different data sources. The best way of determining the connection string is to consult the documentation for the data source to which you want to attach.

Q What if I don't know where the database will be at runtime?

A For file-based data sources such as Jet, you can add an Open File Dialog control to the form and let the user browse and select the database. Then concatenate the filename with the rest of the connection information (such as the provider string).

Workshop

The Workshop is designed to help you anticipate possible questions, review what you've learned, and get you thinking about how to put your knowledge into practice. The answers to the quiz are in Appendix B, "Answers to the Quizzes."

Quiz

1. What is the name of the data access components used in the .NET Framework?
2. What is the name given to a collection of DataRows?
3. How do I get data into and out of a DataTable?
4. What object is used to connect to a data source?
5. What argument of a connection string contains information about the type of data being connected to?
6. What object provides update, delete, and insert capabilities to a DataAdapter?
7. What two .NET data providers are supplied as part of the .NET Framework?
8. What method of a DataTable object do you call to create a new row?

Exercises

1. Create a new project that connects to the same database used in this example. Rather than displaying a single record in two text boxes, put a list box on the form and fill the list box with the names of the people in the database.
2. Further extend the project you built in exercise 1 by adding a Name text box below the list. When the user clicks a name in the list, show the name in the text box. If the user clicks another name, update the database with any changes made in the text box to the newly selected name.

21

PART V
Deploying Solutions and Beyond

Hour

22 Deploying a Visual Basic .NET Application

23 Introduction to Web Development

24 Building a Real-World Application

HOUR 22

Deploying a Visual Basic .NET Application

Now you've learned how to create a Visual Basic .NET application, and you're probably just itching to create some project and send it to the world. Fortunately, Visual Basic .NET includes the tools you need to create a setup program for an application. In this hour, you'll learn how to use these tools to create a setup program that a user can run to install an application you've developed. In fact, you'll be creating a setup program for the Picture Viewer application you created in Hour 1, "Jumping In with Both Feet: A Visual Basic .NET Programming Tour."

The highlights of this hour include the following:

- Creating a custom setup program
- Installing the output of a project
- Changing the installation location of a file
- Specifying build options
- Adding files to an installation

- Creating a custom folder on installation
- Creating a shortcut on the Start menu

Creating a Custom Setup Program

A custom setup program (the program the user runs to install a program) is the result of building a special type of project in Visual Basic .NET. Throughout most of this book, you've created projects of the type Windows Application. To create a custom setup program, you start with a special type of .NET project.

Start Visual Basic .NET and choose to create a new project now. In the New Project dialog box, click the Setup and Deployment Projects item to display its contents, and then click Setup Project (see Figure 22.1). This is the project type to use when you distribute Windows applications; use the Web Setup Project item when distributing Web projects. Enter the name **TYVB Picture Viewer** and click OK to create the project.

FIGURE 22.1

Create a setup project to distribute Windows applications.

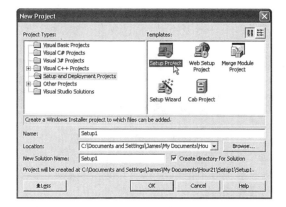

The name you give your setup project is the name that appears in the Setup Wizard when the user installs your program. Unfortunately, the name you use for this project can't be the same as the one you used for the project whose output you're distributing (for reasons you'll learn shortly). This is why I had you use TYVB (for *Teach Yourself Visual Basic*) as the project name.

The interface for a Setup Project consists primarily of two panes. The pane on the left side represents the file system of the target machine (the computer on which the software is being installed). The pane on the right shows the contents of the selected item in the left pane (see Figure 22.2). You really can do a lot when creating custom setup programs, but as you'll see, accessing the features to modify your setup program isn't all that intuitive.

FIGURE 22.2

The interface for creating a setup program isn't intuitive.

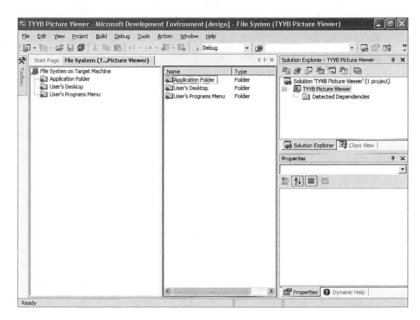

Adding the Output of a Project

For the purposes of creating a setup program, the final file (EXE, DLL, and so on) produced in building a Visual Basic .NET project is called the *output* of the project. The setup program is used to install the output of a project on the user's computer. At this point, the setup program doesn't install anything; you must add the output of another project. The first step to including a project's output is to add the project to the setup program project. Because you're creating a setup program for the Picture Viewer you created in Hour 1, you need to add the Picture Viewer project to the current solution.

Add the project to the solution now by right-clicking the solution name in the Solution Explorer window and then choosing Existing Project from the Add menu. Use the Add Existing Project dialog box to locate your Picture Viewer project (look for the file named Picture Viewer.vbproj) and add it to the current solution. The Picture Viewer project should now appear in the Solution Explorer (see Figure 22.3).

FIGURE 22.3

To distribute the output of a project, the project must be part of the solution.

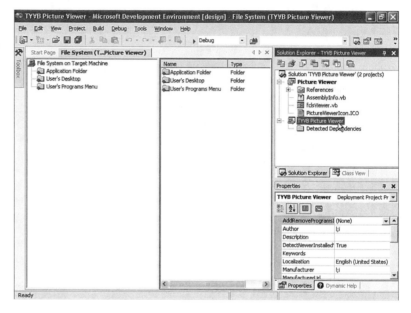

Now that the Picture Viewer project is part of the solution, you have to tell the setup program to install the output of the Picture Viewer project. This is where things get a bit odd because the Project menu changes according to what project you have selected in the Project Explorer. Follow these steps to install the output of the Picture Viewer application:

1. Click the TYVB Picture Viewer project in the Solution Explorer before continuing. If you don't do this, you won't find the appropriate menu items when you open the Project menu.

2. Open the Project menu and then open the Add submenu.

3. Choose Project Output to display the Add Project Output Group dialog box shown in Figure 22.4. Make sure that the project selected is Picture Viewer and that Primary Output is selected as well.

4. Click OK to commit your selections.

5. Next, click Application Folder in the left pane to view its contents. Notice that it now contains the primary output from the Picture Viewer project. This means that the EXE build by the Picture Viewer project will be installed in whatever folder the user designates as the application folder.

FIGURE 22.4

Choosing Primary Output ensures that the distributable file of the project is installed on the user's machine.

Changing the Installation Location of a File

You have complete control over where a file is installed on the user's computer. Most program files (such as the output of the Picture Viewer project) are installed in an application folder. The application folder has the following default path:

```
[ProgramFilesFolder][Manufacturer]\[ProductName]
```

Users can change this when they run your setup program. Right-click the Application Folder icon in the left pane and choose Properties Window from its context menu. In the Properties window, notice that the DefaultLocation property contains the information that defines the default installation location. The items in brackets are tokens that are replaced when the user runs the setup program. The *Manufacturer* token pulls its value from the company name you entered when you installed Visual Basic .NET. To change your default installation folder, you'd change this property (don't do this right now).

Specifying the Build Options of a Project's Output

At this point, the setup program installs the final output of the Picture Viewer program, which is an EXE. However, you have more control over the output of a project than just the file type. For example, you can specify the icon assigned to the EXE file. Right-click the Picture Viewer project in the Solution Explorer and choose Properties from its context menu to display the Picture Viewer Property Pages dialog box. Next click Build in the list on the left to display the Build options for the project (see Figure 22.5).

FIGURE 22.5

Use this dialog box to tailor the output of a project.

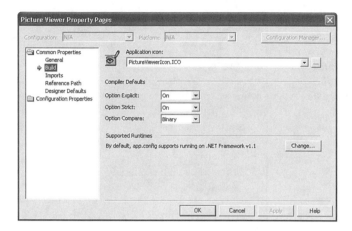

The icon specified appears wherever a shortcut is created for your program. Remember, the default icon assigned to executables isn't all that attractive (and even less meaningful), so you should assign a custom icon to all your projects. Because you did this in Hour 1, there's no need to change the icon now. Before closing this dialog box, ensure that both Option Explicit and Option Strict are turned on.

Adding a File to the Installation Program

You aren't limited to installing the output of a project; you can install any file that you choose. For example, you might want to include sample data or support files with your program. You're now going to install a bitmap with your application so that the user has something to view.

Again select the TYVB Picture Viewer project in the Solution Explorer, or you won't have the appropriate items on the Project menu. Next, add a file by opening the Project menu and then choosing File from the Add submenu. Locate a BMP or JPG on your system, click it to select it, and then click Open to add the file to the install project.

Adding a Custom Folder to the Install

The pane on the left lists folders that correspond to folders on the user's computer. You can add other folders to this list. These folders might already exist on the user's computer (such as the user's Favorites folder) or might be a brand-new folder that your install creates. Add a new folder to the install now by right-clicking the File System on Target Machine item in the left pane (the first item) and choosing Add Special Folder from its context menu. As you can see, you can select from a number of folders that already exist on the user's computer.

Follow these steps to create a custom folder:

1. Choose Custom Folder (see Figure 22.6). The new folder is added to the left pane.

2. Change the name of the new folder to Pictures.

FIGURE 22.6

It's easy to select existing folders and create new ones.

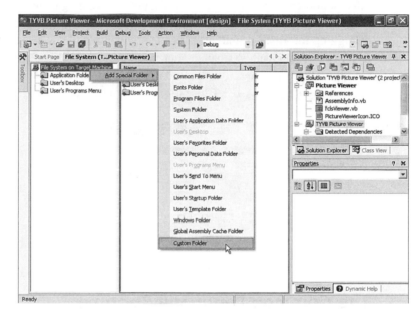

3. Click Application Folder again. Notice that the BMP file you selected for installation appears in the Application Folder.

4. Drag the bitmap to the Pictures folder you just created. Now when the picture is installed, it will be installed in the Pictures folder.

Creating a Shortcut on the Start Menu

The setup program doesn't automatically create shortcuts for your application—you have to create them yourself. Most applications create a shortcut in the Programs folder on the Start menu (or in a subfolder of the Programs folder). You're going to create a shortcut for the Picture Viewer program that will be placed in the Programs folder on the Start menu.

Click the Application Folder to view its contents. Right-click the Primary Output from Picture Viewer item and choose Create Shortcut to Primary Output from Picture Viewer. Visual Basic .NET creates the shortcut item and places it in the Application Folder. Drag the shortcut to the User's Programs Menu item in the left pane. Now, when the user installs your program, a shortcut will be placed in the Programs folder on the user's Start menu.

Defining the Build Configuration for the Setup Program

When you create a setup program, you can choose to include debug information. This information enables you to perform advanced debugging using techniques beyond the scope of this book. When distributing to other machines, you might want to leave out this debugging information and instead create a release build. Release builds are smaller and faster than debug builds. Change your installation to a release build now by choosing Configuration Manager from the Build menu, and selecting Release from the drop-down list (see Figure 22.7). Click Close to save your changes.

FIGURE 22.7

Release builds are smaller and faster than debug builds.

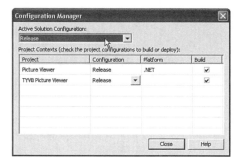

The Common Language Runtime

The common language runtime (discussed in detail in Appendix A, "The 10,000-Foot View") allows any Visual Studio .NET language (Visual Basic .NET, Visual C# .NET, and so on) to run on a computer. For a user to run your Visual Basic .NET application, the common language runtime must exist on the user's computer. You cannot include the common language runtime in your install. Instead, it must either exist on the user's machine, or you must distribute the Microsoft common language runtime installation file, Dotnetfx.exe. There are license restrictions to distributing the common language runtime, so for this example, we'll operate on the assumption that the .NET Framework (the common language runtime) exists on the target machine. For more information about distributing Dotnetfx.exe, including licensing restrictions, please refer to Visual Basic .NET's documentation.

Building the Setup Program

That's it, you're done! All you have left is to actually build the program. Choose Build Solution from the Build menu to create the distributable file. As Visual Basic .NET is building the file (three files actually), a small animation appears in the status bar. This occurs because it can take some time to build a file, especially for large solutions compiling on slower machines with minimum RAM. When Visual Basic .NET is done building

22

the setup program, the status bar will read Build Succeeded. The setup program can be found in the Release subfolder of the TYVB Picture Viewer project folder. The file has the extension of MSI, which indicates that the file is a Windows Installer Package.

Running a Custom Setup Program

Shut down Visual Basic .NET now, saving your work if prompted to do so. Double-click the installation program in the Release folder to start your custom setup program (the file with the .MSI extension is the Windows Installer file that runs your custom setup program). The setup program is a wizard (see Figure 22.8), so installation for an end user is pretty simple. Click Next to pass the Welcome page.

FIGURE 22.8

Your final setup program is in the form of a wizard.

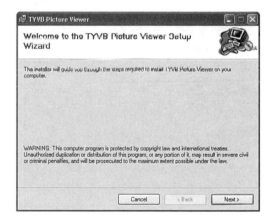

The second page of your setup program is where the user can specify the installation folder. Notice that the default path is what you specified when you created the setup program (see Figure 22.9). The wizard even enables the user to install the application for shared use; you don't have to worry about the details. Clicking Disk Cost shows all installed drives, their disk space, and the disk space required by the setup program. Click Next to accept the default path and continue.

The last important page of your Setup Wizard is used to get confirmation before installing the files (see Figure 22.10). You can add a lot more functionality to your setup program, and doing so might create additional pages in the final setup wizard. However, this example is pretty straightforward, so there's not much to the wizard. Click Next to install the Picture Viewer program. After the program is installed, users will get one last wizard page telling them the installation is complete (see Figure 22.11) .

FIGURE 22.9
The user can change your default installation path.

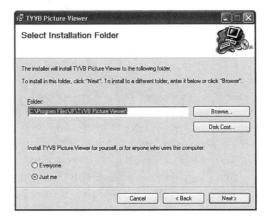

FIGURE 22.10
Clicking Next from here causes your program to be installed.

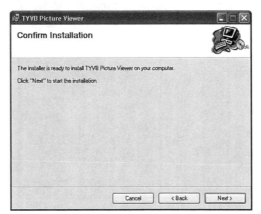

FIGURE 22.11
A successful installation!

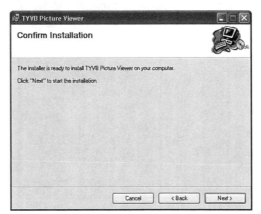

Open the Start menu and look at the contents of your Programs folder; you should see the shortcut to your Picture Viewer program. Click the shortcut to start your program. That's it! You've just created an installation program that installs the Picture Viewer program, and you can now distribute your program to other computers if they have the .NET Framework installed. Refer to Visual Basic .NET's documentation again if you need to distribute Dotnetfx.exe to machines that don't have the .NET Framework installed.

Uninstalling an Application You've Distributed

All Windows applications should provide a facility for easily being removed from the user's computer. Most applications provide this functionality in the Add/Remove Programs dialog box, and yours is no exception. Open the Start menu and choose Control Panel. Next, locate the Add/Remove Programs icon and click it. Scroll down in your Add or Remove Programs dialog box until you find the Picture Viewer program (see Figure 22.12). To uninstall the program, click it to select it and then click Remove.

FIGURE 22.12

Your program can be uninstalled using the Add or Remove Programs dialog box.

Summary

In this hour, you learned how to create a custom setup program to distribute an application you've built using Visual Basic .NET. You learned how to work with folders on the user's computer, how to create shortcuts, how to install files, and how to install the output of a Visual Basic .NET project. Custom setup programs can become quite complex, but even the most advanced ones build on the foundation of skills you learned in this hour. Creating a useful program is a very rewarding experience. Your level of satisfaction will nevertheless increase dramatically the first time a user runs your creation on his computer.

Q&A

Q Should I assume that a user will always have the .NET Framework on her computer?

A Generally, no. When distributing updates to your project, it's probably a safe bet that she's installed the .NET Framework. However, you should either distribute Dotnetfx.exe or include instructions for the end user on where she can obtain the file from Microsoft.

Q Can I install multiple applications in a single setup program?

A Yes. Just add each project as you did the Picture Viewer project, and be sure to include the output of each.

Workshop

The Workshop is designed to help you anticipate possible questions, review what you've learned, and get you thinking about how to put your knowledge into practice. The answers to the quiz are in Appendix B, "Answers to the Quizzes."

Quiz

1. To create a custom setup program, you start by creating what type of Visual Basic .NET project?

2. The final build file of a project (EXE, DLL, and so on) is referred to as the:

3. True or False: To include the output of a project, the project must be added to the solution containing the setup program.

4. Which build option creates smaller and faster builds?

5. How do you add a file to an installation?

6. If the Project menu doesn't have the menu options for creating a setup program, what might be wrong?

7. How do you add folders to the custom setup program?

8. How do you create a shortcut for a file in a setup program?

Exercises

1. Modify the setup program you created in this hour so that the shortcut created appears on the Start menu with the name Picture Viewer, rather its current default name. Also, give the shortcut the same icon you assigned to the Picture Viewer program.

2. Modify the setup program that you created in this hour so that it creates a custom folder within the Programs folder on the Start menu. Install the shortcut to this folder.

HOUR 23

Introduction to Web Development

Visual Studio .NET, more than any previous Microsoft technology, offers incredible Web development tools and functionality. In fact, .NET is very much about programming for the Web. Creating Web applications requires a thorough understanding of all the skills you've acquired in this book—and more. In addition to the complexities of programming that you've dealt with so far, such as creating forms, writing code, and so on, additional concerns exist—such as Web protocols, firewalls, Web servers, and scalability. Teaching you how to create Web applications is beyond the scope of this book. However, it's important that you're at least a little familiar with the concepts and technologies involved with Microsoft's .NET Internet programming strategy. This hour gives you an overview of the .NET Web programming technologies.

The highlights of this hour include the following:

- XML
- SOAP

- ASP.NET
- Web Forms
- XML Web services

Understanding ASP.NET

ASP.NET (Active Server Pages .NET) is the next evolution of ASP (Active Server Pages). ASP.NET is a framework for creating applications that reside on a Web server and are run from within a client browser. ASP.NET enables you to program Web-based client-server applications using tools and methodologies much like those used to create traditional applications.

ASP.NET solutions execute on a Web server running Microsoft Internet Information Server (IIS). Therefore, to create ASP.NET solutions, you'll need to have some knowledge of IIS.

In a nutshell, ASP.NET is the Web technology of .NET used to create XML Web services and to dynamically generate Web pages by serving up Web Forms (both are discussed shortly). For example, you might create an e-commerce site where a user might choose to view all products by category. Using ASP.NET, you could dynamically build and display a Web page containing an appropriate list of products. The server would execute the code to build the new Web page, and then send the page to the user's browser as an HTML document.

Creating Dynamic Web Content with Web Forms

Web Forms are similar to Windows Forms applications (which you've been creating and programming throughout this book). However, Web Forms are designed specifically to run in a browser over the Web. Although Web Forms are designed to run within *any* browser by default, you can target deployment to a specific browser to take advantage of a particular browser's features.

To create a Web Forms application, you choose ASP.NET Web Application on the New Project dialog box (see Figure 23.1). Be aware that to create and test a Web Forms application, you must have a Web server installed. If you don't have a Web server installed and configured, you receive a message similar to that shown in Figure 23.2, and you're prevented from creating the project.

FIGURE 23.1

A Web Forms project is different from a Windows Forms project.

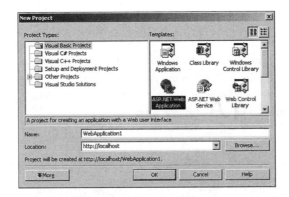

FIGURE 23.2

To create a Web Forms application, you must to install and configure a Web server.

23

Comparing Windows Forms to Web Forms

Creating a Web Forms application can offer many advantages. For example, to deploy a Web Forms application, you have to deploy only to a Web server (not to all client machines). After the program is set up on the server, users can run it simply by pointing their browsers to the proper URL. Contrast this with the need to deploy a Windows Application to hundreds or thousands of users' computers. Another benefit of Web Forms is that applications are essentially platform independent because the code runs on the server and the browser is the only thing running on the client side. When deciding whether to make an application Windows Forms or Web Forms–based, consider the issues discussed in the following sections.

Deployment

As mentioned previously, Windows applications built on Windows Forms are installed and executed on the user's machine. Web Forms, however, run within a browser and therefore don't require deployment to a client machine. Rather than having to install updates on every client as you do with a Windows Forms application, with a Web Forms application you need to update only the server (which must be running the .NET Framework).

Graphics

Windows Forms include the capability to interact with the Windows graphics device interface (refer to Hour 18, "Working with Graphics," for information about the GDI) to create intricate graphics with excellent performance. Web Forms can access the GDI on a Web server. However, round trips are required for screen updates, which can negatively affect the performance of drawing graphics.

Responsiveness

When an application requires a high degree of interactivity with the user (such as screen updates, lots of event code, and data validation), Windows Forms provide the best performance because they run on the client machine. Most interactive processes with Web Forms require round trips to the server, which again can negatively affect the responsiveness of an application.

Text Formatting and Control Positioning

Windows Forms provide an exceptional capability to place controls. Displaying text on a Windows Form, however, requires using controls such as a label or a text box. Making text flow on a Windows Form (such as flowing around other controls when adjusting to the sizing of a form) can be very difficult to accomplish. In addition, formatting text can be problematic because most controls support only one font at a time.

Web Forms, on the other hand, are served to clients as HTTP Web pages, which excel at formatting and flowing text. Web Forms aren't as precise as Windows Forms when it comes to placing controls, however.

.NET Platform Installation

To run a Windows Forms application, a user must have the .NET Framework installed on his computer. Web Forms, however, are installed on the server; therefore, the .NET Framework must be installed on the server, but isn't needed on the client. The client needs only a Web browser.

Security and System Resources

Windows Forms applications can have complete control over system resources such as the registry and also might be restricted by using the operating system's security features. Web Forms are restricted by the user's browser security settings and thus have very limited access to system resources.

XML Web Services

Perhaps the technology that Microsoft is most excited about in .NET is XML Web services. Microsoft describes an XML Web service as "a unit of application logic providing data and services to other applications." It's easiest to think of a XML Web service as an application that resides on a server without a user interface, providing objects to clients. The following are a few practical examples of what can be done with an XML Web service:

- A company could create a stock quote Web service that clients could use to get real-time stock quotes.
- A doctor's office could expose scheduling functions so that clients could use their mobile devices to schedule appointments.
- A government office could expose tax-related objects, which businesses could use to get accurate tax rates.
- A company could expose data that's paid for by subscription. When clients access the data via the Web service's objects, a billing system could track the number of accesses.
- An auction company, such as eBay, could expose its bidding system as an authenticated Web service, and third-party vendors could create their own front ends to placing bids on the auction site.

Obviously, this list just scratches the surface. Microsoft ambitiously envisions everyone exposing application logic as XML Web services. Although this might not become a reality in the near future (indeed, XML Web services might never take off the way Microsoft hopes), many companies are generating a lot of excitement about this technology.

Understanding the Technology Behind XML Web Services

As a programmer, a lot of the details of XML Web services are handled for you by .NET. For example, SOAP and XML are used to marshal objects and method calls across the Web so that you don't have to worry about the details of the plumbing. Because a standard protocol is used to marshal this information, you don't have to worry about the language or the platform used to implement the XML Web service—almost any type of client can consume an XML Web service (Visual Basic, Java, and so on). Clients don't even have to be Windows-based, or even be PCs; Web-enabled phones and other wireless devices can consume XML Web services. Although you don't have to understand the technical details, it's good to have a general understanding of the technology involved.

XML

XML (Extensible Markup Language) is a universal format for transferring data across the Internet. On the surface, XML files are simply text files. This is oversimplifying things, however. The beauty in XML is that XML files themselves contain not only data, but also self-describing information about the data (called *meta data*). The fact that XML files are text makes them relatively easy to move them across boundaries (such as firewalls) and platforms.

NEW TERM Semantic tags are used to describe data in an XML file, and a starting and ending tag are used to define an *element*. The data between a starting and ending tag is the value of the element. Tags are similar to HTML tags and have the following format:

```
<tagname>data</tagname>
```

For example, you could store a color in an element titled BackColor, like this:

```
<BackColor>Blue</BackColor>
```

It's important to note that XML tags are case sensitive; therefore, BackColor is not the same as backcolor, and both elements could exist in the same XML file.

Elements can be nested as long as the starting and ending tags of elements don't overlap. For example, two customers could be stored in an XML file like this:

```
<Customer>
   <Name>John Smith</Name>
   <OrderItemID>Elder Scrolls: Morrowind</OrderItemID>
   <Price>$20.00</Price>
</Customer>
<Customer>
   <Name>Jane Aroogala</Name>
   <OrderItemID>Ultima VII: The Black Gate</OrderItemID>
   <Price>$62.00</Price>
</Customer>
```

XML files can be much more complex, but this simple example should suffice to show you that XML documents are text documents that can store just about any type of data you can think of. In fact, Microsoft is using XML in just about everything, from ADO.NET to XML Web services.

SOAP

To pass structured data across the Web (such as passing objects or calling methods on objects), the sender and receiver must agree on how the data will be transmitted. SOAP (Simple Object Access Protocol) is a new protocol used to exchange structured data in an XML format, and provides a mechanism for making remote procedure calls across the Internet. SOAP is lightweight (that is, it doesn't consume a lot of resources or bandwidth) and makes use of the widely accepted HTTP protocol. SOAP is fundamental to Microsoft's .NET strategy because it allows different applications on multiple platforms to share structured data and interoperate across the Web.

Consuming XML Web Services

Writing code to consume an XML Web service is actually similar to writing code to access an automation server. First you create a Web reference, which is much like creating a reference to an automation library such as Excel or Word. After you've got a reference to the XML Web service, the XML Web service's objects become available in code, and you can browse them as you would traditional objects.

23

To create an XML Web service, you must have a sound understanding of creating objects by programming classes, and you have to have an understanding of ASP.NET—the Web development technology of .NET. The .NET Framework handles the details of using SOAP to enable clients to interact with your XML Web service, so you focus most of your attention on creating useful objects rather than on details of the underlying plumbing.

Summary

Programming for the Web is an exciting proposition, and one that can't be entered into lightly. To create robust Web applications requires an understanding of many technologies, including Web servers, protocols, firewalls, security, object-oriented programming concepts, and much more. By completing this book, you're gaining a solid understanding of application development with Visual Basic .NET, and you're building a set of skills that you can use to move into Web programming. If you're interested in Web development, you should consider purchasing a book dedicated to the subject, such as *Sams Teach Yourself VB .NET Web Programming in 21 Days*.

Q&A

Q Can I use XML files within my applications?

A Yes, you can design your own XML files and use them any way you see fit. For example, you could save a configuration file in an XML file with a scheme you've designed. For more information, look at the documentation on System.XML in the online Help.

Workshop

The Workshop is designed to help you anticipate possible questions, review what you've learned, and get you thinking about how to put your knowledge into practice. The answers to the quiz are in Appendix B, "Answers to the Quizzes."

Quiz

1. What does XML stand for?

2. An element is designated in an XML document using:

3. True or False: Are XML tag names case sensitive?

4. What's the name of the protocol used by .NET to marshal object requests across the Web?

5. What forms engine is used to create forms that run over the Internet?

6. Which forms engine provides for faster response to user interaction?

7. Where is the .NET Framework installed for Windows Forms applications? Web Forms applications?

8. What's the name of the ASP.NET technology used to expose application logic as objects over the Web?

Hour **24**

Building a Real-World Application

As you've worked through this book, you've progressively added to your development skill set. You've covered a lot of material so far, and you might be wondering what's next—how do you put it all together? In this hour, you'll do just that: put everything together. This hour is unique in that I'm really not going to teach you anything new (well, maybe a few things). Instead, you're going to follow explicit instructions to build a working, real-world application. I've included cross-references, so if you need a refresher on a topic you'll know right where to go.

The application you're about to build is CD/Album Catalog program. It's a database application that stores basic information about a CD/album collection, including title, artist name, and associated artwork such as cover art. You'll create forms with toolbars and menus, list views, and much more. All the code you create here follows accepted standards, including using naming conventions and having exception handling. There's nothing in this example that wasn't discussed in a previous hour, but if you get stuck or need more information on a topic than can be found in a corresponding lesson, please visit www.jamesfoxall.com/forums and I'll be happy to provide you with the additional information you need.

Building the Interface

Start by creating a new Windows application titled **Album Catalog**, and follow these steps:

1. Change the Name of the default form to **fclsMain**.
2. Change the Text property of fclsMain to **Album Catalog**.
3. Right-click the default form in the Solution Explorer, choose Rename, and change the name of the file to **fclsMain.vb**.
4. Right-click the project name in the Solution Explorer, choose Properties, and set the Startup object to **fclsMain**.

Designing the Main Window

The interface for the main form will contain a List View control that lists the albums in the database. This List View will show the album title and artist name. In addition, it will display a picture of a camera if artwork is attached to the album information. The form will also have menus and a toolbar for accessing its functionality.

Add an Image List control to the form now and name it **imgMain**. Before adding images to the Images collection, open the TransparentColor property of the Image List control and choose Silver on the Web tab as shown in Figure 24.1.

FIGURE 24.1

Use this shade of gray to make the buttons have a transparent background.

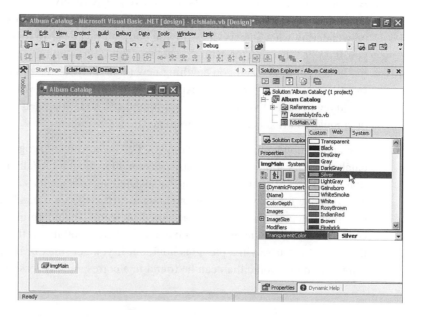

Add the following images to the Image List's Images collection (I've supplied the images with the sample code for this book at both www.samspublishing.com and www.jamesfoxall.com):

1. Open.bmp
2. New.bmp
3. Delete.bmp
4. Edit.bmp
5. Quit.bmp
6. Camera.bmp

> Be sure to add the images to the Images collection in the same order in which they appear in the preceding list. If you don't, the images won't appear on the proper menu or toolbar items.

When you've added all the images, the Image Collection Editor should look like the one shown in Figure 24.2.

FIGURE 24.2

Be sure that the order of your images matches the order shown here.

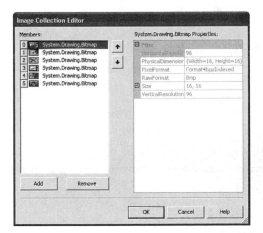

Building the Menu

1. Add a new Main Menu control to the form and name it **mmuMain**.

2. Create a new menu item on the menu bar by entering the text **&File** in the Type Here box. Change the name of the new item to **mnuFile.** Remember, the text you enter to create the menu item becomes the Text property value, not the name.

3. Click the Type Here box below File and enter the text **&New Album**. Change the Name of this item to **mnuNewAlbum**. Set its Shortcut to **CtrlN**.

4. Click the Type Here box below New Album and enter the text **&Delete Album**. Change the name of this item to **mnuDeleteAlbum**.

5. Right-click the Type Here box immediately beneath the Delete Album item and choose Insert Separator from the shortcut menu (see Figure 24.3).

FIGURE 24.3

Use separators to group menu items.

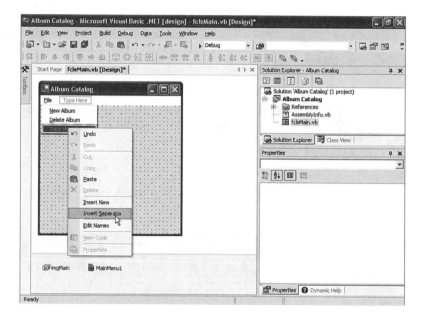

6. Click the Type Here box below separator and enter the text **&Quit**. Change the name of the new item to **mnuQuit** and set its Shortcut property to **CtrlQ**.

7. Click the Type Here box directly to the right of the File menu item and enter **&Edit**. This creates a new top-level menu item; name it **mnuEdit**.

8. Click the Type Here box below Edit and enter the text **&Edit Album**. Change the name of the new item to **mnuEditAlbum**.

The menu is now complete.

Building the Toolbar

1. Add a new Toolbar control to the form and name it **tbMain** and set its ImageList property to **imgMain**.

2. Using the Buttons collection, create the following toolbar buttons:

Button 1:

Property	Value
Name	**tbbOpenDatabase**
ImageIndex	**0**
Text	*(make blank)*
ToolTipText	**Open Database**

Button 2:

Property	Value
Name	**tbbSeparator1**
Style	**Separator**

Button 3:

Property	Value
Name	**tbbNewAlbum**
ImageIndex	**1**
Text	*(make blank)*
ToolTipText	**New Album**

Button 4:

Property	Value
Name	**tbbEditAlbum**
ImageIndex	**3**
Text	*(make blank)*
ToolTipText	**Edit Album**

Button 5:

Property	Value
Name	**tbbDeleteAlbum**
ImageIndex	**2**
Text	*(make blank)*
ToolTipText	**Delete Album**

24

Your ToolBarButton Collection Editor should now look like the one in Figure 24.4.

FIGURE 24.4
The toolbar will contain four buttons and a separator.

Adding the List View to Display Albums

1. Add a new List View control to the form and set its properties as follows:

Property	Value
Name	**lvwAlbums**
Anchor	**Top, Bottom, Left, Right**
FullRowSelect	**True**
HideSelection	**False**
Location	**6,32**
MultiSelect	**False**
Size	**277,224**
SmallImageList	**imgMain**
Sorting	**Ascending**
View	**Details**

2. Add the following three columns to the Columns collection of the List View control:

Column 1:

Property	Value
Name	**colAlbumName**
Text	**Album**
Width	**160**

Column 2:

Property	Value
Name	**colArtistName**
Text	**Artist**
Width	**100**

Column 3:

Property	Value
Name	**colArtWorkFileName**
Text	**ArtWorkFileName**
Width	**0**

Note that specifying a column width of 0 creates a hidden column.

The interface of your main form is now complete, and should look like Figure 24.5.

FIGURE 24.5

This form will serve as the main window in your program.

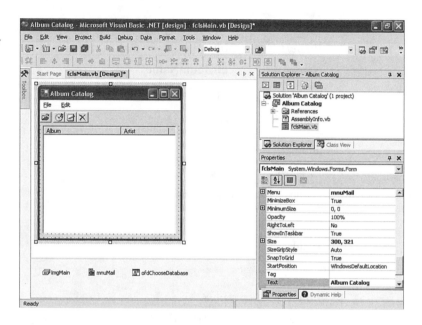

Adding the Browse For Database OpenFileDialog Control

You're going to let the user browse for a database at runtime, so add a new OpenFileDialog control and set its properties as follows:

Property	Value
Name	**ofdChooseDatabase**
Filter	Microsoft Access Databases|*.mdb
Title	**Open Database**

Designing the Album Dialog Box

The secondary form you'll create is the Album dialog box, which will be used to create and edit albums in the database. Choose Add Windows Form from the project menu and create a new Windows form with the name **fclsAlbum.vb**. Set the form's properties as follows:

Property	Value
FormBorderStyle	**FixedDialog**
Icon	**Album.ico**
MaximizeBox	**False**
MinimizeBox	**False**
Size	**298,264**
Text	**Album Maintenance**

1. Add a new label control to the form and set its properties as follows:

Property	Value
Name	**lblTitle**
Location	**8,20**
Size	**40,16**
Text	**Title:**

2. Add a new Text Box control to the form and set its properties as follows:

Property	Value
Name	**txtTitle**
Location	**56,16**
Size	**144,20**
Text	*(make blank)*

3. Add another label control to the form and set its properties as follows:

Property	Value
Name	**lblArtistName**
Location	**8,44**
Size	**40,16**
Text	**Artist:**

4. Add another Text Box control to the form and set its properties as follows:

Property	Value
Name	**txtArtistName**
Location	**56,40**
Size	**144,20**
Text	*(make blank)*

5. Add a PictureBox control to the form and set its properties as follows:

Property	Value
Name	**picArtWork**
BorderStyle	**FixedSingle**
Location	**56,72**
Size	**144,144**
SizeMode	**StretchImage**

6. Add a Button control to the form and set its properties as follows:

Property	Value
Name	**btnChooseCoverArt**
Location	**8,72**
Size	**40,23**
Text	**Art**

7. Add another Button control to the form and set its properties as follows:

Property	Value
Name	**btnOK**
Location	**208,16**
Size	**75,23**
Text	**OK**

8. Add a third Button control to the form and set its properties as follows:

Property	Value
Name	**btnCancel**
Location	**208,46**
Size	**75,23**
Text	**Cancel**

9. Change the AcceptButton property of the form to **btnOK**.

10. Change the CancelButton property of the form to **btnCancel**.

11. You're going to let the user browse their hard drives for artwork files, so add an OpenFileDialog control to the form and set its properties as follows:

Property	Value
Name	**ofdChooseArtWork**
Filter	Windows Bitmaps|*.BMP|JPEG Files|*.JPG
Title	**Choose ArtWork**

Your form should now look like the one in Figure 24.6.

FIGURE 24.6
This form will be used to create and edit album info.

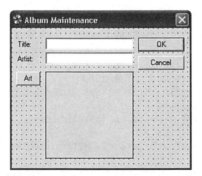

Writing the Code of the CD Cataloger

Now that your forms are complete, it's time to add the code behind them. As you know by now, this involves creating module-level variables as well as code procedures and event procedures.

Writing Code for the Main Window

1. Click the fclsMain.vb [Design] tab to view the main form in the designer.

2. Click the View Code button in the Solution Explorer to access the form's code and enter the following procedure:

```
Private Sub ShowAlbums()
    Dim cnADONetConnection As New OleDb.OleDbConnection
    Dim daDataAdapter As New OleDb.OleDbDataAdapter
    Dim cbCommandBuilder As OleDb.OleDbCommandBuilder
    Dim dtAlbums As New DataTable
    Dim rowPosition As Integer = 0

    Try
        ' Open the database.
        cnADONetConnection.ConnectionString = _
            "Provider=Microsoft.Jet.OLEDB.4.0;Data Source=" & _
            m_strDatabase
        cnADONetConnection.Open()
        ' Get all albums.
        daDataAdapter = _
            New OleDb.OleDbDataAdapter("Select * From tblCDs", _
            cnADONetConnection)
        daDataAdapter.Fill(dtAlbums)
        ' Set up the command builder for navigation.
        cbCommandBuilder = New OleDb.OleDbCommandBuilder(daDataAdapter)

        ' Clear the list.
        lvwAlbums.Items.Clear()

        ' Go through the recordset and show all of the CDs/albums
        Dim objListItem As ListViewItem
        Do Until rowPosition = dtAlbums.Rows.Count
            ' Create a new list item for the album.
            objListItem = lvwAlbums.Items.Add( _
                          dtAlbums.Rows(rowPosition)("Title").ToString, 0)
            objListItem.SubItems.Add( _
                dtAlbums.Rows(rowPosition)("ArtistName").ToString)
            objListItem.SubItems.Add( _
                dtAlbums.Rows(rowPosition)("ArtWorkFileName"). _
                ToString)
            ' If artwork is present, indicate this with an icon.
            If dtAlbums.Rows(rowPosition)("ArtWorkFileName"). _
                    ToString.Length > 0 Then
                ' Show the image of the camera to denote there is
                ' an image for this album.
                objListItem.ImageIndex = 5
            Else
                objListItem.ImageIndex = -1
            End If
            rowPosition = rowPosition + 1
        Loop
        ' Close the connection.
        cnADONetConnection.Close()
```

```
      Catch ex As Exception
         MessageBox.Show("An error has occurred! Error: " & ex.Message, _
                         "Album Catalog", MessageBoxButtons.OK, _
                         MessageBoxIcon.Error)
      End Try
   End Sub
```

3. Enter the following statement immediately below the Inherits statement at the top
   of the module to create a module-level variable. This variable will hold the path
   and filename of the open database.

```
Private m_strDatabase As String
```

4. Place the cursor after the End Sub statement for the ShowAlbums() procedure and
   press Enter a few times. Next, enter the following procedure:

```
Private Sub NewAlbum()
   Try
      ' Make sure a database is loaded.
      If m_strDatabase = "" Then
         MessageBox.Show("No database has been opened.", "Album Catalog", _
                         MessageBoxButtons.OK, MessageBoxIcon.Exclamation)
         Exit Sub
      End If

      ' Load the album maintenance form and let it know
      ' the user is entering a new album
      Dim frmAlbum As New fclsAlbum
      frmAlbum.Database = m_strDatabase
      frmAlbum.ShowDialog()

      ' Refresh the album list.
      Call ShowAlbums()

   Catch ex As Exception
      MessageBox.Show("An error has occurred! Error: " & ex.Message, _
                      "Album Catalog", MessageBoxButtons.OK, _
                      MessageBoxIcon.Error)
   End Try
End Sub
```

5. Place the cursor after the End Sub statement for the procedure you just created and
   press Enter a few times. Next, enter the following procedure:

```
Private Sub EditAlbum()
   Try
      ' Make sure an album has been selected.
      If lvwAlbums.SelectedItems.Count = 0 Then
         MessageBox.Show("There is no album selected.", _
                         "Album Catalog", MessageBoxButtons.OK, _
                         MessageBoxIcon.Information)
         Exit Sub
      End If
```

24

```
        ' Load the album maintenance form and let it know
        ' which album is being edited.
        Dim frmAlbum As New fclsAlbum
        frmAlbum.Database = m_strDatabase
        frmAlbum.ShowAlbum(lvwAlbums.SelectedItems(0).Text, _
                           lvwAlbums.SelectedItems(0).SubItems(1).Text, _
                           lvwAlbums.SelectedItems(0).SubItems(2).Text)
        frmAlbum.ShowDialog()

        ' Refresh the album list.
        Call ShowAlbums()

    Catch ex As Exception
        MessageBox.Show("An error has occurred! Error: " & ex.Message, _
                        "Album Catalog", MessageBoxButtons.OK, _
                        MessageBoxIcon.Error)
    End Try
End Sub
```

6. Place the cursor after the End Sub statement for the EditAlbum procedure you just created and press Enter a few times. Next, enter the following procedure:

```
Private Sub DeleteAlbum()
    Dim cnADONetConnection As New OleDb.OleDbConnection
    Dim daDataAdapter As New OleDb.OleDbDataAdapter
    Dim dtAlbums As New DataTable
    Dim cbCommandBuilder As OleDb.OleDbCommandBuilder

    Try
        ' Make sure an album has been selected.
        If lvwAlbums.SelectedItems.Count = 0 Then
            MessageBox.Show("There is no album selected.", _
                   "Album Catalog", MessageBoxButtons.OK, _
                   MessageBoxIcon.Information)
            Exit Sub
        End If

        ' Open the database.
        cnADONetConnection.ConnectionString = _
                "Provider=Microsoft.Jet.OLEDB.4.0;Data Source=" & _
                m_strDatabase
        cnADONetConnection.Open ()

        ' Find the album in the database.
        daDataAdapter = _
             New OleDb.OleDbDataAdapter("SELECT * From tblCDs " & _
             "WHERE Title = '" & lvwAlbums.SelectedItems(0).Text & _
             "' AND " & "ArtistName = '" & _
             lvwAlbums.SelectedItems(0).SubItems(1).Text & _
             "'", cnADONetConnection)
        daDataAdapter.Fill(dtAlbums)
```

```
        ' Set up the command builder so we can delete a record.
        cbCommandBuilder = New OleDb.OleDbCommandBuilder(daDataAdapter)

        ' Delete the album.
        dtAlbums.Rows(0).Delete()
        ' Commit the changes to the actual data source.
        daDataAdapter.Update(dtAlbums)

        ' Remove the album from the list.
        lvwAlbums.Items.Remove(lvwAlbums.SelectedItems(0))

    Catch ex As Exception
        MessageBox.Show("An error has occurred! Error: " & ex.Message, _
                    "Album Catalog", MessageBoxButtons.OK, _
                    MessageBoxIcon.Error)
    End Try
End Sub
```

7. Click fclsMain.vb [Design] to return to design view. Open the File menu and double-click the New Album menu item. Add the following code to its Click event:

```
NewAlbum()
```

8. Click fclsMain.vb [Design] to return to Design view. Open the Edit menu and double-click the Edit Album menu item. Add the following code to its Click event:

```
Call EditAlbum()
```

9. Click fclsMain.vb [Design] to return to Design view. Open the File menu and double-click the Delete Album menu item. Add the following code to its Click event:

```
Call DeleteAlbum()
```

10. Click fclsMain.vb [Design] to return to Design view. Open the File menu and double-click the Quit Album menu item. Add the following code to its Click event:

```
Me.Close()
```

11. Next you'll add the code for the toolbar. Click the fclsMain.vb [Design] to return to design view. Double-click the Toolbar control and add the following code to the ButtonClick event:

```
Try
    If e.Button Is tbbOpenDatabase Then
        Call OpenDatabase()
    ElseIf e.Button Is tbbNewAlbum Then
        Call NewAlbum()
    ElseIf e.Button Is tbbDeleteAlbum Then
        Call DeleteAlbum()
    ElseIf e.Button Is tbbEditAlbum Then
        Call editalbum()
    End If
```

24

```
Catch ex As Exception
   MessageBox.Show("An error has occurred! Error: " & ex.Message, _
                   "Album Catalog", MessageBoxButtons.OK, _
                   MessageBoxIcon.Error)
End Try
```

12. Create the following new procedure in fclsMain.vb:

```
Private Sub OpenDatabase()
   Try
      ' Let the user browse for and select a database.
      ofdChooseDatabase.ShowDialog()
      If ofdChooseDatabase.FileName <> "" Then
         m_strDatabase = ofdChooseDatabase.FileName
         Call ShowAlbums()
      End If
   Catch ex As Exception
      MessageBox.Show("An error has occurred! Error: " & ex.Message, _
                      "Album Catalog", MessageBoxButtons.OK, _
                      MessageBoxIcon.Error)
   End Try
End Sub
```

13. The last procedure you'll create in fclsMain.vb will enable a user to double-click an album in the list to edit it. Click fclsMain.vb [Design] again to display the form in Design view and then double-click the List view to access its default event. Choose DoubleClick from event drop-down list and enter the following code:

```
Call EditAlbum()
```

Writing Code for the Album Maintenance Dialog Box

The Album Maintenance form (fclsAlbum) will be used to add and edit albums. It will have one method, ShowAlbum, which will be called by the main form to initiate editing an album. In addition, it will have a property titled Database that will accept the full path and filename of the chosen database.

The ShowAlbum method will accept the information for the album being edited so that it knows the record to edit, and it won't have to look up the information in the database. Follow these steps to create the code:

1. Click the fclsAlbum.vb [Design] tab to show the Album Maintenance form.

2. Click the View Code button in the Solution Explorer to access the code behind the form. Add the following below the Inherits statement to create three module-level variables:

```
Private m_strAlbumTitle As String
Private m_strArtistName As String
Private m_strArtWorkFileName As String
Private m_strDatabase As String
```

3. Add the following property procedure (right below the Windows Form Designer generated Code box):

```
Public Property Database() As String
   Get
      Database = m_strDatabase
   End Get
   Set(ByVal Value As String)
      m_strDatabase = Value
   End Set
End Property
```

4. Next, add the following new procedure, which is used to display an album for editing:

```
Public Sub ShowAlbum(ByVal strAlbumTitle As String, _
                     ByVal strArtistName As String, _
                     ByVal strArtWorkFileName As String)
   Try
      ' Keep the original information to know what gets changed.
      m_strAlbumTitle = strAlbumTitle
      m_strArtistName = strArtistName
      m_strArtWorkFileName = strArtWorkFileName

      ' Show the fields to the user.
      txtTitle.Text = strAlbumTitle
      txtArtistName.Text = strArtistName

      ' If an art work file has been specified, show the artwork.
      If strArtWorkFileName.Length > 0 Then
         ' Make sure the file exists.
         If IO.File.Exists(strArtWorkFileName) Then
            picArtWork.Image = Image.FromFile(strArtWorkFileName)
         Else
            MessageBox.Show("The artwork file " & strArtWorkFileName & _
                            " was not found.", "Album Catalog", _
                            MessageBoxButtons.OK, _
                            MessageBoxIcon.Information)
         End If
      End If

   Catch ex As Exception
      MessageBox.Show("An error has occurred! Error: " & ex.Message, _
                      "Album Catalog", MessageBoxButtons.OK, _
                      MessageBoxIcon.Error)
   End Try
End Sub
```

5. This next procedure will save changes made to an existing album or create a new album. If an album is being edited, its name will be stored in the module variable m_strAlbumTitle, and you'll use this fact to determine whether a row is being added or edited.

24

```
Private Sub SaveAlbum()
    Dim cnADONetConnection As New OleDb.OleDbConnection
    Dim objCmd As New OleDb.OleDbCommand
    Dim objTrans As OleDb.OleDbTransaction

    Try

        ' Open the database.
        cnADONetConnection.ConnectionString = _
                    "Provider=Microsoft.Jet.OLEDB.4.0;Data Source=" & _
                    m_strDatabase
        cnADONetConnection.Open()

        ' Start a new transaction. A transaction is used to ensure that
        ' data is written to the disk immediately, and not held in cache.
        objTrans = cnADONetConnection.BeginTransaction

        ' Create a new Command object and attach the transaction to it.
        objCmd.Connection = cnADONetConnection
        objCmd.Transaction = objTrans

        ' Build the query text, depending on if an album is
        ' being added or edited.
        If m_strAlbumTitle = "" Then
            ' Adding a new album.
            objCmd.CommandText = "INSERT INTO tblCDs (Title, ArtistName, " & _
                            "ArtWorkFileName) " & _
                            "VALUES ('" & txtTitle.Text & "','" & _
                            txtArtistName.Text & "','" & _
                            m_strArtWorkFileName & "')"
        Else
            ' Editing an existing album.
            objCmd.CommandText = "UPDATE tblCDs SET Title = '" & _
                    txtTitle.Text & "', ArtistName = '" & _
                    txtArtistName.Text & "', " & _
                    "ArtWorkFileName = '" & m_strArtWorkFileName & _
                    "' WHERE Title = '" & m_strAlbumTitle & _
                    "' AND ArtistName = '" & m_strArtistName & "'"
        End If

        ' Execute the query.
        objCmd.ExecuteNonQuery()

        ' Commit the transaction to the database.
        objTrans.Commit()

    Catch ex As Exception
        ' If a transaction has been started, roll it back.
        If Not (objTrans Is Nothing) Then
            objTrans.Rollback()
        End If
```

```
                     ' Display the error to the user.
                     MessageBox.Show("An error has occurred! Error: " & ex.Message, _
                                "Album Catalog", MessageBoxButtons.OK, _
                                MessageBoxIcon.Error)
                End Try
            End Sub
```

6. Return to the design view of the form and double-click the Art button to access its Click event. Add the following code:

```
Try
   If ofdChooseArtwork.ShowDialog = DialogResult.OK Then
      ' Store the artwork file name.
      m_strArtWorkFileName = ofdChooseArtwork.FileName

      ' Show the artwork.
      picArtWork.Image = Image.FromFile(ofdChooseArtwork.FileName)
   End If
Catch ex As Exception
   MessageBox.Show("An error has occurred! Error: " & _
         ex.Message, "Album Catalog", _
         MessageBoxButtons.OK, MessageBoxIcon.Error)
End Try
```

7. Return to the Design view and double-click the OK button to access its Click event. Enter the following code:

```
Call SaveAlbum()
Me.Close()
```

8. You guessed it: Return to Design view again and double-click the Cancel button. Add the following code to its Click event:

```
Me.Close()
```

Testing Your Application

Congratulations, the application is complete! This was a big project, and it's easy to miss steps. If you're having problems and are having a hard time debugging them, download the complete project with the sample code for this book from either Sams Web site or from mine (www.jamesfoxall.com) and check your work.

I'm sure you know this by now, but press F5 to run your project. The main window will appear as shown in Figure 24.7.

Try clicking the New Album button on the toolbar. You'll receive a message stating that no database has been opened. This is a great example of how a little work on your end goes a long way for the end user. This message is much better than, say, throwing some sort of exception. Try enlarging the form—you'll find that the album list resizes with the form thanks to the magic of the Anchor property. Again, these details really make an application.

24

FIGURE 24.7

Here's your main window—ready and waiting.

Open the File menu and choose Open Database to display the Open Database dialog box and then locate and select the Albums.mdb database provided at the Web site for this book. When you open the database, the album list will display the albums in the database. Notice the camera icon in the list. This denotes that an artwork file has been specified for the album. The database stores only the filename, not the image, so editing this album will cause a message box to appear telling you the image couldn't be found. That's okay—feel free to click the Art button and select a file of your own (see Figure 24.8).

FIGURE 24.8

Providing great functionality doesn't always require a lot of work.

Hopefully, this lengthy example has demonstrated to you how all the various pieces of the development puzzle fit into place—from creating an interface and writing code on through testing and debugging. Your applications will grow in complexity and functionality, but they'll always be built with the same basic principles used in this hour.

I wish you the best of luck on your programming endeavors, and encourage you to stop by www.jamesfoxall.com/forums to discuss your questions and share your success stories!

APPENDIX A

The 10,000-Foot View

You know a lot about Visual Basic. NET now. You can create projects, use forms and controls to build an interface, and you know how to add menus and toolbars to a form. You've also learned how to create modules and procedures and how to write code to make things happen. You can use variables, make decisions, perform looping, and even debug your code. The question you might be thinking now is, "Where to next?"

Throughout this book, I've focused my discussions on Visual Basic. When it comes to Microsoft's .NET platform, however, Visual Basic is just part of the picture. In this appendix, I provide an overview of Microsoft's .NET platform so that you can see how Visual Basic relates to .NET as a whole. After reading this appendix, you'll understand the various pieces of .NET and how they're interrelated. I hope you'll be able to combine this information with your current personal and professional needs to determine the facets of .NET that you want to explore in more detail.

The .NET Framework

The components and technology that make up Microsoft .NET are collectively called the *.NET Framework*. The .NET Framework comprises numerous classes and includes components such as the common language runtime, Microsoft Intermediate Language, and ADO.NET. In the following sections, I'll explain the various pieces that make up the .NET Framework.

Common Language Runtime

A language runtime is what allows an application to run on a target computer; it consists of code that's shared among all applications developed using a supported language. A runtime contains the "guts" of language code, such as code that draws forms to the screen, handles user input, and manages data. The runtime of .NET is called the *common language runtime*.

Unlike runtimes for other languages, the common language runtime is designed as a multilanguage runtime. For example, both C# and Visual Basic use the common language runtime. In fact, currently more than 15 language compilers are being developed to use the common language runtime.

Because all .NET languages share the common language runtime, they share the same IDE, the same forms engine, the same exception-handling mechanism, the same garbage collector (discussed shortly), and much more. One benefit of the multilanguage capability of the common language runtime is that programmers can leverage their knowledge of a given .NET language.

For example, some developers on a team might be comfortable with Visual Basic, whereas others are more comfortable with C#. Because both languages share the same runtime, both can be integrated to deliver a single solution. In addition, a common exception-handling mechanism is built into the common language runtime so that exceptions can be thrown from code written in one .NET language and caught in code written in another.

NEW TERM Code that runs within the common language runtime is called *managed* code because the code and resources used by the code (variables, objects, and so on) are fully managed by the common language runtime. Visual Basic is restricted to working only in managed code, but some languages (such as C++), are capable of dropping to *unmanaged* code—code that isn't managed by the common language runtime.

Another advantage of the common language runtime is that all .NET tools share the same debugging and code-profiling tools. In the past, Visual Basic was limited in its debugging tools, whereas applications such as C++ had many third-party debugging tools available. All languages now share the same tools. That means as advancements are made to the debugging tools of one product, they're made to tools of all products because the tools are shared. This aspect goes beyond debugging tools. Add-ins to the IDE (such as code managers), for example, are just as readily available to Visual Basic as they are to C#—or any other .NET language, for that matter.

Although Microsoft hasn't announced any official plans to do so, it's possible that it could produce a version of the common language runtime that runs on other operating systems, such as Macintosh OS or Linux. If this occurs, the applications that you've written for Windows should run on a newly supported operating system with little or no modification.

Microsoft Intermediate Language

As you can see in A.1, all .NET code, regardless of the language syntax used, compiles to Intermediate Language (IL) code. IL code is the only code the common language runtime understands; it doesn't understand C#, Visual Basic, or any other developer syntax. It's IL that gives .NET its multilanguage capabilities; as long as an original source language can be compiled to IL, it can become a .NET language. For example, people are developing a .NET compiler for COBOL—a mainframe language with a long history. This compiler will take existing COBOL code and compile it to IL so that it will run within the .NET Framework using the common language runtime. COBOL itself isn't a Windows language and doesn't support many of the features found in a true Windows language (such as a Windows Forms engine), so you can imagine the excitement of COBOL programmers at the prospect of being able to leverage their existing code and programming skills to create powerful Windows applications.

One of the potential drawbacks of IL is that it can be susceptible to reverse compilation. This has many people questioning the security of .NET code, and the security of the .NET Framework in general. If code security is a serious concern for you, I encourage you to research this matter on your own.

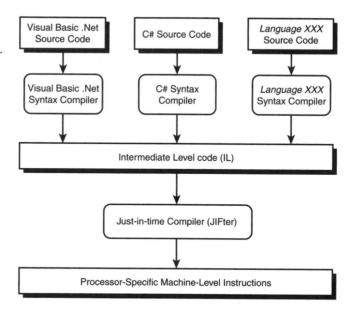

FIGURE A.1

These are the steps taken to turn developer code into a running component.

NEW TERM IL code isn't the final step in the process of compiling and running an application. For a processor (CPU) to execute programmed instructions, those instructions must be in *machine language* format. When you run a .NET application, a just-in-time compiler (called a *JITter*) compiles the IL to machine-language instructions that the processor can understand. IL code is *processor independent*, which again brings up the possibility that JITters could be built to create machine code for computers that are using something other than Intel-compatible processors. If Microsoft were to offer a common language runtime for operating systems other than Windows, much of the differences would lie in the way IL would be compiled by the JITter.

As .NET evolves, changes made to the common language runtime will benefit all .NET applications. For example, if Microsoft finds a way to further increase the speed at which forms are drawn to the screen by making improvements to the common language runtime, all .NET applications will immediately benefit from the improvement. However, optimizations made to a specific syntax compiler, such as the one that compiles Visual Basic code to IL, are language specific. This means that even though all .NET languages compile to IL code and use the common language runtime, it's possible for one language to have small advantages over another because of the way in which the language's code is compiled to IL.

Namespaces

As I mentioned earlier in this book, the .NET Framework is composed of classes—many classes. Namespaces are the method used to create a hierarchical structure of all these classes and they help prevent naming collisions. A naming collision occurs when two classes have the same name. Because namespaces provide a hierarchy, it's possible to have two classes with the same name as long as they exist in different namespaces. Namespaces, in effect, create scope for classes.

The base namespace in the .NET Framework is the System namespace. The System namespace contains classes for garbage collection (discussed shortly), exception handling, data typing, and so much more. The System namespace is just the tip of the iceberg. There are literally dozens of namespaces. Table A.1 lists some of the more common namespaces, many of which you've used in this book. All the controls that you've placed on forms and even the forms themselves belong to the System.Windows.Forms namespace. Use Table A.1 as a guide; if a certain namespace interests you, I suggest that you research it further in the Visual Studio .NET online help.

TABLE A.1 Commonly Used Namespaces

Namespace	Description
Microsoft.Csharp	Contains classes that support compilation and code generation using the C# language.
Microsoft.VisualBasic	Contains classes that support compilation and code generation using the Visual Basic language.
System	Contains fundamental classes and base classes that define commonly used value and reference data types, event handlers, interfaces, attributes, and exceptions. This is the base namespace of .NET.
System.Data	Contains classes that constitute the ADO.NET architecture.
System.Diagnostics	Contains classes that enable you to debug your application and to trace the execution of your code.
System.Drawing	Contains classes that provide access to the Graphical Device Interface (GDI) basic graphics functionality.
System.IO	Contains classes that allow reading from and writing to data streams and files.
System.Net	Contains classes that provide a simple programming interface to many of the protocols found on the network.
System.Security	Contains classes that provide the underlying structure of the common language runtime security system.
System.Web	Contains classes that provide interfaces that enable browser/server communication.
System.Windows.Forms	Contains classes for creating Windows-based applications that take advantage of the rich user-interface features available in the Microsoft Windows operating system.
System.XML	Contains classes that provide standards-based support for processing XML.

A

All Microsoft-provided namespaces begin with either *System* or *Microsoft*. Other vendors can provide their own namespaces, and it's possible for you to create your own custom namespaces as well, but that's beyond the scope of this book.

Common Type System

The Common Type System in the common language runtime is the component that defines how data types are declared and used. The fact that the common language runtime can support cross-language integration to the level it does is due largely to the Common Type System. In the past, each language used its own data types and managed data in its own way. This made it very difficult for applications developed in different languages to communicate because no standard way existed in which to pass data between them.

NEW TERM The Common Type System ensures that all .NET applications use the same data types, provides for self-describing type information (called *metadata*), and controls all the data manipulation mechanisms so that data is handled (stored and processed) in the same way among all .NET applications. This allows data (including objects) to be treated the same way in all .NET languages.

Garbage Collection

Although I've talked a lot about objects (you can't talk about anything .NET related without talking about objects), I've avoided discussing the underlying technical details of how .NET creates, manages, and destroys objects. Although you don't need to know the complex minutiae of how .NET works with objects, you do need to understand a few details of how objects are destroyed.

NEW TERM As I discussed in previous hours, setting an object variable to Nothing or letting it go out of scope destroys the object. However, as I mentioned in Hour 16, "Designing Objects Using Classes," this isn't the whole story. The .NET platform uses a *garbage collector* for destroying objects. The specific type of garbage collection implemented by .NET is called *reference-tracing garbage collection*. Essentially, the garbage collector monitors the resources used by a program, and when consumed resources reach a defined threshold, the garbage collector proceeds to look for unused objects. When the garbage collector finds an unused object, it destroys it, freeing all the memory and resources the object was using.

An important thing to remember about garbage collection is that releasing an object by setting it to Nothing or letting an object variable go out of scope doesn't mean the object will be destroyed immediately. The object won't be destroyed until the garbage collector is triggered to go looking for unused objects.

Now that you've completed this book, you should have a solid working understanding of developing applications with Visual Basic. NET. Nevertheless, you've just embarked on your journey. One of the things I love about developing applications is that there's always something more to learn, and there's always a better approach to a development problem. In this hour, I acquainted you with the bigger picture of Microsoft's .NET platform by exposing you to the .NET Framework and its various components. Consider the information you learned in this hour a primer; what you do with this information and where you go from here is entirely up to you.

I wish you the best of luck on your programming endeavors!

A

APPENDIX B

Answers to the Quizzes

Hour 1

1. Windows Application project
2. Properties window
3. Double-click the control on its form designer
4. The Image property
5. The Click event

Hour 2

1. Change the At Startup property on the Options dialog box available from the Tools menu.
2. Windows Application project
3. Auto Hide
4. Choose Toolbars from the View menu or right-click any toolbar
5. The toolbox

6. The Properties window

7. Solution Explorer

8. Dynamic Help

Hour 3

1. True. Visual Basic .NET is the first version of Visual Basic that is a true OO language.

2. Property

3. The Left Side

4. Instantiation

5. Method

6. True. Such properties are called object properties.

7. Collection

8. Object Browser

Hour 4

1. The operating system, a user, objects

2. False. Each object supports either a set of events specific to itself or no events at all.

3. Click

4. Recursion

5. Double-click the control in the form designer.

6. Sender

7. Update the names of the control's event handlers to reflect the new name.

Hour 5

1. False. The title bar text is determined by the Text property.

2. A system color. System colors are determined at runtime by the user's Windows settings.

3. In the form's title bar, in the taskbar when the form is minimized, and in the Task List when the user presses Alt+Tab.

4. A tool window

5. The ControlBox must be visible.

6. CenterParent

7. The WindowState property

8. True

9. The form's Visible property.

Hour 6

1. False

2. Three: double-click, drag and drop, select and draw

3. In the upper-left corner if it's the only control on the form; otherwise, over the last control placed on the form.

4. Anchor

5. DrawGrid

6. The Format menu

7. IsMdiContainer

Hour 7

1. Label control

2. Text

3. You must set the Multiline property to True.

4. The Click event

5. Accept button

6. A check box

7. Place each set of option buttons on a different container control, such as a group box

8. The Items collection of the control

9. The Insert method of the Items collection

Hour 8

1. Millisecond

2. TabPages Collection

3. The SelectedIndex property of the control

4. True

5. Details

6. SubItems Collection

7. The Count property of the Items collection

8. A node

9. Add it to the Nodes collection of the first node

Hour 9

1. False. They're created using the Main Menu control.

2. Ampersand (&)

3. Click the Main Menu control at the bottom of the form designer.

4. The Checked property.

5. Double-click the item while in Edit mode.

6. The Buttons collection

7. The Style property to Separator.

8. False. All buttons share a ButtonClick event.

9. Set the ShowPanels property to True.

Hour 10

1. Modules

2. True

3. Function

4. False. You use Call to invoke procedures declared with Sub. These procedures don't return values.

5. A parameter

6. A comma (,)

7. Recursion

8. Main

9. Click the statement, open the Edit menu, open the Bookmarks submenu, and then click Add Task List Shortcut.

Hour 11

1. Decimal
2. Object
3. False = 0, True = −1 (Visual Basic stores True as −1 but will convert any nonzero value to True.)
4. Constant
5. Variable
6. First index = 0, last index = 5
7. Scope
8. It's usually best to limit scope.
9. Static variable

Hour 12

1. The caret (^)
2. Mod
3. Multiplication
4. true
5. Not
6. Concatenation
7. DatePart()
8. DateDiff()

Hour 13

1. If…Then
2. Boolean
3. Else
4. True
5. Select…Case
6. Comma (,)
7. No. It's possible that more than one Case statement can be written to match the value of *expression*. However, Visual Basic will execute only the code for the first Case statement that matches.

B

8. False. GoTo can be used to divert code only in the procedure in which the GoTo exists.

9. A code label.

Hour 14

1. Step

2. False. You must know these values at runtime, but it isn't necessary to know them at design time.

3. Next

4. Yes, and this is a common thing to do.

5. Do...Loop

6. No. When you evaluate the expression on the Loop statement, the code within the loop is guaranteed to execute at least once.

7. Exit Do

Hour 15

1. A build error

2. An exception

3. The apostrophe character (')

4. Break point

5. The yellow arrow denotes the next statement to be processed. Red circles are used to mark break points.

6. The Command window

7. False

Hour 16

1. Class

2. Encapsulation

3. No. To access the public variables and routines, an object must be instantiated from the class.

4. True

5. Create a property procedure that includes the Get construct, but not the Set construct.

6. As a private model-level variable.

7. Early binding

8. Late bound

9. Set the object variable to Nothing.

Hour 17

1. The *text* argument.

2. Nothing, which is why you should always specify a caption.

3. Just one.

4. A string.

5. An empty string.

6. KeyPress.

7. Use the Buttons property e object in the event handler.

Hour 18

1. Graphics

2. CreateGraphics()

3. Pens define lines; brushes define fill patterns.

4. Assign a system color to the property

5. Rectangle

6. Ellipses and circles are both drawn using the DrawEllipse() method.

7. DrawString()

8. The form's Paint event

B

Hour 19

1. False. The control returns the name of the file the user wants to open, but it doesn't open the file.

2. The pipe (|) symbol.

3. System.IO.File

4. Two arguments are expected. The first is the name of the current file; the second is the name of the file to create as a result of the copy.

5. Use System.IO.File.Move(), using the same path but a different filename.

6. False.

7. System.IO.Directory. Sometimes Microsoft calls them *folders*, sometimes *directories*. In .NET, however, they're usually directories.

Hour 20

1. Create a reference to a type library.

2. You don't have the component installed on your computer.

3. Wrapper

4. An object variable referencing an object in the server's object model.

5. Read the documentation or use the Object Browser.

Hour 21

1. ADO.NET

2. DataTable

3. Use the Fill and Update methods of the DataAdapter

4. Connection

5. The Provider= argument

6. CommandBuilder

7. The OleDb .NET data provider and the SqlClient .NET data provider

8. NewRow

Hour 22

1. The project type is Setup Project, which can be found in the Setup and Deployment Projects folder.

2. Output of the project

3. True

4. Release builds are smaller and faster than debug builds.

5. Open the Project menu, open the Add submenu, and choose File.

6. You probably have a project *other than* the Setup program project selected in the Solution Explorer.

7. Right-click the File System on the Target Machine item in the left pane of the Setup program project.

8. Right-click the file and choose the appropriate menu item.

Hour 23

1. Extensible Markup Language

2. Starting and ending tags

3. True

4. SOAP (Simple Object Access Protocol)

5. Web Forms

6. Windows Forms

7. The .NET Framework is installed on the user's computer for Windows applications and on the Web server for Web Forms applications.

8. XML Web services

B

INDEX

Symbols

+ (addition operator), 266-267
& (ampersand), 200
' (apostrophe), 22, 320
* (asterisk), 156
\ (backslash), 267
, (comma), 87, 231, 294
/ (division operator), 267
"" (double quotation marks), 249, 274, 326
= (equal sign), 62, 364
^ (exponentiation operator), 268
# (hash symbol), 249, 280
* (multiplication operator), 267
& operator, concatenating strings, 274

() (parentheses), 68, 224, 231, 252, 270. *See also* parameters
| (pipe symbol), 400
+ (plus sign), 14, 48, 104, 194, 275
? (question mark), 326
- (subtraction operator), 267
_ (underscore), 73, 86, 223

A

Abort value, 360
AbortRetryIgnore value, 357
accelerator keys, 200
Accept button, creating, 159-160

AcceptButton property, 159
AcceptReturn property, 155
accessing
Click events, 21
codes, forms, 48
event procedures, 90
object events, 85-87
project properties, 51
actions, 325
active controls, 127, 131
ActiveBorder (system color), 382
ActiveCaption (system color), 382
ActiveCaptionText (system color), 382
ActiveCell object, 419-420
ActiveMdiChild property, 145

ActiveX controls, 50

Add an Item button, 170

Add command (Project menu), 452

Add Existing Project dialog box, 451

Add menu commands, Existing Project, 451

Add method, 169-172, 190-192, 419

Add Module command (Project menu), 221

Add New Item button, 52

Add New Item dialog box, 115, 221, 438

Add *ObjectType* dialog box, 52

Add Project Output Group dialog box, 452

Add Reference feature, 417

Add or Remove Programs dialog box, 459

Add Task List Shortcut command, 236

Add Windows Form command (Project menu), 115, 143, 362, 438, 476

Add() method, 435

Add/Remove Programs icon, 459

addition, performing, 266-267

addition operator (+), 266-267

AddNew function, 341

AddTwoNumbers method, 347

ADO.NET, 425
Data Form Wizard, 438-444
database connections, 427-428
Datatables
creating, 430-431
DataAdapter object, creating, 429-430
DataRow fields, 431-432
example, 438
populating, 430-431
records, 435-437
objects, 426

Adobe Photoshop, 142

Advanced button, 379

advanced window placements, 37

Align command (Format menu), 129

aligning
edges, groups of controls, 129-130
form controls, 126-129
text, 152

All Records in a Grid radio button, 441

Alphabetic button, 42

ampersand (&), 200

Anchor property, 133

anchoring form controls, 132-135

And operator, Boolean logic, 271-272

apostrophe ('), 22, 320

Appearance category, 42

Appearance tab, 379-380

appearances, forms, 101

Application Folder, viewing, 452

Application Folder icon, 453

Application objects, 418

applications, 449. *See also* **example applications**
automating, 421
clients, 340, 421
controlling, 415-416
custom setup programs
adding output, 451-453
build configurations, 456
building, 456
common language runtime, 456
creating, 450-451
custom folders, 454-455
installation programs, 454
running, 457-459
Start menu shortcuts, 455
entry points, 147
.NET, JITter (just-in-time compiler), 492
servers, 340
Setup Project, interfaces, 450
uninstalling, 459
Windows applications, creating, 31

Appointments tab, 184

Archive attribute flag, 409

arguments
brush, 385
Copy method, 405
findtext, 279
font, 385
height, bitmaps, 377
leftY, 385
Move() method, 411
passing, 231
pixelformat, 377-378
replacetext, 279
stringoftext, 385
topX, 385
width, bitmaps, 377
arithmetic, 266-270
arithmetic operators. *See* **mathematical operators**
arrays, 251
data types, 253
data typing, 243
defined, 241
dimensioning, 252
elements, 251, 254
indexing, 252
multidimensional, creating, 253-254
scope, determining, 255
two-dimensional, 253
variables, referencing, 252
arrows
drop-down arrows, 52
yellow arrows (break points), 325
As keyword, 55
Ask Before Closing button, 202-203
Ask Before Closing command (File menu), 203

ASP (Active Server Pages). *See* **ASP.NET**
ASP.NET
IIS (Internet Information Server), 462
XML Web services, creating, 467
asterisk (*), 156
At Startup option, 31
attributes
files, 408-409
objects, exposing as properties, 342-346
Auto Hide, design windows, 36
auto-hidden windows, displaying, 37
automating applications, 421
automation
COM (Component Object Model), Excel, 417
Excel, 416-417
macros, 420
object models, 415
type libraries, references, 416-418
wrappers, 418
automation servers, 416
Excel, showing, 419
Excel workbooks, 419-421
instances, creating, 418
AutoScroll property, 140-141
AutoScrollMargin property, 140-141

AutoScrollMinSize property, 140, 142
AutoSize property, 150-152
autosizing form controls, 132-135

B

BackColor property, 42-43, 102-104, 307, 380
background colors, forms, 102-104
BackgroundImage property, 104-105
background images, forms, 104-105
backslash (\\), 267
bars
status, 213-214
title, 39, 109
baseline values, active forms, 131
beginning spaces (strings), trimming, 278-279
binary information, objects, 50
binding
early, object variables, 349-350
late, object variables, 348-349
object references to variables, 347-351
object variables, 348-350

bit packing, **408**
Bitmap object, referencing, **388**
bitmaps
  Close.bmp, downloading, 160
  Graphics object, creating, 377-378
  height argument, 377
  pixelformat argument, 377
  width argument, 377
black-centered sizing handles, active controls, **127**
bln prefix, **261**
block scope, **255-256**
blocks,
  Try…Catch…Finally, **300**
Bookmarks command (Edit menu), **236**
Boolean data type, **243-244**
Boolean logic
  expressions, evaluating, 265
  False, 271-272
  logical operators, 271-273
  string functions
    characters, determining number of, 275
    InStr() function, 277-278
    Left() function, 275-276
    Len() function, 275
    Ltrim() function, 278

Mid() function, 276-277
Right() function, 276
Rtrim() function, 278
strings, 275-279
Trim() function, 278-279
strings
  manipulating, 274
  replacing text,
    Replace function, 279
  text strings, concatenating, 274-275
  True, 271-272
Boolean values, **246**
borders
  design windows, dragging, 34
  forms, 108-110
  hatched, form controls, 128
  toolbars, 40
BorderStyle property, **42-43**
boxes. *See also* check boxes; dialog boxes; text boxes
  combo, 167
    DropDownStyle property, 175
    Items property, 174, 295
    String Collection Editor, 295
    Text property, 174
  Context Menu, 205

group
  controls, 164
  DataTable records, creating, 435
  properties, setting, 163
  message. *See* messages
  Type Here, 200
break points, **323-325**
BringToFront method, **139**
browsing
  files, 21-23
  scope, 77
brush argument, **385**
bugs, code, **317**
Build button, **43, 104-106, 295, 440**
build configurations, custom setup programs, **456**
build errors. *See* compile errors
Build menu commands
  Build Solution, 456
  Configuration Manager, 456
build options, output (custom setup programs), **453**
Build Solution command (Build menu), **456**
builds, release (custom setup programs), **456**
Button control, **17, 83, 123, 380**
  Accept button, creating, 159-160
  buttons, creating, 157-158

Cancel button, creating, 159-160

pictures, adding to buttons, 160-161

Button icon, 226, 288

button properties, 416

Button property, 88

Button tool, 296

ButtonClick event, 209-210

buttons

Accept, creating, 159-160

AcceptButton property, 159

Add an Item, 170

Add New Item, 52

Advanced, 379

Alphabetic, 42

Ask Before Closing, 202-203

Build, 43, 104-106, 295, 440

Cancel, creating, 159-160

CancelButton property, 160

Categorized, 42

check boxes, Yes/No options, 164-165

Click events, 158-159

clicking, 360

Close, 34, 111

command. *See* Button control

Compute Length, 228-230

Control Box, forms, 110-111

Copy, 404

copying, 18

creating, 17, 157-158

custom dialog boxes, 362-363

DataTable records, 433-436

Destination, 405

DialogResult, assigning, 360

Eat Me, 65

Enlarge, 65

forms, 64, 145

Group Box control, 162-165

grouping (toolbars), 211

Image property, 160-161

ImageAlign property, 161

Location property, 347

Maximize, 109-111

Minimize, 106, 109-111

More, 9

Name property, 307, 312, 347

New Connection, 440

New Project, 31

Open Project, 33

Panel control, 162-163

Perform Division, 324, 327

pictures, adding, 160-161

properties, 18, 399, 402-406, 409

Quit, 24, 203

radio, 165

All Records in a Grid, 441

Check property, 167

Checked property, 297-298

properties, setting, 166

Remove an Item, 170

Run a Do Loop, 313

Save all, 15, 25, 90, 132

Select Picture, 21, 26

Show All Files, 47-48

Show Control Names, 77

Show Form, 118

Show Selected, 172

Shrink, 64

Shrink (Drink Me), 66

Size property, 347

Source, 403-405

Stop Debugging, 67, 74, 109

tbbInvisible, 210

Tell The User, 227-229

Text property, 157, 347

toggle, creating, 209-211

tool, 14

toolbars, 208, 212, 472

View Code, 480, 484

Buttons collection, 208, 211-212, 472

Buttons parameter, 357-360

ByRef keyword, 232

byt prefix, 261

Byte data type, 243

ByVal keyword, 88

C

calendar months, advancing, 282
Call keyword, 228
Call statement, 229
calling, MessageBox.Show() function, 356
calling code procedures, 227-232
calls
    DateAdd() function, dates returned, 282
    functions, 229
Cancel button, creating, 159-160
Cancel value, 360
CancelButton property, 160
Caption property. *See* Text property
capturing mouse events, 372
Case Else construct, code, 294
Case statement, 294, 297
casting, 245
Catch section (Try...Catch...Finally structure), 331
Catch statement, 333-334
catching exceptions, 332
categories, Appearance, 42
Categorized button, 42
CBool() functions, 411
CenterParent value, 112
CenterScreen value, 112

Change event, 83
Char data type, 243
characters
    Len() function, 275
    line continuation, underscore (_), 73
    MaxLength property, 155
    number of, determining, 275
    strings, Len() function, 276
    text boxes, 155-156
Check Box control, check boxes, 164-165
check boxes
    Create Directory for Solution, 9
    Group Box control, 164-165
    properties, setting, 164
    Yes/No options, 164-165
checked menu items, menus, 201
Checked property, 167, 201, 297-298
CheckFileExists property, 401
child forms, 144
child nodes, hierarchical lists, 193
chr prefix, 261
circles, drawing, 384-385
class modules, 50, 220
classes
    code, encapsulating, 338-339
    data, encapsulating, 338-339

    interfaces, 341-342
    methods, creating, 346
    naming collisions, 493
    objects
        attributes, exposing as properties, 342-346
        creating (dimensioning variables), 350-351
        functions, exposing as methods, 346
        instantiating, 346-353
        interfaces, creating, 341-346
        lifetimes, 352-353
        readable properties, creating, 344-345
        references, 347-352
        variables, 348-350
        writable properties, creating, 345-346
    programming, resources, 338
    projects, 340
    properties, adding, 342
    Random, 387
    scope, creating, 493
    standard modules, comparing, 339-340
    System.Drawing.Brushes, 385
classifying objects, 11
Clear() method, 71, 74, 171-172
clearing
    break points, 323
    drawing surfaces, 385
    lists, 171-172

Click events, 83, 157, 391
  accessing, 21
  buttons, 158-159
  picText object, 86
clicking
  buttons, 360
  form controls, 129
Clicks property, 88
client applications, Excel workbooks, 421
client code, 340
clients, 340, 415
clipboard, data, 369
Clng() function, 326-328
Close button, 34, 111
Close() method, 118, 428
Close.bmp (bitmap), downloading, 160
closed design windows, 34
Closed event, 371, 428
CLR (common language runtime), 490-491
code
  bitmaps, creating, 377
  bugs, 317
  Case statement, values, 294
  Click event, 391
  client, 340
  comments, 22, 319-320
  compilers, 242
  constant definitions, 247
  debugging, 317-318
    break points, 323-325
    Command window, 325-329

  comments, adding, 319-320
  error handlers, 330-334
  errors, 320-323
  exceptions, throwing, 321
  Output window, 329-330
  Overflow Exception, 326
  tools, 323
  yellow arrows, 325
decision-making, 287
  Case statement, evaluating values, 294
  If...Then constructs, 288-293
  procedures, branching with GoTo statement, 298-300
  Select Case constructs, 293-298
defining, Case Else construct, 294
developer code, 492
Do...Loop loop, 310
encapsulating, 338-339
enhanced lists, 190-191
entry points, 25
errors, finding with Task List, 322
example applications
  dialog boxes, 484-487
  Main window, 479-484
Excel workbooks, creating, 419

file properties, retrieving, 409-411
forms, accessing, 48
functions, declaring, 225
graphics project example, 388-391
If...Then constructs, 288-293
IL (Intermediate Language), 491-492
indenting, 23
Inflate() method, 383
InputBox() function, 365
InStr() function, 277
interface, writing, 21-24
managed, 490
modules, 219
object properties, referencing, 62
object-based, projects, 70-73
objects, instantiation, 70
Paint event, 390
pens, creating, 378
procedures, 54-55, 298-300
processor independent, 492
processor speed, creating, 309
redundancy, eliminating, 309
Select Case constructs, 293-298
spaghetti, 299
standard modules, 221

unmanaged, 490
VBA, macros, 420
code editors
    displaying, 48
    events drop-down list,
        creating, 86
    modules, 222
**code execution, values,
    249**
code labels, 299
**code modules, creating,
    220-222**
code procedures
    () (parentheses), 224
    calling, 227-232
    code, location of, 224
    declaring, 223-225
    events, 228
    exiting, 232
    function calls, 229
    functions, data types,
        225
    multiple parameters,
        231
    parameters, 224,
        229-232
    recursive, avoiding,
        232-233
    scope, 223
    storing, 50
    Sub, 227
    Sub Main, 233-234
    Task List, 234-236
    ToolTips, 228
    writing, 222-223
code routines. *See* **code
    procedures**
Code view, 48

**code-profiling tools, CLR
(common language run-
time), 490**
Collection Editors
    Image, 207
    ListViewSubItem, 189
    StatusBarPanel, 214
    ToolBarButton, 208,
        211, 474
collections
    Buttons, 208, 211-212,
        472
    Controls, forms, 76
    Count property, 75
    example project, 75-77
    garbage, 494-495
    Images, 185, 207
    Items, 168-171
    Nodes, 192-194
    Panels, 213
    SelectedItems, 190
    TabPages, 183
**color palettes, viewing,
    103**
color properties, 44, 46
color rectangle, 44
colors
    ActiveBorder (system
        color), 382
    ActiveCaption (system
        color), 382
    ActiveCaptionText
        (system color), 382
    BackColor property,
        380
    backgrounds, forms,
        102-104
    Control, 103

Control (system color),
    382
ControlDark (system
    color), 382
ControlLight (system
    color), 382
ControlText (system
    color), 382
creating, 45
Desktop (system color),
    382
Display Properties dia-
    log box, 379-381
dithered, 45
drop-down list, 44
GrayText (system
    color), 382
Highlight (system
    color), 382
HighlightText (system
    color), 382
InactiveBorder (system
    color), 382
InactiveCaptionText
    (system color), 382
Menu (system color),
    382
MenuText (system
    color), 382
system, 45
system colors, 379-382
Window (system color),
    382
**ColumnHeader
    Collection Editor, 187**
columns
    DataRow, referencing,
        431

List View control (example application), 474-475
lists, 187
Columns property, 187
COM (Component Object Model), 417-418
COM tab, 417
combo boxes, 167
  drop-down lists, creating, 174-175
  DropDownStyle property, 175
  Items property, 174, 295
  properties, setting, 295
  String Collection Editor, 295
  Text property, 174
comma (,), 87, 231, 294
command button. *See* **Button control**
Command window, 325-329
CommandBuilder object, 430
commands
  Add menu, Existing Project, 451
  Add Task List Shortcut, 236
  Build menu
    Build Solution, 456
    Configuration Manager, 456
  context menu, Properties, 233
  Debug menu, Stop Debugging, 94, 108, 141, 291, 297

Edit menu, Bookmarks, 236
File menu
  Ask Before Closing, 203
  New, Project, 7, 63
  Open, 33, 47
  Open Database, 488
  Project, 32
  Quit, 201-202, 206
  Save All, 15
Format menu
  Align, 129
  Make Same Size, 130
  Order, 138
  Order, Bring to Front, 139
  Order, Send to Back, 139
  Vertical Spacing, 132
Help menu, Dynamic Help, 56
Insert Separator, 472
New, Project, 33
Project menu
  Add, 452
  Add Module, 221
  Add Reference, 417
  Add Windows, 143
  Add Windows Form, 115, 362, 438, 476
  File, 454
Tools menu, Options, 31, 56
View menu
  Object Browser, 77
  Other Views, 326

Properties Window, 34-35
Show Tasks, 234
Solution Explorer, 47
Tab Order, 136
Toolbars, 39
comments
  ' (apostrophe), 320
  code, 22, 319-320
common language runtime (CLR), 456, 490-491
Common Type System, 494
comparing
  classes and standard modules, 339-340
  equalities of values, 270-271
  forms and windows, 99
comparison operators, equal precedence, 269
comparisons, separating, 294
compile errors, 235
  code, identifying, 320-323
  finding, 322
compilers, 242, 492
Component Object Model (COM), 417-418
components. *See also* **automation servers**
  distributable, defined, 6
  For statement, 304
  projects, 49-50
  running, developer code, 492

Components tab, 40

Compute Length button, 228-230

concatenating strings, 274-275

concatenation, 77

Configuration Manager command (Build menu), 456

configurations, build, 456

conflicts, scope names, 259

Connection tab, 440

connections, databases, 427-428

ConnectionString property, 427-428

constants
benefits, 246
block scope, 255-256
data typing, 243
defining, 246-247
definitions, syntax, 247
global scope, 258-259
magic numbers, 246
module-level scope, 256-257
naming, 248
procedure-level (local) scope, 256
scope, 255, 259

constructs
Case Else, code, 294
Get, readable properties, 344-345
If...Else If...Else...End If, 367
If...Then, 270, 288
ElseIf statement, 291-292

False expressions, 290-291
If statement, 292
nesting, 292-293
use of, 289
Select Case, 92
creative uses, 297-298
examples, building, 295-297
expressions, evaluating for values, 293-295
nesting, 298
Set, writable properties, 345-346

consuming XML Web services, 467

container controls
Group Box control, 162-165
Panel control, 162-163

containers, 184

contents, Properties Window, 41

Context Menu box, 205

context menu commands, Properties, 233

Context Menu control, 205

context menus, 204-206

context-sensitive help, 56

Continue Code Execution action, 325

Control (system color), 382

Control box button, forms, 110-111

control boxes, system menus, 111

Control color, 103

control objects, 61

control positioning, 464

ControlBox property, 111

ControlDark (system color), 382

ControlLight (system color), 382

controlling applications, 415-416

controls, 15, 149
Button, 17, 83, 123, 380
Accept button, creating, 159-160
buttons, creating, 157-158
Cancel button, creating, 159-160
pictures, adding, 160-161
buttons
AcceptButton property, 159
CancelButton property, 160
Click events, 158-159
Group Box control, 162-165
Image property, 160-161
ImageAlign property, 161
Panel control, 162-163
radio, 165-167
combo boxes, 167, 174-175

container
    Group Box control,
        162-165
    Panel control,
        162-163
Context Menu, 205
coordinates, snapping,
    123
double-clicking, 40
dragging and dropping,
    40
drawing, 123
forms
    active, 127
    active controls, 131
    ActiveMdiChild
        property, 145
    adding, 40-41,
        122-123
    aligning, 129
    Anchor property, set-
        ting, 133
    anchoring, 132-135
    AutoScroll property,
        140-141
    AutoScrollMargin
        property, 140-141
    AutoScrollMinSize
        property, 140-142
    autosizing, 132-135
    BringToFront
        method, 139
    buttons, setting prop-
        erties, 145
    clicking, 129
    grids, 123-125
    groups, 125-129, 132
    hatched borders, 128

IsMdiContainer
    property, 143
layering (z-order),
    137-139
location of, 133
manipulating, 123
MdiParent property,
    144
Opacity property,
    139
scrollbars, 141
SelectNextControl
    method, 137
SendToBack method,
    139
sizing, 124, 130-131
sizing handles, 128
Startup object, set-
    ting, 146-147
tab order, creating,
    136-137
tab sequences,
    removing, 137
TabIndex property,
    136-137
TabStop property,
    137
Text property, 143
Graphics object, creat-
    ing, 376-377
grids, snapping, 129
group boxes, 164
Image List, 185-186,
    207, 214
invisible, 19-20
invisible-at-runtime
    controls (invisible
    controls), 19-20

Label
    adding to forms, 306
    AutoSize property,
        150
    properties, 90, 150
    Text property, 91,
        150
lasso, 127-129
list boxes
    Items collection,
        169-171
    list items, retrieving
        information,
        172-173
    lists, 167-172
List View, 186, 470
    columns, 187
    example application,
        474-475
    lists, adding items,
        187-191
Main Menu, 198, 206,
    471
MDI (Multiple
    Document Interface)
    forms, creating,
        142-146
methods, 22
nonvisual (invisible
    controls), 19-20
Open File Dialog, 180,
    398, 400-401
OpenFileDialog, 17-20,
    476-479
PictureBox, 17-18
Pointer (Windows
    Forms tab), 123
Save File Dialog, 19,
    398, 401-403

scrollable forms, creating, 140-142
sizing grips, 213
sizing handles, 153
Status Bar, 213
System Color, 380, 388
Tab, 182-185
tab sequences, removing, 137
Text Box, 204
text boxes
    characters, 155-156
    multiline text boxes, creating, 153-154
    password fields, creating, 156
    properties, 151
    scrollbars, adding, 154-155
    Text property, 151-152
    text, aligning, 152
Textbox, 83
Timer, 84, 180-182
Toolbar, 207, 472
    drop-down menus, creating, 212
    programming toolbars, 209
    separators, 211
    toggle buttons, 209-211
    toolbar buttons, 208
TopMost windows, creating, 139
transparent forms, creating, 139
Tree View, 51, 191-195
user, 50
visible, 17-18

Controls collection, forms, 76
ControlText (system color), 382
conventions, naming, 261-262
conversion functions, data types, 245
coordinates
    DrawString() method, 386
    grids, snapping, 123
Copy button, 404
Copy() method, 404-405
Count property, 75
CounterVariable parameter, 304
CPUs
    machine language formats, 492
    speed, creating code, 309
Create Directory for Solution check box, 9
CreateDirectory() method, 411
CreateGraphics method, 70, 376-377
CreatePrompt property, 402
Ctrl key, controls, 128
current system date and time, retrieving, 284
Cursor property, 113-114
Custom color palette, 45
custom dialog boxes, 361-364
custom displays, forms, 84

custom folders, custom setup programs, 454-455
custom setup programs
    building, 456
    common language runtime, 456
    creating, 450-451
    custom folders, 454-455
    installation programs, 454
    output, adding, 451-453
    running, 457-459
    Start menu shortcuts, 455
Custom tab, 45
Custom value, 379

D

Dash value, 379
DashDot value, 379
DashDotDot value, 379
DashStyle property, 378-379
data
    clipboard, pasting, 369
    encapsulating, 338-339
    Excel workbooks, manipulating, 419-421
    metadata, 466, 494
Data Form Wizard, 438-444
Data Link Properties dialog box, 440
Data Source parameter, 427

data sources
database connections,
427-428
updating, 430
Data tab, 40
data types, 242
arrays, 253
Boolean, 243-244
Byte, 243
casting, 245
Char, 243
conversion functions,
245
Date, 243-244, 280
Decimal, 243-244
default initial values,
248
determining, 243-244
Double, 243
functions, 225
Integer, 243-244
Long, 243-244
naming conventions,
prefixes, 261
Object, 243-244
Short, 243-244
Single, 243-244
storing, 243
String, 243-244
variables, 250
**data typing, strict typing,
251**
DataAdapter object, 426
CommandBuilder
object, 430
creating, 429-430
databases
ADO.NET, 425
connections,
427-428

connections, closing,
428
connections, data
sources, 427
Data Form Wizard,
438-444
DataTables, 429-438
objects, 426
Jet, 427-428
DataReader object, 426
DataRow, fields, 431-432
DataSet object, 426
DataTables, 426
creating, 430-431
DataAdapter object,
creating, 429-430
DataRow fields, refer-
encing, 431-432
example, 438
populating, 430-431
records, 433-437
**Date data type, 243-244,
280**
Date values, 249
**DateAdd() function,
281-283**
**DateDiff() function,
282-283**
DatePart() function, 283
dates, 279
(hash symbol), 280
adding to, 281-282
calendar months,
advancing, 282
current system, retriev-
ing, 284
Date data type, 280
DateTime, 280
files, retrieving, 408

formatting, 283-284
intervals, 282-283
parts of, retrieving, 283
subtracting from,
281-282
values, 285
DateTime, 280
DateTime structure, 284
dbl prefix, 261
**debug information, cus-
tom setup programs,
456**
**Debug menu commands,
Stop Debugging, 94,
108, 133, 141, 291, 297**
Debug object, 329
Debug toolbar, 38
**debug.WriteLine() func-
tion, 230**
**Debug.WriteLine()
method, 266**
**debugging, example
applications, 487**
debugging code, 317-318
break points, 323-325
Command window,
325-329
comments, adding,
319-320
error handlers, 330-334
errors, 320-323
exceptions, throwing,
321
Output window,
329-330
Overflow Exception,
326
tools, 323
yellow arrows, 325

debugging tools, CLR (common language runtime), 490

dec prefix, 261

Decimal data type, 243-244

decimals, numbers, 243

decision-making code, 287

Case statement, values, evaluating, 294

If...Then constructs, 288

ElseIf statement, 291-292

False expressions, 290-291

If statement, 292

nesting, 292-293

procedures, branching with GoTo statement, 298-300

Select Case constructs

creative uses, 297-298

examples, building, 295-297

expressions, evaluating for values, 293-295

declarations

events, 86

variables, explicit, 250-251

Declarations section, 256-258

declared procedures, 257

declaring. *See also* **dimensioning**

code procedures, 223-225

functions, code, 225

variables, static scope, 260

default initial values, data types, 248

DefaultLocation property, 453

defaultresponse parameter, 365

Define Color dialog box, 45

defining

code, Case Else construct, 294

constants, 247

delays, creating, 308

Delete function, 341

Delete() method, 406, 412, 437

deployment, Web Forms or Windows Forms, 463

Description section, 46

descriptions, object properties, 46

design, menus, 204

design time, Items collection, 168

design windows, 33

advanced window placement, 37

Auto Hide, 36

docking, 35-36

floating, 34-37

hiding, 34

showing, 34

types, 34

designers, forms, 48, 226

Desktop (system color), 382

Destination button, 405

destroying objects, 371

Detail option, 186

developer code, turning into running components, 492

device independence, 376

dialog boxes

Add Existing Project, 451

Add New Item, 115, 221, 438

Add *ObjectType*, 52

Add Project Output Group, 452

Add Reference, 417

Add or Remove Programs, 459

code (example applications), 484-487

custom, 631-364

Data Link Properties, 440

Define Color, 45

Display Properties, 379-381

File Properties, 408

Font, 43

ListViewItem Collection Editor, 187

modal, 117

New Project, 7-8, 30-32, 450, 462

Open, 13, 104, 185

Open File, 20, 160, 399-401

Open Project, 30
OpenFileDialog control (example applications), 476-479
Options, 31, 56
Picture Viewer Property Pages, 453
Print, 117
Project Properties, 233
Project Property Pages, 25, 125
Properties, 51
Save File, 402
Select Picture, 26
tabbed, creating, 182-185
DialogResult property, 360-364
Dim keyword, 247, 258
Dim statement, 115, 247, 253, 256
dimensioning
arrays, 252
private module-level variables, 257
variables, 247-248, 350-351
directories, 411-412
Directory attribute flag, 409
display positions, forms, 111-112
Display Properties dialog box, 379-381
display settings, 11
displaying
auto-hidden windows, 37

closed design windows, 34
code editors, 48
form designers, 48
forms, 112-113, 442-443
Help topics, 56
hidden design windows, 34
lists, 167-168
messages, 356
Buttons parameter, 357-360
buttons, clicking, 360
Icon parameter, 357-360
text, creating, 361
static text, 150
system menus, 111
text, form title bars, 101-102
toolbars, 38
displays, custom, 84
Dispose() method, 73, 378
distributable components, defined, 6
dithered color, 45
division, performing, 267
division operator (/), 267
Do...Loop structure, 255
Do...Loop loop, 309-313
Dockable, 36
docked design windows, sizing, 35
docking
design windows, 35-36
floating design windows, 35

multiple floating design windows, 37
toolbars, 39
toolboxes, 122-123
dots, 71-72, 88
Double data type, 243
double quotation marks (""), 249, 274, 326
downloading Close.bmp (bitmap), 160
downward casting, 245
drag handles, toolbars, 39
dragging containers, 184
dragging and dropping, 40
DrawEllipse() method, 372, 384
DrawGrid property, 125
DrawImage() method, 391
drawing
circles, 384-385
colors, system colors, 379-382
controls, 123
ellipses, 384-385
GDI (Graphics Device Interface), 376
graphics, 378
persisting, 386
project example, building, 387-392
Graphics object, creating, 376-378
lines, 384
pens, 378-379

rectangles, 382-384

shapes, 384-385

text, 385-386

drawing surfaces, clearing, 385

Drawing.Drawing2D object, 379

DrawLine() method, 384

DrawRectangle() method, 384

DrawString() method, 385-386

DRIVER parameter, 427

drop-down arrows, 52

drop-down boxes, gray squares, 134

drop-down lists

color, 44

creating, 174-175

IntelliSense, 89, 92

Buttons parameter, 357

early-bound objects, 351

Excel, 418

Option Strict, 251

Properties Window, 42

Startup Object, 233

drop-down menus, creating, 212

DropDownMenu property, 212

DropDownStyle property, 175

dte prefix, 261

Dynamic Help (Help menu), 56

E

e parameter, 88, 390

early binding, object variables, 349-350

early-bound objects, IntelliSense drop-down lists, 351

Eat Me button, 65

edges, groups of controls, 129-130

Edit menu commands, Bookmarks, 236

editors. *See also*

Collection Editors

code

displaying, 48

events drop-down list, creating, 86

modules, 222

Image Collection Editor (example application), 471

String Collection Editor, 295

elements

arrays, 251, 254

XML, nesting, 466

ellipses, drawing, 384-385

Else statements, 290

ElseIf statement, 210, 291-292

empty strings, 248

Enabled property, 153-154, 180

encapsulating, code or data, 338-339

End Function statement, 225

End If statement, 23, 290

End parameter, 304

End Sub statement, 225, 388

End Try statements, creating, 331

ending tags (XML), 466

engines, Windows Forms, 99-100

enhanced lists, 186

all items, removing with code, 191

columns, creating, 187

items, 187-191

Enlarge button, 65

entries, Excel, 417

entry points, 25

applications, 147

projects, 234

single, procedures, 300

enumeration, DashStyle property, 379

environments. *See* **VB environments**

equal precedence, comparison operators, 269

equal sign (=), 62, 364

equalities, values, 270-271

error handlers, 330-334

Error icon, 359

errors

code, 320-323

compile, 235

finding with Task List, 322

Invalid Property Value, 43

Stack Overflow
  Exception, 233
Sub Main was not
  found in
  Forms_Example.
  Form1, 106
evaluating strings, 290
evaluating expressions
  Boolean logic, 265
  values, Select Case construct, 293-295
event declarations, 86
**event handlers, 21, 90-93,
  390**
event parameters, 86-89
**event procedures, 82, 87,
  91, 228**
**event-driven program-
  ming**
  event parameters, 87-89
  events, 82-87
events, 81. *See also* **methods**
  Button control, 83
  ButtonClick, 209-210
  Change, 83
  class interfaces,
    341-342
  Click, 83, 157
    accessing, 21
    buttons, 158-159
    code, 391
    picText object, 86
  Closed, 371, 428
  e parameter, 88
  event-driven program-
    ming, 82
  KeyDown, 367
  KeyPress, 367

KeyUp, 367
Label control, 90-91
Load, 388, 428-430
mouse, 370-372
MouseDown, 87, 90,
  157, 370
MouseEnter, 370
MouseHover, 370
MouseLeave, 370
MouseMove, 157, 370
MouseUp, 157, 370
objects, accessing,
  85-87
orphaned, 94
Paint, 84, 386, 390
parameters, e, 88
procedures, accessing,
  90
project example, 89-94
recursive, 84-85
Resize, Invalidate()
  method, 392
SelectedIndexChanged,
  185
StackOverFlow excep-
  tion, 84
tabs, 185
text boxes, 156-157
Textbox control, 83
TextChanged, 83, 90,
  157
TextChanges, 84
Tick, 180-181
Timer, 84
Timer control, Interval
  property, 84
triggering, 82-84, 180
**events drop-down list,
  creating, 86**

example applications
  code
    dialog boxes,
      484-487
    Main window,
      479-484
  interfaces, 470-471
  List View, adding,
    474-475
  menus, building,
    471-472
  OpenFileDialog control,
    476-479
  testing, 487
  toolbars, building,
    472-473
  troubleshooting, 487
Excel
  ActiveCell object,
    419-420
  Application object, cre-
    ating, 418
  COM (Component
    Object Model), 417
  entries, not visible, 417
  IntelliSense drop-down
    list, 418
  object model, 418
  Range object, 420
  Select method, 420
  showing, 419
  workbooks, 419-421
**Excel workbooks, button
  properties, 416**
**exception objects,
  Message property, 333**
exceptions
  Catch statement, 333
  catching, 332

error handlers, 333-334

Invalid Cast, 323

Overflow Exception, 326

StackOverFlow, 84

throwing, 321

Exclamation value, 358

.exe file extension, 49

Existing Project, command (Add menu), 451

Exists() method, 404, 411

Exit Do statement, 310

Exit For parameter, 304

Exit For statement, 306

Exit Function statement, 232

exit points, single, 300

Exit Sub statement, 232

Exit Try statement, 333

exiting

For...Next loop, 306

procedures, 232

Try...End Try structure, Exit Try statement, 333

explicit variable declaration, 250-251

exploring variables, 250

exponentiation, performing, 268

exponentiation operator (^), 268

exposing functions as methods, 346

exposing object attributes as properties, 342-346

expressions

arithmetic operations, 268

complex, operator precedence, 270

evaluating, 293-295, 310-311

False, 290-291

Not operator, 290

Select Case construct, 92

True or False, 290

variables, 249

Extensible Markup Language (XML), tags, 466

extensions. *See* file extensions

External Help, 56

F

False (Boolean logic), 246, 271-272

False expressions, 290-291, 310-311

fcls prefix, 12

fields

DataRow, referencing, 431-432

passwords, text boxes, 156

File command (Project menu), 454

file extensions

.exe, 49

.frm, 50

.resx, 50

.sln, 47

.vb, 49, 115

File menu commands

Ask Before Closing, 203

New, Project, 7, 33, 63

Open, 33, 47

Open Database, 488

Project, 32

Quit, 201-202, 206

Save All, 15

File Name text box, 405

File Properties dialog box, 408

FileAttributes object, 408

filenames, projects, 52

files

Archive attribute flag, 409

attributes, 408-409

browsing, 21, 23

copying, 404-405

dates, retrieving, 408

deleting, 406-407

Directory attribute flag, 409

Hidden attribute flag, 409

installation locations, custom setup programs, 453

manipulating with System.IO.File object

attributes, determining, 408-409

copying, 404-405

date and time, retrieving, 408

deleting, 406-407

existence of, determining, 403-404

moving, 405-406
properties, 407-411
renaming, 407
moving, 405-406
multiple, selecting, 401
Normal attribute flag, 409
not existing, prompt, 402
Open File dialog box, 399-401
Open File Dialog control, 398-401
project, 52-53
properties, 407-411
ReadOnly attribute flag, 409
renaming, 407
resource, 50
Save File Dialog control, 398, 401-403
source, viewing, 50
System attribute flag, 409
Temporary attribute flag, 409
text, 50, 405
times, retrieving, 408
Fill() method, 429
Filter property, 20, 400
FilterIndex property, 400
filters, | (pipe symbol), 400
Finally section (Try...Catch...Finally structure), 331
Find and Replace window, 116
findtext argument, 279

Fixed3D value, 43
FixedDialog property, 109
FixedSingle value, 43
FixedToolWindow property, 109
flags, 408-409
floating
toolbars, 39
toolboxes, 123
floating design windows, 34-37
folders
Application, viewing, 452
custom, custom setup programs, 454-455
Picture Viewer, 47
projects, 8
Release, 457
Visual Basic Projects, 8
font argument, 385
Font dialog box, 43
Font object, 385
Font property, 43
fonts, objects, 386
For statement, components, 304
For...Next loop
example building, 306-309
exiting, 306
For statement, 304
Next statement, 304-305
Step parameter, 305-306
Form Design view, 48, 85

form designer, displaying, 48, 67
form objects, 61
Form1.resx, 48
Form1.vb [Design] tab, 226
Format menu commands
Align, 129
Make Same Size, 130
Order, 138
Order, Bring to Front, 139
Order, Send to Back, 139
Vertical Spacing, 132
Format() function, 283-284
Format16bppGrayScale value, 377
Format16bppRgb555 value, 377
Format24bppRgb value, 378
formats, machine language, 492
formatting
dates, 283-284
text, 464
times, 283-284
FormBorderStyle property, 108-110
forms, 9, 50
accessing codes, 48
appearances, changing, 101
backgrounds, 102-105
borders, 108-110

buttons
    adding, 64
    properties, 169, 226,
        399, 402-406, 409
check boxes, Yes/No
    options, 164-165
child, 144
Close (X) button, 364
Control Box button,
    adding, 110-111
ControlBox property,
    111
controls, 15-17
    active, 127
    ActiveMdiChild
        property, 145
    adding, 122-123
    aligning, 129
    Anchor property, set-
        ting, 133
    anchoring, 132-135
    AutoScroll property,
        140-141
    AutoScrollMargin
        property, 140-141
    AutoScrollMinSize
        property, 140-142
    autosizing, 132-135
    BringToFront
        method, 139
    buttons, setting prop-
        erties, 145
    clicking, 129
    coordinates snap-
        ping, 123
    grids, 123-125
    groups, 125-129, 132
    groups, sizing, 126
    hatched borders, 128

IsMdiContainer
    property, 143
lasso, 127-129
layering (z-order),
    137-139
location of, 133
manipulating, 123
MdiParent property,
    144
Opacity property,
    139
scrollbars, 141
SelectNextControl
    method, 137
SendToBack method,
    139
sizing, 124, 130-131
sizing handles, 128
creating
    tab sequences,
        removing, 137
    TabIndex, 136-137
    TabStop property,
        137
    Text property, 143
Controls collection, 76
custom displays, 84
designers, displaying,
    226
display positions, speci-
    fying, 111-112
displaying, 112-113,
    442-443
graphics, persisting,
    386
Graphics object, creat-
    ing, 376-377
group boxes, 164
hiding, 117-118

icons, 13, 105-107
images, 104-105
instantiation, 114
interfaces, 17-20
Label controls, adding,
    306
labeling, 90
Maximize button,
    adding, 110-111
MDI (Multiple
    Document Interface),
    creating, 142-146
Minimize button,
    adding, 110-111
modal, 117
Modal property, 117
modality, 116-117
mouse pointers, chang-
    ing, 113-114
names, changing, 101
nonmodal, 116-117
parent, 144-145
repainting, 84
scrollable, creating,
    140-142
Show method, 117
ShowDialog method,
    117
showing, 114-116
ShowInTaskbar proper-
    ty, 110
size, modifying, 14-15
sizing, 213
Solution Explorer, 47
Startup objects, 106,
    146-147
state, 112
system menus, display-
    ing, 111

taskbars, 107
testing, 442-443
text boxes
adding, 90
properties, 398, 401, 409
Text property, 12
title bars, text, displaying, 101-102
tool windows, 110
toolbox, adding controls, 40-41
transparent, creating, 139
unloading, 117-118
Visible property, 115
Web Forms, 462-464
windows, comparing, 99
Windows Forms, 99-100, 463-464
FormulaR1C1 property, 420
Framework, .NET platform, 490
.frm file extensions, 50
FullRowSelect property, 190
function calls, 229
Function keyword, 55, 225, 232
Function procedure, 343
functions
AddNew, 341
CBool(), 411
CIng(), 326-328
conversion, data types, 245
data types, 225

DateAdd(), 281-283
DateDiff, dates or times, 283
DateDiff(), 282-283
DatePart(), 283
debug.WriteLine(), 230
declaring, code, 225
Delete, 341
exposing as methods, 346
Format(), 283-284
InputBox(), 365-367
InStr(), 277-278
IsDate(), 285
IsNumeric(), 289-290, 328
Left(), text strings, 275-276
Len(), 275-276
LTrim(), 278
math, recursive events, 85
MessageBox.Show()
Buttons parameter, 357-360
buttons, clicking, 360
calling, 356
Icon parameter, 357-360
messages, creating text, 361
Mid(), text strings, 276-277
MsgBox(), 357
Not(), 202
Replace, 279
Right(), text strings, 276

RTrim(), 278
strings
characters, 275
containing other strings, 277-278
InStr() function, 277-278
Left() function, 275-276
Len() function, 275
LTrim() function, 278
Mid() function, 276-277
Right() function, 276
RTrim() function, 278
spaces, trimming, 278-279
text, retrieving, 275-277
Trim() function, 278-279
TimeOfDay, 182
Trim(), 278-279

G

g prefix, 262
garbage collection, 494-495
GDI (Graphics Device Interface), 376
General page, 51
Get construct, readable properties, 344-345
GetAttributes() method, 408, 411

**GetCreationTime()
method, 408-410**
**GetLastAccessTime()
method, 408-410**
**GetLastWriteTime()
method, 408-410**
global scope, 258-259
**GoTo statement, proce-
dures, 298-300**
**granularity, form grids,
124**
graphics. *See also* **pictures**
backgrounds, 104-105
bitmaps, 377
circles, drawing, 384-
385
Click event, code, 391
colors, system colors,
379-382
drawing surfaces, clear-
ing, 385
drawing, 378
ellipses, drawing,
384-385
forms, removing, 105
GDI (Graphics Device
Interface), 376
lines, drawing, 384
Load event, 388
Paint event, 386, 390
pens, 378-379
persisting, 386
printing, 377-378
project example, build-
ing, 387-392
rectangles, 382-384
shapes, drawing,
384-385

text, drawing, 385-386
tiling, 104
Web Forms, 464
Windows Forms, 464
**Graphics Device
Interface (GDI), 376**
Graphics object
Clear() method, 385
creating, 376-378
Dispose() method, 378
DrawEllipse() method,
384
DrawLine() method,
384
DrawRectangle()
method, 384
DrawString() method,
385-386
printing graphics, 377
shapes, drawing meth-
ods, 384
**gray squares, drop-down
boxes, 134**
**GrayText (system color),
382**
grids
controls, snapping, 129
form controls, 123-125
hiding, 125
GridSize property, 124
**Group Box control,
162-165**
group boxes
controls, 164
DataTable records,
creating, 435
forms, 164
properties, setting, 163

grouping
projects (solutions), 49
toolbar buttons, 211
groups, form controls
aligning, 126-127
even spacing, 132
property values, setting,
132
selecting, 125-129
sizing, 126

H

Handled property, 369
handlers. *See* **event handlers**
handles
drag (toolbars), 39
sizing, 127-128, 153
Handles keyword, 94
hash symbol (#), 249
**hatched borders, form
controls, 128**
**height argument,
bitmaps, 377**
Height property, 14, 172
Help, 56
**Help menu commands,
Dynamic Help, 56**
**Hidden attribute flag,
409**
**hidden design windows,
34**
hiding
Description section, 46
design windows, 34-36
forms, 117-118

grids, 125
tabs, 184
toolbars, 38
windows, 10
hierarchical lists, 191-195
hierarchies, VB, 32
Highlight (system color), 382
HighlightText (system color), 382
hotkeys, 200

I

Icon parameter, 357-360
Icon property, 13, 106
icons
Add/Remove Programs, 459
Application Folder, 453
Button, 226, 288
Data Form Wizard, 438
Error, 359
forms, adding, 105-107
Module, 221
objects, 13
project type, 31
project type template, 31
Question, 359
Textbox, 227, 288
Windows Application, 31
IDE (integrated development environment), 7
Form1.vb [Design] tab, 226

Properties window, 11
resolution, 11
tabs, 10
windows, 10
If statement, 292
If...Then construct, 270
If...Else If...Else...End If constructs, 367
If...Then constructs, 288
ElseIf statement, 291-292
False expressions, 290-291
If statement, 292
nesting, 292-293
use of, 289
If...Then statement, 210, 291
Ignore value, 360
IIS (Internet Information Server), ASP.NET, 462
IL (Intermediate Language), 491-492
Image collection, 207
Image Collection Editor, 185, 207, 471
Image List control, 185-186, 207, 214
Image property, 160-161
ImageAlign property, 161
ImageIndex property, 188
images. *See also* **graphics; pictures**
Images collection, 185
ImageSize property, 186
InactiveBorder (system color), 382

InactiveCaptionText (system color), 382
increment values, loops, 305-306
indenting code, 23
independence, device, 376
indexing, arrays, 252
Inflate() method, syntax, 383
information
binary, objects, 50
list items, retrieving, 172-173
user, obtaining, 365-367
Information value, 358
Inherits statements, 258
InitialDirectory property, 399
initiating loops, 304
InputBox() function, 367
code, 365
parameters, 365
return values, 366
Insert method, 170-172
Insert Separator command, 472
installation programs, files, (custom setup programs), 454
installations, .NET platform, 464
instances, automation servers, 418
instantiating objects, 346-353
instantiation, 70, 114
InStr() function, 277-278
int prefix, 261

Integer data type, 243-244
integrated development environment. *See* **IDE**
IntelliSense, 65
IntelliSense drop-down lists, 89, 92, 418
  Buttons parameter, 357
  early-bound objects, 351
interactions
  creating, 363-364
    displaying messages, 356-361
    keyboard interactions, 367-370
    mouse events, 370-372
    user information, 365-367
  keyboards, 367-370
  users, 355
interface code, writing, 21-24
interfaces. *See also* **forms**
  classes, 341-342
  example applications, 470-471
  GDI (Graphics Device Interface), 376
  invisible controls, 19-20
  MDI (Multiple Document Interface), 142-146
  objects, 339-346
  projects, creating, 69
  Setup Project, 450
  SDI (Single Document Interface), 142

  user, creating, 89-90, 226-227
  visible controls, 17-18
Intermediate Language (IL), 491-492
Internet Information Server (IIS), ASP.NET, 462
Interval property, 84, 180
intervals between dates or times, determining, 282-283
intMyInteger variable, 260
intPauseCounter variable, 308
Invalid Cast exception, 323
Invalid Property Value error, 43
Invalidate() method, 392
invisible controls, 19-20
invisible-at-runtime controls (invisible controls), 19-20
IsDate() function, 285
IsMdiContainer property, 143
IsNumeric() function, 289-290, 328
items
  adding to Items collection, 169-170
  retrieving, 172-173
  removing from Items collection, 170-171
Items collection
  items, 169-171
  manipulating, 168-169

Items property, 169, 174, 187, 295
iterative processing, 75

J-K

Jet databases, 427-428
JITter (just-in-time compiler), 492
jump locations, procedures, 299
just-in-time compiler (JITter), 492

keyboard interactions, 367-370
keyboard shortcuts
  Alt+F, 203
  Alt+P, 206
  Alt+Tab, 105-107
  assigning, 206-207
  Ctrl+Alt+A, 326
  Ctrl+Q, 206
  F1, 56
  F4, 34
  F5, 325-327
  F10, 325
  F11, 325
  Shift+8, 267
keyboards
  KeyDown event, 367
  KeyPress event, 367
  KeyUp event, 367
KeyChar property, 369
KeyDown event, 367
KeyPress event, 367

keys
accelerator, 200
Ctrl, controls, 128
hotkeys, 200
Shift, 128-129
Tab, 43
KeyUp event, 367
keywords
As, 55
ByRef, 232
ByVal, 88
Call, 228
Dim, 247, 258
Function, 55, 225, 232
Handles, 94
Me, 228
Mod (modulus arithmetic), 268
New, 115, 347, 351-352
Private, 223, 257-258
Public, 223, 258
Return, 225
Static, 260
Sub, 54, 223, 232
To, 294
While, 310

L

Label controls, 90
AutoSize property, 150
forms, 306
properties, 90, 150
Text property, 91, 150
Label tool, 90
labeling forms, 90

labels
BackColor property, 307
code, 299
Location property, 307
Name property, 307
properties, setting, 306
Size property, 307
Text property, 307
languages
CLR (common language runtime), 490-491
IL (Intermediate Language, 491-492
procedural (programming), 82
XML (Extensible Markup Language), tags, 466
Large Icons option, 186
LargeImageList property, 189
lasso, controls, 127-129
late binding, object variables, 348-349
layering form controls (z-order), 137-139
Layout toolbar, 38
Left() function, text strings, 275-276
leftY argument, 385
Len() function, 275-276
Length property, of variables, 275
libraries, 78, 416-418
library nodes, 78
lifetimes of objects, 352-353

line continuation characters, underscore (_), 73
lines
drawing, 384
wavy, code errors, 321
linking controls and context menus, 205
list boxes
Height property, 172
Items property, 169
lists
clearing, 171-172
displaying, 167-168
Items collection, 168-171
items, retrieving information, 172-173
sorting, 173
properties, setting, 167
SelectedIndex property, 172-173
SelectedItem property, 172-173
SelectionMode property, 172-173
Sorted property, 173
List option, 186
List View, example applications, 474-475
List View controls, 186-187, 470
columns, creating, 187
lists
adding items, 187-190
removing items, 191
selecting items, 190
ListBox tool, 123

lists. *See also* **drop-down lists**
  clearing, 171-172
  displaying, 167-168
  enhanced, 186
    all items, removing with code, 191
    columns, 187
    items, 187-191
  events drop-down, creating, 86
  hierarchical, 191-195
  items, information retrieval, 172-173
  Items collection, 168-171
  Project Types, 31
  sorting, 173
  Task List, 234-236, 318, 322
ListViewItem Collection Editor dialog box, 187
ListViewSubItem Collection Editor, 189
literal values, variables, 249
literals, "" (double quotation marks), 274
lng prefix, 261
Load event, 388, 428-430
local scope (procedure-level scope), 256
Location property, 112, 183, 288-289
Location text box, 8
logic. *See* **Boolean logic**
logical operators, Boolean logic, 271-273

Long (GetAttributes() method), 408
Long data type, 243-244
loops, 303
  closing, 304-305
  code, redundancy, 309
  creating, 255, 310
  delays, creating, 308
  Do…Loop, 309-313
  For…Next, 304-309
  increment values, specifying, 305-306
  initiating, 304
  recursive, 233
  While, End While, 313
LTrim() function, 278

M

m prefix, 262
machine language formats, 492
macros, VBA code, 420
magic numbers, constants, 246
Main Menu control, 198, 206, 471
Main window
  code (example application), 479-484
  designing, 470-471
Make Same Size command (Format menu), 130
managed code, 490
managers, Configuration Manager, 456

managing projects, 46
  components, 49-50
  files, 52-53
  setting properties, 51-52
  Solution Explorer, 47-49
Manual value, 112
Manufacturer token, 453
marquee. *See* **lasso**
math functions, recursive events, 85
mathematical operators
  + (addition), 266-267
  / (division), 267
  ^ (exponentiation), 268
  * (multiplication), 267
  - (subtraction), 267
  precedence, determining, 268-270
MaxButton property, 110-111
maximized display, forms, 112-113
Maximize button, 109-111
MaxLength property, 155
MDI (Multiple Document Interface), 142-146
MdiParent property, 144
Me keyword, 228
Me.Close statement, 24
memory leaks, 73
Menu (system color), 382
menus
  accelerator keys, 200
  ampersand (&), 200
  designing, 204
  drop-down, creating, 212

example applications, building, 471-472
hotkeys, 200
items, 198-201
opening, 200
programming, 202-207
Project, 52
shortcut, Properties window, 46
Start, shortcuts, 455
submenus, New, 32
system, displaying, 111
Toolbar control, 207-211
Type Here box, 200
MenuText (system color), 382
Message property, 333
MessageBox statement, 323
MessageBox.Show() function, 224
Buttons parameter, 357-360
buttons, clicking, 360
calling, 356
Icon parameter, 357-360
messages, creating text, 361
MessageBox.Show() method, 77
MessageBox.Show() statement, 55
MessageBoxButtons, values, 357
MessageBoxIcon, values, 358

messages
displaying, 356
Buttons parameter, 357-360
buttons, clicking, 360
Icon parameter, 357-360
text, creating, 361
text, creating, 361
meta data, 466, 494
methods, 22. *See also* **events**
Add(), 169-172, 190-192, 419
AddTwoNumbers, 347
bit packing, 408
BringToFront, 139
class interfaces, 341-342
Clear(), 71, 74, 171-172, 191, 195
Close(), 118, 428
Copy(), 404-405
CreateDirectory(), 411
CreateGraphics, 70, 376-377
creating, 346
Debug.WriteLine(), 266
defined, 68
Delete(), 406, 412, 437
Dispose(), 73, 378
DrawEllipse(), 372, 384
DrawImage(), 391
DrawLine(), 384
DrawRectangle(), 384
DrawString(), 385-386
Exists(), 404, 411
Fill(), 429

functions, exposing as, 346
GetAttributes(), 408, 411
GetCreationTime(), 408-410
GetLastAccessTime(), 408-410
GetLastWriteTime(), 408-410
Inflate(), syntax, 383
Insert, 170, 172
Invalidate(), 392
MessageBox.Show(), 77, 224
Move(), 405-407, 411
NewRow, 435
Next, 387
Refresh, 308
Remove, 170-172, 191, 194
RemoveAt, 171-172
Select, 420
SelectNextControl, 137
SendToBack, 139
Show, 115-117
ShowCurrentRecord(), 433
ShowDialog(), 22, 117, 363-364
triggering, 68-69
Update(), 429, 435
WriteLine(), 330
Microsoft Excel. *See* **Excel**
Microsoft.Csharp namespace, 493
Microsoft.VisualBasic namespace, 493

Mid() function, text strings, 276-277

MinButton property, 110-111

Minimize button, 106
  forms, adding, 110-111
  title bars, 109

minimized display, forms, 112-113

Mod keyword (modulus arithmetic), 268

modal dialog boxes, 117

modal forms, 116-117

Modal property, 117

modal windows, 117

models, object, 415

Module icon, 221

module-level scope, 256-257

modules
  class, 50, 220
  code, 219-222
  code editor, 222
  code procedures, declaring, 223
  Declarations section, 257-258
  procedures, 226
  reserved words, 66
  standard, 220-221, 339-340

modulus arithmetic, performing, 268

months, advancing, 282

More button, 9

mouse, events, 370-372

mouse pointers, forms, 113-114

MouseDown event, 87, 90, 157, 370

MouseEnter event, 370

MouseHover event, 370

MouseLeave event, 370

MouseMove event, 157, 370

MouseUp event, 157, 370

Move() method, 405-407, 411

moving
  floating design windows, 34
  menu items, 201

MsgBox() function, 357

multidimensional arrays, creating, 253-254

Multiline property, 125, 153-156

multiline text boxes, creating, 153-154

Multiple Document Interface (MDI), 142-146

multiple files, selecting, 401

multiple floating design windows, docking, 37

multiple parameters, procedures, 231

multiplication, performing, 267

multiplication operator (*), 267

Multiselect property, 401

N

name conflicts (scope), 259

Name property, 12, 43, 180, 183

Name text box, 8-9, 31

names
  forms, changing, 101
  objects, 49
  output, 52
  spaces in, 223

namespaces, 492-494

naming
  code labels, 299
  constants, 248
  objects, 12
  projects, 8, 31
  tabs, 183
  variables, 248

naming collisions, 493

naming conventions
  data types, prefixes, 261
  prefixes, 262
  scope, denoting with variable prefixes, 262

negation, performing, 267

nesting
  If...Then constructs, 292-293
  If...Then statements, 291
  Select Case constructs, 298
  XML elements, 466

.NET platform, 489
  applications, JITter (just-in-time compiler), 492

CLR (common language runtime), 490-491

Common Type System, 494

Framework, 490

garbage collection, 494-495

IL (Intermediate Language), 491-492

installation, Web Forms or Windows Forms, 464

namespaces, 492-494

reference-tracing garbage collection, 494

New Connection button, 440

New keyword, 115, 347, 351-352

New Project button, 31

New Project dialog box, 7-8, 30-32, 450, 462

New submenu, 32

New, Project command (File menu), 7, 33, 63

NewRow method, 435

Next method, 387

Next statements, 304-305

No value, 360

nodes

child, hierarchical lists, 193

hierarchical lists, 192-195

library, 78

parent, hierarchical lists, 193

Nodes collection, 192-194

None value, 358-360

nonmodal forms, 116-117

nonmodal windows, 116

nonvisual controls (invisible controls), 19-20

Normal attribute flag, 409

normal display, forms, 112-113

Not operator, Boolean logic, 272-273

Not operator expression, 290

Not() function, 202

Notepad

text files, creating, 405

viewing source files, 50

numbers

decimals, 243

magic, constant, 246

random, creating, 387

numeric values, 249

O

obj prefix, 261

Object Browser, 77

Object Browser command (View menu), 77

Object data type, 243-244

object libraries. *See* **type libraries**

object models, 415, 418

object properties, 41, 71

changing, 42-44

color, 44-46

descriptions, 46

viewing, 42-44

object-based code, projects, 70-73

object-oriented programming (OOP), 60, 220, 338

objects, 11, 60. *See also* **System.IO.File object**

ActiveCell, 419-420

adding to projects, 52

ADO.NET, 426

Application, creating, 418

attributes, exposing as properties, 342-346

binary information, 50

Bitmap, referencing, 388

class modules, 220

classes, 338-342

classifying, 11

clients, 415

collections, 75-77

CommandBuilder, 430

controls, 15-17, 61

creating, 339-340, 350-351

customizing, 78

DataAdapter, 426, 429-430

DataReader, 426

DataSet, 426

DataTables, 426

creating, 430-431

DataAdapter object, creating, 429-430

DataRow fields, referencing, 431-432

example, 438
populating, 430-431
Debug, 329
defined, 60
deleting, 437
destroying, 73, 340, 371
dots, 71-72
Drawing.Drawing2D,
  379
early-bound,
  IntelliSense drop-
  down lists, 351
editing, 435
events, 84-87
exception, Message
  property, 333
FileAttributes, 408
Font, 385
fonts, 386
form size, modifying,
  14-15
form, 61
functions, exposing as
  methods, 346
Graphics
  Clear() method, 385
  creating, 376-378
  Dispose() method,
    378
  DrawEllipse()
    method, 384
  DrawLine() method,
    384
  DrawRectangle()
    method, 384
  DrawString()
    method, 385-386
  printing graphics,
    377

shapes, drawing
  methods, 384
icons, 13
instantiating, 70,
  346-350, 352-353
IntelliSense drop-down
  lists, 89, 92
interfaces, 339-346
lifetimes, 352-353
memory leaks, 73
methods, 68-69, 346
naming, 12, 49
navigating, 433-434
OleDBConnection,
  426-427
OleDbDataAdapter, 429
Pens, 72, 378
picText, 86
projects, 69-75
properties, 11, 341
  example, 63-67
  getting, 61-63
  procedures, 343
  read-only, 63
  setting, 61-63
  values, 62
Random, 387
Range, 420
readable properties, cre-
  ating, 344-345
Rectangle, 383
references
  binding to variables,
    347-351
  releasing, 351-352
servers, 415
SqlConnection, 426-427
SqlDataAdapter, 429

Startup object property,
  147
StartUp, 25, 106
Startup, setting,
  146-147
templates, 340
Text property, 12
variables, 348-350
viewing, 48
writable properties, cre-
  ating, 345-346
objGraphics, 378
**OK buttons, custom dia-
  log boxes, 363**
OK value, 357, 360
OKCancel value, 357
**OLE controls (user con-
  trols), 50**
**OleDBConnection object,
  426-427**
**OleDbDataAdapter
  object, 429**
On Error statements, 334
**OOP (object-oriented
  programming), 220, 338**
Opacity property, 139
**Open command (File
  menu), 33, 47**
**Open Database com-
  mand (File menu), 488**
**Open dialog box, 13, 104,
  185**
**Open File dialog box, 20,
  160, 399-401**
**Open File Dialog control,
  180**
  buttons, properties, 399
  CheckFileExists proper-
    ty, 401

Filter property, 400
FilterIndex property, 400
InitialDirectory property, 399
methods, ShowDialog(), 400
Multiselect property, 401
properties
    CheckFileExists, 401
    Filter, 400
    FilterIndex, 400
    InitialDirectory, 399
    Multiselect, 401
    Title, 399
ShowDialog() method, 400
text boxes, properties, 398
Title property, 399
Open Project button, 33
Open Project dialog box, 30
OpenFileDialog control, 17-20, 398, 476-479
operating systems, triggering events, 84
operator precedence, 270
operators
    + (addition), 266-267
    & (concatenating strings), 274
    / (division), 267
    ^ (exponentiation), 268
    * (multiplication), 267
    - (subtraction), 267

comparison, equal precedence, 269
logical, Boolean logic, 271-273
Not, expressions, 290
precedence, determining, 268-270
Option Explicit setting, 251
Option Strict drop-down list, 251
Options command (Tools menu), 31, 56
Options dialog box, 31, 56
Or operator, Boolean logic, 272-273
Order command (Format menu), 138
Order, Bring to Front command (Format menu), 139
Order, Send to Back command (Format menu), 139
orphaned events, 94
Other Views command (View menu), 326
output, custom setup programs, 451-453
output names, 52
Output Type option, 52
Output window, 329-330
Overflow Exception, 326
OverwritePrompt property, 402

P

packing, bit, 408
pages, 183
    General, 51
    Tab control, containers, 184
    Visual Studio Start Page, 30-32
Paint event, 84, 386, 390
palettes
    color, viewing, 103
    Custom color, 45
Panel control, 162-163
panels, status bars, 213
Panels collection, 213
panes, Properties, 42
parameters
    Buttons, 357-360
    code procedures, passing, 231-232
    ConnectionString property, 427
    CounterVariable, 304
    Data Source, 427
    defaultresponse, 365
    DRIVER, 427
    e, 88, 390
    End, 304
    events, 86-89
    Exit For, 304
    Icon, 357-360
    InputBox() function, 365
    multiple, code procedures, 231
    passing by reference, 231
    passing by value, 231

procedures, 224, 229
Provider, 427
PWD, 427
SERVER, 427
Start, 304
Step, 304-306
title, 365
UID, 427
parent forms, 144-145
parent nodes, hierarchical lists, 193
parentheses (), 68, 224, 231, 252, 270. *See also* **parameters**
passing, arguments or parameters, 231
password fields, text boxes, 156
PasswordChar property, 156
passwords
Jet databases, 428
PasswordChar property, 156
paths, specifying (projects), 32
Pen objects, DashStyle property, 378
pens, 72, 378-379
Perform Division button, 324, 327
periods (dots), 88
persisting graphics, 386
Photoshop, 142
picText object, 86
Picture Viewer
custom setup programs, 451
folder, 47

program, 47
project, 47, 451-452
Picture Viewer Property Pages dialog box, 453
PictureBox control, 17-18
pictures
buttons, 160-161
storing, 185-186
pipe symbol (|), 400
pixelformat argument, 377-378
pixels, 15
platforms, .NET, 489
CLR (common language runtime), 490-491
Common Type System, 494
Framework, 490
garbage collection, 494-495
IL (Intermediate Language), 491-492
namespaces, 492-494
reference-tracing garbage collection, 494
plus sign (+), 14, 48, 104, 275
Pointer, 41
Pointer (Windows Forms tab), 123
pointers, mouse, 113-114
points, break points, 323-325
positioning control, 464
Practical Standards for Microsoft Visual Basic, **262**

precedence
equal, comparison operators, 269
operator, overriding, 270
prefixes, 261-262
Print dialog box, 117
printing
graphics, 377-378
Output window, Debug object, 329
Private keyword, 223, 257-258
private module-level variables, dimensioning, 257
Private procedures, 228
procedural languages (programming), 82
procedure-level (local) scope, 256
procedures, 54-55
() (parentheses), 224
branching with GoTo statement, 298-300
code
calling, 227-232
declaring, 223-225
location of code, 224
parameters, passing, 231-232
scope, 223
storing, 50
writing, 222-223
declared, 257
events, 228
accessing, 90
creating, 87, 91
triggering, 82-84, 180

exiting, 232
Function, 343
functions, 225, 229
jump locations, 299
modules, 226
multiple parameters, 231
parameters, 224, 229
Private, 228
properties, structure, 343
recursive, 232-233
scope, determining, 255
ShowCurrentRecord(), 437
single entry points, 300
single exit points, 300
Sub, 227, 343
Sub Main, 233-234
Task List, 234-236
ToolTips, 228
processing, iterative, 75
processor-independent code, 492
processors, speed, 309
programming
event-driven, 82-89
menus, 202-207
MessageBox.Show() statement, 55
OOP (object-oriented programming), 60, 220, 338
procedures, 54-55
toolbars, 209
variables, 54
programming classes, resources, 338

programs
creating, 10
custom
build configurations, 456
building, 456
common language runtime, 456
creating, 450-451
custom folders, 454-455
installation programs, files, 454
output, adding, 451-453
running, 457-459
Start menu shortcuts, 455
defined, 49
distributable components, 6
installation, files, 454
MDI (Multiple Document Interface), windows, 142-143
Picture Viewer, 47
terminating, 24
user interaction, 355
custom dialog boxes, creating, 361-364
displaying messages, 356-361
keyboard interactions, 367-370
mouse events, 370-372
user information, 365-367
writing, 10

Project command (File menu), 32
project management, 46
components, 49-50
project files, 52-53
setting properties, 51-52
Solution Explorer, 47-49
Project menu commands, 52
Add, 452
Add Module, 221
Add Reference, 417
Add Windows, 143
Add Windows Form, 115, 362, 438, 476
File, 454
Project Properties dialog box, 233
Project Property Pages dialog box, 25, 125
project type icon, 31
project type template icon, 31
Project Types list, 31
projects
classes, adding, 340
creating, 7-10, 31-32
defined, 6, 49
entry points, 234
event example, 89-94
filenames, 52
folders, 8
forms, 9
graphics example, building, 387-392
interfaces, creating, 69
naming, 8, 31

object-based code, writing, 70-73
objects, adding, 52
opening, 32
paths, specifying, 32
Picture Viewer, 47, 451-452
properties, accessing, 51
running, 25-27, 322
saving, 15, 32, 222
Setup Project, interfaces, 450
solutions, grouping, 49
testing, 74-75
text files, 50
user interfaces, creating, 226-227
prompts, files not existing, 402
properties
AcceptButton, 159
AcceptReturn, 155
ActiveMdiChild, 145
adding to classes, 342
Anchor, 133
AutoScroll, 140-141
AutoScrollMargin, 140-141
AutoScrollMinSize, 140-142
AutoSize, 150-152
BackColor, 42-43, 102-104, 307, 380
BackgroundImage, 104-105
BorderStyle, 42-43
Button, 88
buttons, 18, 169-170, 311, 347

CancelButton, 160
Caption. *See* Text property
check boxes, 164
Checked, 167, 201, 297-298
CheckFileExists, 401
class interfaces, 341-342
Clicks, 88
color, 44-46
Columns, 187
columns, List View control (example application), 474-475
combo boxes, setting, 295
ConnectionString, 427-428
ControlBox, 111
Count, 75
CreatePrompt, 402
Cursor, 113-114
DashStyle, 378-379
DefaultLocation property, 453
dialog boxes, OpenFileDialog control (example applications), 476-479
DialogResult, 362-364
DrawGrid, 125
DropDownMenu, 212
DropDownStyle, 175
Enabled, 153-154, 180
files, 407-411
Filter, 20, 400
FilterIndex, 400
FixedDialog, 109

FixedToolWindow, 109
Font, 43
FormulaR1C1, 420
FromBorderStyle, 108-110
FullRowSelect, 190
GridSize, 124
group boxes, 163
Handled, 369
Height, 14, 172
Icon, 13, 106
Image, 160-161
ImageAlign, 161
ImageIndex, 188
ImageSize, 186
InitialDirectory, 399
Interval, 84, 180
IsMdiContainer, 143
Items, 169, 174, 187, 295
KeyChar, 369
Label control, 90, 150
labels, setting, 306
LargeImageList, 189
Length, 275
list boxes, 167
ListView control, 187, 474
Location, 112, 183, 288-289
MaxButton, 110-111
MaxLength, 155
MdiParent, 144
Message, 333
MinButton, 110-111
Modal, 117
Multiline, 125, 153-154, 156
Multiselect, 401

Name, 12, 43, 180, 183
object attributes,
  342-346
objects, 11, 61, 41, 341
  changing, 42-44
  descriptions, 46
  example, 63-67
  getting, 61-63
  setting, 61-63
  values, 62
  viewing, 42-44
Opacity, 139
OpenFileDialog control,
  20
OverwritePrompt, 402
PasswordChar, 156
procedures, structure,
  343
projects, 51-52
radio buttons, 166
read-only, objects, 63
readable, creating,
  344-345
ScrollBars, 154
SelectedIndex, 172-173,
  184
SelectedItem, 172-173
SelectionMode, 172-
  173
ShowInTaskbar, 107,
  110
ShowPanels, 214
Size, 14, 112, 183, 289,
  307, 347
Sorted, 173
StartPosition, 111-112
Startup object, 147, 234
SubItems, 189
subproperties, 104

Tab control, 182
TabIndex, 136-137
TabPages, 183
TabStop, 137
Text, 12, 91, 143,
  150-153, 157, 174
text boxes, 151, 398,
  401, 409
TextAlign, 152, 210
TextBox tool, setting,
  125
Timer control, 180
Title, 399
toolbar buttons, exam-
  ple application,
  472-473
TopMost, 139
TransparentColor, 186,
  470
Tree View control, 192
View, 188-189
Visible, 115-117
Width, 14
WindowState, 112-113
writable, creating,
  345-346
X, 88
Y, 88
**Properties command
(context menu), 233**
Properties dialog box, 51
Properties pane, 42
**Properties window, 11,
35, 61, 132**
  contents, 41
  drop-down list, 42
  forms, 101
  object properties, 41-46
  shortcut menu, 46

**Properties Windows
command (View menu),
34-35**
property values
  active forms, 131
  form-control groups,
    setting, 132
**Protected (reserved
word), 87**
**protocols, SOAP (Simple
Object Access Protocol),
466**
Provider parameter, 427
Provider tab, 440
Public keyword, 223, 258
public variables, 342
PWD parameter, 427

Q

Question icon, 359
question mark (?), 326
Question value, 358
Quick Tour, 47
Quit button, 24, 203
**Quit command (File
menu), 201-202, 206**
**quotation marks, double
(""), 249, 274, 326**

R

radio buttons, 165
  All Records in a Grid,
    441
  Check property, 167

Checked property, 297-298
properties, setting, 166
Random class, 387
random numbers, creating, 387
Random object, 387
Range object, 420
read-only properties, objects, 63
readable properties, creating, 344-345
ReadOnly attribute flag, 409
records, DataTables
creating, 435-437
deleting, 437
editing, 435
navigating, 433-434
Rectangle object, 383
rectangles, 383
color, 44
creating, 382
drawing, 384
selections, creating, 127
recursive events, 84-85
recursive loops, 233
recursive procedures, 232-233
red, green, and blue (RGB), 44
redundancy, loops, 309
reference, parameters, 231
reference-tracing garbage collection, 494
references
objects, 347-352
type libraries, creating, 416-418

referencing
array variables, 252
Bitmap object, 388
object properties, 62
variables, 247
Refresh method, 308
release builds, custom setup programs, 456
Release folder, 457
Remove an Item button, 170
Remove method, 170-172, 191, 194
RemoveAt method, 171-172
repainting forms, 84
Replace function, 279
replacetext argument, 279
reserved words, 66, 87, 248
Resize event, Invalidate() method, 392
resolution, 11, 15
resource files, 50
resources, programming classes, 338
responsiveness, Web Forms or Windows Forms, 464
.resx file extensions, 50
Retry value, 360
RetryCancel value, 357
Return keyword, 225
return values, InputBox() function, 366
returned values, code procedure declarations, 225

RGB (red, green, and blue), 44
Right() function, text strings, 276
routines, code. *See* code procedures
RTrim() function, 278
Run a Do Loop button, 313
running
components, developer code, turning into, 492
custom setup programs, 457-459
projects, 322
runtime, Items collection, 169
runtime errors, code, 320-323

S

Sams Publishing Web site, Close.bmp (bitmap), 160
Sams Teach Yourself Object-Oriented Programming with Visual Basic. NET in 21 Days, 220
Save All button, 15, 25, 90, 132
Save All command (File menu), 15
Save File dialog box, 402
Save File Dialog control, 398, 403
buttons, properties, 402

CreatePrompt property, 402

OverwritePrompt property, 402

properties, 402

text boxes, properties, 401

SaveFileDialog, 19, 402

saving projects, 15, 32, 222

scope

block scope, 255-256

creating, 493

defined, 255

denoting with variable prefixes, 262

determining, 255

global, 258-259

module-level, 256-257

name conflicts, 259

procedure-level (local), 256

sizes of, 259

static, variables, 260

variables, prefixes, 262

scope designator, 223

scope name conflicts, 259

scrollable forms, creating, 140-142

scrollbars

adding to text boxes, 154-155

form controls, 141

ScrollBars property, 154

SDI (Single Document Interface), 142

sections

Declarations, 256-258

Description, 46

security, Web Forms or Windows Forms, 464

Select Case constructs, 92

creative uses, 297-298

examples, building, 295-297

expressions, evaluating for values, 293-295

nesting, 298

Select method, 420

Select Picture button, 21, 26

Select Picture dialog box, 26

SelectedIndex property, 172-173, 184

SelectedIndexChanged event, 185

SelectedItem property, 172-173

SelectedItems collection, 190

selection rectangle, creating, 127

SelectionMode property, 172-173

SelectNextControl method, 137

semantic tags (XML), 466

SendToBack method, 139

separating comparisons, 294

separators, creating, 211

SERVER parameter, 427

servers, 415. *See also* **Web services**

applications, 340

automation, 416, 419-421

Set construct, writable properties, 345-346

setup programs, custom

building, 456

common language runtime, 456

creating, 450-451

custom folders, 454-455

installation programs, files, 454

output, adding, 451-453

running, 457-459

Start menu shortcuts, 455

Setup Project, interfaces, 450

Setup Wizard, 457

shapes, 382-385

Shift key, controls, 128-129

sho prefix, 261

Short data type, 243-244

shortcut menus

context menus, 204-206

Properties window, 46

shortcuts, Start menu, 455. *See also* **keyboard shortcuts**

Show All Files button, 47-48

Show Control Names button, 77

Show Form button, 118

Show method, 115-117

Show Selected button, 172

Show Start Page, 31

Show Tasks command (View menu), 234
ShowCurrentRecord() method, 433
ShowCurrentRecord() procedure, 437
ShowDialog() method, 22, 117, 363-364, 400
ShowInTaskbar property, 107, 110
ShowPanels property, 214
Shrink (Drink Me) button, 66
Shrink button, 64
Simple Object Access Protocol (SOAP), 466
Single data type, 243-244
Single Document Interface (SDI), 142
single entry points, procedures, 300
single exit points, procedures, 300
single-clicking, 11
Size property, 14, 112, 183, 289, 307, 347
sizing
   Description section, 46
   docked design windows, 35
   floating design windows, 34
   form controls, 124-126, 130-135
   forms, modifying, 14-15
   toolbars, 39
sizing grips, 213

sizing handles
   active controls, 127
   controls, 153
   form controls, 128
.sln, file extension, 47
Small Icons option, 186
snapping form-control coordinates, 123
sng prefix, 261
SOAP (Simple Object Access Protocol), 466
Solid value, 379
Solution Explorer
   forms, 47
   objects, viewing, 48
   project management, 47-49
   window, 116, 451
Solution Explorer command (View menu), 47
solutions, 6, 49
Sorted property, 173
sorting lists, 173
Source button, 403-405
source files, viewing, 50
sources, data, 427-430
spacing
   form control groups, 132
   strings, trimming, 278-279
spaghetti code, 299
speed, processors, 309
SqlConnection object, 426-427
SqlDataAdapter object, 429
squares, gray, 134
st prefix, 262

Stack Overflow Exception, 84, 233
standard modules, 220
   classes, comparing, 339-340
   code, 221
Standard toolbar, 38, 52
Start menu, shortcuts, 455
Start parameter, 304
starting tags (XML), 466
StartPosition property, 111-112
Startup objects, 25, 106, 146
   drop-down list, 233
   property, 147, 234
   setting, 51
statements
   Call, 229
   Case, 294, 297
   Catch, 333-334
   Dim, 115, 247, 253, 256
   Else, 290
   ElseIf, 210, 291-292
   End Function, 225
   End If, 23, 290
   End Sub, 225, 388
   End Try, creating, 331
   Exit Do, 310
   Exit For, 306
   Exit Function, 232
   Exit Sub, 232
   Exit Try, 333
   For, components, 304
   GoTo, procedures, 298-300
   If, 292

If...Then, 210, 291
Inherits, 258
Me.Close, 24
MessageBox, 323
MessageBox.Show(), 55
Next, 304-305
On Error, 334
Try...End...Try statements, 331
WriteLine(), 250
yellow arrows, 325
states, forms, 112
Static keyword, 260
static scope, variables, 260
static text, displaying, 150
static variables, creating, 260
status bars, 213-214
StatusBarPanel Collection Editor, 214
Step Into action, 325
Step Out action, 325
Step Over F10 action, 325
Step parameter, 304-306
Stop Debugging button, 67, 74, 109
Stop Debugging command (Debug menu), 94, 108, 133, 141, 297
Stop value, 358
storing
    array elements, 254
    code procedures, 50
    data types, 243
    pictures, 185-186
    values, 249

str prefix, 261
strict typing, 250-251
String Collection Editor, 295
String data type, 243-244
stringoftext argument, 385
strings, 54
    & operator, concatenating strings, 274
    characters, Len() function, 276
    concatenating, + (plus sign), 275
    empty, 248
    evaluating, 290
    functions, 275-279
    InStr() function, 277-278
    Left() function, 275-276
    Len() function, 275
    LTrim() function, 278
    manipulating, 274
    Mid() function, 276-277
    Right() function, 276
    RTrim() function, 278
    spaces, trimming, 278-279
    text, 274-275, 279
    Trim() function, 278-279
    zero-length, 326
structure scope. *See* **block scope**
structured error handling. *See* **Try...Catch...Finally structure**

structures
    DateTime, 284
    Do...Loop, 255
    ElseIf statement, 292
    property procedures, 343
    Try...Catch...Finally, 330-331
    Try...End...Try, 331-333
Sub (reserved word), 87
Sub keyword, 54, 223, 232
Sub Main, 51
Sub Main procedure, 233-234
Sub Main was not found in Forms_Example.Form1 error, 106
Sub procedures, 227, 343
SubItems property, 189
submenus, New, 32
subproperties, 104
subtraction, performing, 267
subtraction operator (-), 267
surfaces (drawing), clearing, 385
syntax. *See* **code**
System attribute flag, 409
System Color control, 380, 388
system colors, 45, 379-382
system menus, displaying, 111
System namespace, 493

System palette tab, 381
system resources, 464
System tab, 45
System.Data namespace, 493
System.Diagnostics namespace, 493
System.Drawing namespace, 493
System.Drawing.Brushes class, 385
System.IO namespace, 493
System.IO.Directory object, 411-412
System.IO.File object
    buttons, properties, 404-406, 409
    CBool() functions, 411
    Copy() method, 404-405
    Delete() method, 406
    Exists() method, 404
    files
        attributes, determining, 408-409
        copying, 404-405
        date and time, retrieving, 408
        deleting, 406-407
        existence of, determining, 403-404
        moving, 405-406
        properties, code to retrieve, 409-411
        properties, retrieving, 407-408
        renaming, 407

GetAttributes() method, 408, 411
GetCreationTime() method, 408-410
GetLastAccessTime() method, 408-410
GetLastWriteTime() method, 408-410
Move() method, 405-407
text boxes, properties, 409
System.Net namespace, 493
System.Security namespace, 493
System.Web namespace, 493
System.Windows.Forms namespace, 493
System.XML namespace, 493
systems
    Common Type System, 494
    operating, triggering events, 84

T

Tab control, 182-185
Tab key, 43
tab order, form controls, 136-137
Tab Order command (View menu), 136
tab sequences, controls, 137

tabbed dialog boxes, creating, 182-185
tabbed floating design windows, creating, 37
TabIndex property, 136-137
TabPage Collection Editor, 183
TabPages property, 183
tabs
    adding, 184
    Appearance, 379-380
    Appointments, 184
    COM, 417
    Components, 40
    Connection, 440
    Custom, 45
    Data, 40
    events, 185
    Form1.vb [Design], 226
    hiding, 184
    IDE, 10
    naming, 183
    pages, 183
    Provider, 440
    removing, 184
    showing, 184
    System, 45
    System palette, 381
    Toolbox, 10, 16, 36
    Web, 45, 104, 470
    Windows forms, 40, 122
    Windows Forms, Pointer, 123
TabStop property, 137
tags, XML, 466
Task List, 234-236, 318, 322

taskbars, forms, 107
tasks, 235-236
tbbInvisible button, 210
Tell The User button,
   227-229
templates, objects, 340
Temporary attribute flag,
   409
testing
   client applications,
      Excel workbooks, 421
   event project example,
      93-94
   example applications,
      487
   form modality, 117
   forms, 112-113
   projects, 74-75
text
   ""(double quotation
      marks), literals, 274
   aligning, 152
   brush argument, 385
   drawing, 385-386
   DrawString() method,
      coordinates, 386
   entering in boxes,
      151-152
   font argument, 385
   Font object, 385
   fonts, objects, 386
   form title bars, display-
      ing, 101-102
   leftY argument, 385
   literals, 274
   messages, creating, 361
   sending to Output win-
      dow, 230
   static, 150

stringoftext argument,
   385
strings, replacing,
   Replace function, 279
topX argument, 385
Text Box control, 204
text boxes
   AcceptReturn property,
      155
   adding to forms, 90
   characters, 155-156
   DataTable records, cre-
      ating, 436
   Enabled property,
      153-154
   events, 156-157
   File Name, 405
   Location, 8
   multiline, creating,
      153-154
   Multiline property,
      153-156
   Name, 8-9, 31
   password fields, creat-
      ing, 156
   properties, 151, 398,
      401, 409
   scrollbars, adding,
      154-155
   ScrollBars property,
      154
   text, aligning, 152
   Text property, 151-153
Text Editor toolbar, 38
text files
   creating, 405
   projects, 50

text formatting, Web
   Forms or Windows
   Forms, 464
Text property, 9, 12, 143,
   150-153, 157
text strings
   concatenating, 274-275
   Left() function, 275-276
   Mid() function, 276-277
   Right() function, 276
   text, retrieving, 275-277
TextAlign property, 152,
   210
Textbox control, 83
Textbox icon, 227, 288
TextBox tool, 43, 122, 125
TextChanged event,
   83-84, 90, 157
throwing exceptions, 321
Tick event, 180-181
tiling images, 104
TimeOfDay function, 182
Timer control, 182
   Interval property, 84
   Tick event, 180-181
Timer event, 84
times, 279
   adding to, 281-282
   calendar months,
      advancing, 282
   current system, retriev-
      ing, 284
   Date data type, 280
   dates, 283
   DateTime, 280
   files, retrieving, 408
   formatting, 283-284

intervals between,
determining, 282-283
subtracting from, 281
title bars
forms, text, displaying,
101-102
Maximize button, 109
Minimize button, 109
toolbars, 39
title parameter, 365
Title property, 399
To keyword, 294
**toggle buttons, creating,
209-211**
**tokens, Manufacturer,
453**
tool buttons, 14
tool windows, 110
toolbar buttons
creating, 472
drop-down menus, cre-
ating, 212
Toolbar control, 207, 472
drop-down menus, cre-
ating, 212
separators, 211
toggle buttons, 209-211
toolbars, 208-209
**ToolBarButton
Collection Editor, 208,
211, 474**
toolbars, 207
borders, 40
buttons, 208, 211
Debug, 38
docking, 39
drag handles, 39
example applications,
building, 472-473

floating, 39
hiding, 38
Layout, 38
programming, 209
resizing, 39
showing, 38
Standard, 38, 52
Text Editor, 38
title bars, 39
undocking, 122
**Toolbars command (View
menu), 39**
toolbox
adding controls to
forms, 40-41
ContextMenu, 205
docking, 122-123
floating, 123
ImageList, 185
Label tool, 90
ListView, 187
MainMenu, 198
OpenFileDialog, 398
SaveFileDialog, 402
StatusBar, 213
tabs, 36
ToolBar, 207
TreeView, 192
Toolbox tab, 10, 16
Toolbox window, 10
tools
Button, 296
code-profiling, CLR
(common language
runtime), 490
debugging, CLR (com-
mon language run-
time), 490

debugging code
break point actions,
325
break points,
323-325
Command window,
325-329
Output window,
329-330
dragging and dropping,
40
Label, 90
ListBox, 123
Object Browser, 77
TextBox, 43, 122, 125
**Tools menu commands,
Options, 31, 56**
ToolTips, 207, 228
TopMost property, 139
**TopMost windows, creat-
ing, 139**
topX argument, 385
**trailing spaces (strings),
trimming, 278-279**
**transparent forms, creat-
ing, 139**
**TransparentColor prop-
erty, 186, 470**
Tree view, 51, 56, 191-195
**triggering methods,
68-69**
**triggering events, 82-84,
180**
Trim() function, 278-279
**trimming spaces
(strings), 278-279**
troubleshooting
example applications,
487

memory leaks, 73
project tests, 74
True, string evaluations, 290
True (Boolean logic), 271-272
True Boolean value, 246
True expressions, 290, 310-311
Try section (Try...Catch...Finally structure), 331
Try statements, End Try statements, 331
Try...End Try structure, 331-333
Try...Catch...Finally block, 300
Try...Catch...Finally structure
  Catch section, 331
  error handlers, 330-334
  Finally section, 331
  Try section, 331
two-dimensional arrays, 253
Type Here boxes, 200
type libraries, references, 416-418
types, data, 243
typing, strict, 250

U

UID parameter, 427
underscore (_), 73, 86, 223

undocking toolbars, 122
unloading forms, 117-118
unmanaged code, 490
Update() method, 429, 435
updating, data sources, 430
upward casting, 245
user controls, 50
user interfaces, creating, 89-90, 226-227
usernames, Jet databases, 428
users
  events, triggering, 83
  information, obtaining, 365-367
  interactions, 355
    custom dialog boxes, creating, 361-364
    displaying messages, 356-361
    keyboard interactions, 367-370
    mouse events, 370-372
    user information, 365-367

V

values. See also properties
  Abort, 360
  AbortRetryIgnore, 357
  baseline, active controls, 131

Boolean, 246
button properties, 347
Cancel, 360
CenterParent, 112
CenterScreen, 112
code procedure declarations, 223-225
Custom, 379
Dash, 379
DashDot, 379
DashDotDot, 379
DashStyle property, 379
Date, 249
DateAdd() function, 281
dates, 285
default initial, values, 248
DialogResult, 360
equalities, comparing, 270-271
evaluating expressions for, Select Case construct, 293-295
Exclamation, 358
Fixed3D, 43
FixedSingle, 43
Format16bppGrayScale value, 377
Format16bppRgb555 value, 377
Format24bppRgb value, 378
Ignore, 360
increment values, loops, 305-306
Information, 358
literal, variables, 249
Manual, 112

MessageBoxButtons, 357
MessageBoxIcon, 358
No, 360
None, 358-360
numeric, 249
object properties, 62
OK, 357, 360
OKCancel, 357
parameters, passing, 231
pixelformat argument, 377-378
Question, 358
Retry, 360
RetryCancel, 357
return, InputBox() function, 366
Solid, 379
StartPosition property, 112
Stop, 358
storing, 249
Warning, 358
WindowsDefaultBounds, 112
WindowsDefaultLocation, 112
Yes, 360
YesNo, 357
YesNoCancel, 357
variables, 54, 62, 242
arrays, 251-254
block scope, 255-256
creating, 250
data typing, 243, 250-251
declaration, explicit, 250-251

defined, 241
dimensioning, 247-248, 350-351
event parameters, 86-89
exploring, 250
expressions, 249
global scope, 258-259
intMyInteger, 260
intPauseCounter, 308
Length property, 275
literal values, 249
module-level scope, 256-257
naming, 248
object references, binding to, 347-351
objects, binding, 348-350
prefixes, denoting scope, 262
private module-level, dimensioning, 257
procedure-level (local) scope, 256
public, 342
referencing, 247
scope, 255, 262
scope name conflicts, 259
static, creating, 260
static scope, declaring, 260
strict typing, 250
VB (Visual Basic), 29-30
Help, 56
hierarchies, 32
VB environments
controls, adding to forms, 40-41

design windows, 33-37
programming, 54-55
project management, 46
components, 49-50
project files, 52-53
setting properties, 51-52
Solution Explorer, 47-49
Properties window, 41-46
toolbars, 38-39
.vb file extension, 49, 115
VBA code, macros, 420
Vertical Spacing command (Format menu), 132
View Code button, 480, 484
View menu commands
Object Browser, 77
Other Views, 326
Properties Window, 34-35
Show Tasks, 234
Solution Explorer, 47
Tab Order, 136
Toolbars, 39
View property, 188-189
viewing
Application folder, 452
color palettes, 103
object properties, 42-44
objects, 48
source files, 50
views
Code, 48
Form Design, 48, 85

List View, example applications, adding, 474-475

Tree, 56

visible controls, 17-18

Visible property, 115, 117

Visual Basic Projects folder, 8

Visual Basic. *See* **VB**

Visual Studio Start Page, 30-32

W

Warning value, 358

wavy lines, code errors, 321

Web development, 461

ASP.NET, 462

control positioning, 464

deployment, 463

graphics, 464

IIS (Internet Information Server), 462

.NET platform installation, 464

responsiveness, 464

security, 464

system resources, 464

text formatting, 464

Web Forms, 462-463

XML Web services, 465-467

Web Forms, 462-464

Web services

SOAP (XML technology), 466

XML, 465-467

Web sites

Close.bmp (bitmap), downloading, 160

Sams Publishing, Close.bmp (bitmap), downloading, 160

Web tab, 45, 104, 470

While keyword, 310

While…End While loop, 313

width argument, bitmaps, 377

Width property, 14

Window (system color), 382

window placements, advanced, 37

windows. *See also* **design windows; Properties window; Solution Explorer**

auto-hidden, displaying, 37

closing, 10

Command, 325-329

Dynamic Help, 56

events, triggering, 84

Find and Replace, 116

forms, comparing, 99

hiding, 10

IDE, 10

Main

code (example applications), 479-484

designing, 470-471

MDI (Multiple Document Interface) programs, 142-143

modal, 117

nonmodal, 116

Output

Debug object, 329

debugging code, 330

error handling, 332

text, sending to, 230

Task List, 318

tool, 110

Toolbox, 10

TopMost, creating, 139

Windows Applications, 31

Windows Forms, 99-100, 463-464

Windows Forms tab, 40, 122-123

WindowsDefaultBounds value, 112

WindowsDefaultLocation value, 112

WindowState property, 112-113

wizards

Data Form Wizard, 438-444

Setup, 457

words, reserved, 66, 87, 248

workbooks, Excel

button properties, 416

client applications, testing, 421

creating, 419

data manipulation, 419-421

wrappers, COM (Component Object Model), 418
writable properties, creating, 345-346
WriteLine() method, 330
WriteLine() statement, 250
writing
  code procedures, 222-225
  interface code, 21-24
  object-based code, projects, 70-73
  programs, 10

z-order (layering form controls), 137-139
zero-length strings, 326

X-Z

X property, 88
XML (Extensible Markup Language)
  elements, nesting, 466
  tags, 466
  Web services, 465-467
Xor operator, Boolean logic, 272-273

Y property, 88
yellow arrows, break points, 325
Yes value, 360
Yes/No options, check boxes, 164-165
YesNo value, 357
YesNoCancel value, 357

Your Guide to Computer Technology

www.informit.com

License Agreement

By opening this package, you are also agreeing to be bound by the following agreement:

You may not copy or redistribute the entire DVD-ROM. Copying and redistribution of individual software programs on the DVD-ROM is prohibited.

This software is sold as-is without warranty of any kind, either expressed or implied, including but not limited to the implied warranties of merchantability and fitness for a particular purpose. Neither the publisher nor its dealers or distributors assumes any liability for any alleged or actual damages arising from the use of this program. (Some states do not allow for the exclusion of implied warranties, so the exclusion may not apply to you.)

Visual Studio .NET 2003

This program was reproduced by Sams Publishing under a special arrangement with Microsoft Corporation. For this reason, Sams Publishing is responsible for the product warranty and support. If your disc is defective, please return it to Sams Publishing, which will arrange for its replacement. PLEASE DO NOT RETURN IT TO MICROSOFT CORPORATION. Any product support will be provided, if at all, by Sams Publishing. PLEASE DO NOT CONTACT MICROSOFT CORPORATION FOR PRODUCT SUPPORT. End users of this Microsoft program shall not be considered "registered owners" of a Microsoft product and therefore shall not be eligible for upgrades, promotions or other benefits available to "registered owners" of Microsoft products.